In the Shadow of the Rising Sun

Shanghai under Japanese Occupation

The authors of this volume consult newly available Chinese and Western archival materials to examine the Chinese War of Resistance against the Japanese in the Shanghai area. They argue that the war in China was a nationalistic endeavor carried out without an effective national leadership. Wartime Chinese activities in Shanghai drew upon social networks rather than ideological positions, and these activities cut across lines of military and political divisions. Instead of the stark contrast between heroic resistance and shameful collaboration, wartime experience in the city is more aptly summed up in terms of bloody struggles between those committed to normalcy in everyday life and those determined to bring about its disruption through terrorist violence and economic control. The volume offers an evaluation of the strategic significance of the Shanghai economy in the Pacific War. It also draws attention to the feminization of urban public discourse against the backdrop of intensified violence. The essays capture the last moments of European settlements in Shanghai under Japanese occupation. This is the first serious scholarly endeavor to examine the Sino-Japanese War from a regional as well as international perspective.

Professor Christian Henriot is professor of history at Lumière-Lyon 2 University and director at the Institut d'Asie Orientale (Institute of East Asian Studies). He is the editor of *New Frontiers: Imperialism's New Communities in East Asia, 1842–1952* (1999), and the author of *Prostitution in Shanghai: A Social History* (Cambridge, 2001); *Shanghai 1927–1937: Municipal Power, Locality, and Modernization* (1993); and *Atlas de Shanghai: Espace et représentations de 1849 à nos jours* (1999).

Professor Wen-hsin Yeh is professor of history at the University of California, Berkeley, and the former chair of the Center for Chinese Studies. She is the editor of *Wartime Shanghai* and *Becoming Chinese: Passages to Modernity and Beyond* and the author of *The Alienated Academy* (1990, 2000) and *Provincial Passages* (1996). Professor Yeh has published articles in *The American Historical Review*, *The China Quarterly*, and the *Journal of Asian Studies*.

Cambridge Modern China Series

Edited by William Kirby, Harvard University

In the Shadow of the Rising Sun

Shanghai under Japanese Occupation

— as opposed to the Am occupation itself — we have almost nothing — a vacuum. —

Edited by

CHRISTIAN HENRIOT

Institut d'Asie Orientale
Lumière-Lyon 2 University

WEN-HSIN YEH

University of California, Berkeley

CAMBRIDGE
UNIVERSITY PRESS

PUBLISHED BY THE PRESS SYNDICATE OF THE UNIVERSITY OF CAMBRIDGE
The Pitt Building, Trumpington Street, Cambridge, United Kingdom

CAMBRIDGE UNIVERSITY PRESS
The Edinburgh Building, Cambridge CB2 2RU, UK
40 West 20th Street, New York, NY 10011-4211, USA
477 Williamstown Road, Port Melbourne, VIC 3207, Australia
Ruiz de Alarcón 13, 28014 Madrid, Spain
Dock House, The Waterfront, Cape Town 8001, South Africa

http://www.cambridge.org

First published 2004

Printed in the United States of America

Typeface Times New Roman 10/13 pt.   *System* LATEX 2$_\varepsilon$ [TB]

A catalog record for this book is available from the British Library.

Library of Congress Cataloging in Publication Data

In the shadow of the rising sun : Shanghai under Japanese occupation / Edited by
Christian Henriot, Wen-hsin Yeh.
    p.   cm. – (Cambridge modern China series)
Includes bibliographical references and index.
ISBN 0-521-82221-1
1. Shanghai (China) – History.   2. Sino-Japanese Conflict, 1937–1945 – China – Shanghai.
I. Title: Shanghai under Japanese occupation.   II. Henriot, Christian.   III. Yeh, Wen-Hsin.
IV. Series.
DS796.S257I56   2003
940.53′51132–dc21   2003048468

ISBN 0 521 82221 1 hardback

Contents

Handwritten annotation: Where on the I's authorities / in reoccupied Shan.? / "culture" do Japan factored in?. 12

vii

Contents

Preface

With the end of the Cold War and the passing of an earlier generation, historical research on the Chinese War of Resistance (1937–1945) against the Japanese has entered a new era. Archives have opened up while films and photographs appeared. Changing political circumstances, both in China and on Taiwan, have made it possible for new perspectives to emerge. The rise of the right wing in Japanese politics and its refusal to acknowledge wartime atrocities have turned issues of history and memory into flash points in contemporary East Asian international politics. The government of China's Communist Party, meanwhile, finds itself caught between opposing forces. On the one hand, nationalistic sentiments run high when people recall wartime hardships. On the other hand, practical considerations, especially those in connection with China's preeminent goal to achieve economic modernizations, dictate Chinese restraint in response to hard memories. Despite an enhanced capacity to record and recall the war, it is in China's economic interest in the 1990s to let bygones be bygone.

More than a half century has elapsed, meanwhile, since the end of the war. A new generation has come to the fore, wanting to learn about their parents' or even grandparents' war. Mo Yan's gripping tale, *Red Sorghum*, is artfully framed as a child's account of episodes of invasion that had become family lore. More than one English-language fiction have appeared, including some that made it to the *New York Times* bestseller list, with the formulaic framing of a young Asian-American woman's desire to learn about her grandmother's life in the old world. These new voices raise new questions and introduce new perspectives. The diasporic dispersal of the Chinese in the post-1945 world means that war memories are refracted through divergent trajectories of later experiences. These remembrances, sometimes represented with borrowed idioms and from comparative perspectives, also become embroiled in later-day cultural politics.

ix

Earlier in the century, Chinese authorities, under both the Nationalists and the Communists, had maintained that there had been a national war of Chinese resistance against the Japanese. The two parties, rivals of a subsequent civil war (1946–1949), disagreed over issues such as who had borne the brunt of enemy forces and who had betrayed the joint cause. There was consensus, nonetheless, that the war was a hard-earned Chinese victory, and that there were shameful collaborators as well as patriotic resistors among the Chinese.

In the 1990s, researchers gained access to previously closed government archives, especially to Chiang Kai-shek's pre-1949 papers held at the Academia Historica on Taiwan. These materials made it possible for scholars to reconstruct, for the first time, critical moments in Republican political history that shaped the course of the larger events. They permit a better view of how the War of Resistance had occurred after decades of regional arming and civil conflicts in China, and that there were, besides the Nationalists and the Communists, many more regionally based actors who fought in this mosaic of Chinese struggles against the Japanese. The War of Resistance, in other words, was a nationwide Chinese endeavor that was conducted without an effective national leadership. It was a watershed event for the country as a whole. Yet, without the mediation of national institutions, it became a series of struggles of pronounced regional characteristics.

This insight placed the Chinese war experience in a new light. We now realize that several wars and multiple fronts engulfed the land for nearly a decade. Conventional accounts had built upon a "master narrative" about a single Chinese nation-state at war. This narrative, we find, hardly does justice to the complexity of the events and the differences in experience. The scope and intensity of the organized violence had rallied the Chinese people to reflect upon the shape of a unified nation and their common destiny. But these aspirations were articulated in local contexts. The time has come for us to adopt a regional rather than a national perspective in the design of new research questions.

The present volume traces its origin to a conversation one afternoon on a late spring day in Berkeley, when talk turned to issues of collaboration and resistance and the research challenge it represents, both when reconstructing war experience from wartime propaganda and when separating this war from the Cold War. The chapters in this volume examine the war as experienced in just one city, Shanghai. Broadly speaking, we pose three sets of questions.

Shanghai was one of the first modern cities to come under attack in the 1930s. What did it mean, we ask, when a civilian population of more than three million, drawn from multiple nations, found itself relentlessly subjected to the harshness of armed hostility for years? How did the brutality of siege and occupation distort or disrupt the civic patterns of authority and association of prewar days? In what way did the violence reconfigure the material landscape of the city?

A modern city like Shanghai was a nexus of relationships reaching beyond its territorial boundaries. Yet as soon as Nationalist Chinese troops withdrew toward the hinterland, Shanghai's foreign concessions became "lone islets" (*gudao*) of commerce and modernity in the midst of vast expanses of Japanese-occupied towns and villages. A second question thus has to do with Shanghai's strategic place in the conduct of war. How "local" or "regional" did Shanghai become when coming under siege? Did the military checkpoints stop the flow of goods and people in and out of the city? What sorts of resources were mobilized to enable alternative channels of communication?

For much of the war, the Shanghaiese coexisted with allies and enemies right in their midst. Struggles like these afforded fewer opportunities for heroism than messy compromises or protracted negotiations. These were not, in other words, materials that lent themselves to tall tales of clear-cut solutions and furious struggle. Our third question thus has to do with the ambivalence of resistance and collaboration and the overall question of political allegiance and patriotic commitment. If neither willing collaboration nor overt resistance, then what was the spectrum of viable political choices in the occupied city? What were the issues that ultimately defined the meaning of human struggle in the city?

Instead of an exclusive focus on politics and warfare, the authors of this volume examine culture and economy, two areas that defined the city and made Shanghai unique in the Chinese context. It begins with a paradox, that in Shanghai, where nearly 200,000 lives were lost within the first three months of the armed conflict, the population essentially endured the war as both a siege and an occupation. Wartime Shanghai was neither Chongqing nor Yan'an, where Chinese authorities, whether Nationalist or Communist, mobilized the civilians for resistance. Despite the intensity of the initial fighting, business in Shanghai resumed as usual and entertainment went on as if there were neither memories nor remembrances. Underground agents used the foreign concessions of the city, to be sure, to stage assassinations, especially during the first four years of the war. Yet sounds and signs on the airwaves and from the film screens directed the minds not to lofty heroism but to simple bliss at home.

What this volume seeks to offer, then, is not only a first study of the Sino-Japanese War in a local context; it is also a ground-level perspective of an international city of commerce and culture caught in the midst of a national war. Few of Shanghai's urbanites earned credentials as war heroes. Yet what they lived through were not times of peace. It remains an essential chapter in the larger Chinese story of war and how the people in that city went on with their lives and defined the terms of their triumphs as well as losses.

Each author in this volume has intellectual debts that he or she may wish to acknowledge. For the volume as a whole, a preliminary workshop was held in April 1996 at the Center for Chinese Studies, University of California at Berkeley. A conference was subsequently held in October 1997, in Lyon. The editors wish to acknowledge the support of the Chiang Ching-kuo Foundation for International Scholarly Exchanges and the Région Rhône-Alpes. Funding from these sources made it possible to pay for the travel and other expenses associated with these gatherings. In addition, we wish to acknowledge the support of the French Ministry of Foreign Affairs and of Lumière-Lyon 2 University. The faculty, staff, and students in modern Chinese studies at Berkeley and Lyon generously contributed their time and thoughts. This volume would have been much impoverished without their active participation.

Introduction

CHRISTIAN HENRIOT AND WEN-HSIN YEH

Metropolitan Shanghai never was a city at war, though Shanghai at large was among the first battle scenes in the Sino-Japanese War. This is a paradox and even a challenge in a statement that will sound provocative and controversial to the reader. No one will deny the reality of war in the city. Shanghai was the first large metropolis to bear the full brunt of modern warfare in World War II. Three months of bitter fighting left tens of thousands of casualties among the Chinese and Japanese troops. Hundreds of thousands of civilians from the Chinese-administered districts abandoned their homes and belongings to seek refuge in the foreign settlements. Entire neighborhoods were burned to the ground as a result of indiscriminate shelling and uncontrolled fires. The deliberate or accidental dropping of bombs by Japanese and Chinese planes – "collateral damages" in military jargon – brought the horror of war into the very heart of the city, on the world-famous Bund and near the Great World amusement center. When the fighting was over, the Chinese living outside of the settlements were often exposed to the arbitrary power and brutality of the occupant. Yet, after the withdrawal of Chinese troops and administration in November 1937, the foreign concessions of the city progressively returned to a state of "quasi normalcy." Except for the strategic bombings of industrial districts by U.S. airplanes in 1944–1945, full-scale warfare between professional military forces was never again part of the Shanghai experience.

As fighting ended, a new era of urban violence began. Shanghai became a major stake over which various contending parties, especially the Japanese military authorities, the Chongqing-based Nationalist government, and the successive puppet regimes competed fiercely for control. The contenders resorted to terrorist strategies and employed deadly means. But despite the struggle and the bloodshed or precisely because of them, Shanghai was not a city mobilized

1

1. The tragic bombing of the Great World Theater on August 14, 1937, left 3,000 victims. Source: Courtesy of the Fabre Family.

for war. Major features such as the unification of people in space and time, the organization of resistance, or the mobilization of resources for the armed conflict were largely missing. On the first issue, the organization of time and space became even more fragmented in Shanghai. Territorial and political divisions, as we know, were not new to the city, but war introduced new patterns. The Chinese districts came under Japanese military occupation, even as their administration was entrusted to puppet municipal governments. The foreign settlements came under siege, surrounded as they were by the Chinese districts, and had to face increasingly stringent measures of blockade. Nevertheless, they continued to have access to the outside world by sea up to 1941. In the Chinese municipality, power shifted in succession to men appointed or monitored by the Japanese army. In the foreign settlements, the Western-dominated municipal authorities declared a state of "neutrality" despite their resentment at being threatened by an Asian power. Neither the British nor the American home government was about to declare war against Japan over Shanghai extraterritoriality. Eventually, the predominantly Anglo-American International Settlement became the sole refuge for anti-Japanese activists when Vichy France actually

2. Death by the thousands around the Great World Theater. Source: Courtesy of the Fabre Family.

allowed almost free access to the French Concession to the Japanese special services.[1]

The peculiar spatial and political division of Shanghai created an opportunity for the organization of actions of resistance. After all, for decades gangsters had taken advantage of the divisions of jurisdiction to evade pursuit and arrest by moving from one place to the other.[2] Although the Japanese consul and the army exercised strong pressures on the Shanghai Municipal Council in the International Settlement to quell all anti-Japanese activities, Japanese interest did not dominate the foreign territories. Foreign authorities yielded to Japanese pressures by accepting the latter's censorship, police surveillance, and sometimes arrests, but their main worry did not come from civilian resistance by Shanghai's Chinese students, intellectuals, or artists. The authorities were

---

[1] Wen-hsin Yeh's "Prologue" in *Wartime Shanghai* offers the most sophisticated presentation of the chain of events in Shanghai during the Japanese occupation. Wen-hsin Yeh (ed.), *Wartime Shanghai*, London and New York, Routledge, 1998, pp. 1–17.

[2] On police and bandits in Shanghai, see Wakeman, Frederic, *Policing Shanghai, 1927–1937*, Berkeley, University of California Press, 1994 and Martin, Brian, *The Shanghai Green Gang. Politics and Organized Crime, 1919–1937*, Berkeley, University of California Press, 1996.

concerned, instead, about the resistance put up by the professional agents of the Chinese Nationalist army and secret services in the form of terrorist actions (mostly assassinations and bomb attacks). When the Chinese collaborators and the puppet authorities established their own apparatus, especially the infamous No. 76 secret police on Jessfield Road, Shanghai became the scene of a series of extremely violent acts of terrorism. Nationalist agents targeted prominent Chinese public figures, Nationalist or non-Nationalist, who had been approached by the Japanese or the puppet authorities as leaders of collaboration. The collaborators struck back, attacking all those involved *volens nolens* in the propaganda (journalists), political (lawyers, magistrates), and economic (bankers and their employees) battle between the contending parties.[3] Acts of hideous brutality and violence, however, did not involve the population at large. These forms of action remained the domain of professionals and, for that matter, left most Chinese residents in Shanghai at the fringe of resistance or active mobilization for war purposes.

The third missing element in a logic of war economy in Shanghai is precisely the absence of a harnessing of resources to support the war effort by either side. At the onset of the war, the city was a huge safe with the highest concentration of capital in China, a thriving commercial hub, and an unrivaled industrial power engine. Although the armed conflict inflicted heavy damages on industrial plants and induced many capitalists to send their money to Hong Kong for safety, this handicap was overcome by the influx of capital and equipment from inland Chinese cities and, after a short lapse of time, the return of the absconded capital. Production resumed within months of the cessation of hostilities. In late 1938, Shanghai had regained its initial potential and enjoyed a strong revival of its economy. Local entrepreneurs, Chinese, Japanese, as well as Westerners, actively sold their locally produced goods to all parties. Depending on their nationality, they probably had national preferences when it came to selecting their customers. There is also no doubt that goods put out by Chinese firms were shipped or transshipped to Nationalist forces in inland China.[4] Finally, the Chongqing government maintained a relative influence on the local economy through various agencies and its currency. Yet the economic system worked in a freewheeling mode since no single authority functioned to place the financial, commercial, and industrial resources of Shanghai under a war-supporting scheme. When the Wang Jingwei government and the Japanese

---

[3] Wakeman, Frederic E., *The Shanghai Badlands: Wartime Terrorism and Urban Crime, 1937–1941*, New York, Cambridge University Press, 1996.

[4] Schoppa, Keith, "The structure, dynamics, and impacts of the Shanghai-coastal Zhejiang trading system, 1938–1944," paper presented at the international conference on "Wartime Shanghai, 1937–1945," Lyon, October 15–17, 1997.

eventually carried out a form of command economy (*tongzhi jingji*) made of monopolies on commodities in early 1943, it only led to the gradual collapse of production and paralysis in the city.[5] Throughout the war, and despite the declared hostilities, this volume argues, the foreign concessions of the city continued to operate along their prewar patterns of economic activities, albeit within a much more restrictive context.

Many economic actors chose to stay in Shanghai during the war. Others moved far beyond the limits of the city. Either alternative entailed risks of sorts. A decision to remain in Shanghai meant vulnerability in an uncertain economic environment. Supplies were difficult to obtain, prices were on the rise, and there existed the permanent threat of a Japanese takeover of the foreign settlements. This last fear eventually became a reality in December 1941. The other possibility – to move one's machinery, or capital, or simply oneself to Chongqing and the Nationalist-controlled areas – entailed an almost equally hazardous future in China's underdeveloped hinterland that was ill equipped for industrial operations. Meanwhile, Shanghai offered an opportunity for great games, great risks, and eventually great profits. Imported commodities were plentiful, overseas markets were accessible, banks stored huge amounts of idle capital, real estate offered a safe investment alternative, and plenty of urbanites whiled away their days shopping. Finally, the city remained a unique springboard for foray into the surrounding countryside. These markets were firmly under the control of either the thriving smuggling rings or a variety of state agencies. Shanghai was a marketplace for social connections (*guanxi*) where all the major and minor players converged. War or no war, Shanghai concessions remained a nerve center for business, industry, intelligence, and intrigue.

Throughout the fighting and the occupation, Shanghai maintained its connections to its hinterland. Imports continued despite the restrictions imposed by the Japanese army on the movement of goods. As late as 1941, there was no dearth of smuggled materials crisscrossing the boundaries. Chinese merchants used the dense network of the rivers of the lower Yangzi area or the transshipment facilities of the string of harbors along the South China coast to elude military controls and barriers. The communist guerrillas in Central China frequently commissioned special agents to organize the purchase of controlled commodities and equipment. Although these acquisitions remained several degrees below the large-scale smuggling activities of the secret services–backed companies,

[5] Henriot, Christian, "War and economics: the control of material resources in the lower Yangzi and Shanghai area between 1937 and 1945," paper presented to the international conference "The Role of the Republican Period in Twentieth Century China: Reflections and Reconsiderations," Venice, June 30–July 3, 1999.

they bear testimony to the fluidity of Shanghai's relations with its hinterland. The flow ceased only when the Wang Jingwei government enforced a strict system of controlled economy. Its purpose, however, was not to seal off Shanghai, but to place all the material resources of Central China under the command of a coordinated set of official agencies or committees. Whereas the explicit purpose of this policy was the full mobilization of resources for the war effort, its clumsy implementation, compounded by the corruption and inefficiency of the said agencies, resulted in a devastating – albeit unintended – paralysis of the whole economic system. Only then did metropolitan Shanghai become insulated from the economy of its hinterland.

There are many good reasons, therefore, to reconsider the idea that after the withdrawal of Chinese troops in November 1937, the foreign concessions in Shanghai became a lone islet (*"gudao"*). The term was coined in the aftermath of the Chinese withdrawal and has become a standard expression for the period prior to Japanese occupation. It conveys various conflicting meanings: that of *gu'er* (orphan) or *gujun* (lone army [of resisters]). It can also mean a haven, an oasis that afforded protection in a realm of violence. Above all, it means the singularity of Shanghai in the Chinese war experience. For those who coined the term, its immediate meaning may have been closer to "isolation, abandonment, orphan." The larger world beyond its confines had been transformed by the Japanese military. The Chinese government had retreated to the deep hinterland. The enemy was all around. There was hardly any sense of heroism in this initial definition. *Gudao* conjured up powerlessness and vulnerability. But as time passed, people resumed their old habits and everyday life while the rest of the country continued to struggle and suffer. During the war, but probably more so after the Japanese surrender – that is, when the time had come to reward the winners and punish the losers – *gudao* served to buttress Shanghai's claim of its commitment to resistance and to survival against all odds. The combined values of heroism and singularity were injected into the term to characterize the Shanghai experience during the war. It was a term that shielded its inhabitants from the accusation of collaboration and absolved them of the guilt of survival. After all, the people of Shanghai were orphans abandoned by their elders during the war.[6]

Like "Résistance" in postwar Gaullist France, *gudao* has to be deconstructed in order to engage in a historical re-assessment of the Japanese occupation in Shanghai. It is a convenient and simplistic cover-up for a complex period dominated by postures and actions that do not fit in a "resistance vs. collaboration"

---

[6] Fu Poshek, *Passivity, Resistance, and Collaboration: Intellectual Choices in Occupied Shanghai, 1937–1945*, Stanford, Stanford University Press, 1993.

mold.[7] There was no time for a "postwar" period in China since the victors of the day (Nationalists and Communists) became at once the enemies of tomorrow and headed off to a military struggle. The question of resistance and collaboration became a secondary issue in the civil war between the Chinese Communist Party (CCP) and the Guomindang (GMD). There was no time for reflection on the war experience under the Japanese. Nor was the civil war an appropriate framework for a consideration of issues of collaboration and resistance during the Sino-Japanese War. After 1949, the Nationalists and the Communists told their divergent war stories respectively. On the mainland, wartime memory was reconstructed according to the canons of Marxist historiography. On Taiwan, it became part of a larger effort to explain the collapse of the Nationalist regime and the victory of the Communists. Nationalist leaders had no interest in a close examination of their possible compromises and misconduct during the war. Postwar politics dictated that a black and white picture should serve as a much more convenient posture. By and large, much was said about the evils of militarism and imperialism while little was done by way of historical research to examine the actual experience of war at the local level.[8]

In real life, there was a wide array of attitudes toward the Japanese occupation. Few, indeed, engaged in outright collaboration with the enemy. Despite a long history of political and cultural relations, the Japanese had not been able to build up the kind of sympathetic following that the Germans could rely on in France among political elites.[9] In Central China and in Shanghai, the Japanese could not even rely on the network of proxies from the pool of former warlords they had supported in the 1920s–1930s. When the Japanese Navy decided to establish the Dadao (Great Way) government in the city in late 1937, it had to "import" its main leaders from Taiwan. This government probably was an exceptional example of a collaborationist institution in Shanghai. It turned out to be a dismal failure, despite ambitious plans to extend its reach to the whole Central China region. Its successors, the Fu Xiao'an and Chen Gongbo municipal

---

[7] On the issue of collaboration by the Vichy regime and the postwar "épuration" in France, see Lottman, Herbert, *L'épuration, 1943–1953*, Paris, Fayard, 1986; and Rousso, Henry, *The Vichy Syndrome: History and Memory in France Since 1944* (Arthur Goldhammer, trans.), Cambridge, Mass., Harvard University Press, 1991 (Paris, Seuil, 1987).

[8] Although the Japanese case is not unique, it is interesting to note that the Japanese communities that lived in China, especially in Shanghai, have been absent from most historical accounts until very recently. On the general issue of foreign communities, see Bickers, Robert and Henriot, Christian (eds.), *New Frontiers: Imperialism's New Communities in East Asia, 1842–1952*, Manchester, Manchester University Press, 2000. The first historical study by Japanese scholars to address the issue of the Japanese community in Shanghai is Takahashi, Kôsuke and Furumaya, Tadao (eds.), *Shanhai shi* (The History of Shanghai), Tokyo, Toho shoten, 1995.

[9] See Ory, Pascal, *Les collaborateurs, 1940–1945*, Paris, Seuil, 1976.

administrations, proved no more malleable to Japanese ends. Some will argue that the prewar colonial situation in Shanghai – the foreign settlements had been in existence for almost ninety years – had prepared the ground for "collaboration" between the various sectors of Chinese society and Japan. After all, Westerners were invaders and the masters of a political sysem that called for collaboration on the part of the Chinese. True enough, significant parts of Shanghai had developed under Western colonialism. But Westerners prevailed in a system under the appearance of a rule of law. It was also a system of governance that had stemmed from collaboration in the economic sphere. The Japanese military presence in Shanghai developed under different circumstances. From a Chinese perspective, some might argue that there was hardly a difference in nature. Yet a Western colonial legacy and a system of collaboration such as had developed in Shanghai do not mean, as this volume will show, that the Chinese in Shanghai thus became "naturally" and indiscriminately receptive to *any* form of foreign dominance or political coercion.

Japanese occupation sealed the fate of the Western presence in Shanghai. Foreign authorities of the International Settlement and the French Concession resorted to different tactics in their dealings with the Japanese, the puppet administrations, and the Chongqing Nationalists. Yet neither showed much commitment to the local population beyond what happened to coincide with its self-interest. The concessions, thanks to the colonial standing, offered some protection to those Chinese who had fled Japanese occupation. During the initial phase of the war, this served the interest of the Nationalist government in Chongqing and the Shanghai Chinese among the local elite. Japanese military authorities made repeated attempts to interfere with the functioning of the concession municipality. The Shanghai Municipal Council (SMC) adopted a middle-of-the-road strategy that ultimately entailed repeated compromises at the expense of Chinese sovereign rights, institutions, and nationalism. The French Concession adopted a tough stance in the early years of the war, but gave in to most Japanese demands when the French government fell for Japan under Marshall Pétain. In both cases, the authorities were concerned primarily with the preservation of their existing interests – a dream that fell apart on December 8, 1941 for the SMC – and future presence – an illusion that crumbled in July 1943 for the French – in Shanghai. The SMC carried on its duties under Japanese command until its staff members were interned as "enemy nationals" in 1943. The French consul and concession authorities, by contrast, escaped the humiliation of formal submission to the Japanese army. In both cases, however, there was a similar pattern of collaboration with the invaders.

Among both the Shanghai workers and business elite, Japanese and puppet Chinese manipulation of anti-Western sentiments failed to generate enough support for pro-Japanese collaboration. The workers were severely hit by the rising cost of basic necessities, especially food. They organized numerous strikes to express their discontent and disarray. The war period, in particular the years 1940–1941, saw a short-lived though extensive movement of workers' protests. The puppet authorities and the Japanese special services realized the potentialities of the workers' dissatisfaction in their struggle against Western companies and, through them, against Western political dominance in the city. They facilitated or often provoked the establishments of clubs and simili-unions to engineer strike movements or to monitor those that erupted spontaneously. Like its Nationalist predecessor, the Wang Jingwei regime was eager to control the "world of labor" and harness it in its anti-Western campaign, but it failed to attract the sympathy of the workers. Fundamentally, however, its major weakness laid in its inability to formulate and materialize a genuine policy toward the workers. Among its Japanese allies, there was even a clear aversion to the development of unions, as a labor movement was perceived to be potentially dangerous for social stability. Eventually, the puppet authorities made halfhearted and instrumental inroads into the working classes, but they failed to enlist them under their banner.

The local elites in general also proved to be unwilling partners. The business community, especially the major figures of the prewar period, either remained in the relative safety of the foreign settlements or, when the pressure became too high, absconded to Hong Kong or Chongqing. The Japanese and Wang Jingwei managed to attract only a handful of established Shanghai capitalists. Nevertheless, war also offered opportunities for expansion and profits for those who placed the interests of their company ahead of political considerations. Some even saw the war, its restrictions, and built-in system of state involvement as a privileged moment to place themselves as intermediaries– "fixers" in the words of Sherman Cochran's Xu Guanqun – and to use their privileges to conquer market shares. Were these characters very dissimilar to the Shanghai British businessmen who equated British national interests with their company's financial prospects, and therefore had no qualms about their deals with their country's enemy after 1941? Were they "conscious" collaborators? They probably did not think of themselves as collaborators or traitors.[10] They argued that the success of their businesses was a guarantee for the success of China in the long term. They refused to believe that they were contributing to the immediate interests of the Japanese occupiers or the puppet regimes.

---

[10] For an interesting discussion of these notions, see Wasserstein, Bernard, "Ambiguities of occupation: Foreign resisters and collaborators in wartime Shanghai," in Wen-hsin Yeh (ed.), *Wartime Shanghai*, London and New York, Routledge, 1998, pp. 24–41.

For the merchant organizations and their leaders, the policy of no contact with the enemy or its Chinese representatives came to an end when the Japanese army took over the International Settlement. Frustrated by four years of failed attempts to throw their net over Shanghai's industry and trade, the Japanese pursued an aggressive policy of creating Sino-Japanese professional associations (*tongye gonghui*). The entrepreneurs, who had failed to respond to the Japanese call to cooperate and lost their properties in the occupied parts of the city, could no longer avoid playing by the rules of the city's occupiers. The mediation of the Wang Jingwei government made collaboration more palatable than a straightforward *entente* with the Japanese. Yet, the entrepreneurs were torn between their political allegiance to Chongqing and a pragmatic desire to put their plants back into production under the Japanese. The Rong family treaded a careful path in order to avoid direct involvement in collaboration, shamelessly sending nonfamily executives of the company to serve in the professional associations or monopoly committees set up by the Wang Jingwei government. Having secured protection from both sides of the political contenders, they came out of the war with a clean record and escaped postwar sanctions.

Although the confusing mix of trade and politics and the subtle system of relationships between entrepreneurs and officials can be traced back to the Nanking decade, the war and the occupation marked the forceful intrusion of the state into the control of material resources.[11] It promulgated and enforced various sets of increasingly stringent regulations in order to harness the productive machinery for the war effort. The coexistence of rival authorities or agencies often resulted in the adoption of competing and contradictory regulations. In the case of the local authorities, these measures were designed to ensure the procurement of basic necessities to the people, an objective that was never met. The wealthy region around Shanghai became a bounty for army-backed Japanese companies. They organized the systematic, though unsuccessful, plundering of material resources, especially agricultural products. The Japanese civilian community swelled to unknown heights – 100,000 people – taking advantage of the

---

[11] On state-bourgeoisie relations under the Nationalist regime, see Eastman, Lloyd E., *The Abortive Revolution: China Under Nationalist Rule, 1927–1937*, Cambridge, Mass., Harvard University Press, 1974; Coble, Parks M., *The Shanghai Capitalists and the Nationalist Government, 1927–1937*, Cambridge, Mass., Harvard University Press, 1980; Bush, Richard, *The Politics of Cotton Textiles in Kuomintang China*, New York, Garland Publishing, 1982; Fewsmith, Joseph, *Party, State, and Local Elites in Republican China*, Honolulu, University of Hawaii Press, 1985; Bergère, Marie-Claire, *The Golden Age of the Chinese Bourgeoisie*, Cambridge, Cambridge University Press, 1989.

privileges offered by military dominance.[12] Chinese merchants, to be sure, managed to defend their share and shipped commodities to Shanghai until mid-1940. But the measures of control imposed by the Japanese army and the privileges enjoyed by Japanese companies led to the strangulation of Shanghai at the turn of the year. The Japanese extracted at best a half success, however, since they were only able to stifle, but never to exploit to their own advantage, the city's potential for production.

Gradually Shanghai was cut off from the sources of supply without which its industries could not function. The severe food shortages of the 1942–1944 period pushed the population to the brink of starvation. Shanghai lost its critical economic relevance in the waging of the war. Japanese confiscation of food and other surpluses in Central China was a major cause of scarcity. The other factor, however, was the parallel and proportionate development of the "black market." The latter served to offset the defects of the official distribution system. It was also a surrogate to market mechanisms that the state authorities had suppressed. In this regard, the most striking feature of the "controlled economy" was the actual involvement of official organs in smuggling and black marketeering. Most of the large-scale trade relations were carried out primarily by underground organizations emanating from the very authorities – Japanese, Nationalist, and puppet – that prohibited smuggling and imposed severe regulations on merchants. The very agencies that had been employed to stifle the market mechanisms, especially the military and the secret services, turned out to have their hand in this "illegal" traffic.

How was the war experienced in Shanghai? In what way did such experience find expression in Shanghai's wartime culture? If no major structural changes took place in the city's economy until the imposition of massive state control in the 1940s, did the War of Resistance usher in a comparable reorganization of the city's cultural life? Or did it reinforce and perpetuate established ways of being?

On the surface, the city's economic rebound in 1938 provided the backdrop for a high degree of "normalcy" in the city's cultural arena. Returning popular entertainers in 1938 found that Shanghai was as commercially oriented as ever. For much of the war, entertainment and advertising dominated the radio programs. Resistance and patriotism were barely audible on the city's airwaves despite the full-scale armed conflict that was being waged elsewhere on Chinese soil.

---

[12] Henriot, Christian, "Little Japan in Shanghai: An insulated community, 1875–1945," in Bickers, Robert and Henriot Christian (eds.), *New Frontiers: Imperialism's New Communities in East Asia, 1842–1952*, Manchester, Manchester University Press, 2000, pp. 146–169.

This normalcy in public media in the Shanghai concessions was the result of Japanese military pressure instead of "natural" Chinese apathy to the war. For months following the outbreak of violence in Shanghai, patriotism and the call for resistance had dominated the city's radio broadcasting programs. These expressions proved to be short-lived. It was not because Chinese fervor had subsided, but because Japanese suppression had intensified. Despite the brisk sale in radio units, Chinese-operated radio stations were simply driven out of existence so long as they resisted Japanese demands of registration and control.

But the call to arms was not completely silenced in the pages of Shanghai's wartime journals and periodicals. Middle-class Chinese housewives were called upon to contribute their efforts to wartime goals. Yet instead of women working in the public arena, this was patriotism in everyday practice while performing the duties of being a mother or a wife. Prewar feminine virtues such as frugality, pragmatic competence, and dedication to the family continued to characterize the representation of the exemplary female. Wartime patriotic rhetoric "consolidated and strengthened a conservative strain in social life" and reconfirmed the primacy of women's reproductive functions over and above their potential public and economic roles. Women were urged to dedicate themselves to caring for family members and managing domestic responsibilities. These representations were juxtaposed, meanwhile, with horrid images of the breaking up of families and the violation of individuals, women in particular, in time of foreign invasion.

The political use of feminine domestic virtue in this new discourse of patriotism, despite its conservative overtone, nonetheless served to bring women into the public arena. During the occupation period in the 1940s, Shanghai witnessed a feminization of its print culture in the practice of reading as well as of writing. Women writers such as Su Qing and Eileen Chang (Zhang Ailing) became prominent public figures in the print arena. The feminine subjects and domestic concerns in their work served to function as a tacit commentary on the sense of loss and fragmentation during the war. Women's speech in that regard restructured the discursive pattern of political speech in public. Women writers, in short, were the principal architects reconstructing the textual universe that fashioned the Shanghai experience with war.

Wartime culture in Shanghai, then, exhibited two sets of seemingly contradictory characteristics. On the one hand, there were plenty of signs of business as usual, with the entertainment industry and the advertising agencies being as busy as ever, catering to the wealthy and comfortable as if there had never been war. Editors of print periodicals filled their journal issues with articles about how to run households and serve flavorful meals. These writings catered to the blessed and content as if everyone had had a roof over their heads and no child would ever go hungry. But this very appearance of "normalcy" was itself the product of a radical restructuring of the terms of permissible speech in public, as a result of both enemy-imposed censorship and state-sponsored propaganda. In lieu of war and politics, women and domesticity emerged to become the public preoccupations of the day, as if the fate of the Chinese nation hinged upon its women living up to expectations about their traditional virtue. The use of the commercial and traditional language camouflaged the suppression that had distorted the structure of public discourse; an expression of this distortion was the feminization of public discourse in print culture. All subjects were taboo but women. Women writers came to the fore and commanded enormous popularity. Representations of women, along with the public consumption of these representations, became meanwhile an enterprise of tremendous political complexity.

Was the war a watershed event in modern Chinese experience? Did the widespread suffering and the massive devastation usher in new awareness in their aftermath? Even when the War of Resistance was still waging, the armies of the Nationalists and the Communists had already clashed in the lower Yangzi valley. There were no clear separations between the war against an external foe and the war against a domestic rival. Remembrances of the Sino-Japanese War were complicated by the outbreak of armed civil conflicts between the Nationalists and the Communists and politicized in the subsequent civil war. It had become, in that sense, almost a forgotten war.

There were, in short, multifaceted experiences of war in Shanghai across class, gender, and ethnic lines. Although it affected almost everybody in one way or the other, it made a difference to be a woman or a man, a worker or a businessman, a Chinese or a foreign national. Yet, apart from the most economically or politically privileged (who often belonged to the same groups), war meant unconditional risk for one's life, well-being, and future. Divisions within society, as before the war, were many, but the war failed to produce major changes within society.

In Shanghai, the War of Resistance contributed to a stronger sense of units and shared destiny, but it failed to generate new patterns of social interaction. Wartime mobilization, to be sure, intensified social organizations that had been in existence before 1937. The merchant associations played their traditional role of assistance to the needy, defense of their members' interests, and representation of local society. The Shanghai people rallied around the Nationalist government and embraced the cause of war against Japan. The original mobilization drive, however, did not metamorphose into organized and sustained forms of active resistance among the Shanghai *shimin*. To paraphrase Alain Roux's observation on the working class in the Chinese revolution,[13] the Shanghaiese were outsiders in a war that was fought primarily by professionals, mostly members of the military and secret services, in the name of competing claims for legitimacy. Paradoxically, the advantageous context of relative immunity the foreign settlements offered gave the Nationalists a free hand not only to take the initiative in acts of resistance, but to monopolize their organization and implementation, de facto ruling out people's participation. The violent turn of events that unfolded between the Nationalist and the puppet agents took its toll on the morale of the population. When the haven of the settlements disappeared in 1941, resistance just crumbled.

---

[13] Roux, Alain, "Chine 1945–1949: la classe ouvrière dans une révolution à l'envers," *Cahiers d'histoire*, 28 (1987), pp. 8–44.

Part I

Chapter 1

Shanghai Industries under Japanese Occupation

Bombs, Boom, and Bust (1937–1945)

CHRISTIAN HENRIOT

The fate of Shanghai industries during the war is a central issue.[1] The city represented the main industrial center of the country, with the highest concentration
of firms and urban proletariat. It had experienced a tremendous transformation
since its opening to foreign trade in 1842 and the development of modern industries after the Shimonoseki treaty of 1895. Although Manchuria also underwent
a similar process of development, it did not lead to the same level of concentration and, above all, it became so as a Japanese semi-colony. During and after
World War I, Shanghai's booming economy literally took off thanks to a process
of substitution that saw the multiplication of a wide array of industrial firms,
most notably textile and flour mills. Although less well known, the manufacture
of machinery also reached a very high level during the 1930s.[2] Shanghai had
become the vanguard of China's economic modernization.

By 1937, Shanghai was also the major commercial and financial hub of the
country on which the Nationalist regime depended to a large extent for its
revenue. The city drained huge amounts of resources from the hinterland, it
served as a transformation and redistribution center, and it attracted tens of
thousands of job seekers from the surrounding provinces. In spite of the criticisms Rhoads Murphey has addressed to his own work on the role of Shanghai,
the city was not a world unto itself. Its development did have linkage effects
on the regional economy and the prosperity of its industries had a direct resonance on the life of millions of peasants.[3] Therefore, the bombing of the city,

---

[1] This essay is based on documentary research conducted in association with Feng Yi, junior
research fellow at the Institut d'Asie Orientale.

[2] Rawski, Thomas, "The Growth of Producer Industries, 1900–1971," in Willmott, W. E. (Ed.),
and Perkins, Dwight H. (Ed.), *China's Economy in Historical Perspective*, Stanford, Stanford
University Press, 1975, pp. 203–233.

[3] Murphey, Rhoads, *Shanghai: Key to Modern China*, Cambridge, Harvard University Press, 1953;
Treaty Ports and China's Modernization: What Went Wrong? Michigan Papers in Chinese Studies

its occupation by the Japanese army, its progressive sealing off from the rest of the country, and the institution of monopolies by the Japanese authorities on vital raw materials all altered the role and the influence of Shanghai in a fundamental way. As Robert Barnett once wrote: "Shanghai became a hostage to politics."[4]

The evolution of Shanghai industries under Japanese occupation therefore requires a careful examination of the general political and economic context in China and more specifically in Central China. It cannot be fully understood without studying the monopolistic policies implemented by the Japanese army in order to take control of the agricultural, mineral, and industrial resources of the Lower Yangzi area.[5] Although this essay will focus primarily on the situation in Shanghai, it will show that the city was not the "lone island" so often referred to in contemporary accounts, and not just in economic terms. Changes in its hinterland had a direct and often negative impact on many sectors of the economy. Yet it is only after Pearl Harbor and the occupation of the International Settlement that the city was more effectively cut off from its hinterland and overseas markets.

Three sets of questions will be addressed in this chapter. The first looks at the extent of the damage suffered by Shanghai industries during the conflict that swept the city from August 13 to the end of November 1937. The second line of inquiry is about the nature of the recovery of the local economy after the cessation of hostilities. I shall examine how far and how fast industrial firms managed to resume production and which factors presided over these changes. Finally, my attention will focus on the creeping paralysis that enveloped the city's economic system during the second part of the war, as well as on the changes induced by wartime conditions and the policies introduced by the Japanese and Chinese authorities in the industrial structure. Throughout this study, there will be a concern as to what extent the Japanese were able to muster local resources, especially Shanghai industries, to serve their military ambitions in China.

no. 7, Ann Arbor, University of Michigan, 1971; *The Outsiders: The Western Experience in India and China*, Ann Arbor, University of Michigan Press, 1977.

[4] Barnett, Robert W., *Economic Shanghai: Hostage to Politics, 1937–1941*, New York, Institute for Pacific Relations, 1941.

[5] The issue of Japanese policies and their consequences in Central China have been addressed in Henriot, Christian, "War and Economics: The Control of Material Resources in the Lower Yangzi and the Shanghai Area Between 1937 and 1945," paper at the international conference, "The Role of the Republican Period in Twentieth Century China: Reflections and Reconsiderations," Venice, 30 June–3 July 1999.

3. The flow of refugees crossing Garden Bridge into the International Settlement.
Source: Unknown.

WAR DAMAGES AND LOSSES

A complete assessment of the losses and damages incurred by Shanghai industries during the war is probably an insoluble question. Three different constraints prevent us from reaching a definite and fully reliable image. First, the assessment of war damages became at once a political issue. Nationalistic considerations on the Chinese side led to an inflation of the figures, as in 1932.[6] Both government and entrepreneurs had an interest in raising the stakes from the perspective of postwar indemnities.[7] Second, most of the damage took place in areas that were occupied by the Japanese army. Therefore, the collection of data was uneven. In the International Settlement, the SMC did a fairly reliable survey. In the Chinese municipality, however, the legitimate government collapsed and the puppet authorities were certainly not in a position to undertake any serious study. Most of the assessments published were produced by professional organizations or private bodies whose methodology we cannot control.[8] In other words, we have to make do with incomplete data. Third, apart from the plants that were fully destroyed, the data rarely indicate the extent of "damage" in great detail. Furthermore, there were also transfers of machinery and other equipment by the Japanese army during the period of hostilities. Such moves are not easy to distinguish from real destruction. Finally, available figures tend to be contradictory.

When war broke out, economic life collapsed. The conflict started in the eastern and northern districts (Yangshupu, Zhabei, and Hongkou) and progressively engulfed the whole city, even if actual fighting took place only in the Chinese municipality. The territory of the settlements were by and large immune from fighting, although heavy bombing and shelling sometimes caused

---

[6] On the first Sino-Japanese conflict and its consequences, see Henriot, Christian, *Shanghai 1927–1937. Municipal power, locality and modernization*, Berkeley, University of California Press, 1993, chap. 3.

[7] The Nationalist government established a special committee for war indemnities, but it was a late initiative and it was concerned with retrieving and summarizing data at the national level. In a study of the history of this committee, the name of Shanghai appears only three times. Qi Jingde, *Zhongguo dui ri kangzhan sunshi diaocha* (A historical account of the surveys of China's losses during the war with Japan), Taipei, Guoshiguan, 1987. Han Qitong, a member of the Academia Sinica, made an independent survey after the war. Although it has been hailed as the best scientific study of China's war losses, it suffers from the same limitations referred to above. All the figures have been computed at the national level, and the damages have been expressed in monetary terms. In spite of its usefulness, there is no way to retrieve any data related to Shanghai. Han Qitong, *Zhongguo duiri zhanshi sunshi zhi guji 1937–1945* (An estimate of China's losses in the war against Japan, 1937–1943), Shanghai, Zhonghua shuju, 1946.

[8] The Shanghai General Chamber of Commerce collected claims from its members, but this was a fairly late initiative and the available records look very incomplete.

collateral damage in the settlements. There was an exception, however. The eastern industrial district of Yangshupu became the focus of considerable fighting between Chinese and Japanese troops. This was the area where the largest factories were located. According to a report by the French commercial attaché, approximately 60 percent of the larger industrial plants were to be found in the eastern district. The rest was concentrated in the western part of the city.[9]

The distribution of small plants was slightly different. Whereas 60 percent of them were located in the eastern district, 10 percent had their seat in the northern district, 20 percent in the western district, and 10 percent in the central district.[10] The above figures are crude indications, but they show that certain sectors of industry were heavily concentrated in the northern districts. Zhabei housed hundreds of workshops, which were bombed and burned to the ground. Hongkou, the area where the Japanese population had its quarters, was also massively destroyed. It was said that 35 percent of the plants located in Zhabei as well as 20 percent of those in Nanshi and Pudong were destroyed.[11] One-half of the Zhabei flour mills were turned into ashes.[12]

In a book published in 1938, Hsü Shuhsi indicated that 905 plants had been fully destroyed and a thousand more had been partially damaged or destroyed.[13] These figures were drawn from the report published by the industrial section of the SMC in May 1938.[14] This list included only the plants located in the International Settlement. Before the war, there were 3,801 registered plants in the settlement (this figure does not include the western external road area). The destroyed plants represented around one-fifth of Shanghai's industrial potential. They employed more than 30,000 workers. Table 1.1 lists the number of destroyed plants by sector.

Machine and textile factories were severely hit. Together, they represented one-half of the total. They formed, with flour mills, the core of Shanghai industry. The textile industry was made up of a small group of large plants, mainly cotton mills, and a large group of smaller ventures, especially in

---

[9] *Bulletin d'informations économiques*, 1 October 1937, p. 3, Consulat général de Shanghai, Archives diplomatiques de Nantes, box 45 (série noire). On the distribution of Shanghai industries, see Alain Roux's work, *Le Shanghai ouvrier des années trente: Coolies, gangsters et syndicalistes*, Paris, L'Harmattan, 1993.

[10] *Bulletin d'informations économiques*, 1 October 1937, p. 3, Consulat général de Shanghai, Archives diplomatiques de Nantes, box 45 (série noire).

[11] Huang Wenzhong, *Zhongguo zhanshi jingji teji*, Shanghai, Zhongwai chubanshe, 1940, p. 146.

[12] *Shanghai zhi gongshangye* (Shanghai's commerce and industry), [Shanghai], Zhongwai chubanshe, 1941, p. 21.

[13] Hsü, Shuhsi, *Japan and Shanghai*, prepared under the auspices of the Council of International Affairs, Shanghai, Kelly & Walsh, 1938, p. 42.

[14] *The Municipal Gazette*, vol. 31, 1938, p. 3.

Table 1.1 *The SMC survey of destroyed factories in the International Settlement*

Machinery and metal products	410	Woodworking	23
Textiles	136	Other	21
Printing, paper	75	Leather, rubber	19
Metal industry	72	Bricks, glass	8
Chemicals	49	Vehicles	3
Clothing	44	Scientific and musical instruments	3
Food, drinks, tobacco	40	Furniture	2

Source: The Municipal Gazette, vol. 31, 1938, p. 3.

the silk industry.[15] Machine manufacturing and repair comprised around 200 small workshops located mostly in Hongkou (80%).[16] From the SMC report, it appears that around 90 dyeing plants, 15 knitting mills (out of 50), 51 silk reeling mills (out of 100), 118 silk weaving mills (out of 400), 8 of the 48 largest tobacco plants, and 8 flour mills (out of 15) were wiped out.[17]

There were sixty-five cotton mills before the hostilities with 2,676,000 spindles and 30,000 looms.[18] Only ten of them were located in war-free areas.[19] Only ten or eleven of the thirty Chinese-owned cotton mills (237,074 spindles, 8754 looms) in Shanghai were located in war-free areas, and seven of them managed to work throughout the hostilities. For the others, the damage was uneven, although only six were completely destroyed or seriously damaged.[20]

---

[15] On the development of the textile industry in Shanghai, see Bergère, Marie-Claire, *Capitalisme national et impérialisme: la crise des filatures chinoises en 1923*, Cahiers du Centre Chine 2, CRDCC, Paris, Ecole des Hautes Etudes en Sciences Sociales, 1980 and Bergère, Marie-Claire, *The Golden age of the Chinese bourgeoisie*, Cambridge, Cambridge University Press, 1989.

[16] *China Weekly Review*, 3 August 1940, p. 347.

[17] *Bulletin mensuel*, May 1938, p. 3.

[18] There were 31 Chinese mills, 30 Japanese mills, and 4 British mills. They had respectively 1,114,408, 1,331,412, and 221,336 spindles. Wang Jishen, *Zhanshi shanghai jingji*, vol.1, Shanghai jingji yanjiusuo, 1945, p. 191; *Zhanhou shanghai zhi gongshang ge ye*, Shanghai, Zhongguo jingji yanjiuhui, Minyi shuju, 1940, p. 38.

[19] *Bulletin d'informations économiques*, 1 October 1937, p. 3.

[20] Although the various sources I have consulted indicate a total of 21 damaged Chinese cotton mills, there is always one mill missing from their listing, while the total number of destroyed spindles is correct. Hopeless! A detailed summary of war damage tells the following: 2 fully destroyed (59,400 spindles), 6 seriously damaged (219,255 spindles), 13 moderately damaged (449,426 spindles), 11 untouched (385,932 spindles). It is therefore extremely difficult to reconcile these figures and to estimate the real number of *spindles* or *looms* that were actually destroyed. A postwar study states that only 130,000 spindles were transferred from the Yangshupu district to the International Settlement. But one can also imagine that the Japanese seized a large number of spindles. Shou Bai, "Shanghai fangzhiye zhi jinxi," *Shangye yuebao*, vol. 21, no. 1, January 1941, pp. 1–2; Li Shengbo, "Shi nian lai zhi mianfangzhi gongye," in Tan Xihong

The Japanese cotton mills also suffered. They lost 17 percent of their equipment during the conflict.[21] Silk reeling mills were almost all located in Zhabei and Hongkou (97%). Thirty were entirely destroyed and three were severely damaged. Only ten or eleven escaped the hostilities untouched. The equipment of the destroyed plants represented 68 percent of the city's potential.[22] Fifteen out of fifty knitting plants were destroyed, though nine managed to move their machinery before the destruction of the buildings. Dyeing plants were legion in Shanghai. There were around 270 houses at the time of hostilities. More than one-half were located in Hongkou, Zhabei, and Nanshi. More than 190 concerns, large and small, were reported by the trade association to have been destroyed. The survivors moved en masse into the settlement at the end of the hostilities and twenty new ones were soon established.[23]

The tobacco industry was much less affected. Of the forty-eight tobacco plants, six were destroyed, three were seriously damaged, and eight suffered minor destruction. Twelve were located in safe areas. Nevertheless, eight of the eighteen large Chinese-owned plants were destroyed.[24] Chinese rubber factories numbered thirty-four before the war. Five were reduced to ashes, while ten were severely damaged. Fifteen of them suffered mild destruction and four escaped trouble altogether.[25] The Commercial Press (*Shangwu yinshuguan*) and 200 small printers were entirely destroyed.[26] Of the fifteen flour mills, eight were destroyed, incurring losses estimated at 2 million yuan, while those of glass

---

(Ed.), *Shi nian lai zhi zhongguo jingji (1937–1945)* (China's economy during the past ten years), Shanghai, Zhonghua shuju (coll. Jindai zhongguo shiliao congkan xuji), 1948, p. 79. Throughout China, only 19 of the 88 Chinese-owned cotton mills escaped destruction. Despatch, 31 July 1939, Consular trade report, E326, Box 1415, National Archives at College Park; *Shanghai zhi gongshangye*, p. 24.

[21] Inoue Kiyoshi, *Nitchû sensô to Nitchû kankei* (The Sino-Japanese war and Sino-Japanese relations), Tokyo, Hara shobo, 1988, p. 338. The Japanese cotton mills suffered in the following way: 2 fully destroyed (50,656 spindles), 7 seriously damaged (349,924), 5 moderately damaged (409,084 spindles), and 16 untouched (553,392 spindles). Shou Bai, "Shanghai fangzhiye zhi jinxi," *Shangye yuebao*, vol. 21, no. 1, Jan. 1941, pp. 1–2.

[22] There were 44 silk reeling mills in operation in Shanghai before the war. From a maximum of 112 in the early 1930s, the number of plants had undergone a severe reduction following the economic crisis of 1931–1935. "Shanhai ni okeru seishigyô no jôkyô" (The situation of the silk industry in Shanghai), *Shanhai* (Shanghai), no. 1026, 1943, p. 97; *Shanghai zhi gongshangye*, p. 6; Zhou Qibang, "Zhongguo zhanshi gongye gaikuang" (General situation of China's wartime industry), *Zhongguo gongye yuekan* (China Industrial Monthly), vol. 1, no. 1, 1943, p. 37.

[23] Wang Jishen, Zhanshi shanghai jingji, p. 198; *Shanghai zhi gongshangye*, p. 21; *An annual report of Shanghai commodity prices* (from the annual report of the Industrial section of the Shanghai Municipal Council), Shanghai, National Tariff Commission, 1938, p. 27.

[24] *Shanghai zhi gongshangye*, p. 24.

[25] *Shanghai zhi gongshangye*, p. 36; *An annual report of Shanghai commodity prices*, p. 27.

[26] *Bulletin d'informations économiques*, 17 April 1939, p. 2.

Table 1.2 *Chinese-owned firms
destroyed during the hostilities*

Wool	22
Cotton spinning	31
Silk reeling	112
Miscellaneous	83
Machines	103
Dyeing	6
Paper	14
Leather	8
Glass	31
Matches	6

Source: Huang Wenzhong, *Zhongguo
zhanshi jingji teji*, Shanghai, Zhongwai
chubanshe, 1940, p. 146.

factories – one-half were erased – were valued at 1–2 million yuan.[27] Most of these factories, plants, and workshops were Chinese-owned. Except for textile mills, the available data do not provide a breakdown by ownership. There is no doubt that Chinese industrialists were the main losers. Table 1.2 gives an idea of the destruction.

The total number of firms destroyed (416) is certainly below the reality. Immediately after the war, the Bureau of Social Affairs estimated that 2,270 Chinese-owned plants had been destroyed or damaged causing a total loss of 800 million yuan.[28] In a later estimate, the same bureau indicated that 4,998 plants out of a total of 5,255 had suffered.[29] As indicated above, the SMC estimated that 905 firms had been completely destroyed while a thousand had suffered damages. An Osaka-based Japanese research center gave the figure of 1958 destroyed plants, valued at 500 million yuan, before the fall of Nanshi.[30] It is clear that in order to emphasize the extent of the damage, official sources often did not distinguish between "fully destroyed" and "damaged."[31] In 1939,

[27] Report, 26 July 1939, Consular trade report, E326, Box 1415, National Archives at College Park; Chôsabu, "Shanghai kôgyô kai no gaikyô" (The situation of Shanghai industrialists), *Shanhai* (Shanghai), no. 986, 1939, p. 91.

[28] *Bulletin d'informations économiques*, 1 December 1937, p. 3.

[29] Zhou Qibang, "Zhongguo zhanshi gongye gaikuang," p. 36.

[30] *Kangzhan zhong de zhongguo jingji* (The Chinese economy during the war), Shishi wenti yanjiuhui bian, Kangzhan shudian, 1940, pp. 154–155.

[31] I have also come across two other sets of figures, one by Cai Lian, of the Institute of Social Sciences at the Academia Sinica, who pushed the figure to 600–700 million yuan, and another by *Yinqianjie* (The World of Banking) in which damages amounted to 8,000 million yuan. *Kangzhan zhong de zhongguo jingji*, pp. 154–155; *Yinqianjie*, vol. 3, no. 6, p. 400.

the Chinese-owned Kincheng Banking Corporation (Jincheng yinhang) made a much-reduced assessment of war damages. The losses of Chinese factories in Shanghai and its immediate vicinity from the commencement of hostilities up to March 1939 totaled 155,764,000 yuan. Of this sum, 85,484,000 represented direct material damages as a result of the three-month military operations, while the remaining was the aggregate capital of the 47 Chinese industries confiscated by the Japanese.[32] The discrepancy between official and private figures is too obvious. It reflects the difficulty to separate economics from politics, and that of establishing a standard set of criteria to assess war damages.

Shanghai's industrial potential was further depleted by the move of factories to inland provinces. Since this migration started only in August 1937 when heavy fighting had already begun around the city, the displacement of factories and their equipment was actually limited. The national government was caught unprepared and tried to coordinate the departure of the more vital plants. Nevertheless, it was left to the initiative of the owners and few financial resources were actually mobilized to help the candidates migrate. By February 1938, 123 factories had left Shanghai along with 1,500 workers and 12,000 tons of equipment. They hardly represented more than 2 percent of the original number of factories. It could not seriously affect the industrial potential of the city.[33]

From the preceding presentation, it appears that whatever the sources used, the data for an assessment of war damages to Shanghai industry are far from transparent. It is obvious that many small and medium-sized establishments in many sectors were fully destroyed. Larger plants, especially cotton mills, although they also suffered, seem to have escaped extensive destruction. As we do not have reliable figures on the destruction or confiscation of *equipment*, no definite judgment can really be made.[34] If this hypothesis holds true, these two observations could explain the capacity of Shanghai industrialists to resume operations fairly rapidly. Small and medium-sized plants did not require much capital to start up anew, while large plants may have been in a position to make use of undamaged equipment after resettling in a safer area. As we shall see, there was no dearth of capital to rely on in the city.

---

[32] *China Weekly Review*, 15 July 1939, p. 212. This sum represented 58% of the total amount of damages suffered by factories and plants in the coastal provinces (779 establishments valued at $267,709,700).

[33] On this subject, see the well-documented paper by Huang Liren, "Kangri zhanzheng shiqi gongchang neiqian de kaocha" (An investigation of factories moving into the hinterland of China during the war of resistance against Japan), *Lishi yanjiu* (Historical research), no. 4, 1994, pp. 120–136.

[34] For instance, the Japanese were said to have expropriated 275,000 spindles to compensate themselves. *China Weekly Review*, 29 June 1940, p. 159.

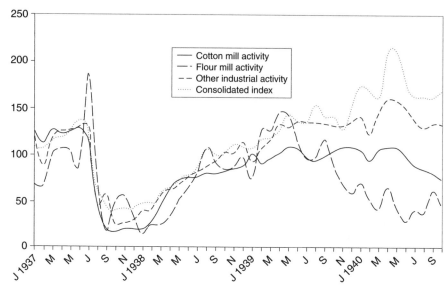

Figure 1.1 The U.S. consulate's business barometer (1937–1940)

RECOVERY AND BOOM (1938–1940)

To monitor the evolution of the local economy, the U.S. general consulate in Shanghai in the 1930s designed a system of economic indicators called the "Business barometer." Although it focused on specific domains, I shall take this "barometer" as a crude indicator of economic changes. In Figure 1.1, the barometer shows a drastic drop in economic activity and industrial production after August 1937. For three months, economic life was almost nil. There was then a continuous though moderate upward movement throughout 1938. By the end of the year, these indicators had come close to their prewar levels. The recovery proceeded over the whole year until the demand created by an increased population and by the military requirements stimulated the economy. During the following two years, the local economy definitely emerged from depression and entered a phase of boom.

If we look at the industrial index in Figure 1.1 we can observe that the flour and cotton industries passed the 100 ceiling in October 1938 and January 1939 respectively. Other industrial activities had also recovered by the end of 1938. Afterward, development was far from constant. Difficulties emerged as early as mid-1940, even if industrial production had enough momentum to maintain a fairly high level of production throughout the whole period. In 1939 and

1940, the average industrial index reached 115 and 108 respectively.[35] Textile and flour factories, however, were declining very rapidly. A toll was levied on all supplies of all categories of goods moving into Shanghai from the interior, to such a degree that the U.S. commercial attaché considered that the city had virtually the status of a rationed and heavily taxed concentration camp.[36] By 1941, difficulties accumulated. Economic blockades, lack of transportation facilities, and more stringent policies of economic control began to slow down the pace of industrial activity.

How did recovery proceed? Large factories began to resume operation in the spring of 1938, while the summer saw an acceleration of the process. All the Japanese factories had stopped during the time of hostilities. They resumed operation in February–March 1938.[37] Among these, fourteen cotton mills resumed production and two new ones were established.[38] In August 1938, small industrial plants also experienced a recovery. These included the small workshops in the field of dyeing, machine manufacturing, and weaving which sought refuge in the foreign settlements and western external road area. Between August and December 1937, 422 new plants moved into the International Settlement.[39] By May 1938, the SMC counted 1,861 plants in its territory with 130,796 workers, most of them in the western part of the settlement and the external road area.[40] By May 1938, 339 more had followed this example and by October, 2,540 plants (152,596/154,296 workers) were in operation in the International Settlement.[41]

---

[35] "Shanghai business barometer (February 1941)," 30 April 1941, Consular trade report; see also *China Weekly Review*, "China's cotton industry since the hostilities," 22 April 1939, p. 241, and "Textile industry in Shanghai booming," 3 June 1939, p. 17.

[36] *Confidential weekly economic report*, 23 November 1940, Consular trade report. In a confidential report disclosed by the *China Weekly Review*, the SMC attributed to the Japanese army a major role in the high-price situation. The army imposed on every cow a levy of 25 yuan, on every sheep 10 yuan, and on every goat from 5 to 7 yuan. A truckload of vegetables was taxed 25 yuan and a handcart load had to pay 3 yuan. Rice was taxed 15 to 20 yuan a picul. *China Weekly Review*, 6 March 1940, p. 94.

[37] There were 48 Japanese factories in Shanghai at the time of the conflict. Factory owners belonged to the Association of Shanghai Industrialists (Shanghai gongye tongzhihui). Yoda Yoshiie, *Nitchû sensô shi shiryô* (Documents sur l'histoire de la guerre sino-japonaise), vol. 4, Nitchû sensô shi shiryô henshû iinkai (Ed.), Tokyo, Kawade shobô shinsha, [1975], p. 647.

[38] *Shanghai zhi gongshangye*, p. 38.

[39] *Zhongguo gongye yuekan* (China industrial monthly), vol. 1, no. 6, 1943, p. 30.

[40] The other plants were located in the central (312) and northern districts (381). The low figure for the eastern district is surprising since the extent of destruction was not so severe. It may include only the firms located in the part of the eastern district under actual SMC control. Most of the area remained under the control of the Japanese army. *Bulletin mensuel*, May 1938, p. 3.

[41] *Bulletin mensuel*, May 1938, pp. 2–3, October 1938, p. 109; *Bulletin d'informations économiques*, 24 October 1939, p. 9.

Table 1.3 *Index of industrial production in Shanghai (1936 = 100)*

Year	1937	1938	1939	1940	1941
Cotton	81.7	69.8	104.5	99.0	63.3
Silk	72.6	95.5	116.8	104.2	97.3
Flour	77.5	72.5	112.1	49.0	22.3
Wool	89.1	59.5	164.8	173.1	49.5
Rubber	65.9	25.3	42.1	45.9	50.9
Dyeing	81.9	73.0	213.9	232.9	196.0
Machine	99.6	56.0	112.1	153.9	125.0
Paper	115.6	147.4	242.5	350.5	396.0
General index	82.4	72.5	102.9	105.5	80.0

Source: *Shenbao nianjian* (The Shenbao yearbook), Shanghai, Shenbaoshe, 1944, p. 715 [based on *Zhongyang jingji yuekan*, vol. 2, no. 6].

At the end of the year, the figure had grown to 4,709.[42] The year 1939 saw the establishment of 347 large plants and 669 small ones.[43] In 1940, 51 large plants and 171 small ones opened.[44] At the end of 1941, there were more than 6,000 plants, well over the 5,525 figure of 1937.[45] Yet, not all of them were in operation. In the northern and eastern districts, however, the situation remained unchanged. Few plants were able to resume operation.[46] A striking feature of the new establishments was their small size.[47] A dispatch of the U.S. commercial attaché shows that in the first term of 1940, the 165 newly opened factories had an average of 22 workers. The size of the factories depended on their location. Those that were located in the areas that had escaped the hostilities were significantly larger (77 vs. 38).[48]

Table 1.3 indicates that the year 1939 was a major turning point.[49] The foreign settlements of Shanghai witnessed extensive industrial recovery and expansion. In cotton spinning, weaving, and dyeing, output compared favorably with the

[42] Before the war, they sold 40% of their production in Jiangsu and Zhejiang, 30% in Central China, and 30% in South and North China. After the occupation and blockades imposed by the Japanese, the market kept shrinking. *Shanghai zhi gongshangye*, p. 24.

[43] *Shanghai zhi gongshangye*, p. 2.

[44] "Newly opened factories in the International Settlement," 31 May 1940, Consular trade report.

[45] *Zhongguo gongye yuekan* (China Industrial Monthly), vol. 1, no. 6, 1943, p. 30.

[46] *Bulletin d'informations économiques*, 29 August 1938, p. 3.

[47] Chôsabu, "Shanhai kô gyôkai no gaikyô," pp. 88–92.

[48] "Newly opened factories in the International Settlement," 31 May 1940, Consular trade report.

[49] The U.S. commercial attaché notes that the industrial statistics of the SMC became less reliable in 1939 but they still remained the best indicator available. Despatch, 23 October 1939, Consular trade report.

levels of 1936 and profits were exceptionally high. The output of flour mills was 12 percent greater than that of 1936; nevertheless, flour mills hardly had any favorable period, except 1939, while the rubber industry, so dependent on imports from Southeast Asia, failed to overcome the difficulties of the war.[50] The machine industry also benefited from the demand from other industries. The most interesting phenomenon was the number and variety of manufacturing establishments that grew up, most of them moderate and small-sized plants.

In 1939 and 1940, Shanghai industries in most cases returned to their prewar level of production and, in many cases, even exceeded this level.[51] Keith Schoppa has studied how Chinese traders found ways of securing access to the Chinese-controlled regions by shipping Shanghai factory goods to Hong Kong and then moving the goods on small craft to small Japanese-controlled ports in the vicinity where "fees" could be arranged.[52] By offering bribes to lesser officials, Chinese mills in Shanghai also managed to secure materials for production.[53] Another major factor in the recovery was the tremendous amount of "idle capital" that accrued to Shanghai.[54] According to a Japanese source, 1,000 million yuan left Shanghai for Hong Kong when the war broke out. In spring 1938, there was a reversal of this trend. As fighting was closing in on Hong Kong, Shanghai appeared to be a safer place. In 1939, Shanghai experienced a new influx of capital. In June, the deposits in local banks amounted to 2,800 million yuan, a figure that jumped to 3,500 million yuan by the end of the year.[55] The amount of capital available exceeded by fourfold the most pessimistic assessments of war damages.

Various factors contributed to this initial recovery. Shanghai received a large influx of population from cities in Jiangsu and Zhejiang who sought refuge in the settlements. It increased the demand for consumer goods. Many also

---

[50] On the fate of this industrial sector, *China Weekly Review*, 23 November 1940, pp. 390–391.

[51] Dyeing and weaving mills underwent considerable expansion, from 270 establishments in 1937 before the hostilities to 414 mills by the end of 1939. They were very sensitive to the fluctuations in cotton and silk production. When the Japanese army blocked the Fujian coast in 1940, more than 100 establishments were forced to suspend operation while another 140 mills were under operation. *China Weekly Review*, 16 November 1940, p. 361.

[52] Schoppa, Keith, "The structure, dynamics, and impacts of the Shanghai-coastal Zhejiang trading system, 1938–1944," paper presented at the international conference on "Wartime Shanghai, 1937–1945," Lyon, 15–17 October 1997.

[53] "Confidential weekly economic report," 23 November 1940, Consular trade report.

[54] Wu Chengxi, "Zhanhou shanghai jinrong biandong zhi yiban de qingxiang," *Jinrong daobao*, vol 1, no. 1, March 1939, pp. 4–7.

[55] *Shanhai keizai no hensen* (The evolution of the Shanghai economy), Shanhai, Obayashi jimusho, 1943, pp. 71–72.

brought with them capital they sought to protect and reinvest in the city. The rising cost of cotton in the second half of 1938 which resulted from hoarding, but also from increasing demand by the military and the civilian population, gave a boost to cotton mills. As a result, the other industrial sectors related to textiles all experienced a new upshot.[56] In the autumn of 1938, the reestablishment of links with Hong Kong and South China generated a rise in the volume of trade as Shanghai products could be shipped to inland China. Nevertheless, the city's industries found it increasingly difficult to reach their markets, for both supplies and sales, in North China – the northern provinces became integrated into the Yen bloc – and the Yangzi valley, where the Japanese army replaced the *fabi* with compulsory military scrip.[57]

In Central China, the movement of goods also became subject to permits issued by the Japanese authorities. This was designed to guarantee the regular supply of cheap agricultural products for the army's needs in North China, Manchuria, and Japan. In the course of 1938, the Japanese set up various enterprises under the umbrella of the Asia Development Board whose purpose was to monitor and systematically plunder the major sectors of the economy in Central China.[58] Production costs also soared as a result of the multifarious taxes on all goods brought into Shanghai by either the Japanese or the puppet "Reformed" government or by the Shanghai Dadao government.[59] Last, the instability of the national currency (*fabi*) contributed to speculative behaviors.

---

[56] Although it is difficult to assess which markets Shanghai textile industries served, it is obvious that both the Japanese and Chinese armies were in need of cotton and silk products. As to the civilian population, one of the main outlets was North China where most of the factories had been destroyed.

[57] *Bulletin mensuel*, October 1938, p. 107.

[58] The ADB was founded in December 1938, while its Central China Liaison Bureau was set up in March 1939 in Shanghai. *Shanhai yôran* (Shanhai handbook), Shanhai Nihon shôkô kaigisho, Shanghai, 1939, p. 188. A major instrument for economic penetration and domination was the Central China Development Company which was itself made up of several subcompanies covering essential domains of economic activity, for instance the trade in silk cocoons, shipping, mining, and power production. By 1941, the *China Weekly Review* observed that its operations "remained cloaked in mystery," but "the foundations of this quasi-military enterprise were built on loot." *China Weekly Review*, 8 February 1941, p. 344; 18 January 1941, p. 234.

[59] Reconstruction was also impaired by the rising cost of building materials. Basic items such as sand, tiles, bricks, and bamboo were scarce. The plants that had been destroyed were rehabilitated or reconstructed at a higher cost. In his annual report for 1939, the U.S. commercial attaché wrote: "During 1939, Shanghai experienced the most extensive building activity of any of the cities of China, but it was confined mostly to the foreign settlements . . . actual construction was much greater than in 1936, but buildings and materials were on much lower quality levels, in fact were the cheapest possible consistent with quick returns on investments." "China annual economic report for 1939," 15/2/40, p. 17, Consular trade report, 1940, Box 1498; "Sino-Japanese hostilities have greatly increased the cost of domestic building materials," Report by H. H. Smith, U.S. Consul, 27 June 1938, Consular trade archives.

To protect themselves against future depreciation, Shanghai residents invested in commodities. The volume of trade of the large department stores reached its prewar level and even exceeded it. In the second semester of 1938, the department stores made huge profits.[60] The more serious the currency problem became, the more Shanghai residents turned to the purchase of goods for hoarding and further exchange. Although the movement was irregular, the volume of sales had doubled by 1939 and quadrupled by the end of 1940.

After the end of hostilities, the Japanese army barred the Chinese population from entering the areas under its control. The measure also applied to foreigners. Although this policy was justified for security reasons, it gave the Japanese enough time to survey the remaining factories and to remove the stocks and the machinery that could be used for their military purpose or as a compensation for collateral damages to Japanese firms.[61] Chinese entrepreneurs had many difficulties getting back to their plants. When they eventually obtained special passes, they could only observe that the doors had been sealed and that they were enjoined to get in touch with Japanese mills.[62] When the Japanese-occupied districts were finally opened to the Chinese population, the army continued to press the Chinese industrialists to resume operations "in collaboration with" Japanese firms. Blunt refusal was tantamount to having their installations confiscated. By May 1938, few entrepreneurs had accepted the Japanese dictate. To avoid possible troubles in dealing with the Japanese, many important figures in Chinese industry went to Hong Kong to seek refuge until such pressures receded.[63] In many cases, however, the Chinese entrepreneurs had no choice but to comply. In early 1940, thirty Chinese plants had agreed to "cooperate" (*gongtong jingying*) with the Japanese.[64] Moreover, through persuasion, pressure, and mostly arbitrary confiscation, the Japanese seized more than two hundred enterprises in Shanghai, mostly in the sectors of textile, food, and chemicals.[65]

---

[60] *China Press*, 23 February 1939 [from ADN 46, noire); Despatch of the U.S. commercial attaché, 25 July 1939, Consular trade report, 1939.

[61] The *North China Daily News* sent one of its reporters to investigate the war-torn areas: "Gangs of Chinese coolies under a Chinese foreman, and controlled by the Japanese, have for weeks past been making house to house, factory to factory, visits on Chinese property, removing not only metal which might rightly be termed scrap, but all types of metal fabrication from boilers down to small motors. The process which is going on hardly comes within the ordinary definition of looting . . . but amounts to the careful and systematic removal of every piece of metal which can be found on Chinese property." *North China Daily News*, 4 February 1938.

[62] *North China Daily News*, 10 May 1938 [taken from *Bulletin mensuel*, May 1938, p. 3].

[63] *Bulletin mensuel*, May 1938, p. 1.

[64] Huang Wenzhong, *Zhongguo zhanshi jingji teji*, pp. 171–172.

[65] There were 90 confiscations, 66 "fusions," 31 "rentals," and 16 "acquisitions," while the total number of newly created Japanese enterprises was 65. Yoda Yoshiie, *Nitchû sensô shi shiryô*, p. 58.

By May 1939, forty Chinese cotton mills were under military control.[66] As Park M. Coble's chapter on the Rong family in this volume documents, textile industrialists had to play a very subtle game to protect their assets and avoid a too obvious compromise with the puppet and Japanese authorities.

After the establishment of the Wang Jingwei government in Nanjing, the Chinese authorities attempted to obtain the return of the confiscated factories. A committee for the return of Chinese factories to their original owners was organized in August 1940 in Nanjing, with offices in Shanghai and Canton. Progress was slow. The Japanese required financial compensation for actual or alleged repairs and improvements that were so great as to prove a significant obstacle to the Chinese owners.[67] In some instances, the Japanese purchased plants from the Chinese, but at a price fixed by them.[68] Chinese firms were returned to their owners in successive installments. By January 1943, eleven plants had been restituted. They were said to represent 108 enterprises out of an official total of 140 confiscated firms. It is obvious that this figure, which includes the whole country, was well below the actual number of firms seized by the Japanese army. It was a mere symbolic gesture to give the Wang Jingwei government some political face.[69]

Japanese pressures caused a drastic change in the local industrial geography. Chinese companies sought to escape confiscation by moving their equipment to the safety of the settlements. The Japanese-controlled areas lost a lot of industrial equipment and production capacity as a result of this migration.[70] Besides Shanghai factories, many workshops and plants originally located in the cities and towns of Jiangsu and Zhejiang province also moved into the foreign settlements or its western extension.[71] Western Shanghai was also a place where

---

[66] Inoue Kiyoshi, *Nitchû sensô to Nitchû kankei*, p. 340. In March 1939, the *Shanghai Evening Post* indicated that the Japanese policy of taking over Chinese industrial firms in the Lower Yangzi valley had proceeded at a regular pace. In Shanghai, 17 mills representing 686,420 spindles (cotton), 72,426 spindles (silk), and 6,721 looms had been transferred to Japanese interests. *Shanghai Evening Post*, 4 March 1939 [from ADN 46, noire]. The Japanese also planned very early the total seizure of the Chinese industrial firms located in the International Settlement. In January 1938, the Army, the Navy, and the Consulate formed a team to make a detailed census of all the factories and to examine to what extent they could serve to repair the Japanese plants that had been damaged during the hostilities. Inoue Kyoshi, *Nitchû sensô to Nitchû kankei*, p. 340. By October 1940, the Japanese controlled 70% of the cotton spindleage and over 80% of the cotton weaving looms of Shanghai. *China Weekly Review*, 5 October 1940, p. 154.

[67] *Weekly economic report*, 7 September 1940, Consular trade report.

[68] *Monthly economic report*, 26 August 1940, Consular trade report.

[69] *Chôkô sangyô ihô* (Yangzi Industries Report), no. 24, 20 February 1943, pp. 15–18.

[70] *Bulletin mensuel*, September 1938, p. 21.

[71] To the west of the settlements and beyond its official borders, there was an area which for decades had enjoyed a particular status. The so-called extra-settlement road area, though legally

land was less expensive than in the settlements. Many factories decided to settle there with the hope that they would also enjoy the protection of the foreign authorities. From the beginning of the hostilities to the end of the year, 422 factories moved into the western and central areas of the International Settlement. Another 288 new enterprises joined them during the following three months.[72] The flow never stopped: Chinese industrialists set up shop by the hundreds.[73] The Western residents, who were alarmed by developments that affected their lifestyle, organized an association to press the SMC to ban the establishment of new industrial firms in these areas. Their attempt stumbled on the SMC's legal posture and sympathetic attitude toward Chinese entrepreneurs.[74] By the end of 1938, there were 4,700 industrial firms in the International Settlement, twice the prewar figure.[75]

Actually, the Chinese puppet authorities and the Japanese army tried to monitor these developments very closely. On March 23, 1938, the Dadao government set up a "Society for the economic reconstruction of the Western district of Shanghai" in the western external road area. It was replaced in August by the "Society for the economic reconstruction of Shanghai" under the supervision of the Special Service Section of the Japanese army. All the plants were required to register with the new society to be allowed to transport their commodities.[76] In fact, by 1940, police restrictions over the movement of workers, the extortion of exorbitant fees for permits to bring raw materials into the area and to export

---

part of the Chinese municipality, was placed under the actual administration of the SMC and offered a certain degree of safety. This area became a tug of war between the SMC and the puppet government. In the early years of the war, because of its ambiguous status, it became a land of lawlessness where all kinds of illegal traffic and activities (opium, gambling, etc.) flourished. For a contemporary journalistic account, see the *China Weekly Review*. Frederic Wakeman has written a very vivid study of this period and place. Wakeman, Frederic E., *The Shanghai Badlands: Wartime terrorism and urban crime, 1937–1941*, New York, Cambridge University Press, 1996.

[72] "Memorandum on conditions in the Western extra-settlement area" (30 May 1938), Shanghai Municipal Council, Mulu "Shanghai gonggong zujie gongbuju weishengchu B 15 (2)," File 2108 "Shanghai xibu diqu gongchang jianchuang qingkuang" (1938–1939), p. 169.

[73] "Some 300 new factories and workshops were opened or reopened in Shanghai during the month of February [1939] . . . Of these 30 were in the eastern district, and 140 in the western extra settlement area." *China Weekly Review*, 18 March 1939, p. 75. American diplomats made the same observations for 1940. "Newly opened factories in the International Settlement," Despatch no. 317 (Richard P. Butrick), 31 May 1940; "Factories in the Shanghai International Settlement," 24 July 1940, Consul Arnold, Consular trade report, 1940, Box 1497.

[74] On the SMC's position, see "Memorandum on conditions in the Western extra-settlement area" (30 May 1938); on the Western residents' protests, see *The China Press*, 19 March 1938, 2 April 1938; *North China Daily News*, 21 March 1938, 31 March 1938, 1 April 1938.

[75] *Kangzhan zhong de zhongguo jingji*, p. 215.

[76] *Bulletin mensuel*, August 1938, p. 26.

finished goods, and the stories constantly recurring of the kidnapping of owners to extort ransom under torture, were said to have caused a lack of enthusiasm among Chinese entrepreneurs to set up shop in this area.[77] In reality, SMC figures tend to show that entrepreneurs did continue to go into this area in spite of the risks involved.

This drastic geographical redistribution notwithstanding, economic recovery proceeded at a hasty pace as long as the lines of communication with the surrounding provinces, especially in terms of transportation facilities, could be maintained at a reasonable level.[78] The blockade of certain regions, the institution of a system of permits, then of a monopolistic system led to a reduction in the flow of domestic supply and an increasing dependence on overseas markets.[79] The war period was marked by the growing intervention of the military and state authorities in the economy through the institution of monopolies on various commodities, either with the purpose of securing resources for their own needs, or with the intention of stabilizing a situation that seemed to get out of hand, especially prices.[80] The Japanese policy with regard to cotton was to move as much as possible of the domestic supply to Japan or other Yen-bloc regions, hence neither the Japanese nor the Chinese mills in Shanghai enjoyed free access to the domestic market. They were forced to depend to an increasing extent on India and other foreign sources for the supply of cotton.[81]

---

[77] "Newly opened factories in the International Settlement," 31 May 1940, Consular trade report.

[78] In early 1939, the Yangzi river was still closed to all vessels except the Japanese companies. Only the small junks could move rather freely, but they could carry only a small part of the cargo that used to transit on the river. All the Chinese and foreign shipping companies were excluded. *Bulletin d'informations économiques*, 31 January 1939, p. 16.

[79] A branch office of the Asia Development Board was established in March 1939 in Shanghai under the authority of Admiral Tsuda. It was the main actor in the exploitation of the resources of Central China through the institution of a system of permits for the transportation and trade of agricultural commodities, then of monopolies exercised by associations under its control. "Industrial situation in Shanghai," FO 371, File 23515, F4952, 1 April 1939, Public Record Office.

[80] In Japan proper, the government adopted a series of legislative texts to transform the productive system into a command economy devoted solely to the war effort. See for example the presentation of these dispositions published for the edification of Chinese industrialists by the *Zhongguo gongye yuebao*. The author stated that the needs of the military and the war effort had a priority over all the rest. The whole system of production had to be subject to a regime of control to allow the maximal mobilization of resources, even if the level of consumption of the population was to suffer. Isobe, Kiichi, Guan, Huaicong (trans.), "Zhanshi gongye tongzhi zhengce" (The wartime policy of control over industry), *Zhongguo gongye yuekan*, vol. 1, no. 5, 1943, pp. 16–24.

[81] "Confidential weekly economic report," 23 November 1940, Consular trade report. Whereas cotton imports stood at 387,440 tons in 1936, 141,151 in 1937, and 146,855 in 1938, in 1939 and 1940 they reached the unprecedented figures of 2,318,026 and 2,301,801 tons respectively. *Zhanhou shanghai zhi gongshang ge ye*, p. 46; *Shanghai Nihon shôkô kaigisho nenpô* (Annual

This situation generated a rise in the price of raw materials. The outbreak of hostilities in Europe had an adverse effect on the price of many commodities and introduced new difficulties into a situation already suffering from foreign exchange fluctuations.[82] To curtail their operating costs, factories had to reduce output or to cease operations altogether.[83] On the other hand, as in World War I, the stoppage of imports from Europe was also conducive to the development of industries of substitution not just for the Shanghai and China markets, but also for Southeast and South Asian countries where Chinese goods replaced Western products.

During the first three years of the war, Shanghai managed to recover beyond expectations. Because of the fierce fighting and heavy destruction of late 1937 and the obstructions created by the Japanese army, local merchants and industrialists devised ways to provide adequate supplies to factories and to dispose of their production on the market. The limitations on the circulation of goods was partly circumvented thanks to the existence of the foreign settlements which allowed an almost free access to external markets both for imports and exports. Shanghai's industries were extremely responsive to the new context. Chinese entrepreneurs adapted to the new demand created by the war situation. This recovery, however spectacular, was also based on fragile ground. The safety and supply of Shanghai industries were heavily dependent on the existence of the foreign settlements and on the access to overseas markets extraterritoriality allowed.

DECLINE AND PARALYSIS (1941–1945)

With the institution of restrictions on the movement of goods in the second half of 1940 by the Japanese army, especially the blockade of the Fujian and Zhejiang coast, the regions that had supplied Shanghai with raw materials were virtually sealed off. Their closure also meant the loss of a huge market for the city's industrial products. In March 1941, Shanghai's industrial activity had come down to 88 percent of the 1936 level. Long-term war conditions, which ruled out such prerequisites as the availability of raw materials, cheap labor, and

report of the Japanese Chamber of Commerce and Industry), Shanghai, Shanhai nihon shôkô kaigisho, p. 34.

[82] In spite of active support by Western governments, the official *fabi* lost ground vis-à-vis foreign currencies. In 1938 a selling adjustment was made following the drop in exchange, but the market was not able to absorb a second adjustment in 1939. The introduction of a new currency by the Wang Jingwei government only increased the confusion and further contributed to a debasement of the *fabi*.

[83] "Industrial situation in Shanghai," FO 371, File 23515, F10635, 11 August 1939, Public Record Office.

extensive shipping facilities, caused the situation to worsen. Smuggling could somehow alleviate these constraints, though not to the same degree as a free-flow trading system.[84] Furthermore, the hike in fuel prices and the restricted supply of electrical power proved to be the most severe blows to Shanghai's ability to produce goods at competitive prices.[85] Depression definitely set in.[86]

During the summer of 1941, two events contributed to an acceleration of the mounting crisis. In July, the Japanese banned the export of fifteen products, including textiles, that were considered essential to the war effort. Shanghai industries then lost an outlet and a source of foreign currency. In the same month, the American and British governments decided to freeze all Japanese assets in their respective countries and to stop commercial relations with Japan and its occupied territories. This was a terrible blow to Shanghai, which relied extensively on raw materials imported from American and British colonies to replace domestic sources. This decision also pushed the national currency (*fabi*) further down.[87] Prices soared to previously unknown levels, while production took a deep plunge. By October 1941, the crisis took a more dramatic turn. Transportation was further curtailed for lack of gas and oil and the poor condition of motor vehicles. The scarcity of primary materials led to the recycling of existing goods. Most iron fences around government buildings and large business quarters disappeared and a nationwide campaign to collect all metal articles was launched.[88]

The attack on Pearl Harbor and the beginning of the Pacific War further aggravated the situation. Locally, the political and economic context changed radically with the occupation of the International Settlement. Chinese factories had preserved their autonomy thanks to the haven provided by the regime of extraterritoriality. The existence of independent foreign authorities had provided a venue for relatively free imports. With the Japanese occupation, Chinese factories lost their freedom and became subject to Japanese decisions. Furthermore, all the foreign firms belonging to "enemy nationals" were confiscated

---

[84] See the chapter by Frederic Wakeman and the chapter by Brian Martin in this volume.

[85] "Shanghai business barometer" (February 1941), 30 April 1941, Consular trade report.

[86] "Shanghai business barometer" (March 1941), 31 March 1941, Consular trade report.

[87] The instability of the national currency and its continued depreciation against the British pound and the U.S. dollar, in spite of the efforts made by both governments to support the Nationalist war effort, made imported raw materials more expensive. The introduction of a new currency in 1940 by the Wang Jingwei government made the situation even more confused, although it was unable to impose the use of the CRB until after the takeover of the International Settlement by the Japanese army. The official rate of exchange imposed by the government drove prices up even further.

[88] Letter from commercial attaché, 6 October 1941, "Shanghai business barometer" (February 1941), 31 March 1941, Consular trade report.

and placed under military command.[89] Although they were later entrusted to Japanese firms for their exploitation, those that were not related to war necessities were closed altogether.[90] The decrease in imports of raw materials was a major cause of decline, although the industries directly related to military needs still enjoyed a certain expansion.[91] The metal industry was severely curtailed for lack of raw materials. The same was true of tobacco in spite of a strong demand.[92] Industrial firms were increasingly confronted with the lack of supply in primary materials and the continuing rise of prices.

The policy of monopoly and fixed prices through which the Japanese army and the Wang Jingwei government desperately tried to gain some control over the economy only created havoc throughout the whole system. The controlled economy (*tongzhi jingji*) instituted after 1942 was beset by irrational pricing methods, inefficient management, fierce competition between Japanese and Chinese agencies, and above all widespread corruption.[93] In the context of runaway inflation and lack of supply, an active black market developed for all essential agricultural and industrial commodities.[94] Industrialists could not get out of the vicious circle, which made hoarding and black-marketeering much more profitable than actual production. The compulsory purchase of major industrial products at state-fixed prices did not even cover the costs of production. Although a few industrial firms managed to survive and even thrive, either because their products did not require massive quantities of raw materials, or because their managers were especially apt at finding the right channels for their purchases and sales, most faced decline, or chose to subcontract part of their machinery to small ventures based in the countryside around Shanghai.[95]

The rising cost of energy and the curtailment of the production of electricity became a severe impediment to the operation of industrial plants. The rising

---

[89] In Shanghai, the Japanese confiscated 71 "enemy" industrial enterprises (52 British and 19 American factories). Yoda Yoshiie, *Nitchû sensô shi shiryô*, pp. 83–84.

[90] Wang Jishen, *Zhanshi shanghai jingji*, p. 191.

[91] *Shanhai keizai nenkan* (Yearbook of the Shanghai economy), [Shanghai], 1944, p. 261.

[92] *Zhongguo gongye yuekan* (China industrial monthly), vol. 1, no. 2, 1943, p. 36.

[93] The organization of the "controlled economy" is presented in Huang Meizhen, "The Control of Materials by Japan and Its Puppet Government in the Central China-Occupied Area Around Shanghai." For relevant materials on this topic, see Mulu, "Shanghai tebieshi zhengfu jingjiju 1–14," Files 4 "Tiaozheng jingji xingzheng zhiquan"; 263 "Quanguo shangye tongzhi zonghui ji fushu jigou"; 264 "Tongzhi zhuyao wuzi ji guanli pingding wujia"; 257 "Qudi zhanshi wuzi yidong"; 298 "Chuli moshou wuzi," Shanghai Municipal Archives.

[94] Pan Yangrao, "Shanghai gongye fuxing wenti" (Shanghai's industrial problems), *Zhongguo gongye yuekan*, vol. 1, no. 2, 1943, pp. 3–4.

[95] Sherman Cochran has studied a remarkable case of successful entrepreneurs during the Japanese occupation. See Cochran, Sherman, "Marketing medicine across enemy lines: Chinese 'fixers' and Shanghai's wartime centrality" in this volume.

cost of electricity had made its effect felt well before 1941.[96] The authorities of the two foreign settlements had imposed heavy tax surcharges and introduced consumption quotas.[97] After Pearl Harbor, although the price of energy kept increasing, the real issue was about the brutal decline in coal supply which in turn caused the production of energy to drop sharply.[98] The Shanghai Power Company had to reduce its production by 40 percent.[99] By 1942, the general level of production of electricity was half that of 1936.[100] At the beginning of 1943, a review of the situation of each sector by the *Zhongguo gongye yuekan* indicated that in most cases, plants operated at half of their capacity.[101] In December, energy quotas were further curtailed. At this level, Chinese factories could only use 5.5 percent of their productive capacity.[102] Although the Wang Jingwei government decided to make 1944 the year of increased production (*zengchan nian*), all indicators (number of plants in operation, consumption of electricity, production) confirmed the decline of industrial production.[103]

By the end of 1942, the *Zhongguo gongye yuekan* (Chinese industrial monthly) identified no more than 1,145 plants in operation in Shanghai (120,000 workers). Their number had decreased by two-thirds in comparison with 1937, while the number of workers had been cut by one-half.[104] In mid-1943, there

[96] *China Weekly Review*, 10 August 1940, pp. 384–385. Despite more costly operations, Shanghai utilities (electricity, water, telephone, and gas) underwent a limited growth. *China Weekly Review*, 6 July 1940, pp. 191–192.

[97] *Bulletin d'informations économiques*, 13 March 1939, p. 1. *Weekly economic report*, 7 September 1940, Consular trade report; "Shanghai business barometer" (February 1941), 31 March 1941, Consular trade report; *Bulletin mensuel*, February 1941, p. 71, September 1941, p. 61 and p. 72.

[98] The city used to rely on domestic coal imported from North China and to a lesser extent from nearby Anhui province. After the Japanese seizure of the northern provinces, Shanghai had to turn to imports from India, Borneo, and Indochina, a venue which disappeared almost completely after summer 1941. The share of imports increased tremendously, from 137,505 tons in 1937 to 789,207 in 1938, 950,075 in 1939, 1,366,482 in 1940, and 1,497,363 by November 1941. Rationing measures could not make up for the deficit in supply. Wu Chunxi, "Shanghai gongshang dongtai zhi" (Notes on the trends in Shanghai trade and industry), *Zhongguo jingji*, vol. 2, no. 2, 1944, p. 23; "Shanghai meijin xiaofei shichang zhi fenxi" (An analysis of the coal consumption market in Shanghai), *Zhongguo gongye yuekan* (China industrial monthly), vol. 1, no. 6, 1943, pp. 29–36.

[99] *Bulletin mensuel*, February 1941, p. 71. To reduce the consumption of electricity, the authorities of the two settlements also adopted in 1940 a summer time starting on March 15 every year.

[100] Pan Yangrao, "Shanghai gongye fuxing wenti" (Shanghai's industrial problems), *Zhongguo gongye yuekan*, vol. 1, no. 2, 1943, pp. 3–4.

[101] *Zhongguo gongye yuekan*, vol. 1, no. 2, 1943, p. 36.

[102] Wu Chunxi, "Shanghai gongshang dongtai zhi" (Notes on the trends in Shanghai trade and industry), *Zhongguo jingji*, vol. 2, no. 2, 1944, p. 19.

[103] Wang Yizong, "Zengchan nian zhong de gongye jianchan qingkuang," p. 1.

[104] *Zhongguo gongye yuekan* (China industrial monthly), vol. 1, no. 2, 1943.

Table 1.4 *Number and percentage of factories in operation in 1943 and 1944*

Sector	Number 1943	Number 1944	In operation (%) 1943	In operation (%) 1944
Wood	104	131	82	60
Furniture	22	27	68	44
Metal	120	138	86	65
Machines	1218	1399	78	62
Ships	48	64	60	55
Bricks	52	68	65	50
Chemistry	320	510	82	82
Textiles	753	841	75	60
Cloth	288	373	74	62
Rubber/Leather	53	62	77	60
Food	165	238	70	62
Paper/Printing	412	479	86	60
Medicine and scientific instruments	55	96	78	60
Other	162	181	65	60

Source: Wang Yizong, "Zengchan nian zhong de gongye jianchan qingkuang" (The decline of production in the year of production increase), *Zhongguo jingji*, vol. 2, no. 9, 1944, p. 2.

were 1,617 plants, though with a much reduced staff. On average, industrial firms had lost 58 percent of their workers.[105] The textile, paper, printing, motor vehicle, and furniture industries were the more seriously affected.[106] In February 1944, there were 4,607 enterprises employing more than ten workers in the city. Of these 4,607 enterprises, however, only 2,910 (63%) were in operation. The strongest sectors were still the machine (1,399) and textile (841) industries. Altogether, they employed 87,041 workers (24,752 in textiles and 15,179 in mechanical industries).[107] See Table 1.4.

Even among Japanese industrialists, there was a real concern for the crisis caused by the cost of living and the lack of raw materials. As early as 1942, a

---

[105] In the two settlements, the authorities initiated an ambitious plan for the repatriation of the population to the countryside. Besides employment considerations, there was a real concern for the increasing share of the destitute population in the city. Food was in short supply and prices were pushed to a level that excluded large sectors of the population. Despite these forceful efforts, the repatriation movement seems to have had limited success. On the SMC's action, see Mulu "Shanghai gonggong zujie gongbuju weishengchu" 15 (1), files 998–1007, "Jiuji weiyuanhui, 1941–1942"; for a public view, see *Shanghai Times*, 9, 14, 15, 17, 21, 28, 29 January 1942; 5,11, 17, 18, 26 February 1942.

[106] *Zhongguo gongye yuekan* (China industrial monthly), vol. 1, no. 6, 1943, p. 30.

[107] Wang Yizong, "Zengchan nian zhong de gongye jianchan qingkuang," p. 1.

study group formed by Shanghai economic circles was asking for a relaxation of monopolistic policies which, in their eyes, were no longer necessary after the complete occupation of Shanghai.[108] Their plea obviously went unnoticed. In its 1944 edition, the *Shanhai keizai nenkan* (Shanghai economic yearbook) observed that the high cost of living made life unbearable for industrial workers. Many of them had left and returned to the countryside or turned to other activities. It was feared that this process might eventually lead to a lack of skilled labor. The *Shanhai keizai nenkan* called for a better supply of cheap rice to the workers and a general increase in wages to keep them in the plants. It also suggested giving a priority to certain sectors such as heavy industry through a more severe regulation of employment.[109] In spite of these veiled criticisms, both the Wang Jingwei government and the Japanese military authorities followed their own agenda with little consideration for Shanghai industrialists.[110]

The "idle capital" which remained in the city increasingly shifted toward more speculative ventures. In 1943, among the 174 new enterprises established in the first quarter of the year, 88 were financial companies. Together with investment companies, they represented 60 percent of the whole group, whereas industrial companies numbered only 10 (6%).[111] The general atmosphere and the lack of secure channels of investment for available capital were conducive to haphazard movements of concentration of enterprises and the constitution of conglomerates.[112] Their sole purpose, most often, was the seizure of the commodities (raw materials, etc.) stored in these enterprises. The process of concentration, a positive phenomenon in itself, was not related to a concern for rationality and better production. It was oriented toward protecting oneself from monetary instability. Although enterprises merged as early as 1937, the

---

[108] *Shanhai zai hensei ni kansuru hôshin oyobi sochi yôryô (an)* (Measures and general direction for the reconstruction of Shanghai [Proposal]), [Shanghai], Shanghai shisei kenkyûkai, 1942, vol. 1, pp. 7–11.

[109] *Shanhai keizai nenkan*, pp. 262–263.

[110] Visits to Wang Jingwei and protests by Shanghai capitalists failed to bring any substantial change to government policies. On these visits, see *Chôkô sangyô ihô*, pp. 26–27; Memo (26 August 1943), *Jingji qingbao* (Economic secret report), August 1943, Mulu "Shanghai tebie shi jingchaju 36-1/2," File 28; Report (25 November 1943), *Jingji qingbao*, November 1943, File 40, Shanghai Municipal Archives.

[111] According to a survey of the Banking Study Society (Yinhang xuehui), 61 of the 111 financial establishments in existence until 1942 were created before 1937. Six were created in 1939 and 1940, 19 in 1941, and 28 in 1942. During the first quarter of 1943, 53 more made their appearance. Mo Yuansheng, "Ben nian di yi ji xinchuang de qiye," *Zhongguo gongye yuekan*, vol. 1, no. 2, 1943, p. 60.

[112] After Pearl Harbor and until May 1942, 1,400 million yuan sought refuge in Hong Kong. In spite of this drain, "idle capital" was still estimated at 7,500 million yuan. *Shanhai keizai no hensen*, p. 74.

process developed only after 1941.[113] Another author noted the development of more than three hundred enterprise companies *(qiye gongsi)* which concentrated their activities on real estate and trade to make high and quick profits by taking advantage of the lack of legislation. They did not play any role in the development of industrial plants.[114]

After 1940, the Japanese inflicted two deadly blows to Shanghai industries and, to a larger extent, to the whole local economy. The reinforcement of monopolies and the institution of blockades definitely cut off the city from the surrounding countryside. Following the Pearl Harbor attack, access to world markets was terminated. Shanghai lost its raison d'être. Without regular and adequate supplies of raw materials, without markets in which to sell its products, local industry was doomed to bankruptcy. Shanghai was a center of transformation that could not exist without its hinterland or foreign markets. The formidable scale of smuggling notwithstanding – and, as Frederic Wakeman has clearly established, all sorts of important transactions took place between companies set up by the Nationalist, puppet, and Japanese army and special services – the flow of incoming products and materials could not match the requirements of the Shanghai industrial engine.[115] Up to 1940, the city could walk on its own two legs, the increasingly severe foot-binding imposed by the Japanese notwithstanding. Between 1941 and 1944, the two legs were virtually chopped off. Shanghai was lame.

CONCLUSION

Although a clear assessment of the damage suffered by Shanghai industries is an impossible task, we have seen that the losses were real and caused a severe setback to the city's potential. Nevertheless, the influx of huge amounts of capital from the surrounding provinces and from all over China and the migration of workshops from the countryside into the foreign settlements contributed to partially offset war losses. Shanghai industrialists were able to turn to their advantage the opportunities offered by the war in China and later in Europe. Industrial and commercial firms, both Chinese and Japanese, reaped enormous profits in 1938–1940, even if inflation has to be discounted.

[113] Shi Hao, "Shanghai xinxing qiye caituan de lunlang yu pipan" (An outline and critique of the new developing enterprise conglomerates in Shanghai), *Zhongguo jingji*, vol. 2, no. 11, 1944, pp. 1–13.
[114] Wang Yizong, "Zengchan nian zhong de gongye jianchan qingkuang" (The decline of production in the year of production increase), *Zhongguo jingji*, vol. 2, no. 9, 1944, pp. 8–9.
[115] On the extent of smuggling in wartime Shanghai and China, see Wakeman, Frederic, "Shanghai smuggling," in this volume.

Two different cycles – before and after 1941 – have been identified. They were directly related to the policies implemented by the Japanese army in Central China and to the freezing of economic relations by the United States and Great Britain. The system of monopolies instituted in Japan at the outset of the war was also enforced in Central China. Its main purpose was the plundering of Chinese resources for the Japanese war effort. Although it did affect Shanghai industries, causing shortages and price hikes, it was not a serious threat as long as local firms had easy access to international markets and were able to ship their products to inland China. On the whole, however, Shanghai became more dependent than ever on international trade. The extent of this dependence was revealed instantly in mid-1941 when this vital channel was shut down.

Post-1937 Shanghai industries did not reproduce the prewar situation. The structure and the geography of local industry changed. It had an impact on housing as well as on the composition of the workforce. Factories and workshops created a whole new industrial district in western Shanghai, which remained in place after the war, up to the present. The other main difference was the reduced scale of the plants. In all sectors, the large plants that were destroyed were replaced by small workshops, which employed fewer workers per unit and required a smaller investment. In part, it can be explained by the fact that the plants that moved into the foreign settlements, either moved only a part of their original equipment, or moved the part that had not been destroyed. Another reason for the existence of so many small workshops was the migration of many such enterprises from the cities and towns around Shanghai. Altogether, the level of technology probably declined.

The large industrial plants inherited from the prewar period were caught in the rigorous monopolistic system established by the Japanese and puppet authorities (price controls, compulsory sale and purchases, etc.) and suffered a serious decline after 1941. Their competitors, the small workshops, could circumvent such controls more easily and make use of the black market. But their multiplication was also a sign of a major shift in the local economy. Under the circumstances of both scarcity and monopoly created by the authorities, Chinese industrialists, and more general capital-holders, resorted more and more to speculative ventures or to real estate. The sources of capital for industrial investment dried up as firms competed only for primary materials to be hoarded for future transactions, not for production.

The fate of Shanghai industries tends to show that the Japanese army failed to use the industrial potential of the city to its own advantage. It may be argued that its stringent measures of economic control may have succeeded in preventing or more probably in limiting the supply of goods to the Nationalist-controlled areas. Chinese firms did also produce goods that served the Japanese army's needs. On the whole, however, the policies of control that were implemented blindly resulted in a growing paralysis of Shanghai industries, including Japanese firms. Even after 1942, when the remainder of Nationalist political and economic influence had been wiped out of the city, the Japanese army failed to turn Shanghai into a base for its war effort in China and Southeast Asia, despite pleas and proposals by its own nationals. The proliferation of Japanese administrative and research agencies in Central China was more a liability than an asset. The army was unable to decide on a fixed plan or to elaborate on any long-term blueprint for its presence in China. In other words, short-term military considerations, marred by tensions and conflicts with unwilling and corrupt Chinese puppet authorities, seem to have overdetermined the course of its action.

BIBLIOGRAPHY

An annual report of Shanghai commodity prices (from the annual report of the industrial section of the Shanghai Municipal Council). Shanghai, National Tariff Commission, 1938.

Barnett, Robert W., *Economic Shanghai: Hostage to Politics, 1937–1941*. New York, Institute for Pacific Relations, 1941.

Bergère, Marie-Claire, *Capitalisme national et impérialisme: la crise des filatures chinoises en 1923*. Cahiers du Centre Chine 2, CRDCC, Paris, Ecole des Hautes Etudes en Sciences Sociales, 1980.

Bergère, Marie-Claire, *The Golden age of the Chinese bourgeoisie*. Cambridge, Cambridge University Press, 1989.

Bulletin d'informations économiques, 1 October 1937. Consulat général de Shanghai, Archives diplomatiques de Nantes, box 45 (série noire). On the distribution of Shanghai industries, see Alain Roux's work, *Le Shanghai ouvrier des années trente: Coolies, gangsters et syndicalistes*. Paris, L'Harmattan, 1993.

China Weekly Review, 1937–1945.

Chôkô sangyô ihô (Yangzi Industries Report), 1942–1943.

Chôsabu, "Shanhai kôgyô kai no gaikyô" (The situation of Shanghai industrialists). *Shanhai* (Shanghai), no. 986, 1939, p. 91.

Cochran, Sherman, "Marketing medicine across enemy lines: Chinese 'fixers' and Shanghai's wartime centrality." Chap. 3 in this volume.

Consular trade report, E326, Box 1415, National Archives at College Park.

Han Qitong, *Zhongguo duiri zhanshi sunshi zhi guji 1937–1945* (An estimate of China's losses in the war against Japan, 1937–1943). Shanghai, Zhonghua shuju, 1946.

Henriot, Christian, *Shanghai 1927–1937: Municipal power, locality and modernization*. Berkeley, University of California Press, 1993.

Hsü, Shuhsi, *Japan and Shanghai*, prepared under the auspices of the Council of International Affairs. Shanghai, Kelly & Walsh, 1938.

Huang Liren, "Kangri zhanzheng shiqi gongchang neiqian de kaocha" (An investigation of factories moving into the hinterland of China during the war of resistance against Japan). *Lishi yanjiu* (Historical research), no. 4, 1994, pp. 120–36.

Huang Meizhen, "The Control of Materials by Japan and Its Puppet Government in the Central China-Occupied Area Around Shanghai, unpublished paper."

Huang Wenzhong, *Zhongguo zhanshi jingji teji*. Shanghai, Zhongwai chubanshe, 1940.

"Industrial situation in Shanghai," FO 371, File 23515, F10635. 11 August 1939, Public Record Office.

Inoue Kiyoshi, *Nitchû sensô to Nitchû kankei* (The Sino-Japanese war and Sino-Japanese relations). Tokyo, Hara shobo, 1988.

Isobe, Kiichi, Guan, Huaicong (trans.), "Zhanshi gongye tongzhi zhengce" (The wartime policy of control over industry). *Zhongguo gongye yuekan*, vol. 1, no. 5, 1943, pp. 16–24.

Kangzhan zhong de zhongguo jingji (The Chinese economy during the war). Shishi wenti yanjiuhui bian, Kangzhan shudian, 1940.

Li Shengbo, "Shi nian lai zhi mianfangzhi gongye," in Tan Xihong (ed.), *Shi nian lai zhi zhongguo jingji (1937–1945)* (China's economy during the past ten years). Shanghai, Zhonghua shuju (coll. Jindai zhongguo shiliao congkan xuji), 1948.

Memo (26 August 1943), *Jingji qingbao* (Economic secret report), August 1943. Mulu "Shanghai tebie shi jingchaju 36-1/2," File 28; Report (25 November 1943), *Jingji qingbao*. November 1943, File 40, Shanghai Municipal Archives.

Mo Yuansheng, "Ben nian di yi ji xinchuang de qiye." *Zhongguo gongye yuekan*, vol. 1, no. 2, 1943, p. 60.

Mulu "Shanghai gonggong zujie gongbuju weishengchu B 15 (2)." File 2108, "Shanghai xibu diqu gongchang jianchuang qingkuang" (1938–1939), p. 169.

Murphey, Rhoads, *Shanghai: Key to Modern China*. Cambridge, Harvard University Press, 1953.

    Treaty Ports and China's Modernization: What Went Wrong? Michigan Papers in Chinese Studies, no. 7. Ann Arbor, University of Michigan, 1971.

    The Outsiders: The Western Experience in India and China. Ann Arbor, University of Michigan Press, 1977.

North China Daily News, 1938.

Pan Yangrao, "Shanghai gongye fuxing wenti" (Shanghai's industrial problems). *Zhongguo gongye yuekan*, vol. 1, no. 2, 1943, pp. 3–4.

Rawski, Thomas, "The Growth of Producer Industries, 1900–1971," in Willmott, W. E., and Perkins, Dwight H., (eds.), *China's Economy in Historical Perspective*. Stanford, Stanford University Press, 1975, pp. 203–233.

"Shanghai meijin xiaofei shichang zhi fenxi" (An analysis of the coal consumption market in Shanghai). *Zhongguo gongye yuekan* (China industrial monthly), vol. 1, no. 6, 1943, p. 29–36.

Shanghai zhi gongshangye (Shanghai's commerce and industry). [Shanghai], Zhongwai chubanshe, 1941.

Shanhai keizai nenkan (Yearbook of Shanghai economy). [Shanghai], 1944.

Shanhai keizai no hensen (The evolution of the Shanghai economy). Shanhai, Obayashi jimusho, 1943.

Shanhai Nihon shôkô kaigisho nenpô (Annual report of the Japanese Chamber of Commerce and Industry). Shanghai, Shanhai nihon shôkô kaigisho.

"Shanhai ni okeru seishigyô no jôkyô" (The situation of the silk industry in Shanghai). *Shanhai* (Shanghai), no. 1026, 1943, p. 97.

Shanhai yôran (Shanghai handbook). Shanhai Nihon shôkô kaigisho, Shanghai, 1939.

Shanhai zai hensei ni kansuru hôshin oyobi sochi yôryô (an) (Measures and general direction for the reconstruction of Shanghai [Proposal]). [Shanhai], Shanhai shisei kenkyûkai, 1942, vol. 1.

Shi Hao, "Shanghai xinxing qiye caituan de lunlang yu pipan" (An outline and critique of the new developing enterprise conglomerates in Shanghai). *Zhongguo jingji*, vol. 2, no. 11, 1944, pp. 1–13.

Shou Bai, "Shanghai fangzhiye zhi jinxi." *Shangye yuebao*, vol. 21, no. 1, January 1941, pp. 1–2.

Wakeman, Frederic, "Shanghai smuggling," Chap. 5 in this volume.

Wakeman, Frederic E., *The Shanghai Badlands: Wartime Terrorism and Urban Crime, 1937–1941*. New York, Cambridge University Press, 1996.

Wang Jishen, *Zhanshi shanghai jingji*, vol.1. Shanghai jingji yanjiusuo, 1945.

Wang Yizong, "Zengchan nian zhong de gongye jianchan qingkuang" (The decline of production in the year of production increase). *Zhongguo jingji*, vol. 2, no. 9, 1944, pp. 8–9.

Wu Chengxi, "Zhanhou shanghai jinrong biandong zhi yiban de qingxiang." *Jinrong daobao*, vol 1, no. 1, March 1939, pp. 4–7.

Wu Chunxi, "Shanghai gongshang dongtai zhi" (Notes on the trends in Shanghai trade and industry). *Zhongguo jingji*, vol. 2, no. 2, 1944.

Yoda Yoshiie, *Nitchû sensô shi shiryô* (Documents sur l'histoire de la guerre sino-japonaise), vol. 4, Nitchû sensô shi shiryô henshû iinkai, (ed.), Tokyo, Kawade shobô shinsha, [1975].

Zhanhou shanghai zhi gongshang ge ye. Shanghai, Zhongguo jingji yanjiuhui, Minyi shuju, 1940, p. 38.

Zhongguo gongye yuekan (China industrial monthly), 1943.

Zhou Qibang, "Zhongguo zhanshi gongye gaikuang" (General situation of China's wartime industry). *Zhongguo gongye yuekan* (China industrial monthly), vol. 1, no. 1, 1943, p. 37.

Chapter 2

Chinese Capitalists in Wartime Shanghai, 1937–1945

A Case Study of the Rong Family Enterprises

PARKS M. COBLE

When war erupted between China and Japan in the summer of 1937,[1] Japanese forces swept over the lower Yangzi area and brought this economic heartland under Japanese control. Because the "China Incident" remained an undeclared conflict until December 1941, the Japanese left unoccupied most of the foreign concessions of Shanghai – the International Settlement and the French Concession – save for the portion of the settlement north of the Suzhou Creek which was a center of Japanese presence. The unoccupied zones, containing the financial center of the Bund, the famous shops of Nanjing Road, and the posh residential and shopping areas in the French Concession, became a "solitary island" (*gudao*) in the midst of Japanese-occupied China. The city of Shanghai, which had already developed as a "divided city," became even more so during 1937 to 1941.

The outbreak of war was a disaster for most Chinese capitalists of Shanghai. Industrialists saw their plants destroyed or confiscated by the Japanese. Merchants found shops looted and devastated, commercial routes closed. Shipping on the Yangzi came to a halt, rail traffic fell sharply. In the divided city, however, fortunes were divided as well. Chinese businessmen whose enterprises were located on or near the key battlefields in the Shanghai area, such as in Zhabei and Wusong, suffered almost total loss. By contrast, those fortunate to be in

[1] The larger study of which this chapter is a part has benefited from grants from the Committee on Scholarly Communications with the People's Republic of China for research at the Shanghai Academy of Social Sciences, from a faculty development leave from the University of Nebraska, and from a travel grant from the Stanford East Asia National Resource Center. The author thanks the Shanghai Academy of Social Sciences; the Harvard-Yenching Library; the Fairbank Center for East Asian Research at Harvard; the East Asian Collection at the Hoover Institute; and the University of Nebraska-Love Library for access to collections. The author also thanks Sherman Cochran, Joshua Fogel, Po-shek Fu, Takeshi Hamashita, Huang Hanmin, Christian Henriot, William Kirby, Sophia Lee, Andrea McElderry, Keith Schoppa, Wei Peh-t'i, Yeh Wen-hsin, and the late Lloyd E. Eastman for their assistance.

4. The victor's march into the city. Source: Courtesy of the Fabre Family.

the solitary island were able to keep possession of their facilities. Others had enterprises and plants in the Japanese sector north of the Suzhou Creek which escaped much of the destruction but fell under Japanese control. Japanese military authorities blocked access to these properties by both businessmen and workers and ultimately confiscated most of them. The fate of Chinese enterprises therefore varied tremendously, often from block to block in the divided city.

In the midst of such wreckage, most Chinese capitalists – conditioned to survival in an inhospitable climate – tried to salvage what they could. Although much historical writing on the war emphasizes those businessmen who heroically followed Chinese armies to the interior, in fact only a very few were able and willing to retreat with the Nationalist forces. The majority of Shanghai capitalists took the most expedient route and tried to relocate their existing business to the solitary island if they were not there already. For those businessmen who could relocate their factories, shops, and banks to the safety of the foreign concessions, the war actually provided an opportunity for profit. The refugee-swollen city offered both cheap labor and great demand. Trade with unoccupied China was often possible through ports on the southeast coast. For bankers, the war brought an influx of capital from the regional areas into Shanghai, which had already been the center of China's finances. Many Chinese capitalists, therefore, weathered the storm of war remarkably well, at least until 1941.

The nature of Chinese enterprises was key to their survival – the family firm was dominant. Although Chinese companies could be organized as limited-liability corporations, William Kirby's study "China Unincorporated" reveals that even in the 1930s, few chose to organize in this way.[2] Instead, family organization with personal control by a senior leader was the preferred style. This highly personalistic control was suited to an environment in which legal norms were unclear, the political structure weak, and the future uncertain. As Siu-lun Wong has written, "The father, as head of a family firm has maximum flexibility in his action. . . . The father-entrepreneur is also able to transfer funds from one line of business to another for mutual sustenance. Capital is mobile within the family group of enterprises because it belongs to a common, unified *jia* budget."[3]

In war conditions, these characteristics served Chinese businessmen well. The uncertainty of the wartime environment required the ability to operate rapidly and secretly. Decisions on moving resources to the solitary island or to attempt relocation to the interior had to be made quickly. Formal consultation with a board of directors might well have delayed action until the issues were moot. The father-entrepreneur was also able to use sons, sons-in-law, and nephews for secret negotiations and contacts. Often Chinese businessmen tried to maintain smooth relations with Chongqing while operating in Shanghai and Hong Kong or even the occupied zone. Use of family members provided a mechanism for such actions. A son could be dispatched to the interior, act on behalf of the family firm, and be trusted even in the absence of regular communication.

Yet this very strength of the family firm was also its Achilles heel. It was highly dependent on the leadership of the senior figure. His death or incapacitation (great risks in wartime) could leave the firm bereft of leadership. As David Faure has noted, "The continuation of a Chinese family business beyond the lifetime of the patriarch is fraught with difficulties. As a family business, the division between personal expenses and business expenses was never very clear-cut."[4] Without the presence of the patriarch, disputes over control of funds often led to family divisions. A study of the experiences of Shanghai's capitalists during the war reveals both the strengths and limitations of the family firm. The

[2] William C. Kirby, "China Unincorporated: Company Law and Business Enterprise in Twentieth-Century China," *The Journal of Asian Studies*, vol. 54, no. 1 (February 1995), pp. 43–63.

[3] Siu-lun Wong, "The Chinese Family Firm," *British Journal of Sociology*, vol. 36, no. 1 (1985), pp. 63–64.

[4] David Faure, "The control of equity in Chinese firms within the modern sector from the late Qing to the early Republic," in Brown, Rajeswary A., ed., *Chinese Business Enterprise in Asia* (London: Routledge, 1995), p. 66.

flexibility of the business form permitted businessmen to find opportunities in the midst of disaster. The limitations of single-person leadership often led to disaster when the patriarch died.

The experiences of the Rong family group illustrate both the perils and opportunities which war brought to Shanghai businessmen. Their fate was not typical simply because the Rong group was the largest such company. With so many properties, Rong mills were in all of the major zones of Shanghai. A study of the survival of the Rong group during the war thus reveals the wide variety of conditions experienced by Shanghai-area capitalists.

Founded by Rong Zongjing and his brother Rong Desheng, the Rong group included the Shenxin textile mills (ten in all) and the Maoxin and Fuxin flour mills (sixteen in all). The Rongs had plants not only in Shanghai but in their native Wuxi, in Hankou, and even north China. By the mid-1930s, the Rongs held 20 percent of all spindles in Chinese-owned textile mills and produced one-sixth of the milled flour.[5] Although Shenxin or Fuxin would commonly be referred to as one company, each mill was actually organized as an unlimited liability company, and Rong Zongjing was named director-general of every factory in the group.[6]

The war seemed to deal a crippling blow to the Rong empire. The fighting destroyed over one-third of their spindles, 60 percent of their looms, and 18 percent of their flour grinders; enemy forces seized much of the rest. Yet out of this rubble, the Rongs survived and even earned substantial profits. More crippling to the firm was the death of senior figure Rong Zongjing, whose health suffered under war conditions. After the war erupted, Zongjing departed Shanghai for Hong Kong and died there on February 10, 1938, at the age of sixty-six. His younger brother, Desheng, had difficulty controlling his nephews, and the Rongs began to disagree over what strategy to pursue in wartime. Some spoke of a split between the Ximo Road group (where Rong Zongjing's home was located) and the Zhi'en Road group (site of Rong Desheng's home).[7]

[5] Shang Fangmin, "Jindai shiye jia Rongshi xiongdi jingying zhi daoxi" (Modern industrialists, the Rong brothers and their way of management), *Minguo dang'an* (Republican Archives), 1992, no. 2, pp. 86–91; Huang Hanmin, "Rongjia qiye dizao zhe – Rong Zongjing, Rong Desheng" (The founders of the Rong industries – Rong Zongjing, Rong Desheng), in Xu Dixin, ed., *Zhongguo qiye jia liezhuan* (Biographies of China's entrepreneurs; Beijing: Jingji ribao chuban, 1988), vol. 1, pp. 97–109; Wan Lin, "Wuxi Rongshi jiazu baofa shi" (The history of the sudden rise of the Rong family of Wuxi), *Jingji daobao* (Economic report), December 14, 1947, no. 50, p. 1.

[6] William Kirby, "China Incorporated," p. 51.

[7] Qian Zhonghan, "Minzu ziben jia Rong Zongjing, Rong Desheng" (National capitalists – Rong Zongjing, Rong Desheng), *Jiangsu wenshi ziliao xuanji* (Selections from literary and historical materials, Jiangsu province), no. 2 (1963), pp. 131–139; Qian Zhonghan, "Wuxi wuge zhuyao chanye ziben xitong de xingcheng yu fazhan" (The formation and development of Wuxi's five

SURVIVING THE BATTLE OF SHANGHAI

The fate of individual mills varied greatly depending on their location. When war erupted, the Rongs lost control of five of their seven textile mills in Shanghai. Two were virtually destroyed – the Shenxin #1, having 72,800 spindles, and the Shenxin #8, with 50,000 spindles. Located in the Western Roads section of Shanghai, both were bombed by the Japanese on October 27, 1937, heavily damaging the mills, killing 70 workers, and injuring 350. The Western Roads area had been the subject of a longstanding dispute between Chinese and foreigners in Shanghai. Not part of the International Settlement, it nonetheless had many foreign residents. The Western-dominated Shanghai Municipal Council therefore attempted to exercise jurisdiction over the area.[8]

The Rongs had gambled that their mills in this location would be protected by foreign presence and hence continued operation after war erupted. This strategy both exposed the workers to great danger when the Japanese attacked and precluded removing equipment from the mills to a safer location in the International Settlement proper. Only about ten truckloads of raw cotton and cloth were salvaged. Later the sites of these two mills were occupied by the Japanese military, which turned them over to the Japanese Toyoda Textile Company which had a mill next to the property and would partially rebuild the two. Under Toyoda the mills had a combined total of 40,000 spindles and 1,300 looms.[9]

most important capitalist systems), *Wenshi ziliao xuanji* (Selections from literary and historical materials), no. 24, p. 109; Huang Hanmin, "Rongjia qiye dizao," vol. 1, p. 109; Rong Shuren, "Wojia jingying mianfen gongye de huiyi" (Memoirs of management of the flour milling industry by my family), *Gongshang shiliao* (Historical materials on industry and commerce; Beijing: Wenshi ziliao chuban she, 1981), vol. 2, pp. 52–53; Gong Tingtai, "Rongshi jiazu de shiye juzi – ji Rong Zongjing, Rong Desheng xiongdi" (The Rong family industrial leaders – remembering Rong Zongjing and Rong Desheng), *Jiangsu wenshi ziliao*, no. 34 (1989), pp. 111–138; Shanghai shehui kexue yuan, Jingji yanjiu suo, ed., *Rongjia qiye shiliao* (Historical materials on the Rong family enterprises; Shanghai: Shanghai renmin chuban she, 1980), vol. 2, p. 187. On the eve of the war, the Rong mills held 570,000 spindles. An estimated 207,484 or 36.4 percent were lost during the war. The number of looms was 5,304, of which 3,226 or 60.8 percent were lost. The number of flour grinders was 347, of which 18.4 percent were lost.

[8] For information on the Western Roads issue, see Frederic Wakeman, Jr., *The Shanghai Badlands: Wartime Terrorism and Urban Crime, 1937–1941* (Cambridge: Cambridge University Press, 1996).

[9] Rong Collection, Shanghai shehui kexue yuan, Zhongguo qiye shi ziliao yanjiu zhongxin (The center for material for research of Chinese enterprise history, Shanghai Academy of Social Sciences [hereafter Rong Collection, SASS], R01-2, p. 59 and R03-2, *Shenxin xitong qiye shiliao* (Historical material on the Shenxin system enterprises), vol. 3, no. 1, pp. 26–32; *Rongjia qiye shiliao*, vol. 2, pp. 3–4, 120; M. C. Bergère, "Zhongguo de minzu qiye yu ZhongRi zhanzheng: Rongjia Shenxin fangzhi chang" (China's national industry and the Sino-Japanese War: the Rong family's Shenxin textile company), in Zhang Xianwen et al., eds., *Minguo dang'an yu minguo*

Three additional Shenxin mills, #5, #6, and #7, suffered much less damage but were in areas which the Japanese occupied. The Shenxin #5, with 49,000 spindles, was located in the Pudong section of Shanghai. It was abandoned almost immediately when an air battle occurred right over the plant, frightening away the workers. Shortly thereafter, Japanese forces occupied the plant. Shenxin #6 and #7, both located in the Yangshupu section, had over 80,000 and 53,000 spindles, respectively, in 1937. Both suffered limited damage in the fighting; #7 also suffered a warehouse fire. Despite this damage, these mills could easily be brought back into production. But by whom? Japanese military authorities sealed off the properties, denying the Rongs access. For a time in 1938 it appeared that the Japanese might return control in exchange for active collaboration by the Rongs with puppet regimes (discussed below). Ultimately the military authorities entrusted the management and rehabilitation of these properties to Japanese firms. Shenxin #5 went to the Yūhō Textile Company (Yūhō bōseki kabushiki kaisha); Shenxin #6 went to the Shanghai Textile Company (Shanhai bōseki kabushiki kaisha); and #7 went to the Kanegafuchi Company.[10]

The actions by Japanese authorities were designed not only to ensure control of the economy in China but in part to compensate Japanese firms for losses in the China War. In the Shanghai area before July 1937, for instance, thirty of sixty-four textile mills were Japanese owned. During the fighting, two of these – the Toyoda #1 and #2 mills – were totally destroyed; seven others were heavily damaged. Five mills suffered light damage, and only sixteen escaped unharmed. Total losses by Japanese firms in Shanghai reached well over 200,000 spindles. Japanese losses were even more dramatic in Qingdao, where they had totally dominated prewar textile production. Retreating Chinese armies destroyed nine Japanese mills with over 667,000 spindles and 11,544 looms. An additional Japanese mill in Wuhan was seized by the Chinese army and used to make military uniforms. Later the plant was moved to Chongqing. Japanese mill owners were eager to recoup these

shixue shu taolun lunwen ji (A collection of essays on the study of Republican history and the Republican archives; Beijing: Dang'an chuban she, 1988), pp. 533–534; Chen Zhen, Yao Luo, eds., *Zhongguo jindai gongye shi ziliao* (Material on the history of modern Chinese industry; Beijing: Sanlian chuban she, 1957), vol. 1, p. 384; Xu Weiyong and Huang Hanmin, *Rongjia qiye fazhan shi* (The development of the Rong family enterprises; Beijing: Renmin chuban she, 1985), pp. 132–134.

[10] *Rongjia qiye shiliao*, vol. 2, pp. 36–37; Chen Zhen, Yao Luo, eds., *Zhongguo jindai gongye shi ziliao*, vol. 1, pp. 391, 394; M. C. Bergère, "Zhongguo de minzu qiye yu ZhongRi zhanzheng," pp. 533–534; Rong Collection, SASS, R05, *Shenxin 2, 5 chang juan*, pp. 32–34; Xu Weiyong and Huang Hanmin, *Rongjia qiye fazhan shi*, p. 137; Rong Collection, SASS, R03-2, *Shenxin xitong*, vol. 3, no. 1, pp. 13–17, 65–66.

losses and clamored for restitution from the pool of confiscated Chinese mills.[11]

COLLABORATION?

As noted above, Japanese authorities hinted that Chinese businessmen might be partially compensated for confiscated property or be made junior partners with Japanese firms if they were willing to collaborate with the occupation authorities. Evidence suggests that the Rongs flirted with this idea shortly after the fall of Shanghai. The press mentioned Rong Zongjing, along with twenty other prominent business figures, as an organizer of the Shanghai Citizens Association (Shanghai shimin xiehui). This body had an announced goal of restoring economic production in the occupied sectors of Shanghai, an effort which would no doubt have involved the restoration of Chinese control of seized businesses. Guomindang officials considered the organization to be a part of the puppet *Dadao* government being organized by the Japanese government and labeled the participants in the group collaborators. Rong Zongjing, mentioned in the press as one of the three cochairs of the body, came under considerable pressure to withdraw from participation. Hoping to defuse criticism, Rong told reporters that the association was not a government organization; members were merchants, not politicians. The group was a strictly humanitarian body, Rong argued, attempting to aid refugees living in the foreign concessions by restoring the economy of Zhabei, Nanshi, Pudong, and Wusong which would allow them to return home. Rong admitted that the group had been negotiating with the Japanese military authorities, but denied that the body was part of the *Dadao* government.

Despite Rong's denials, Guomindang authorities considered the group collaborationist and GMD agents used violent tactics to discourage participation. On December 31, 1937, Lu Bohong, manager of the Nanshi Electric Company and a member of the board of directors of the association, was shot and killed, a clear warning to the others. Rong Zongjing's house came under surveillance. The intimidation had the desired effect. Businessmen such as Wang Yuqing, manager of Fuxin mills, announced that they were not participating in the venture, and the association became inactive. A panicky Rong Zongjing departed Shanghai for the safer environs of Hong Kong. Zongjing's experience had been

---

[11] Rong Collection, SASS, R03-3, *Shenxin xitong*, vol. 4, no. 1, p. 40; Du Xuncheng, *Riben zai jiu Zhongguo de touzi* (Japanese investment in old China; Shanghai: Shanghai shehui kexue yuan chuban she, 1986), pp. 199–201.

a lesson for the Rongs; although remaining aloof from the Japanese had its difficulties, collaboration was risky.[12]

Following his older brother's death in Hong Kong, Rong Desheng, now the senior family member, continued to avoid collaboration as much as possible. He rejected attempts by the Japanese to gain his participation in puppet organizations in exchange for possible restoration of Rong property. Yet pressure continued; in 1940, his second son, Rong Er'ren, was held fifty-eight days by puppet police in Pudong. Even then Desheng refused to ask puppet authorities for assistance in exchange for political favors. Because of their refusal to collaborate actively with Japanese and puppet authorities, whatever the motivation, the Rongs were not able to regain possession of their mills in the occupied areas of Shanghai during the 1937–1941 period.[13]

THE "SOLITARY ISLAND" (*GUDAO*)

Of their textile mills in Shanghai, therefore, the Rongs retained control only of their Shenxin #2 and Shenxin #9 mills. These were located in the International Settlement and were not occupied until December 1941. The #2 mill had been founded in 1919 and by 1935 had 53,123 spindles. The Rongs purchased Shenxin #9 in 1931, and by 1937 it had 129,280 spindles and 615 looms. Despite pressure from the Guomindang government to relocate in the interior, the Rongs decided to make the Shanghai concessions the base of their operations. Rong Desheng, the younger brother who had initially fled Wuxi for Hankou with his sons, returned to Shanghai to lead the family.[14]

The foreign concessions were "solitary islands" of neutrality in a sea of Japanese control, yet Chinese firms were not fully secure. As an added measure of protection many Chinese companies, the Rongs included, used the cover of foreign registration. The Rongs "leased" their two mills to foreign owners, in paper transactions, so as to provide the protection of a foreign flag. The Shenxin #2, for instance, was ostensibly rented to an American company, Associated American Industries, Ltd., for a five-year period beginning on April 16, 1938. The American firm in turn obtained funds for this transaction from the

---

[12] Frederic Wakeman, Jr., *The Shanghai Badlands*, p. 25; *Rongjia qiye shiliao*, vol. 2, pp. 18–23; Xu Weiyong and Huang Hanmin, *Rongjia qiye fazhan shi*, p. 140; Gong Tingtai, "Rongshi jiazu de shiye juzi," pp. 130–132. On the formation of the *Dadao* government, see Timothy Brook, The Great Way Government of Shanghai," in this volume.

[13] Gong Tingtai, "Rongshi jiazu de shiye juzi," p. 133. Rong Er'ren was released when Fuxin manager Rong Bing'gen paid the puppet police the equivalent of US$30,000. See *Rongjia qiye shiliao*, vol. 2, p. 88.

[14] Rong Collection, SASS, R05, p. 42; RO8, p. 44.

Bank of China and Shanghai Bank which then appointed a joint committee to operate the plant. This committee was composed, quite naturally, of the original management. Shenxin #9 underwent a similar transformation in May 1938 but used a British cover and also was registered in Hong Kong.[15]

Since the Rongs retained control of only two of their seven mills in Shanghai, one might suppose that their economic fortunes declined substantially. Yet in many respects the Rongs actually did rather well in the war. Plagued by over-capacity on the eve of the conflict, the Rongs were able to make fuller use of their remaining mills – both increased in output. Although Shenxin #2 had almost the same number of spindles, its output of yarn increased over 43 percent from 1937 until 1940. For Shenxin #9 the Rongs actually increased the number of looms to 815 and spindles to 148,220, making it the largest mill in China. Its output of cotton yarn production increased 52 percent from 1937 to 1940; cotton cloth, 37 percent.[16] Although the market in the immediate hinterland of Shanghai was cut off, the Rongs increased their sales in Southeast Asia by stressing their identity as Chinese. In the aftermath of Japanese aggression in China, the large communities of overseas Chinese began to boycott Japanese products and turned to the "Golden twin horses" brand of the Rong family.

But production and profit are not the same thing, of course. Increased output from existing equipment and a tilt in the supply-demand ratio created a formula for higher earnings. In 1936, Shenxin's seven mills in Shanghai earned a total profit of almost 1.6 million yuan, with Shenxin #1 being the most profitable. Shenxin #2 had lost over 150,000 yuan that year, while #9 earned only 417,000 yuan. In 1938, both earned substantial profits; #2 earned over 2.7 million yuan, #9 over 6.9 million. Thus, from the standpoint of profits, the Rongs earned more with only two mills in "island Shanghai" in 1938 than they had from all seven Shanghai mills in the prewar period. War had reduced the supply of cotton yarn and cloth while demand remained firm. The good times did not last; the strains of war eventually drove profits down. In 1941, Shenxin #2 earned less than half the income of 1938 (adjusted for inflation); Shenxin #9 just over one-third as much. Still, the Rongs did reasonably well during the first years of the war.[17]

Even wartime inflation benefited the Rongs to a certain extent. The Rongs had endured some difficult years during the mid-1930s and had accumulated

---

[15] *Rongjia qiye shiliao*, vol. 2, pp. 43–46; Chen Zhen, Yao Luo, eds., *Zhongguo jindai gongye shi ziliao*, p. 394.

[16] *Rongjia qiye shiliao*, vol. 2, pp. 68, 73–74, 191; and Rong Collection, SASS, R08, pp. 48, 52–53, R05, pp. 35–41.

[17] *Rongjia qiye shiliao*, vol. 2, pp. 68, 73–74, 191; and Rong Collection, SASS, R08, pp. 48, 52–53, R05, pp. 35–41.

substantial debt. The effects of the world depression, the suspension of business in early 1932 when fighting had erupted in Shanghai, and the adverse impact of the American silver purchase policy, had created rather unfavorable economic conditions for Shenxin in the mid-1930s. The company had, in fact, teetered on the verge of bankruptcy for a time before conditions improved in 1936 and 1937. Total debts of Shenxin and Fuxin mills were estimated to be 80 million yuan in 1936. With wartime inflation, old loans were rapidly repaid. By 1941 Shenxin #2 and #9 were debt-free; debts of other units were reduced to 20 million yuan. When in May 1942, the Wang Jingwei government required the exchange of old *fabi* for its currency at a two-for-one ratio, this was reduced to only 10 million yuan. Adjusted for inflation, this was the equivalent of only 4.56 percent of this sum in 1936 yuan. The Rongs thus quickly repaid the remaining debt and by the end of June 1942 the company was debt-free. The Shenxin mills even began paying dividends, although this good fortune ignited tensions among the shareholders over the spoils.[18]

ORGANIZATIONAL ISSUES

Wartime profits did not smooth relations within the Rong family. Because only two of the mills of the Rong group continued to operate under their control, and the investments in each of the mills varied, some members of the Rong clan profited more than others. This disparity resulted from the organizational structure of the Rong enterprises. The Rong brothers had established a general headquarters for Shenxin, but the company was not organized as an incorporated limited-liability concern controlled by a board of directors. The general office handled the purchase of materials and sales of goods, but individual factories were organized separately. The Rongs had raised capital investment individually for each mill, but rights for shareholders had not been clearly established. The real authority in Shenxin was not in the institution of the general headquarters but in the person of Rong Zongjing and his brother.[19] This looseness of organization was common among Chinese enterprises of prewar China.

In the Rong firm, Rong Zongjing had combined the position of head of the company and head of family. Upon his death, however, the reliance on personal rather than institutional arrangements became more of an issue, especially under wartime conditions. Desheng was neither forceful enough nor healthy enough to assume dominant leadership at the general headquarters. Although Rong

---

[18] Gong Tingtai, "Rongshi jiazu de shiye juzi," pp. 125–132; *Rongjia qiye shiliao*, vol. 2, pp. 74, 166–173; Xu Weiyong and Huang Hanmin, *Rongjia qiye fazhan shi*, p. 132.

[19] Rong Collection, SASS, R03-4, *Shenxin xitong*, vol. 7, no. 2, p. 131.

Zongjing's son Hongyuan took over as general manager, he could not control his brothers and cousins. The surviving #2 and #9 mills became increasingly independent of the general headquarters, as did the Hankou Shenxin #4. The Maoxin and Fuxin flour companies also split off, with Rong Desheng dominating Maoxin and Wang Yuqing, Fuxin.[20]

As the #9 mill became more profitable, for instance, the manager, Wu Kunsheng, moved to make it more independent of the general headquarters, repaying to the center capital owed from the prewar period and accepting less interference in management decisions. When the mill distributed profits to the investors, the senior Rong branch of Rong Zongjing's heirs, now headed by Rong Hongyuan, held considerably more of the investment than Rong Desheng and his heirs. It gained more of the profits, creating dissension within the family.

In January 1939, the firm reallocated the stock to provide for both Rong branches and the managers of #9, but this did not resolve disagreement. The paperwork defining stockholder rights in the firm was held in a safe deposit box at a British bank, custody of which was jointly held by Rong Hongyuan and Rong Weiren (Desheng's eldest son). When Weiren died, his widow attempted to retrieve the documents, resulting in a quarrel between the two branches. Additional disputes arose because some of the stock from the 1939 distribution had been sold to outsiders who then raised questions about their rights.

On August 20, 1941, the capital of the mill was re-set at 50 million yuan (in CRB banknotes of the Nanjing government), with a new distribution. The senior branch, headed by Rong Hongyuan and his brothers Rong Hongsan and Rong Hongqing, still controlled the majority – 59.8 percent, with 25.6 percent held by Rong Desheng and his children. Smaller amounts were held by the managers, including 4.8 percent by Wu Kunsheng. The firm was defined as a partnership, which meant that the shares of ownership could not be transferred to a third party. In this way, the privacy of the family firm was to be maintained.[21]

In the meantime, Rong Er'ren, realizing that he was being shut out of real authority in Shenxin #9, began to press for changes in Shenxin #2. With the death of his brother Weiren, he was now a key figure among Desheng's sons. In July 1938, Er'ren drafted an economic plan for Shenxin #2. Key to his plan was the repayment of bank loans. Accumulated debts had left #2's management in the hands of bank authorities on the eve of the war. Er'ren's plan, however, was predicated on Shenxin #2 becoming independent of the general headquarters of Shenxin and coming under Er'ren's domination. When Rong Hongyuan became aware of this plan, he devised a counterproposal. The debt of Shenxin #2 and #5

---

[20] Rong collection, SASS, R03-3, *Shenxin xitong*, vol. 4, no. 2, pp. 107–109.
[21] *Rongjia qiye shiliao*, vol. 2, pp. 166–169; Rong Collection, SASS, R08, pp. 28–30.

(then under Japanese control) would be retired together and the two reorganized as one group, but as a unit of the general headquarters of the Shenxin company. The competing plans led to an intense dispute between the two factions which was finally resolved, much as disputes over #9. In an understanding reached in May 1942 (when conditions were no longer so profitable), the two sides agreed that the debt of #2 and #5 would be retired together and that they would be reorganized as one unit. The stock was set at 30 million yuan (in Nanjing currency) in June 1942, with 56.7 percent going to Rong Hongyuan and his brothers; 43.3 percent to Rong Desheng and his sons. Rong Hongyuan took the title general manager, while Rong Er'ren was manager. Despite the title, it was agreed that day-to-day control would rest with Er'ren. In late 1942 a distribution of dividends occurred, with the senior Rongs getting 2,811,000 yuan and the junior branch, 2,149,000. The following year, 1943, the distribution was 6,664,000 for the seniors, 5,499,000 for the juniors, but with a modest 370,000 being returned to the general company headquarters and high-level personnel. The increase in total dividends from 1942 to 1943, incidentally, was a result of inflation. The actual value of the total dividends dropped nearly 20 percent when adjusted for inflation.[22]

These resolutions still left minority investors in Shenxin #1 and #8, which had been destroyed in the early fighting, out in the cold. They had received no income since the war began, while Shenxin #2 and #9 earned handsome profits. Many of these protested that since Shenxin as a group was an unlimited-liability firm, they should be entitled to compensation for their losses from the profits being earned by other branches. This dispute was not easily resolved and the acrimony continued through the war era. In early 1943 (when all of Shanghai was under Japanese control), several launched a protest with the puppet Ministry of Industry in Nanjing. The bickering also festered at a meeting of Shenxin #1 and #8 shareholders on April 7, 1943, which was chaired by Rong Hongyuan. Several stockholders protested his leadership on the grounds that the position of chair of the board was not hereditary. As a consequence, Hongyuan withdrew and was replaced as chair by Zhang Zhipeng.[23]

Under Zhang's direction, a committee of seven minority stockholders was appointed to examine the account books of the Shenxin system and report back. When the group arrived at the Shenxin office, however, they were not allowed to view the accounting records on the grounds that these were the private property of the Rong family. The minority shareholders then approached puppet official Chu Minyi through an intermediary with the hope of examining the books of

---

[22] *Rongjia qiye shiliao*, vol. 2, pp. 169–171, 192; Rong Collection, SASS, R05, p. 77.
[23] Rong Collection, SASS, R03-2, *Shenxin xitong*, p. 78; *Rongjia qiye shiliao*, vol. 2, pp. 171–172.

the Shenxin properties and getting the right to participate in the management of the concern. The Rongs, however, outflanked the dissidents, having already approached Chu.

In the meantime, Rong Er'ren sought to use the anger of the minority stockholders against his cousin Hongyuan. He promoted yet another scheme for the general reorganization of Shenxin with the hope of increasing his authority. He suggested a revised and strengthened role for the Shenxin central headquarters in a new "Greater Shenxin" structure. He told the stockholder committee, "You are Shenxin's seven gentlemen (*qi junzi*).[24] When the Greater Shenxin is set up, it will be of your effort." The minority stockholders, however, lacked the clout to force restructuring of Shenxin. Rong Desheng and the older leaders resisted the idea of changing the family firm into a limited-liability company. On January 5, 1944, the minority shareholders agreed to recognize the existing organizational structure for Shenxin #2, 5, 6, 7, and 9, but would pursue the eventual reorganization of Shenxin #1, 8 as a limited-liability company. The latter form of organization would provide for specified legal rights for shareholders.[25]

It is not surprising that the senior Rongs resisted change. The loose structure of Shenxin had allowed them to garner profits from #2 and #9 while minority shareholders in the other mills gained nothing. Little of the profit from the #2 and #9 mills had been returned to the general headquarters of Shenxin. The central office actually lost money in 1938 and 1939 (1,666,780 yuan and 1,593,870 yuan, respectively) before earning 775,710 in 1940. The central office lost funds because so many unemployed personnel from #1, 6, 7, and 8 depended on the general headquarters for support, straining its resources. Under these circumstances, most of the Rongs preferred to isolate #2 and #9 (and their profits) from the liabilities of the general headquarters.[26]

The continual disputes between the senior and junior branches of the Rong family led Desheng to attempt to establish a separate firm to be controlled by his side. As early as 1941, Desheng had been planning for the Tianyuan Industrial Company (Tianyuan shiye gongsi) which would include textiles, flour, electricity, and a foundry. Desheng would be the general manager and his seven sons would serve as assistant general managers. It would be entirely separate

---

[24] *Rongjia qiye shiliao*, vol. 2, p. 176. The phrase *qi junzi* was widely used in conjunction with the seven leaders of the National Salvation Movement who had been arrested before the war. See Parks M. Coble, *Facing Japan: Chinese Politics and Japanese Imperialism, 1931–1937* (Cambridge: Harvard East Asian Monograph Series, 1991), pp. 334–342.

[25] *Rongjia qiye shiliao*, vol. 2, pp. 171–177, 194.

[26] Rong Collection, SASS, R03-3, *Shenxin xitong*, vol. 4, no. 2, p. 109.

from Rong Zongjing's branch of the family. The firm was still in the planning stages, however, when the war ended.[27]

These disputes reflect both the strengths and weaknesses of the family firm as an organizational form. Wartime conditions coupled with the deaths of key personnel put great strains on the family enterprise and led to quarrels. At the same time, the flexibility of the family firm may have been essential to its survival in the insecure and rapidly changing environment of war. Had the company had a more formal bureaucratic structure it might not have survived the early phase of the war.

FLOUR MILLS

The Rongs were also able to save some of their flour milling empire in Shanghai, the Fuxin mills. Three of their mills, Fuxin #1, #3, and #6, were located in the Zhabei section of Shanghai and sustained heavy damage. Japanese troops also occupied all three sites and then in 1938 entrusted the properties to the Japanese Mikyō flour company. Three other mills, Fuxin #2, #7, and #8, however, were in the foreign concessions and remained under Rong control. As with the Shenxin textile mills, the Rongs placed the Fuxin properties under foreign registration. Even with half the number of mills as prewar, Fuxin was profitable during Shanghai's "flourishing" period of 1938 and 1939. The influx of refugees kept demand, and profits, high. Fuxin #2 and #8, which had produced 3.4 million bags of flour in 1937, produced 4.8 million in 1939. Profits rose even faster. Fuxin #2 and #8 had lost 323,720 yuan in 1937; Fuxin #7, 31,860 yuan. They quickly turned profitable. Fuxin #2 and #8 earned 2.1 million yuan in 1939; Fuxin #7, 1.3 million.[28]

The biggest difficulty for the mills was the source of wheat. Shipments from north China were disrupted by the war, so Fuxin turned to imported wheat. A negligible source before 1939, imported wheat accounted for almost 84 percent of the purchases of the three mills in that year. The outbreak of the war in Europe, however, played havoc with supplies, and output began to drop. Fuxin #2 and #8 could only manage 1.4 million bags in 1940. Fuxin #7 dropped from 3.8 million bags in 1939 to 1.1 million in 1940. High prices kept profits up for a time, but Fuxin #2 and #8 began losing money in 1941, Fuxin #7, in 1942.[29]

---

[27] Xu Weiyong and Huang Hanmin, *Rongjia qiye fazhan shi*, pp. 145–146; Rong Collection, SASS, R01-3, pp. 141–142; R03-3, *Shenxin xitong*, vol. 4, no. 2, p. 109.

[28] Rong Collection, SASS, R03-4, *Shenxin xitong*, vol. 7, no. 1, p. 8; R15, p. 83; Xu Weiyong and Huang Hanmin, *Rongjia qiye fazhan shi*, p. 132.

[29] *Rongjia qiye shiliao*, vol. 2, pp. 10, 37, 46, 75–76, 79, 164, 193; Chen Zhen, ed., *Zhongguo jindai gongye shiliao*, vol. 4, pt. 1, pp. 423–424.

AN END TO THE "SOLITARY ISLAND"

When the Pacific War erupted, the sanctity (incomplete as it was) of the International Settlement evaporated. Shenxin #2 and #9 textile mills and Fuxin #2, #7, and #8 flour mills all came under Japanese control. The British and American registry, previously used to provide protection, was now a detriment. Japanese military police seized Shenxin #2 and #9, and five other textile mills in Shanghai, on the grounds that they were enemy property.[30] Unlike 1937, however, when they parceled out seized mills to Japanese firms, military leaders were more ready to restore property to Chinese industrialists. The Pacific War placed new strains on the Japanese economy and *zaibatsu*. Personnel and capital were in short supply; Japanese companies were often unable to operate the new properties. Tokyo also sought to strengthen the Wang Jingwei government so active collaboration by Chinese capitalists was welcome.

The Rongs, who had been reluctant to deal with the occupiers as long as they could operate in the solitary island, now began a carefully orchestrated campaign to make discreet overtures to the Japanese. One key strategy was to bring in new personnel with close ties to the Japanese. As an assistant manager, Shenxin hired Tong Luqing who had studied in Japan, and Jiang Junhui, a Japanese language professor in Shanghai when war erupted, joined the board of managers of Shenxin #9. Jiang was then secretary of the puppet government's Cotton Control Commission which controlled access to raw cotton. Wen Lanting, who headed the commission, was invited to join the board of directors of Shenxin on February 1, 1942. Shenxin #9 even hired a Japanese adviser.[31] The goal, of course, was to regain control of their mills, and having achieved that, to protect their access to raw materials.

The Rongs and other groups which lost property in December 1941 opened direct negotiations with the Japanese military. Jiang Shangda, a textile industrialist in Shanghai, represented the Chinese side. Jiang sought to counter pressure from the Japanese mill owners in Shanghai who did not wish any property returned to the Chinese. Jiang argued that restoring production would not only win over the Chinese population, but provide the cloth, uniforms, and blankets needed by the Japanese army. To press these arguments, Jiang Shangda dispatched Jiang Junhui to Tokyo.[32]

Jiang Shangda took advantage of one other tie, to Japanese right-wing leader Ōkawa Shūmei. Ōkawa was a mainstay of the radical right, an earlier associate

---

[30] *Rongjia qiye shiliao*, vol. 2, pp. 104–105; Rong Collection, SASS, R08, p. 27.

[31] *Rongjia qiye shiliao*, vol. 2, pp. 106–107; Qian Zhonghan, "Wuxi wuge zhuyao chanye ziben," p. 118; Huang Hanmin, "Rongjia qiye dizao zhe," vol. 1, p. 109.

[32] *Rongjia qiye shiliao*, vol. 2, pp. 107–108; Rong Collection, SASS, R01-3, pp. 73–74.

of Kita Ikki, and had been imprisoned for his role in the May 15 Incident in
Tokyo. A strong advocate of Pan-Asianism and a Shōwa Restoration, Ōkawa
was highly regarded by many Japanese military commanders in China. (He
was tried as a class A war criminal after the war.) Ōkawa came to Shanghai
and negotiated between the Japanese mill owners association and the military,
pressing for the return of all seven plants to Chinese control. Such a policy was
considered necessary for implementation of a true Pan-Asianist ideal.[33]

With this solid backing, the seven mills, including Shenxin #2 and #9, were
returned to their Chinese owners. A formal ceremony of rendition occurred
in May 1942. The group left out of these negotiations had actually been the
Nanjing puppet authorities, who nominally had real authority. Jiang Shangda
and the Japanese did invite Mei Siping, Minister of Industry of the puppet
government, to attend the rendition ceremony, but he had not been an active
party in the negotiations.[34]

As the Japanese became even more interested in working with Chinese capitalists, the Rongs attempted to regain control over properties lost since 1937,
including the old Shenxin #5, #6, and #7 as well as the rebuilt #1 and #8. In
April 1942, after the Wang government issued a proclamation on return of
property, Rong Hongyuan submitted a petition thanking the Japanese for
"protecting" the properties during the war and asking for the return of these
old mills under the broad principles of Sino-Japanese cooperation through
the Greater East Asia Co-Prosperity Sphere. Obstacles remained. Japanese
firms had invested the repair of the facilities and demanded compensation.
The Japanese Yūhō Company returned Shenxin #5, on July 24, 1943, but only
after protracted negotiations about the amount of compensation. Similar negotiations with Shanghai bōseki brought the return of Shenxin #6, but it was in
poor shape and was out of production until the end of the war.[35] Problems of
a different sort developed over the return of Shenxin #7. The site of this mill
was occupied by the Japanese navy, which hoped to convert the facility into
a ship manufacturing plant. On April 16, 1943, Rong Hongyuan appealed for
the Japanese consulate to assist in getting the property released. The Imperial
Navy, finally realizing that its plans could not be brought to fruition, returned
control to the Rongs in July 1943.[36]

---

[33] *Rongjia qiye shiliao*, vol. 2, pp. 107–108.

[34] *Rongjia qiye shiliao*, vol. 2, pp. 107–108; Rong Collection, SASS, R01-2, pp. 186–187; R01-3,
pp. 76–77; R03-2, *Shenxin xitong*, vol. 3, no. 1, p. 67.

[35] *Rongjia qiye shiliao*, vol. 2, pp. 117–118, 121–122; Rong Collection, R03-3, *Shenxin xitong*,
vol. 4, no. 1, p. 41.

[36] Rong Collection, SASS, R03-3, *Shenxin xitong*, vol. 4, no. 1, p. 45; Qian Zhonghan, "Wuxi wuge
zhuyao chanye ziben," p. 118; Sherman Cochran, "Business, Governments, and War in China,

Even more difficulties surrounded the return of Shenxin #1 and #8. Gutted in the early fighting, the two mills were rebuilt as one unit under the Toyoda company. The Japanese firm claimed that their repairs were equal to three-fourths of the value of the plant and demanded that the Rongs either sell the plant to them or compensate them for the repairs. Toyoda decided on a purchase price for the mill of 2.5 million yen. The Rong management contested Toyoda's figures, saying that the major buildings were old facilities, as were most of the looms and spindles. Before the war the two mills contained 120,000 spindles, they noted. In 1943 only 40,000 remained.

The dispute with Toyoda made the return of the mills problematic. This situation exacerbated the stockholder dispute initiated by the minority stockholders in #1 and #8 (discussed above). Many of these stockholders were suspicious of the Rongs' leadership, feeling that they were pursuing the interests of the other mills, while writing off Shenxin #1 and #8. When the stockholders met on April 7, 1943, and again on July 10, 1943, they refused to sell their title to Toyoda or agree to a joint management proposal, despite the urging of the Wang government. Stockholders wanted to regain the property and reorganize it as a limited-liability company, so they instructed Rong Hongyuan to demand full return of the facility. Unable to reach an agreement, Shenxin did not regain control of the #1 and #8 plant until the war's end, when only 5,000 spindles were found immediately usable.[37]

The post–Pearl Harbor situation was thus fraught with difficulties for the Rongs. Although they desired to regain as much of their property as possible, and revealed a willingness to work with puppet authorities and the Japanese military in doing so, they still rejected the idea of a junior partnership with a Japanese firm, and attempted to keep collaboration as low key as possible.

WARTIME DECLINE IN PRODUCTION

Even with their mills restored, the Rongs found the glory days of "flourishing Shanghai" over. The returned properties were not in good shape. Shenxin #5 had lost about one-half of its spindles, #6 was partially gutted, and #7 had only 30,000 of the earlier 54,000 spindles remaining. A more serious problem was the disruption of trade by the Pacific War. Raw materials were in short supply,

---

1931–1949," in Akira Iriye and Warren Cohen, eds., *American, Chinese, and Japanese Perspectives on Wartime Asia, 1931–1949* (Wilmington, Del.: Scholarly Resources, 1990), p. 124; Chen Zhen, Yao Luo, eds., *Zhongguo jindai gongye shi ziliao*, vol. 1, pp. 391–395; *Rongjia qiye shiliao*, vol. 2, pp. 115–123.

[37] *Rongjia qiye shiliao*, vol. 2, pp. 124–131, 172, 188; Rong Collection, SASS, R03-2, *Shenxin xitong*, vol. 3, no. 1, pp. 75–79.

and what was available was assigned elsewhere. In 1942, Rong Hongyuan estimated that 60 percent of China's raw cotton was appropriated by the Japanese military for shipment to Japan. Of the remaining 40 percent of the harvest in China, three-fourths was assigned to Japanese mills and only one-fourth to Chinese-owned mills. Although Shenxin #2 and #9, for instance, resumed production in June 1942, their output was much reduced. Shenxin #2 produced only 10 percent of the cotton yarn and thread in 1942 that it had in 1936; Shenxin #9, only 7.5 percent. Shenxin #9 had used 321,812 piculs of cotton in 1940; only 12,050 in 1942. Overall the Rongs' mills operated at only 20 percent of capacity in 1942.[38]

Japanese efforts to control the economy also plagued production. The Commerce Control Commission (Quanguo shangye tongzhi zonghui), established in the spring of 1943, continued the efforts of the Japanese military to keep its procurement costs low. The subordinate Cotton Control Commission, operated by the Wang Jingwei government, placed severe restrictions on the sale price of cotton and cotton goods. The price levels which the puppet government set were not sufficiently adjusted for wartime inflation. The Japanese military, for instance, had set 714 yuan per picul of raw cotton as the payment price in 1942, a level maintained by the cotton commission. By the spring of 1943 this was less than half of the market value of cotton, so most farmers tried to avoid the forced procurement process. As the market system broke down, farmers simply curtailed or hoarded production and supplies became unavailable. Similarly, Wang Jingwei authorities set prices for the procurement of cotton yarn and cloth on August 9, 1943. For 20 count cotton yarn the price was 10,000 yuan per *jian*, and for 12 pound cloth, 375 yuan per bolt. In September 1943, the market price for yarn was over 35,000 per *jian* and for cloth, 975 per picul. By June 1944, the government was only paying 6–7 percent of market value in its procurement purchases. Under these conditions Shenxin mills could not operate profitably, at least not without evading the rules of the occupation forces.[39]

In return for restoration of their mills, the Japanese required a quid pro quo from the Rongs – public support for the Japanese and the Wang Jingwei regime. To the end of the conflict, however, Rong Desheng tried to minimize the family's involvement. When dispatching representatives to join the organizations of the puppet government, the Rongs rarely sent someone bearing the family name. Instead, individuals such as Tong Luqing and Jiang Junhui, who had been

---

[38] Rong Collection, SASS, R03-3, *Shenxin xitong*, vol. 4, no. 1, pp. 22–23; R05, p. 70; R08, pp. 52–54; M. C. Bergère, "Zhongguo de minzu qiye yu ZhongRi zhanzheng," p. 539; *Rongjia qiye shiliao*, vol. 2, pp. 121–123, 139–141, 188–189.

[39] Xu Weiyong and Huang Hanmin, *Rongjia qiye fazhan shi*, pp. 165–167.

employed because of their Japanese connections, were sent forward. Tong and Jiang, for instance, both served on Nanjing's Cotton Control Commission, and Tong on the Commerce Control Commission.[40]

Despite this cooperation with the Japanese, Rong Desheng strove to keep good relations with Chongqing, not wanting to jeopardize the family's future if the Allies were victorious. In September 1943, he dispatched his son, Rong Er'ren, to Chongqing with a large sum for investment. Er'ren also registered all family property with the Guomindang government to avoid being labeled a traitor. Through early use of foreign registry and later substantial cooperation with puppet authorities, the Rong enterprises in Shanghai thus survived the war and even profited, especially before December 1941. By compromising with the Japanese, while maintaining relations with Chongqing, the Rongs survived the last years of the war and remained one of the major enterprises in China.[41]

CONCLUSION

The experiences of the Rong family industrialists were not typical of all Chinese capitalists embroiled in the war. The Rongs were bigger and more diverse in their holdings than others. Nonetheless, a study of the Rongs tells us much about wartime conditions.

Certainly the war was destructive. Factories, mills, shops, ships, and banks were physically damaged, occupied, and used for barracks, stripped for scrap metals, and turned over to Japanese firms. Nonetheless, in a divided city such as Shanghai, the experience of the Rongs demonstrated how variable the destruction was. Factories and enterprises in Chinese sections of Shanghai which were active battlefields were largely destroyed, as Shenxin mills #1 and #8. Plants in the foreign sector north of the Suzhou Creek usually escaped destruction but were confiscated by the Japanese, as Shenxin #6 and #7. By contrast, those fortunate enough to be located in the "solitary island" usually escaped destruction and could actually profit from wartime conditions during 1937–1941. The Rongs were sufficiently diverse that they experienced all three situations. Most Chinese businessmen had a more singular experience – either their enterprises were destroyed or confiscated or fortune smiled.

---

[40] Qian Zhonghan, "Wuxi wuge zhuyao chanye ziben," p. 118; Tang Zhenchang, ed., *Shanghai shi* (A history of Shanghai; Shanghai: Shanghai renmin chuban she, 1989), p. 803; *Rongjia qiye shiliao*, vol. 2, pp. 106–108.

[41] Rong Collection, SASS, R01-3, pp. 141–142; R03-2, *Shenxin xitong*, vol. 3, no. 1, pp. 91–92; Qian Zhonghan, "Wuxi wuge zhuyao chanye ziben," p. 118; Sherman Cochran, "Business, Governments, and War in China," p. 125; *Rongjia qiye shiliao*, vol. 2, pp. 179–180; Xu Weiyong and Huang Hanmin, *Rongjia qiye fazhan shi*, pp. 195–196.

Wartime China also revealed the adaptability of Chinese capitalists. Accustomed to operating under stressful conditions without strong legal or political protection, Chinese capitalists were quick to seize opportunity whenever possible. The Rongs then grabbed profits as rapidly as they were able from their remaining properties. Yet the war also revealed some of the problems with the family firm. The death of the senior figure led to a rift within the family group. Minority stockholders who were excluded from the profits of the early war era became discontented.

Finally, the actions of many Chinese capitalists did not serve them well in the postwar environment. Both Guomindang and Communist authorities accused many of the capitalists of pursuing profit rather than patriotism. In a political environment generally unfriendly to capitalism, the wartime behavior of Chinese capitalists did little to improve their weak position in the postwar world. The Rongs attempted to avoid collaboration as long as possible, but even they made significant compromises after 1941. On numerous occasions they worked with Japanese and puppet authorities, seriously damaging their credibility as patriotic capitalists. Only careful maneuvering late in the war preserved their postwar status.

Chapter 3

Marketing Medicine across Enemy Lines

Chinese "Fixers" and Shanghai's Wartime Centrality

SHERMAN COCHRAN

During the period of the [Japanese wartime] occupation, we [Chinese] businessmen continued to put profits above all other considerations. To make a profit, we fought with each other in a life or death struggle and never thought of giving in to rivals. At the time, the most important thing for [Chinese] leaders of industry and commerce in Shanghai's foreign concessions was to become fixers (*lulutong*, a Shanghainese slang expression literally meaning "one who takes every road") so as to maneuver successfully in the market, and I was a typical example of a fixer. Those called fixers managed to have good relationships with all political parties, including the Japanese [military] authorities, Wang Jingwei's puppet government at Nanjing, and the Nationalist government's underground agents sent from Chongqing. I was pretty successful at establishing friendships with leading figures in all of these political groups during the war.[1]

Fixers, as described above, are shadowy figures in the history of wartime Shanghai and, for that matter, in the history of other cities under other wartime occupations. Fixers in Shanghai between 1937 and 1945 are worth bringing to light for many reasons and perhaps above all because of their roles in

---

[1] Xu Guanqun, "Xinya yaochang sanshinian laide huigu" (Reflections on my thirty years at New Asia Pharmaceuticals), 1964. The original copy of this unpublished manuscript is in the office of the New Asia Pharmaceutical Company, Shanghai.

On many projects I have consulted colleagues at the Institute of Economics in the Shanghai Academy of Social Sciences, and I am grateful for their advice and guidance over the years. With respect to this particular project, I want to express my special thanks to them because, without their help, I would not have had access to the principal sources cited here. In addition, I owe a great debt to Zheng Liren for joining me in conducting research on this topic.

5. A Chinese soldier under search before entering the French Concession
(November 1937). Source: Courtesy of the Fabre Family.

maintaining the city's position as China's most central metropolis for commerce and popular culture. On the eve of the war, Shanghai had unquestionably
reached the pinnacle of China's urban hierarchy by surpassing all other Chinese
cities as a nationwide exporter of consumer goods and print media (newspapers,
magazines, advertisements),[2] but the question of whether Shanghai retained this
preeminent position during the war is still at issue. Some historians have concluded that the city lost its centrality during the war, and they have formulated
an interpretation that may be called the Island Shanghai thesis. According to this
thesis, the Japanese invasion undid Shanghai's centrality by isolating the city in
two stages: In 1937, Japan seized all of Shanghai except the foreign concessions
which became a "solitary island" (*gudao*) surrounded by Japanese forces; then
in 1941 the Japanese extended this occupation to encompass Shanghai's foreign
concessions too. As a result, according to the Island Shanghai thesis, Shanghai
became marooned both commercially and culturally. As a center for trade, it

---

[2] Zhang Zhongli, ed., *Jindai Shanghai chengshi yanjiu* (Urban studies on modern Shanghai), 148–
152 and 1130–1159; Leo Ou-fan Lee and Andrew J. Nathan, "The Beginnings of Mass Culture:
Journalism and Fiction in Late Ch'ing and Beyond," 368–375; G. William Skinner, "Regional
Urbanization in Nineteenth-Century China," 17 and 24n.

lost access to markets in its hinterland and the rest of China, and as a center for popular culture, according to Chang-tai Hung in the first book published on China's wartime popular culture, Shanghai lost its centrality because of a process of "decentralization of culture from coastal cities to the interior . . . that shifted China's attention to the countryside."[3]

Before accepting the Island Shanghai thesis as valid, it is worth taking into account the role played by Shanghai-based Chinese fixers as catalysts for production, distribution, and consumption of both commerce and culture in wartime China. These fixers are difficult to investigate because they were notoriously secretive, but one of them, Xu Guanqun (1899–1972), the self-identified fixer quoted in the epigraph above, has provided a window on their world by preserving detailed records of his business, New Asia Pharmaceutical Company (Xinya zhiyao chang), and by writing a revealing and unpublished memoir which describes his dealings with leading wartime figures not only in business but in the wider arenas of politics, medicine, science, and literature.[4] As shown in Tables 3.1 and 3.2, his company's capital and sales rose in a linear progression, and its distributing network dramatically expanded throughout China and Southeast Asia during the war. By the end of the war Xu formed the New Asia Enterprise Group (Xinya qiye jituan), capitalized at more than a billion yuan, which had New Asia Pharmaceutical Company as its cornerstone and included thirty-five enterprises in medicine, printing, paper-making, dyes, textiles, hardware, banking, insurance, and real estate.[5]

How did Xu as a Chinese fixer compile this remarkably successful record in wartime? And what is its significance for Shanghai as a center of China's commerce and culture? The following essay addresses these questions by examining Xu's negotiations with Japanese and Chinese governments at the beginning of the war and his use of science to achieve commercial expansion and cultural influence during the war.

---

[3] Chang-tai Hung, *War and Popular Culture: Resistance in Modern China, 1937—1945*, 281–282 and 285.

[4] The tone of Xu Guanqun's memoirs is not easy to explain. In the early 1960s he wrote proudly of his wartime achievements as though he still had the unreconstructed mentality of a fixer, even though by then he had lived in Shanghai as a citizen of the People's Republic of China for more than ten years and had witnessed massive campaigns in which Chinese capitalists had been denounced and punished for wartime profiteering and traitorous collaboration with the enemy. Perhaps he was unguarded about his capitalist past because he wrote in 1962–1963 during a brief hiatus between mass campaigns (the Great Leap Forward which ended by 1961 and the Socialist Education Campaign which began in 1963). On the campaigns against Chinese capitalists in Shanghai during the 1950s, see John Gardner, "The *Wu-fan* Campaign in Shanghai: A Study in the Consolidation of Urban Control."

[5] Xu, "Xinya," 131–133.

Table 3.1 *New Asia Pharmaceutical Company's Capital and Sales Revenue,*
1926–1945

Year	Capital (in yuan)*	Capital (equivalent in U.S. dollars)	Sales Revenue (in yuan)*	Sales Revenue (equivalent in U.S. dollars)
1926	1,000	508		
1927	10,000	4,608		
1930	50,000	15,337		
1932	50,000	9,506	355,000	67,490
1933	250,000	83,333	614,000	204,667
1934	250,000	85,034	705,000	239,796
1935	250,000	75,075	825,000	247,748
1936	500,000	166,666	1,000,000	333,000
1937	500,000	150,150	1,303,000	391,291
1938	1,000,000	224,719		
1939	1,000,000	130,039	3,968,000	515,995
1940	3,000,000	165,016		
1941	8,000,000	400,000		
1942	30,000,000	750,000		
1943	120,000,000	204,012	52,566,000	893,676
1944	120,000,000	60,000	248,077,000	124,038
1945	120,000,000	72,003	121,075,000	72,648

* The currencies used were as follows: before 1935, yinyuan (silver yuan); during 1935–1941, fabi (the currency of the Nationalist government); during 1942–1945, zhongchuquan (the currency of Wang Jingwei's Japanese-sponsored government).
   The figures in U.S. dollars are rough approximations because foreign exchange rates are based solely on the currency of the Nationalist government in unoccupied China, not the currency of the Japanese-sponsored government in occupied China.

Sources: Chen and Yuan, 7. For exchange rates, see C. F. Remer, *Foreign Investments in China* (New York: Macmillan, 1933), 172; Kia-ngau Chang, *The Inflationary Spiral: The Experience in China, 1939–1950* (New York: The Technology Press of the Massachusetts Institute of Technology, 1958), 278–282, 300–301, 382–383; Arthur N. Young, *China and the Helping Hand, 1937–1945* (Cambridge, Mass.: Harvard University Press, 1963), 435–437.

WARTIME ALLIANCES

When Japan invaded China in the summer of 1937, it threatened to cut off Xu Guanqun and his Shanghai headquarters from a long-distance marketing network which he had built up in the early 1930s. In response to this threat, Xu made every effort to hold together his nationwide business in a politically divided country under foreign occupation. Like the majority of Shanghai's capitalists, he declined to follow Chiang Kai-shek's government as it moved its capital from Nanjing westward first to Wuhan (1937–1938) and then to Chongqing

Table 3.2 *Wartime Expansion of New Asia Pharmaceutical Company*

	1926–1936	1938–1945
Headquarters	Shanghai	Shanghai
Headquarters of branch companies (*fen gongsi*) in China	None	- Shanghai (for Jiangsu and Zhejiang) - Hankou (for Hunan, Hubei, Jiangxi, and Henan) - Chongqing (for Sichuan, Guizhou, Yunnan, and Tibet) - Guangzhou (for Guangdong, Guangxi, and Fujian) - Tianjin (for Hebei, Shanxi, Shandong, and Inner Mongolia) - Xi'an (for Shaanxi, Gansu, Ningxia, Qinghai, and Xinjiang)
Headquarters of branch companies outside China	None	Hong Kong, Singapore, Bangkok, Manila
Medicine-making plants	Shanghai (1 plant)	Shanghai (4 plants), Chongqing, Beijing, Hong Kong
Sales agencies	27 agencies (all in China)	41 agencies in China, 10 agencies in Southeast Asia

Sources: Xiyao, 278–280; Xu, "Xinya," 66–70; Chen and Yuan, 6, 224; file Q38-40-11: 104, 107–108.

(1938–1945), but like several other Chinese capitalists, Xu transported some equipment from his Shanghai plants first to Wuhan and then to Chongqing. In 1938 he established at Chongqing a new branch, the New Asia Southwest China Company, and in 1940 he opened there a pharmaceutical plant capitalized at one million yuan.[6] He moved this equipment and opened this new branch, as he later recalled, for commercial rather than patriotic reasons. "Our base for our business was well established in Shanghai, and we had to maintain our primary strength here for the sake of future development," he explained. "But it would have been wrong not to heed the call to move inland. In fact, moving inland was a great opportunity to open vast markets in the provinces of the Southwest.

[6] Xu, "Xinya," 42–43; Shanghai shehui kexue yuan jingji yanjiu suo (Shanghai Academy of Social Sciences, Institute of Economics), *Shanghai jindai xiyao hangye shi* (A history of the modern medicine trade in Shanghai) (Shanghai: Shanghai shehui kexue yuan chubanshe, 1988), 279–280. Hereafter this book is cited as *Xiyao*.

Why should we have let this opportunity slip through our fingers?"[7] During the war, Xu continued to reach out from his Shanghai base even after it came under the Japanese occupation, and he was able to exploit markets in other parts of wartime China because of his political alliances across enemy lines.

Political Alliances. In the course of the war, Xu cultivated Chinese and Japanese leaders of almost all groups in positions of political authority throughout China. Within Shanghai, Xu maintained a key contact with a close associate of Du Yuesheng, the Chinese head of the Green Gang which played an influential role in the city's labor-management relations and business-government relations before and during the war. In 1938 Du fled to Hong Kong and did not return to Shanghai until the end of the war, and during the war he was represented in Shanghai by his associates, notably Gu Kemin, a banker whom Xu had recruited onto New Asia's board of directors in 1936. Soon thereafter Xu became Gu's sworn brother, and at the end of the war when Xu himself fled from Shanghai to Hong Kong, he and his partners showed the extent of their reliance on Gu by leaving New Asia in Gu's hands.[8]

In Shanghai, Xu also worked with the Japanese occupying forces and leading Chinese collaborators. He was able to take advantage of preexisting contacts because he had already formed ties in prewar Japan through his co-founder and partner at New Asia, Zhao Rudiao, who had studied in Japan, learned Japanese, and worked for a Japanese trading company in China. When Xu had traveled to Japan in 1936, he had depended on Zhao as his translator and intermediary,[9] and after the Japanese invasion of 1937, Xu had Zhao available to mediate with the Japanese authorities and their Chinese collaborators in Shanghai.

In the early years of the war, 1937–1941, Xu assumed official positions in the government of Shanghai's International Settlement, and in these positions he served with Chinese who gave him access to the Japanese authorities. In 1939 and again in 1941, he was elected to the Shanghai Municipal Council, and he aligned himself with fellow Council member Yuan Ludeng and two of Yuan's associates, Wen Lanting and Lin Kanghou, who were known at the time as "The Three Elders of Shanghai" and were later described by Xu as "notorious collaborators" and "leading Chinese traitors" (*da Hanjian*). Through them he made contacts with the Japanese military police and intelligence service.[10]

---

[7] Xu, "Xinya," 42.

[8] Xu, "Xinya," 34, 148, 155; *Xiyao*, 279, 288. On Du, see Brian Martin's essay in this volume.

[9] Xu, "Xinya," 38–40; *Xiyao*, 278; Chen Lizheng and Yuan Enzhen, *Xinya de licheng – Shanghai xinya zhiyaochang de guoqu xianzai he jiangli*, 5.

[10] Xu, "Xinya," 67 and 102; *Xiandai Shanghai dashiji* (Great events in modern Shanghai), 740 and 796; *Xiyao*, 171–172. Cf. Wang Ke-wen, "Collaborators and Capitalists: The Politics of 'Material

In December 1941, when Japan occupied Shanghai's foreign concessions, Xu began working directly with the Japanese authorities. He presented himself as a Chinese leader by citing his credential as president of the Association of Shanghai Pharmaceutical Manufacturers (Shanghaishi zhiyao changye tongye gonghui) (which he had founded in 1933), and he merged this association with a related one, the Shanghai Association of the New Medicine Trade (Shanghai xinyaoye tongye gonghui) for the purpose of dealing with the Japanese authorities.[11] In 1942 Xu and other Chinese in the pharmaceutical industry lost their direct control over distribution of medicine in China, but only briefly. At first, beginning in April 1942, they had to distribute through a Japanese administrative organization, the Central China Commission for Control of Medicine (Huazhong yiyaopin tongzhi lianhehui), and they were subordinated to its Japanese head, Nakajima Seiichi, a manager in the Japanese-owned Takeda Chemical Industries. Less than a year later, by March 1943, Xu and other Chinese capitalists achieved greater control over distribution with the establishment of the Japanese-sponsored National Commission for the Control of Commerce (Quanguo shangye tongzhi zonghui) which was characterized by the Japanese as a "self-governed merchant group." In August 1943, Xu was recommended for the commission's board of directors by Mei Siping, minister of the interior and one of the most influential figures in Wang Jingwei's Japanese-sponsored government. From then until the end of the war, Xu served as a member of its board and sold medical products (especially alcohol) to Japanese customers, including the Japanese army.[12]

In Japanese-occupied parts of China outside Shanghai, Xu maintained close relations with Chinese Japanese-sponsored governments. In Beijing, the head of New Asia's branch company for North China had close relations with Wang Kemin, the top Chinese official in the North China Provisional Government which was set up by the Japanese in 1937. In Nanjing, the capital of the Japanese-sponsored government for central China, Xu worked through Chu Minyi, the foreign minister and vice president of the executive yuan of this government which was led from 1940 to 1945 by Chu's brother-in-law, Wang Jingwei. It was

---

Control' in Wartime Shanghai," 5; and Yuan Yuquan, "Rikou jiaqiang luedou huazhong zhanlue wuzi paozhi shangtonghui jingguo," 83–85.

[11] *Xiyao*, 301–303, 319–320; Chen and Yuan, 5; Xu, "Xinya," 25. The organization resulting from this merger was known as the Alliance of the New Medicine Trade and the Pharmaceutical Industry (Xinyaoye zhiyaoye lianhehui). It existed barely a year (until April 1943) when it once again was divided into two organizations because of orders from Wang Jingwei's government that all prewar guilds and trade associations should be restored (*Xiyao*, 301–302).

[12] Wang, 49–50; Gan Gu, ed., *Shanghai bainian mingchang laodian* (One hundred years of famous factories and old shops in Shanghai), 32; *Xiyao*, 170–171, 287, 302; Chen and Yuan, 27.

because of Chu's intervention that Xu was able to reopen New Asia's offices in the Japanese-occupied cities of Hangzhou, Hankou, Guangzhou, and Fuzhou during the early 1940s. "We in the new medicine industry knew Chu Minyi most intimately (*shouxi*) of all the ranking officials in Wang Jingwei's inner circle," Xu later recalled.[13]

Outside Japanese-occupied China, Xu had connections with Chiang Kai-shek's Nationalist government. He arranged for protection of New Asia's goods in areas under the Nationalists' control by winning support from members of the Nationalists' underground in Shanghai. In particular, he financed a unit in Shanghai led by Wu Kaixian and Wu Shaoshu, two prominent figures in the Nationalist party and members of the C. C. Clique, a conservative political faction which took charge of the Nationalist party's intelligence network before the war and became extremely influential with Chiang Kai-shek before, during, and after the war. The C. C. Clique, in return, helped to protect New Asia's branch company in Chongqing and its distributing network in the Upper Yangzi region.[14]

The only major political group with which Xu did not have close relations while he was in Shanghai during the war was the one led by the Chinese Communists. Not until he moved to Hong Kong at the end of the war in 1945 did he begin doing business with the Communists' underground agents.[15] But the Communists were the exception. With other major parties, Xu came to terms during the war.

Xu's success at negotiating this extraordinary range of alliances with leaders of almost every political stripe served more than one of his purposes. It not only protected his distributing network's access to markets both in and outside Shanghai; it also opened financial channels and allowed him to tap sources of capital from outside the city as well as within it.

Financial Arrangements. In finance, as in politics, Xu successfully brokered agreements with political rivals outside wartime Shanghai. In financing New Asia, he was particularly adept at raising capital from members of one faction of the Nationalist government, the Political Study Clique (*Zhengxue xi*), without antagonizing this faction's bitter rival, the C. C. Clique.[16] As noted

---

[13] Xu, "Xinya," 68, 127; *Xiyao*, 171–172.

[14] Xu, "Xinya," 68–69. On Wu Kaixian and Wu Shaoshu in wartime Shanghai, see Brian Martin's essay in this volume. On the C.C. Clique, see Hung-mao Tien, *Government and Politics in Kuomintang China 1927–1937*, 47–52; and Lloyd E. Eastman, *Seeds of Destruction: Nationalist China in War and Revolution, 1937–1949*, 27–28, 100–102, 109–116.

[15] Xu, "Xinya," 162–163.

[16] On the rivalry between the C.C. Clique and the Political Study Clique before, during, and after the war, see Tien, 70–71; and Eastman, *Seeds*, 111–113, 125–127.

earlier, during the war Xu received the C. C. Clique's protection for New Asia's distributing network outside Shanghai in regions of China under the control of the Nationalist government. At the same time, Xu did not let the C. C. Clique's opposition to the Political Study Clique prevent him from making financial arrangements with members of the Political Study Clique who owned banks based in Chongqing as well as Shanghai.

Before the war, Xu had issued New Asia's stocks (*gu piao*) and bonds (*gongsi zhai*) through several Shanghai-based banks owned by members of the Political Study Clique, but when the war broke out in 1937, some of these banks fled with Chiang Kai-shek's Nationalist government to Chongqing. In 1939, Xu made New Asia's first and second issues of stock in wartime by relying exclusively on banks still remaining in Shanghai. Then in 1940, when Xu announced that he was about to issue more stock in New Asia, he discovered that bankers who had moved their banks to Chongqing managed to reestablish themselves in Shanghai. The first step was taken by Zhang Jia'ao, head of the Bank of China and an influential member of the Political Study Clique, who sent an emissary to conduct negotiations with bankers in Shanghai. As a result, the bankers from Chongqing and Shanghai jointly formed an investment firm, the Nanyang Enterprise Company (Nanyang qiye gongsi), and in 1940 Xu issued New Asia's stock through this firm.[17]

In the early 1940s, Xu started his own financial institutions in Shanghai, and they also had relations with Chongqing. On December 1, 1941, he and other Chinese industrialists opened the China Industrial Bank (Zhongguo gongye yinhang) in Shanghai's foreign concessions with the aim of circumventing the Nationalist government's regulations, which limited the amounts of money that depositors could withdraw from their accounts. Prior to the bank's opening, Xu's plans for it encountered resistance from the Nationalist government in Chongqing. One of his banking partners, Zhu Boquan, was offered money by Du Yuesheng's agents if he would withhold his investment from the proposed bank, and Xu's application to register the bank with the Nationalist government in Chongqing received no reply. Nonetheless, Xu won Zhu's support and opened the bank, which immediately prospered. A little over a year later, Xu added an investment firm, New Asia Reconstruction Company (Xinya jianye gongsi), and he again heard from Chongqing. This time he was contacted by the Shanghai Commercial and Savings Bank and the China Vegetable Oil Company, both of which were owned by members of the Political Study Clique in the Nationalist government in Chongqing. From their owners he received expressions of interest in this venture, and he accommodated, appointing their representatives

---

[17] Xu, "Xinya," 119–121.

along with Shanghai banks' representatives to the board of directors of his new investment firm, which was initially capitalized at 10 million yuan.[18]

In all of these cases, Xu allowed neither political rivalries nor wartime battle lines to block his financial transactions with investors from outside Shanghai. Far from being financially restricted, Xu seems to have found more room to maneuver during the war. On the one hand, the war did not prevent him from tapping his prewar sources of capital, and on the other hand, it did allow him to carry out financial transactions beyond the reach of the Nationalist government's attempts to intervene from Chongqing. As a result, Xu was able to build up New Asia's capital and sales throughout most of the eight-year war. In the late 1930s and early 1940s, his company's capital and sales revenue surpassed its prewar levels and did not fall below these levels until hit by a runaway inflation between 1943 and 1945 (see Table 3.1). As a trained accountant, Xu was never one to let his funds lie idle, and during the war he invested them in New Asia's operations to expand the company and make it more scientific.

POPULARIZING SCIENCE

Xu's political and financial deals opened the way for his wartime commercial ventures but by no means guaranteed their success. It is true that in wartime his product to some extent sold itself; in fact, almost all of Shanghai's big Chinese pharmaceutical companies grew rapidly during the war because of a great demand for medical products.[19] But even compared to these other pharmaceutical firms, New Asia grew at an extraordinary rate and emerged as a giant. Why did it become so big so fast? As wartime refugees fled from Shanghai and other coastal cities westward into smaller cities and the countryside, did Xu appeal to Chinese consumers by making New Asia seem less Shanghai-centered and more rural-oriented? The answer to this last question is no. During the war, Xu popularized New Asia's goods by making them seem Chinese, but he did so by identifying them with Chinese science in Shanghai rather than with Chinese resistance in the countryside.

Science in Research and Development. Xu Guanqun made New Asia more scientific and more Chinese by adding to its staff an illustrious group of Chinese research scientists. Before the war, like almost all pharmaceutical manufacturers in the world prior to the 1930s, he had no scientists on his staff doing full-time

[18] Xu, "Xinya," 128–133.
[19] Sherman Cochran, "Intra-Asian Marketing: Aw Boon Haw's Commercial Network, 1910–1937"; Cochran, "Marketing Medicine and Advertising Dreams in China, 1900–1950."

serious research and no substantial laboratory in which they could conduct experiments.[20] In 1935, Xu had opened at Shanghai his first modest laboratory, the New Asia Chemical and Pharmaceutical Research Institute, but not until the war was under way did he give New Asia major research facilities by building three large laboratories. In 1937 he opened the New Asia Medical Materials Plant for designing and making surgical instruments, adhesive plasters, gauze, bandages, and absorbent cotton. In 1938 he added the New Asia Serum Plant which produced vaccines to prevent or treat cholera, typhoid, smallpox, diphtheria, rabies, dysentery, tetanus, meningitis, pertussis, and plague. In 1941 he founded his most sophisticated laboratory, the New Asia Biological Research Institute, specializing in antibiotics, including penicillin.[21]

To staff these laboratories, Xu recruited distinguished Chinese scientists trained in Japan and the West as well as China. In the early 1930s, he and his Japanese-trained partner Zhao Rudiao had acquired New Asia's first technology and technical expertise by relying on Japanese technical advisers; and in 1935, when he had opened his first laboratory, he had appointed as director Zeng Guangfang, a native of China with a Pharm.D. degree from Tokyo (Teikoku) University, who had employed Japanese technicians and had used Japanese-made equipment in the laboratory. But after the war began, Xu recruited for New Asia's top research positions Chinese scientists trained in the West rather than Japan. He selected as director of the New Asia Serum Plant Cheng Muyi, a Chinese bacteriologist trained at Harvard and formerly the director of the Nationalist government's Central Institute for Medical Testing, and as associate director, he chose Wu Liguo who had been trained in France. At the New Asia Biological Research Institute he appointed as director Yu He, another American-trained bacteriologist who had been educated at Harvard. Xu employed under these directors additional research scientists who had received training and gained experience in several different institutions and countries. His Chinese scientists trained in China included former members of China's Academia Sinica (Zhongyang yanjiu yuan), former faculty members from China's leading universities, and recent graduates from China's universities

---

[20] The only exceptions to this generalization were in Germany where the leading pharmaceutical company, Bayer, already was producing synthetic drugs developed in its laboratories as early as 1900. In the United States and Britain, the leading pharmaceutical companies did not open their first laboratories for serious research until the decade preceding the war: Eli Lilly in 1929, Merck and Company in 1933, Squibb in 1938. See Alfred D. Chandler, Jr., *Scale and Scope: The Dynamics of Industrial Capitalism*, 478; David L. Cowen and William H. Helfand, *Pharmacy: An Illustrated History*, 164 and 214; and James Harvey Young, *Pure Food: Securing the Federal Food and Drug Act of 1906*, 113–120.

[21] Xu, "Xinya," 44, 49–50, 125.

(where New Asia recruited every year); and his scientists trained abroad included Chinese holders of advanced degrees in medical science from universities in Japan, the United States, Britain, Germany, and France. As Xu proudly recalled, by the end of the war fully 10 percent of New Asia's staff members were experts and trained technicians in one field of medical science or another.[22]

These scientists developed medical products which New Asia manufactured almost entirely in new plants built during the war. As shown in Table 3.2, New Asia had only one medicine-making factory in Shanghai before the war, and during the war it added six – three more in Shanghai plus one each in Chongqing, Beijing, and Hong Kong – which employed more than a thousand workers.[23] These plants were needed outside Shanghai as well as within it to supply New Asia's growing long-distance distributing network.

Science in Distribution. While recruiting scientifically trained researchers for New Asia's laboratories, Xu also gave scientific training to pharmacists and sales managers who served as its distributing agents. Between 1937 and 1945, he relied less and less on his native-place associates (who, writing in retrospect, have grumbled ever since about their loss of authority and influence at New Asia during the war),[24] and he began recruiting candidates according to their educational credentials rather than their native-place connections. He gave some of these recruits training in science as pharmacists at one of his company's schools, and he gave others training in scientific management as sales managers at another of his company's schools.

In February 1939, Xu opened at Shanghai the Guangcheng Professional School for Advanced Pharmacy (Guangcheng gaoji yaoxue zhiye xuexiao) (which was named after his father, Xu Guangcheng). Xu ran the school entirely within New Asia, appointing himself as chairman of its board, his partner Zhao Rudiao as its president, and his long-time chief pharmacist Liu Buqing as its dean.[25] While Xu intended that this school, like New Asia's research

---

22 Xu, "Xinya," 37–39, 49, 125, 197; *Xiyao*, 276, 278; Yu, 32; Chen and Yuan, 13.

23 Chen and Yuan, 66.

24 Qi Heming, "Xu Guanqun yu Xinya yaochang" (Xu Guanqun and New Asia Pharmaceutical Mills), 51,70.

25 Xu's appointments to the school's board of trustees illustrated his techniques for cultivating political figures in positions of authority. In deference to the Japanese, he appointed to the school's board three of Shanghai's leading Chinese collaborators, Wen Lanting, Yuan Ludeng, and Lin Kanghou. To give representation to Wang Jingwei's Japanese-sponsored government for Central China, Xu appointed as a trustee Chu Minyi who was Wang's brother-in-law and a high official in Wang's government. And Xu's choice as a representative of the Green Gang among the school's trustees was Gu Kemin, Xu's sworn brother and leader of the gang in wartime Shanghai (Xu,"Xinya," 102).

laboratories, should raise the standards of pharmaceutical medicine in China, he did not invest in it for purely altruistic reasons. Although not requiring its graduates to take jobs at New Asia, he counted on them to promote the company's medicines wherever they were employed. As Xu spelled out this rationale:

> We knew that it would cost our company a substantial amount of money to run a private professional school. But we also felt that it was very important for our company to have a basic rank and file (*jiben duiwu*). We called the graduates trained by ourselves our "Army of Sons and Brothers" (*zidi bing*), and we counted on their loyalty.[26]

Xu thus inculcated loyalty in his pharmacy students as ardently as in his salesmen, referring to them as members of his "Army of Sons and Brothers," the same militaristic expression that he used to describe his sales organization.[27]

In retrospect, Xu expressed satisfaction that the graduates of this school fulfilled his expectations, and it seems likely that they did. After all, upon completing their professional education within his company, they were deeply in his debt, and as they fanned out and took up posts in China's leading pharmacies, they were undoubtedly inclined to promote New Asia's medical products.

While training pharmacists with the expectation that they would informally promote New Asia's products, Xu also trained middle managers with formal responsibility for marketing these goods. Xu had founded New Asia's Staff Training Institute to teach recruits "scientific management" at Shanghai in early 1937, and during the war he assigned Chinese graduates of this institute responsibility for managing New Asia's elaborate four-tiered marketing system on a national and an international scale. At the top, Xu presided from New Asia's Shanghai headquarters over a commercial empire that pushed beyond its prewar borders to encompass all of China proper (excluding the Northeast), Tibet, Ningxia, Qinghai, Xinjiang, and seven Southeast Asian countries. At the second level were ten branch companies (six in China and four in Southeast Asia), each responsible for distribution in a sales region (*yingye qu*) which covered between two and five provinces in China or a country in Southeast Asia (see Table 3.2). At the third level, each sales region was divided into subregions with an office (*banshichu*) managing distribution in each subregion. And at the fourth level, each subregion was divided into smaller territories with an agency (*dailichu*) handling local distribution.[28]

---

[26] Xu, "Xinya," 102.
[27] Xu, "Xinya," 79.
[28] Xu, "Xinya," 66–72; *Xiyao*, 279–281; Chen and Yuan, 5–8.

From Shanghai, Xu sent "posted representatives" (*zhuwai daibiao*) to manage this organization. He assigned to these posted representatives the task of recruiting local merchants to handle New Asia's goods at all levels, but he did not leave supervision to them alone. To monitor them and local merchants, he regularly dispatched from Shanghai teams of inspectors (*fangwen yuan*), and according to the confidential minutes of the meetings of New Asia's board of directors, he took these on-the-spot inspections very seriously.[29] On February 27, 1943, for example, he made the following statement of policy with its implied threat: "Every Saturday the General Promotion Office (*tuiguangchu*) must report on the inspectors' work to the general manager [Xu himself] who may personally review an inspector's work at any time."[30]

During the war, New Asia's sales force continued to promote the company's goods as it had before the war, but now with greater intensity. It was able to achieve greater intensity not only because it had more numerous offices and better trained staff members but also because it had at its disposal more promotional publications.

Science in Advertising. During the war, even as Xu recruited specialists in other aspects of his business – scientists to develop his medical products and pharmacists and distributing agents to market them – so too did he recruit editors, literary figures, and artists to promote his goods through popular publications. Even as he built New Asia's laboratories to do scientific research and trained pharmacists in science and sales managers in scientific management, so too did he call upon the magazine's contributors to popularize science and to show the compatibility between modern science and traditional Chinese culture.

In 1938, Xu set out to show the compatibility between modern medical science and traditional Chinese medicine by founding *The New Voice of Chinese Medicine* (Guoyao xinsheng), a Chinese-language monthly medical journal for practitioners of traditional Chinese medicine. Xu hired as its editor-in-chief Ding Fubao, a Chinese author and doctor who had become famous in China for writing books criticizing traditional Chinese medicine in light of Western biological science even while he continued to practice traditional Chinese medicine in Shanghai. Under Ding's editorship, the magazine was given a hand-sewn binding of the traditional Chinese kind, and 2,000–4,000 copies of each issue were printed at .30 yuan per copy.[31]

---

[29] Xu, "Xinya," 64–66, 69–72; *Xiyao*, 278–280; Chen and Yuan, 17–19; Tan Yulin, "Xu Guanqun," 263.

[30] Xinya huaxue zhiyao gongsi dang'an (Files on New Asia Chemical and Pharmaceutical Company), Q38-40-11, Shanghai City Archives.

[31] Xu, "Xinya," 58–59; *Xiyao*, 282; Qi, 54–55.

Through this journal, Xu sought to convince traditional Chinese doctors that New Asia's products were based on a kind of science that would serve traditional Chinese medicine as well as modern Western medicine. In this task, Xu had to overcome traditional Chinese doctors' anti-Western bias which had been deepened by their fierce rivalry with Chinese advocates of purely Western-style medical science since the 1920s. Keeping his distance from this dispute, Xu convinced both sides to buy New Asia's goods. As he later recalled, "At the time, [Chinese] Western-style doctors (*Xiyi*) and [Chinese] Chinese-style doctors (*Zhongyi*) didn't mix any better than fire and water. . . . As for those of us selling medicine, we didn't really care whether they were Chinese-style or Western-style doctors or which side they were on. We sold to them all."[32] Besides introducing this new medical journal, Xu also continued to publish his prewar medical journal, his drug catalogues, and his popular magazine, *Healthy Home* (Jiankang jiating) (founded in 1936), which became his most effective advertising weapon of all.[33] During the war Xu converted *Healthy Home* from a quarterly (which it had been before the war) into a monthly, and he personally dictated editorial policies for promoting sales by popularizing science.

In this magazine, Xu's point of departure was the term in its title, "Healthy Home," which he redefined for his own purposes. In the prewar period, Chinese intellectuals had originally borrowed the term health (*jiankang*) as a loan word from Japanese[34] and had used the phrase "healthy home" to show the fundamental incompatibility between traditional Chinese values and modern Western values. These Chinese modernizing intellectuals had argued that the traditional Chinese extended family was "unhealthy" because it was based on outdated and oppressive Confucian notions of filial piety, and they had proposed that it

---

[32] Xu, "Xinya," 58. On the rivalry between advocates of Chinese- and Western-style medicine, see Ralph C. Croizier, *Traditional Medicine in Modern China: Science, Nationalism, and the Tensions of Cultural Change*; Zhao Hongjun, *Jindai Zhongxiyi lunzhengshi* (History of the rivalry between Chinese-style and Western-style doctors); and Xiaoqun Xu, "Collective Action and State Sanction: Chinese Native Physicians' Fight for Legitimacy, 1912–1937."

[33] Xu's other wartime medical publications included: *The Catalogue of Superior Medicines from [New Asia's] Star Brand* (*Xingpai liangyao ji*) (in Chinese) which started in 1929 and went through a total of twenty editions by the end of the war (Chen and Yuan, 256–258); *The Journal of New Medicine* (Xin yiyao kan) (in Chinese) which had been founded in 1932 and continued to be published until 1941; and *Modern Therapeutics*, an English-language medical manual whose first edition of 5,000 copies was shipped in 1939 from Shanghai to Singapore for distribution throughout Southeast Asia (Xu, "Xinya," 59–60; *Xiyao*, 282).

[34] On the etymology of the Japanese term for health in the Meiji period, see Tatsukawa Shoji, *Meiji iji orai*, 50–58. I am indebted to Ruth Rogasky for this reference. On the etymology of the related Chinese term *weisheng* (health care, hygiene, or sanitation) and its derivation from the Japanese term *eisei*, see Rogasky, "From Protecting Life to Defending the Nation: The Emergence of Public Health in Tianjin, 1859–1953," ch. 3.

should be abolished in favor of the Western-style nuclear family which, they said, was "healthy."[35]

During the war, Xu reacted against this usage and proposed his own definition. " 'Healthy' (*jiankang*)," he pointed out on page one of *Healthy Home*'s issue for November 1940, "is made up of two Chinese characters, *jian* and *kang*: *jian* as in *jianquan*, meaning sound and perfect, and *kang* as in *kangle*, meaning healthy and happy. So a healthy home (*jiankang jiating*) describes a family in which all the members are living healthy and happy lives because they are sound and perfect in mind and body."[36] By associating health with happiness rather than with liberation from oppressive extended families or filial piety, Xu thus rejected modern Chinese intellectuals' prewar critique of Confucian filial piety and identified health as a modern scientific idea that was compatible with traditional Chinese values.

Throughout the war, Xu sustained his campaign to give new meaning to the term "healthy home." Writing in *Healthy Home* in May 1944, he attacked modernizing Chinese intellectuals for claiming that traditional filial piety and the modern healthy home were not compatible. "Nowadays some self-styled 'modern people' who aspire to distinguish themselves from the rest of us claim that filial piety is an obsolete idea and should be abandoned," Xu observed. But these modernizers were wrong, Xu insisted, because filial piety was "an important Chinese tradition" which should be preserved and adapted to meet the demands of the modern world. He admitted that "old thinking" and "big families" were inherited burdens, but he argued that these problems from the past would solve themselves, disappearing of their own accord as Chinese parents learned to "reproduce eugenically, raise children scientifically, and teach children rationally." Even in a fully modern world of the future, Chinese should continue to value filial piety, he maintained. "Otherwise people will have no moral standard to follow."[37]

Xu did not formulate this new definition of healthy home as an end in itself. He used it as the basis for campaigns to popularize his magazine and New Asia's goods in wartime China. In editorials he attacked *Healthy Home*'s authors for divorcing science from traditional Chinese values as manifested in everyday life. His magazine *Healthy Home*, he complained in 1940, had too closely resembled "a specialized journal devoted to scholarly discourse"

---

[35] Wen-hsin Yeh, "Progressive Journalism and Shanghai's Petty Urbanites: Zou Taofen and the *Shenghuo Weekly*, 1926–1945," 205–214, especially 213–214.

[36] Xu Guanqun, "Women de yuanwang yu nuli – xie zai benkan gexinhao zhiqian" (Our goals and plans – a few words on our magazine's new format and style), 1.

[37] Xu Guanqun, "Fumujie yougan" (Some thoughts on Parents Day), 5–6.

(*zhuanmen yanjiu xueshu taolun de kanwu*), and he proposed that it should become "a magazine for family reading" (*yiban jiating yuedu de kanwu*). He wanted no more writing on "solemn" (*yansu*) and "heavy" (*chenmen*) topics. Instead he called for writing that was "vivid" (*shengdong*), "lively" (*huopo*), and "engaging" (*xinying youqu*). Xu urged anyone submitting a piece for publication to address problems within families, between the sexes, and with children (*jiating wenti, liangxing wenti, ertong wenti*), and to "construct the model healthy family" (*jianshe jiankang jiating de fanben*) whose solutions could be adopted by readers in their own families.[38]

Xu laid down editorial policies which called upon authors to combine science with family life and thereby popularize science with a broad audience. His insistence on this point was evident in the first two editorial policies that he unveiled in 1940:

1. Our magazine will provide our readers with the most up-to-date information on science, education, and health care.
2. Our magazine will be an excellent source of leisure reading which is good for women and children.[39]

These policies showed Xu's determination to make science popular, and during the war these policies were carried out quite fully.

Between 1937 and 1945, numerous contributors to *Healthy Home* wrote pieces that popularized science and showed its compatibility with traditional Chinese family values. In almost every issue of the magazine, authors called upon parents (especially mothers) to raise children scientifically, instill traditional filial piety, and achieve these goals successfully and productively by applying the science of home economics. In "Science and the Family," to cite one example, Zeng Guangfang urged *Healthy Home*'s readers to create "the scientific family" which was to be achieved by using science ("the greatest achievement of the West's material civilization") as means of preserving traditional Chinese family values ("the greatest achievement of China's spiritual civilization").[40] Among popularizers of these ideas were both nonfiction writers, who gave simple explanations of science with easy-to-follow instructions, and fiction writers, who included members of China's best known school of popular literature, the Mandarin Duck and Butterfly school. This latter group has been regarded as resisting change and never innovating – upholding "pre-Western norms and stay[ing] within traditional literary styles" in the words of

---

[38] Xu, "Women," 1.
[39] Xu, "Women," 1.
[40] Zeng Guangfang, "Kexue yu jiating" (Science and the family).

literary critic Perry Link[41] – but some Mandarin Duck and Butterfly writers were more adaptable than has been supposed, and the ones who published in *Healthy Home* closely conformed to Xu Guanqun's editorial policies. For example, one of the most famous Mandarin Duck and Butterfly writers, Chen Diexian (Tianxu Wosheng), contributed a piece to *Healthy Home* on the need to conduct scientific "family experiments" (*shiyan jiating*) for practical purposes such as extracting soda from ashes, refining salt, and salvaging nutrients from burned or spoiled rice.[42]

Whereas these writers used prose to popularize science for the family, commercial artists used visual representations to do the same. During the war, New Asia's advertising department employed more than ten painters, including the pioneer cartoonist Ding Song (1891–1972) who in 1927 had founded China's first organization of cartoonists,[43] and they designed and produced full-page and half-page pictorial advertisements and quarter-page cartoons for every issue of *Healthy Home* during the war. Their pictorial advertisements highlighted the scientific nature of New Asia's goods, and their cartoons proclaimed the superiority of scientific medicine and enumerated the deficiencies of "superstitious remedies" and "non-scientific medicine."[44] So even if looking only at *Healthy Home's* pictures and ignoring its words, anyone picking up the magazine was able to receive Xu Guanqun's message.

During the war Xu invested heavily in these writers, commercial artists, and other Chinese intellectuals who contributed to New Asia's promotional publications. In 1940 he allocated for advertising no less than 500,000 yuan which represented 16.6 percent of the company's total capital at the time, and as his company's sales grew in the early 1940s, his expenditures on advertising probably grew apace. He used this money to produce advertising and organize performances in several different media: posters, window displays, neon signs, commercials (on slides) in movie theaters, and mobile libraries; traveling teams of basketball players, martial arts performers, and harmonica players; and radio programs, including "blitzs" in which New Asia monopolized a station as the sole sponsor for twenty-four hours at a time.[45] In all of these media, Xu identified

---

[41] Perry Link, *Mandarin Ducks and Butterflies: Popular Fiction in Early Twentieth-Century*, 178.

[42] Chen Diexian (Tianxu Wosheng), "Shiyan jiating changshi" (Common sense about family experiments). Other writers from the Mandarin Duck and Butterfly school contributing to *Healthy Home* included Zhou Shoujuan, Fan Yanqiao, Gu Mingdao, Qin Shou'ou, Xu Zhuodai, and Zhang Henshui. On them and their early writings, see Link, *Mandarin Ducks and Butterflies*.

[43] Qi, 54–55; cf. Hung, 30.

[44] See, for example, a cartoon by Zhang Baiwen, "Bukexue de dazhong yisheng" (Non-scientific doctors of the masses).

[45] Xu, "Xinya," 55–61.

New Asia's medical science with Chinese popular culture, and through another vehicle, free clinics (*zhenliaosuo*), he identified New Asia's medical science concretely with wartime conditions. In Shanghai between 1939 and 1945, Xu built ten of these free clinics, all named after New Asia (New Asia Free Clinic No. 1, New Asia Free Clinic No. 2, and so on), plus additional free clinics in Yangzhou, Fuzhou, and other cities and towns. On each clinic's sign, New Asia associated itself with the Red Cross and public health by showing a red cross inside the Chinese character for Asia (ya), and it printed its own name and trademark in bold characters, leaving no doubt about who deserved all the credit for this scientific contribution to the Chinese struggle for survival in wartime.[46]

Science in China and Chinese Science. In all these ways, Xu Guanqun achieved success for New Asia in wartime China by claiming and making good on the claim that its goods were both fully scientific and fully Chinese. Cut off from the West, he employed Chinese scientists to conduct research and develop products in New Asia's newly built laboratories. Breaking into new markets, he trained Chinese pharmacists in science and Chinese sales agents in scientific management and counted on them to extend and sustain New Asia's distributing network. Advertising widely, he founded and published Chinese-language media – medical journals, drug catalogues, and a popular health magazine – and through these media he delivered the message that New Asia's modern medical science was compatible with traditional Chinese practices (such as Chinese medicine) and traditional Chinese values (such as filial piety). Thus, Xu did not merely identify New Asia with Western-style modern medical science; he identified New Asia with a modern medical science that was Chinese. No longer was he ashamed or defensive about Chinese science as he had been in the late 1920s when he had falsified the origins of New Asia's medical products by stamping them "Made in Japan."[47] During the war he confidently and aggressively marketed his company's goods under labels, publications, and advertisements marked "Made in Shanghai."

Xu's representations of his business as Chinese served him well during the war, but at the end of the war he was afraid that he would be charged with treason for collaborating with Japan. So in 1945, after remaining at his Shanghai base throughout the war, he fled to Hong Kong. In retrospect, he claimed that he could have returned to Shanghai without any risk if he had been able to raise the money needed to bribe the Nationalist intelligence service (*juntong*) when

[46] Xu, "Xinya," 101.
[47] Xu, "Xinya," 8; *Xiyao*, 276.

its agents contacted him in Hong Kong in 1945. Be that as it may, even though the Nationalist government did not bring charges against him, he remained in Hong Kong until 1950. Only then, after the founding of the People's Republic, did he return to Shanghai where he resided until his death in 1972 at the age of 73.[48]

FIXERS AND SHANGHAI'S WARTIME CENTRALITY

Like any case study, this one raises the question of representativeness: Was Xu Guanqun representative of fixers in wartime Shanghai, and were these fixers sufficiently numerous and influential to make Shanghai a center for commerce and culture during the war? In lieu of comparable case studies, no definitive answers can be given, but on the basis of other historians' recent research, some tentative conclusions can be reached.

On Shanghai as a center for wartime commerce, historians' recent findings suggest that Xu and other Chinese in the pharmaceutical industry were by no means the only ones to engage in trade between Shanghai and cities in other parts of China during the war. According to Lloyd Eastman, Shanghai "was the chief supplier of goods traded in the Nationalist area" during the war, and in the Nationalist area, "Millions of men engaged in trade, and goods as diverse as tungsten and toothpaste, sheeps' wool and vacuum bottles, automobile tires and opium, passed from one side to the other."[49] Eastman's assertion that Shanghai interacted commercially with wartime China has been greatly elaborated, documented, and refined by Brian Martin, Allison Rottmann, and Frederic Wakeman in their essays for the present volume. Their findings and mine suggest that we should reject or substantially revise the Island Shanghai thesis that wartime Shanghai was commercially isolated.

On Shanghai as a center for wartime culture, Chang-tai Hung has argued in a recent book that the city did not retain its cultural centrality. "In the 1930s," he has acknowledged, "Shanghai . . . had nearly monopolized the country's learning and publishing to an even greater extent than did Paris in France, . . . [and it] became a pacesetter of modern popular culture." He also has conceded that when the war ended in 1945, "most bookstores and newspapers returned to coastal cities [particularly Shanghai]." But between 1937 and 1945, he has concluded, the war "caused the rapid fading of the urban, elitist character of Chinese culture . . . [T]he 'ruralization' of Chinese culture had commenced . . . The War

---

48 Xu, "Xinya," 142–146.
49 Lloyd E. Eastman, "Facets of an Ambivalent Relationship: Smuggling, Puppets, and Atrocities During the War, 1937–1945," 276–278.

of Resistance . . . created a new political culture that shifted China's attention to the countryside."[50]

Hung's conclusion concerning the creation of a new political culture is well documented in his book; his research has brought to light a substantial body of work done during the war by inland-based Chinese dramatists, cartoonists, journalists, and writers. But Hung's conclusion concerning the fading of urban culture, the advent of ruralization, and the shift of China's attention to the countryside is problematic if the above account of Xu Guanqun's wartime publications is any indication. As shown here, Xu's Shanghai-based medical journals, catalogues, and health magazine retained their focus on science as an urban-oriented subject and not only continued but expanded their distribution of publications from Shanghai throughout China and Southeast Asia during the war. Moreover, Xu's case was not unique. According to Susan Glosser's recent research, Chinese entrepreneurs in the milk industry also founded promotional publications and used them to advertise the scientific nature of their goods in Shanghai during the war.[51]

This apparent contradiction between Hung's interpretation and my own might be resolved on a regional basis if the circulation of media in wartime China is ever fully mapped. Perhaps (in line with Hung's findings) inland-based media were more influential than coastal-based media in western regions of China such as the "rear area" (*houfang*) which was not occupied by Japan, and (in line with my findings) coastal-based media were more influential in eastern regions of the country under the Japanese occupation. But even this claim for the regional influence of inland-based media should be subjected to close scrutiny because coastal-based media (like *Healthy Home*) circulated in the rear area as well as along the coast during the war. Accordingly, on the basis of the above essay and other case studies,[52] I think it is unlikely that Chongqing became "the de facto center of journalism" during the war.[53] It is more likely that wartime Shanghai retained its prewar position as the center for China's journalism and popular culture in general.

These questions about Shanghai's commercial and cultural centrality could be more fully answered if more were known about Chinese fixers during the war. At the beginning of this essay, Xu Guanqun was quoted as saying that "the most important thing for [Chinese] leaders of commerce and industry in

---

[50] Hung, 14, 18, 19, 279, 282, 285.
[51] Susan L. Glosser, "Milk for Health, Milk for Profit: Shanghai's Chinese Dairy Industry under Japanese Occupation."
[52] Cochran, "Intra-Asian Marketing" and "Marketing Medicine."
[53] Hung, 185.

Shanghai's foreign concessions was to become fixers . . . and I was a typical example of a fixer." Whether Xu was typical will not be known until research is done on other Chinese wartime fixers. If Xu was typical, then these secretive and elusive figures are worth tracking down because they might very well have played decisive roles in retaining and even increasing Shanghai's centrality in China during the war.

BIBLIOGRAPHY

Chandler, Alfred D, Jr. *Scale and Scope: The Dynamics of Industrial Capitalism.* Cambridge, Mass.: Harvard University Press, 1990.

Chen Diexian (Tianxu Wosheng). "Shiyan jiating changshi" (Common sense about family experiments). *Jiankang jiating* 5 (1939).

Chen Lizheng and Yuan Enzhen. *Xinya de licheng – Shanghai xinya zhiyaochang de guoqu xianzai he jiangli* (New Asia step by step – Shanghai New Asia Pharmaceutical Company in the past, present, and future). Shanghai: Shanghai shehui kexue yuan chubanshe, 1990.

Chen Xinqian and Zhang Tianlu. *Zhongguo jindai yaoxue shi* (A history of modern medicine in China). Beijing: Renmin weisheng chubanshe, 1992.

Cochran, Sherman. "Intra-Asian Marketing: Aw Boon Haw's Commercial Network, 1910–1937." In S. Sugiyama and Linda Grove, eds., *Commercial Networks in Modern Asia*. Richmond, Surrey: Curzon, 2001, pp. 171–181.

Cochran, Sherman. "Marketing Medicine and Advertising Dreams in China, 1900–1950." In Wen-hsin Yeh, ed., *Becoming Chinese: Passages to Modernity and Beyond, 1900–1950*. Berkeley: University of California Press, 2000, pp. 62–97.

Cowen, David L. and William H. Helfand. *Pharmacy: An Illustrated History*. New York: Abrams, 1990.

Croizier, Ralph C. *Traditional Medicine in Modern China: Science, Nationalism, and the Tensions of Cultural Change*. Cambridge, Mass.: Harvard University Press, 1968.

Eastman, Lloyd E. "Facets of an Ambivalent Relationship: Smuggling, Puppets, and Atrocities During the War, 1937–1945." In Akira Iriye, ed., *The Chinese and the Japanese: Essays in Political and Cultural Interactions*. Princeton, N.J.: Princeton University Press, 1980.

Eastman, Lloyd E. *Seeds of Destruction: Nationalist China in War and Revolution, 1937–1949*. Stanford: Stanford University Press, 1984.

File Q38-40-11, di 1-35 ci yewuhuiyi jilu, 1943–48, Shanghai City Archives.

Gan Gu, ed. *Shanghai bainian mingchang laodian* (One hundred years of famous factories and old shops in Shanghai). Shanghai: Shanghai wenhua chubanshe, 1987.

Gardner, John. "The *Wu-fan* Campaign in Shanghai: A Study in the Consolidation of Urban Control." In A. Doak Barnett, ed., *Chinese Communist Politics in Action*. Seattle: University of Washington Press, 1969, pp. 477–539.

Glosser, Susan L. "Milk for Health, Milk for Profit: Shanghai's Chinese Dairy Industry under Japanese Occupation." In Sherman Cochran, ed., *Inventing Nanjing Road: Commercial Culture in Shanghai, 1900–1945*. Ithaca, N.Y.: Cornell East Asia Series, 1999, pp. 207–233.

Hung Chang-tai. *War and Popular Culture: Resistance in Modern China, 1937–1945.* Berkeley: University of California Press, 1994.

Jiankang jiating (Healthy Home). Shanghai, 1937–45.

Lee, Leo Ou-fan and Andrew J. Nathan. "The Beginnings of Mass Culture: Journalism and Fiction in Late Ch'ing and Beyond." In David Johnson, Andrew J. Nathan, and Evelyn S. Rawski, eds., *Popular Culture in Late Imperial China.* Berkeley: University of California Press, 1985.

Link, Perry. *Mandarin Ducks and Butterflies: Popular Fiction in Early Twentieth-Century Chinese Cities.* Berkeley: University of California Press, 1981.

Perry, Elizabeth J. *Shanghai on Strike: The Politics of Chinese Labor.* Stanford: Stanford University Press, 1993.

Qi Heming. "Xu Guanqun yu Xinya yaochang" (Xu Guanqun and New Asia Pharmaceutical Mills). *Wujin wenshi* 7 (December), 1986.

Rogasky, Ruth. "From Protecting Life to Defending the Nation: The Emergence of Public Health in Tianjin, 1859–1953." Ph.D. dissertation, Yale University, 1996.

Rowe, William T. "The Qingbang and Collaboration under the Japanese, 1939–1945." *Modern China* 8.4 (1982): 491–499.

Shanghai shehui kexue yuan jingji yanjiu suo (Shanghai Academy of Social Sciences, Institute of Economics). *Shanghai jindai xiyao hangye shi* (A history of the modern medicine trade in Shanghai). Shanghai: Shanghai shehui kexue yuan chubanshe, 1988.

Skinner, G. William. "Regional Urbanization in Nineteenth-Century China." In Skinner, ed., *The City in Late Imperial China.* Stanford: Stanford University Press, 1977.

Tan Yulin. "Xu Guanqun." In Zhu Xinquan and Yan Ruping, eds., *Minguo renwu zhuan* (Biographies of figures from the Republican period). Beijing: Zhonghua shuju, 1984. Vol. 4, pp. 261–267.

Tatsukawa Shoji. *Meiji iji orai.* Tokyo: Shinchosha, 1986.

Tien Hung-mao. *Government and Politics in Kuomintang China 1927–1937.* Stanford: Stanford University Press, 1972.

Wang Ke-wen. "Collaborators and Capitalists: The Politics of 'Material Control' in Wartime Shanghai." *Chinese Studies in History* 26.1 (fall 1992): 42–62.

Xiandai Shanghai dashiji (Great events in modern Shanghai). Shanghai: Shanghai cishu chubanshe, 1996.

Xiyao. See Shanghai shehui kexue yuan jingji yanjiu suo, 1988.

Xu Guanqun. "Fumujie yougan" (Some thoughts on Parents Day). *Jiankang jiating* 5.4 (May 1944).

Xu Guanqun. "Women de yuanwang yu nuli – xie zai benkan gexinhao zhiqian (Our goals and plans – a few words on our magazine's new format and style). *Jiankang jiating* 2.8 (November 1940).

Xu Guanqun. "Xinya yaochang sanshinian laide huigu" (Reflections on my thirty years at New Asia Pharmaceuticals), 1964. The original copy of this unpublished manuscript is in the office of the New Asia Pharmaceutical Company, Shanghai.

Xu Xiaoqun. "Collective Action and State Sanction: Chinese Native Physicians' Fight for Legitimacy, 1912–1937." Unpublished manuscript, 1995.

Yeh, Wen-hsin. "Progressive Journalism and Shanghai's Petty Urbanites: Zou Taofen and the *Shenghuo Weekly*, 1926–1945." In Frederic Wakeman, Jr. and Wen-hsin

Yeh, eds., *Shanghai Sojourners*. Berkeley: University of California Institute for Chinese Studies, 1992, pp. 186–238.

Young, James Harvey. *Pure Food: Securing the Federal Food and Drug Act of 1906*. Princeton, N.J.: Princeton University Press, 1989.

Yuan Yuquan. "Rikou jiaqiang luedou huazhong zhanlue wuzi paozhi shangtonghui jingguo" (How the Japanese established the Commercial Control Committee to take control of strategic materials in central China). *Dang'an yu lishi* (Archives and History) 4 (1986).

Zeng Guangfang. "Kexue yu jiating" (Science and the family). *JianKang jiating* 1 (1939).

Zhang Baiwen. "Bukexue de dazhong yisheng" (Non-scientific doctors of the masses). *Jiankang jiating* (1939).

Zhang Zhongli, ed. *Jindai Shanghai chengshi yanjiu* (Urban studies on modern Shanghai). Shanghai: Shanghai shehui kexue yuan, 1990.

Zhao Hongjun. *Jindai Zhongxiyi lunzhengshi* (History of the rivalry between Chinese-style and Western-style doctors). Hefei: Anhui renmin chubanshe, 1989.

Chapter 4

Crossing Enemy Lines

Shanghai and the Central China Base

ALLISON ROTTMANN

In the late 1970s, new memoir materials on Communist Party history began to appear in China. These publications, which began to pour from the presses in the 1980s and continued in the 1990s, contain scores of memoirs describing public and clandestine interaction between wartime Shanghai and the Communists' rural base in central China. Unlike official historical sources, memoir sources allow us to see the development of the wartime revolutionary movement and the building of the new party-state as a process of human interaction.[1]

A close examination of one man completing one wartime purchase and transport assignment uncovers the details of human interactions available in reminiscent literature. The narrative that follows is based on the memoirs of a Communist Party member named Liu Yanru, who spent the early war years doing underground work in Shanghai and the later war years running trafficking lines between the city and the party's Central China Base.[2] In Liu Yanru's

---

[1] For a discussion on using memoirs to write the history of the 1949 revolution, see Gregor Benton, *Mountain Fires: The Red Army's Three-Year War in South China, 1934–1938,* preface. On studying the revolution as a process, see Joseph W. Esherick, "Deconstructing the Construction of the Party-State: Gulin County in the Shaan-Gan-Ning Border Region," 1053.

[2] The Central China Base (Huazhong genjudi) refers to Communist-controlled areas mostly in the provinces of Anhui, Jiangsu, and Zhejiang in eastern and central China. After the New Fourth Army was founded in late 1937, the army opened and secured these rural bases, which were behind Japanese lines and also in direct competition with Guomindang forces in the region. From the army's original Guomindang-assigned territory mostly south of the Yangzi River in Anhui, its control spread east and north of the river during the war. Important districts of the base area include southern Anhui (Wannan); the regions north and south of the Huai River in Anhui and Jiangsu (Huainan and Huaibei); northern Jiangsu (Subei); southern Jiangsu (Sunan); eastern

I am grateful to Christian Henriot, Wen-hsin Yeh, and other participants in the Occupied Shanghai Project for their comments on an earlier version of this work. An anonymous reader's insights are also appreciated. This chapter has benefited from support offered by the Institut d'Asie Orientale, Maison Rhone-Alpes des Sciences de l'Homme in Lyon, France and the Committee on Scholarly Communications with the People's Republic of China.

transport work, chains of small actions by loosely connected individuals, crossing through territories of differing political and military obedience, were turned into actions of larger consequence – the development of a wartime rural base that played a key role in the making of Chinese communism. His memoirs not only show that he relied on social connections (*shehui guanxi*) and money to get the job done, but also reveal the specific people he turned to for help and who he had to pay for services. We see what was available in the city but not the countryside, how the Chinese Communist Party (CCP) turned to urbanites and urban resources to meet its wartime needs, and what methods the party was willing to use to accomplish its goals in the countryside.

LIU YANRU'S TRANSPORT ASSIGNMENT

When the war broke out, Liu Yanru was a party member in the Shanghai underground organization.[3] In May 1938, the Shanghai party assigned him to work at the Helpful Friend Society (Yiyoushe), a party-controlled organization for the cultural and educational enrichment of shop clerks and commercial staff.[4] His party-arranged cover job was as an office worker at Yongda Transport Company, whose management was also involved with the Helpful Friend Society. In June 1941, Liu was given the job of escorting a woman who had been injured

Zhejiang (Zhedong); and the Jiangsu-Zhejiang (Su-Zhe), Anhui-Jiangsu (Wansu or Suwan), and Hubei-Henan-Anhui (Eyuwan) border regions.

On the army's and party's development of the Central China Base, see Chen Yung-fa, *Making Revolution: The Communist Movement in Eastern and Central China, 1937–1945;* Gregor Benton, *New Fourth Army: Communist Resistance Along the Yangtze and the Huai, 1938–1941.*

[3] The narrative that follows is based on Liu Yanru, "Zhandou zai diren de fengsuo xian shang" [The Battle Against the Enemy's Blockade], 134–141; "Zhandou zai dixia yunshu xian shang" [Battle Along Underground Transport Lines], 163–171; "Yi tiao shusong geming shu-kan de mimi yunshu xian" [A Clandestine Transport Line for Carrying Revolutionary Books and Periodicals], 338–340.

[4] In late 1937, underground party workers in cooperation with people outside the party organized Yiyoushe. It offered various cultural and educational activities for young staff workers to participate in, usually after work in the evenings. Yiyoushe continued to operate throughout the war years until 1949, consistently growing in membership and in services offered. From the party's point of view, the organization was a recruitment ground for party members, a mass organization for propagating nationalist and socialist ideologies and organizing the city's clerical workers, and a means of developing connections with staff workers in large and small industries and also with business and community leaders.

For more on Yiyoushe, see Zhong Gong Shanghai shiwei dang shi ziliao zhengji weiyuanhui and Yiyoushe shiliao zhengjizu, eds., *Yiyoushe shi er nian* [Twelve Years of the Helpful Friend Society], vol. 1 and vol. 2; Yiyoushe shiliao bianxiezu, ed., "Yiyoushe kaizhan tongzhan gongzuo" [The Helpful Friend Society's Development of United Front Work], 110–120; Luo Suwen, "Xin wang de yanshen: Minguo shiqi Shanghai de Huaren zhiye julebu" [Extending a New Network: Republican Shanghai's Chinese Occupational Clubs].

from Shanghai back to the Huainan district of the Central China Base Area, which was where the New Fourth Army's Second Division was stationed.[5] Liu began to help the army with further jobs of moving people and materials between the base and Shanghai. In 1942, he was officially transferred from the Shanghai party to the Central China Bureau's Urban Work Department to do Shanghai-to-Huainan communications and transportation work.

One of Liu's assignments in the winter of 1943 was to go to Shanghai and purchase military materials for the New Fourth Army and then arrange for their shipment back to the base. He was sent to buy seamless steel tubes for mortar barrels; movie film for making explosive charges; a diesel generator for the Huainan munitions factory; and a printing press, typecasting furnace, and set of copper typecasting molds for the base's printing house. Liu's purchasing budget was 10,000 yuan in Central Reserve Bank notes, which he carried with him out of the base area.[6] The goods Liu was after were not available on the open market but classified as contraband under Japanese material control policies. After buying them, he would have to smuggle them across Japanese blockade lines. As a first step toward solving his transport problem, Liu stopped in the Yangzi River port city of Zhenjiang on his way to Shanghai to meet with boat captains who had cooperated with the party before. These men, who operated small-engine boats, offered their help and advice on smuggling routes.

Liu focused first on buying the seamless steel tubes for the mortar barrels. The Japanese army had done its best to locate and buy up the city's supply of these products. Not wanting to sell to the Japanese at artificially low prices, those in the business had concealed the products. Through the Helpful Friend Society, Liu knew a sales clerk in a hardware store. He used his connection (*guanxi*) with the sales clerk to find out the name of a metal shop that had the tubes in storage. Liu struck a deal with the shop owner and purchased the tubes. Liu's nephew worked at a small shipyard, and there, the tubes were secretly cut to the army's length specifications. Liu arranged for the tubes to be trucked at night to his aunt's family home for storage.

A year or so earlier, Liu had operated a postal trafficking line for shipping progressive publications into the army base and money from the base into Shanghai. He had worked with several publishing houses and bookstores to supply the base with reading materials, and now he turned to his connections

---

[5] Huainan refers to a region south of the Huai River in Anhui and Jiangsu provinces.

[6] In early 1942, the collaborating Wang Jingwei government replaced the Guomindang's falling currency, the *fabi*, with one of its own – Central Reserve Bank notes. The new currency was exchanged for the old at a 2:1 rate.

within Shidai Publishing House for help with buying the printing press, type-casting furnace, copper molds, and film.[7] After purchase, he hid these items in a native-place association's (*huiguan*) coffin repository on North Jiangxi Road.

In the spring, a Zhenjiang boat owner named Chen, whom Liu had met with on his way to Shanghai, contacted him. Chen said that he had recently met someone from his native place (*tongxiang*) who was the second mate on a small steamer that the Japanese navy had commandeered. The vessel's captain was now Japanese, and the ship regularly carried coal along the Yangzi River from Nanjing to Shanghai and then returned to Nanjing empty. Liu decided to try to use this ship to move the equipment from the city to the army base. He told Chen that he wanted to negotiate with this second mate the next time the ship docked in Shanghai at the Japanese navy dock on Jungong Road. Soon, Liu met with Chen, the second mate, and the Japanese captain in a Shanghai hotel room that Liu rented for the meeting. A carriage fee was agreed on and a shipping date set.

Liu's next problem was transporting the materials hidden around the city to the Japanese naval dock and arranging to load the boat. He turned to the Yongda Transport Company, where he had worked as a cover for his underground work with the Helpful Friend Society. The manager of Yongda Transport Company was a supporter of the Helpful Friend Society, and the company's business director was also active in the society and had sons and nephews in the New Fourth Army. These two men knew that Liu Yanru was working for the army, and they agreed to use the transport company's name to rent three trucks and drivers to move the goods. To prevent an inspection of the trucks while en route in the city, Liu relied on a gangster named Zhang Genfu. To ensure smooth passage through the city, Liu paid Zhang to take care of the "local bullies" along the trucks' route.

Early in the morning on the decided day, the trucks traveled separately to the three places where the equipment was hidden and then drove back to the Yongda Company. The drivers, realizing now that their truck loads were military contraband, refused to move the goods to the Japanese navy dock. The drivers objected that if the Japanese inspected their trucks, they would be arrested and their trucks confiscated. After Liu promised to cover any costs, Yongda's manager put in writing that he would stand as guarantor if the drivers were arrested

---

[7] The Shidai Publishing Company was founded in Shanghai in 1941, registering in the Japanese-occupied city under the name of the Soviet Commercial Publishing House (Su shang chubanshe). Until 1953, it published Russian literature as well as the *Shidai Weekly* (Shidai zhouke). Its chief editor was Jiang Zhongfang.

and that the drivers would be compensated if their trucks were confiscated. Only then did the men agree to drive to the Japanese navy dock.

The gangster Zhang Genfu rode with Liu Yanru in one of the trucks, greeting the necessary people along the route. The convoy made it without incident to the naval docks, and the truck crew loaded the ship. Shortly after Liu returned to his hotel, Zhang Genfu turned up with a few friends. They threatened to report Liu to the Japanese military police for transporting war materials without a permit. Liu bought them off once more. Still, as soon as they left, Liu paid his bill and moved out of the hotel.

The ship sailed the following morning. The plan was for the ship to travel to Zhenjiang, a south-bank Yangzi River port city in Jiangsu, and anchor in the middle of the Yangzi, while Liu traveled by train from Shanghai to Zhenjiang. In Zhenjiang, the second mate would come ashore and meet Liu in a hotel. When the second mate showed up at the prearranged meeting spot, he told Liu that the Japanese captain had realized that the "metal equipment" on board was military contraband and was insisting on docking at Zhenjiang so that the Japanese military police could inspect the ship. In response, Liu reminded the second mate that a mutual friend had introduced them and that they had already struck a deal. Moreover, he suggested reminding the Japanese captain of his own role in the arrangement to transport contraband to the New Fourth Army. After apologizing repeatedly for having put a new acquaintance in a difficult spot, Liu said to tell the captain he would raise the shipment price. He suggested accompanying the captain to shore for a bath that evening and then sailing toward Nanjing tomorrow as planned. He instructed the second mate that when the ship approached the Yangzi town of Shawozi near Longtan, it should fly a white flag as a signal and watch for another white flag on shore. The ship should then slow down and a barge would come out into the river to unload the cargo. Once the goods were received, the increase in the shipping price would be paid. The second mate agreed.

That afternoon, Liu took the train from Zhenjiang to Longtan, walked about three miles to the river, and then took a ferry across to the north bank of the Yangzi near Shawozi. At nightfall, he hurried to a contact point at a farmer's home and sent off a letter to the army base's border station telling the army to rush people to the river's edge to help with the shipment. A transport team of about one hundred people was organized and special arrangements made to carry the diesel generator. To prevent word getting out to the enemy, New Fourth Army guerrillas blocked passage to the Liuhe and Yizheng county roads. Other troops were assigned to protect the equipment on the way to the base.

At the riverside, Liu made plans for the army's two receiving barges. That night, he kept watch along the bank in case the ship arrived early. At three o'clock the next afternoon, he saw a steamer approaching flying a white flag. Liu pulled off his white undershirt and waved it. The ship had already slowed down, and the two waiting barges moved in quickly and unloaded the goods. The ship then sailed full steam ahead to Nanjing, while the barges headed for the bank near Shawozi. It was dusk by then and Liu sent a liaison to call the transport team down to the river. To avoid detection by enemies on the opposing Longtan bank, no one was to talk or use hand lights. It was dark by the time the barges were unloaded.

The line of movers on the road was conspicuous, however, to nearby villagers. By dawn, enemy troops based in Yizheng, a county seat thirty miles away from the landing point, started to pursue and attack. New Fourth Army soldiers gave cover to the transport, and the goods made it safely to the border area at Yuetangji. It was impossible, however, for the ten people carrying the heavy diesel generator to move quickly over the small earth dike paths. When the enemy got close, the moving team hid the crate holding the generator in a hollow dike and covered it with rice straw. It was moved later and arrived at the Huainan prefectural office to complete delivery of the entire shipment. Liu Yanru had completed another transport assignment.

WARTIME SHANGHAI AND THE CENTRAL CHINA BASE

During the final United Front negotiations in the summer of 1937, the Guomindang government agreed to the CCP's proposal to organize the steely Red Army survivors of the Jiangxi Soviet and other guerrilla bases in the southeast into a new force to fight behind Japanese lines in central China.[8] The Guomindang designated this Communist force, named the New Fourth Army (Xinsijun), territory along the southern bank of the Yangzi River in Anhui and Jiangsu provinces, as well as a small area north of the river. During the war, the New Fourth Army and party spread its military control and political organization throughout the lower Yangzi region. Although there was not a unified administration governing the bases the army built in central and eastern China, they are collectively known as the Central China Base (Huazhong genjudi).

From its inception, the New Fourth Army's relationship with Shanghai developed quickly. When the head of the Shanghai party visited the army's headquarters in southern Anhui (Wannan) in the summer of 1938, military leaders stressed that the city's help was needed to build the base. The CCP Central Committee soon directed the Jiangsu Provincial Committee, which oversaw the underground party in Shanghai, to mobilize workers, students, intellectuals,

---

[8] For a prehistory of the New Fourth Army, see Gregor Benton, *Mountain Fires*.

activists, and party members to go to the new army's base. Within the city, the Shanghai Party was ordered to spread positive propaganda about the army, offer economic help, and provide cover for the army's logistics work in the city.[9]

Cooperation centered on four areas crucial to the army's efforts: human resources, finance, matériel, and intelligence. For example, the approximate ten thousand people in the army at its start were insufficient to advance the party's wartime goals of resistance and base construction. Not only were more soldiers needed but also other groups of people not easily found in the countryside, such as skilled workers, drivers, writers, medical professionals, artists, cadres, and all kinds of technicians. One Chinese study of the Shanghai–New Fourth Army relationship documents over twenty thousand residents and refugees moving out of Shanghai to the Central China Base during the war.[10] This estimate counts those who joined the army through groups sponsored by or affiliated with party organizations in Shanghai and who usually worked in specialized units in the base like printing shops, hospitals, and schools. It does not include those who made their way to the base alone or accompanied by a friend or two were recruited by army divisions along their own trafficking lines operated independently of party organizations in Shanghai, or went to the base sometime after they had left the occupied city for their hometowns in Shanghai's periphery.

A Central Committee directive to the Shanghai party leadership highlights the New Fourth Army's desire for the city's human resources and the city's ability to provide them. In December 1940, news reached the Central Committee of a plan, per the army's request, for the Shanghai underground to send 10,000 residents and 500 party members from the city to the base. The Central Committee forbade this plan, believing that such a large-scale transfer of people would dangerously expose the Shanghai underground organization. It pointed out that movements like the one to collect winter clothes for the army had already exposed the Shanghai party, and it reiterated the policy that the city's organization was to function in secret. After an important recent New Fourth Army victory in northern Jiangsu, groups of students, unemployed workers, and intellectuals were eager to get to the Central China Base. The Central Committee allowed that the Shanghai party could offer some assistance to those able to get to the base by their own social connections or by public transportation. The underground,

---

[9] Wang Yaoshan, "Shanghai dixiadang yu Xinsijun" [The Shanghai Underground Party and the New Fourth Army], vol. 1, 86; Liu Xiao, "Shanghai dixiadang huifu he chongjian qianhou" [Restoration and Reconstruction of the Shanghai Underground Party from Beginning to End], 42–43.

[10] *Shanghai renmin yu Xinsijun*, 14–16.

however, was authorized to use its own connections and transport routes to move only specific groups of people, like those whose cover in Shanghai had been blown or whose specialized skills were required by the New Fourth Army.[11]

In 1938 and 1939, with the United Front in place and the international concessions still free of Japanese control, the Shanghai Communists organized and worked both above ground and below with various national salvation groups and leaders to sponsor charity bazaars, fund-raising drives, and benefit performances to collect donations for the New Fourth Army. The campaigns to collect donations fall generally into three categories. First, newspapers, banks, and other organizations solicited contributions, usually under the legal names of Save for the Distressed (*jieyue jiunan*) or Relief for Refugees (*jiuji nanmin*). Although the New Fourth Army's name was not revealed to the public in these campaigns, because of the involvement of underground party members and co-operating national salvation elite in the fund raising, part or all of the money raised in these campaigns was earmarked for the army. Second, in the winter of 1939, there was a citywide drive for winter clothing for the army. Finally, charity bazaars and performances were held by organizations affiliated with the national salvation movement to raise money. Among the items donated were warm clothing, shoes, blankets, fabric, tin, medicine, and medical equipment. During the beginning years of the war, an estimated 1.3 million yuan *fabi* went to the New Fourth Army from Shanghai sources. Through the CCP's legal and public Eighth Route Army Office in Shanghai, for instance, 800,000 yuan were sent to the New Fourth Army.[12]

Shanghai's unique *gudao* environment made a certain level of semipublic Communist activity possible. Yet even in the concession areas, exposed party members, as well as the city's national salvation elite, had to avoid becoming assassination targets of the Japanese and collaborating occupation authorities, especially their spy branches. At national salvation associational meetings, for

---

[11] "Zhongyang guanyu Shanghai dang de mimi gongzuo de zhishi" [Central Committee Directive Concerning the Secret Work of the Shanghai Party], 199–200.

[12] Three yuan could support one refugee for one month, and a set of soldier's winter clothing cost about five yuan. Wang Jihua, "Zhiyejie jiuwang xiehui he Shanghai 'gudao' shiqi de kang di douzheng" [The Professional Circles National Salvation Association and the Struggle to Resist the Enemy in the Shanghai "Gudao" Period], 53.

Wang Yaoshan, 88; Li Wenjie, "Shi qi wan ba qian wu bai yuan de jukuan" [The Huge Sum of 178,500 Yuan], 181–182; Yao Huiquan, "KangRi jiuwang gongzuo huiyi" [A Memoir of Anti-Japanese Save-the-Nation Work], vol. 1, 199–201; Yao Huiquan, "Shanghai minzhong yuanzhu Xinsijun de qiangzhi, bupi, jiaoxie" [The Shanghai People's Aid to the New Fourth Army in Firearms, Cloth, and Rubber-Soled Shoes], 178–179; Cao Da, "KangRi shenghuo zaji" [Notes on Living the Resistance War], vol. 2, 242; *Shanghai renmin yu Xinsijun*, 16–17.

instance, participants of all political stripes knew their activities had to be well guarded from enemy spy infiltration. When Guomindang-affiliated agents ignited an assassination war with the Japanese and their Chinese collaborators through all parts of the city, the concession authorities, wanting to avoid occupation, also succumbed to Japanese pressure to suppress resistance activities.[13] This environment, even in the concession areas, pushed the relationship between Shanghai and the Central China Base increasingly underground. From 1940 onward, Japanese control over the city and the Yangzi delta tightened, while cooperation with the Guomindang faltered. Once Japan occupied the foreign concessions in December 1941, strict secrecy ruled all aspects of the urban-rural relationship. Matériel, people, and intelligence all had to be transported covertly.

One method of covert operations was for the various divisions of the army to dispatch their own purchasing agents like Liu Yanru to Shanghai to move goods along secret transportation routes over sea, inland waterways, and rivers. Although transport lines by water became favored by necessity, goods also traveled over land by vehicle, railroad, and foot. Some New Fourth Army purchasing agents worked through party organizations and had the help of the Shanghai underground. Others ran independent lines for their army division or work bureau. The army also had people open up stores that served as fronts for buying and storing goods and as liaison points along trafficking lines. In addition, the army, in cooperation with the Shanghai underground, ran a secret New Fourth Army Office in Shanghai between December 1940 and December 1942 that escorted people, including survivors of the Wannan Incident, nearly daily to the base in northern Jiangsu.[14] The office also transported materials and intelligence. Even after the complete occupation of Shanghai and the surrounding countryside, the New Fourth Army still smuggled out of the city necessary items

---

[13] On the terrorist battles of the early war period, see Frederic Wakeman, Jr., *The Shanghai Badlands: Wartime Terrorism and Urban Crime, 1937–1941.*

[14] The Wannan Incident of January 1941 is also known as the New Fourth Army Incident or the South Anhui Incident. In the tense months before the event, the government had ordered the New Fourth Army to move north of the Yellow River. When the 10,000-troop army finally withdrew from its Wannan headquarters and began the move north, it was surrounded and destroyed by a Guomindang force larger than any one that had faced the Japanese in the previous year. The loss to the New Fourth Army, most of which was already operating north of the Yangzi River, was about one-tenth of its total strength. The incident effectively ended the United Front, and the Guomindang's attack was widely condemned. The definitive study of the Wannan Incident is found in Gregor Benton, *New Fourth Army*, 511–616.

On the New Fourth Army Shanghai Office, see Zhang Daping, "Huiyi Xinsijun Shanghai banshichu" [Recalling the New Fourth Army Shanghai Office], 70–79; Rong Jiansheng, "Xinsijun she zai Shanghai de mimi banshichu" [The Secret Office Set Up by the New Fourth Army in Shanghai], 1–8; Interviews with Zhang Daping, November 1997 and October 1999.

like medicine, communications equipment, batteries, hardware, chemicals, and printing equipment and supplies.

Intelligence, considered more risky than people, was smuggled out as well. In the New Fourth Army Office in Shanghai, workers read all available publications to gather information, which was classified by category in the city and then sent to the base area. Communications might be on film and sewn into clothing; written in extremely small script, rolled up in waterproof foil, and inserted into an empty toothpaste tube; or written in a secret ink of rice water (*mitang*) and then read at the base after applying an iodine solution.[15] Along these routes between the city and the countryside, the traffic was not all one way. Important documents, special equipment, and wounded leaders were also smuggled into Shanghai.

THE COSTS OF WARTIME COOPERATION

Although Communists ran trafficking lines between Shanghai and the surrounding countryside throughout the war, these urban-rural interactions were fraught with danger. Mao Liying's assassination in Shanghai shows the extreme end of the hazard associated with underground work designed to aid the New Fourth Army. Mao was a staff worker in the city's customs office who got involved with national salvation work after the outbreak of the war in August 1937. She joined the Communist Party in May the next year, and when the Vocational Women's Club (Zhiye funü julebu) was founded, she served as its president. In the fall of 1938, the underground assigned her to use her position within the club to sponsor large-scale charity work based in the concession areas to collect money and goods for refugees and the New Fourth Army.[16]

The well-publicized drive was successful, and it attracted the attention of the Japanese military police and their collaborating intelligence service, called

---

[15] Interview with Shen Ou, November 1997.

[16] "Zhifu julebu zhuxi Mao Liying zao qiang ji" [Vocational Women's Club Chair Mao Liying Shot Last Night], *Shen bao*, Dec. 13, 1939, 1; "Mao Liying zuo shishi" [Mao Liying Died Yesterday], *Shen bao*, Dec. 16, 1939, 1; Shanghai shi gonganju gongan shi bangongshi and Luwan, Jing'an gongan fenju gongan shi xiaozu, "Wang wei 'tegong zongbu' mouhai Mao Liying lieshi de jingguo" [The Process of the Wang Collaborator "Secret Service General Headquarters'" Plot to Murder the Martyr Mao Liying], 60–63; "Zhongyang guanyu shenru xuanchuan junwei 'guanyu Wannan shibian de fayan' deng wenti gei Liu Xiao tongzhi de zhishi" [Central Committee Directive to Comrade Liu Xiao on Thoroughly Publicizing the CCP CC Military Commission's "Statement on the Wannan Incident" and Other Issues], 201; Wang Yaoshan, 88–89; *Shanghai lieshi xiaozhuan* [Profiles of Shanghai Martyrs], 167–170. Mao Liying's death secured her status as an icon of the revolution in Shanghai. She is buried in Shanghai's Martyrs Cemetery (Shi lieshi lingyuan).

Number 76 after its location at 76 Jessfield Road and headed by Li Shiqun, a one-time party member as well as a former agent for the Guomindang's Bureau of Statistics and Investigation (Zhongguo Guomindang zhongyang weiyuanhui tongji diaocha ju, or Zhongtong for short). The goals of Number 76 included curbing the anti-Japanese sentiment that Chinese newspapers and patriotic activities in the concessions encouraged, and consequently, the secret service infiltrated the Vocational Women's Club.[17] On the night of December 12, 1939, Mao was gunned down as she left a club meeting. The assassination put an immediate halt to all large-scale benefit work in the city. It also marked a turning point in the party's ability to work above ground through legal organizations like the Vocational Women's Club toward its eventual operation in total secrecy.

Strict discipline in operating procedures was required for the safety of transport workers and the success of their work. Single-line or one-way contact practices (*danxian*) controlled liaisons between Communist agents. Contact practices varied. For a meeting, two meeting times and places were set, for example. A person would wait no more than five minutes for a counterpart to show before leaving an area. If the first meeting was missed, there was the remaining chance to make contact according to the second set of arrangements. Since so few people had their own watches but there were many clocks visible along city streets, public clocks set the standard for meeting times. Operating procedures were learned while on the job. An experienced cadre or transport worker would advise a newcomer on how to go about his or her job, passing on details such as what clothes to wear and how to behave and speak appropriately for the assignment at hand. Through verbal instruction from an experienced agent, liaisons learned skills such as how to disguise documents they carried and dispose of them quickly if necessary and how to avoid and lose an enemy tail.[18]

Cadres from the base on purchasing trips in the city were often left to their own resources, especially if they were operating a traffic line independently of the local party organization. Even a person whose army unit was working in cooperation with the Shanghai underground usually had only one formal contact to turn to for help. One New Fourth Army man who frequently entered Shanghai said that sometimes, before he left the base, the army would radio to the Shanghai underground that he was coming. He would then arrive in the

---

[17] See Wen-hsin Yeh, "Dai Li and the Liu Geqing Affair: Heroism in the Chinese Secret Service During the War of Resistance," 552.

[18] Interview with Zhang Daping, November 1997; Interview with Ding Gongliang, November 1997; Zheng Yuzhi, "Pan Hannian tongzhi dui wo de jiaodao" [Comrade Pan Hannian's Guidance Toward Me], 11–16.

city with a known contact point. Once, for example, he was instructed to go to a well-known accounting instruments store on Nanjing Road. He was to find a certain clerk there and tell him where his own contact point would be. On this trip, the cadre was staying at a former classmate's home while the classmate was away. After a member of the underground met him there for an initial meeting, all other meetings were at different places. A time was selected for future meetings, and a regular interval of days between meetings was set. At each meeting, the next meeting place was chosen.[19]

Civilians drawn into the Communists' urban-rural intercourse also faced risks. Those who left Shanghai for the base describe trips that were both mentally and physically challenging. Toward the end of the war when Wu Mingyi was escorting twenty technicians and engineers to the Jiangsu-Zhejiang base near Lake Tai, his group ran into a Japanese mop-up action (*saodang*). The volunteers first had to hide in a small cave without food for a day. The next night was spent hiding at the foot of a hill in the pouring rain. When the group thought it had found temporary refuge in a temple, the Japanese showed up in the area again, forcing everyone to crawl through the woods to the next village. Very hungry now, they hoped to get something to eat there, but the Japanese attacked that village too. They spent that night hiding in tall grass. They finally made it to Lake Tai to meet their boat escort but after they arrived at their next destination, they encountered yet another mop-up. The group was scattered into nearby corn fields, and although each had to fend his or her own way from there to the base, everyone made it safely.[20]

In the summer of 1945, the New Fourth Army's Fang Guofeng was trying to open a traffic line from Shanghai to a new base on the Jiangsu-Zhejiang border. In the course of his work, Fang offered a boat captain and his crew a good price for transporting a shipment of wine from Wuxi across Lake Tai to Dingshan. Unfortunately, on the day of the shipment a group of collaborating police came down to the dock to plunder. One of them discovered the cases of wine on the boat, and the police swarmed to it, accidentally breaking a bottle in their excitement. Yellow smoke arose from the spilled "wine," which was quickly recognized as nitric acid. The police arrested the entire crew and confiscated the boat and three hundred pounds of nitric acid. Since the men could not tell the

[19] Interview with Xin Yuanxi, November 1997.

[20] Wu Mingyi and Fang Guofeng, "Su-Zhe jiaotong yunshu xian de huiyi" [Recalling the Su-Zhe Communication and Transport Lines], vol. 4, 113–114. For another example of the fear and hardships volunteers experienced, see also Cao Da's escort trips with pharmacists, chemists, and physicians in Caizhengbu caizheng kexue yanjiusuo and Xinsijun yanjiuhui Shanghai gaoxiao zhuantizu, eds., *Shanghai dixiadang zhiyuan Huazhong kangRi genjudi* [The Shanghai Underground Party's Aid to the Central China Anti-Japanese Base Area], 507.

authorities the whereabouts of Fang and truly had not known they were carrying nitric acid, these workers had a very short jail stay. The transport route had to be abandoned though.[21]

Zhang Jin'gen was another civilian who spent a few days in jail because of his association with the army. He was a Zhejiang longshore worker when the New Fourth Army approached him to set up a sea transport firm for covert deliveries to the base in eastern Zhejiang. A collaborator with a grudge against Zhang informed the Japanese military police that Zhang had transported a money press, and Zhang was arrested. Although he was in jail for less than five days, this was long enough for him to be tortured on the rack and with pepper juice down his throat.[22] Whether or not civilians were aware of what they were involved in, any link to the Communists and the Central China Base put them at risk.

GAINING ASSISTANCE

We may accept that members of the Shanghai underground and New Fourth Army assumed the risk of clandestine work based on an ideological commitment to the revolution and a patriotic commitment to the nation. But how did these Communist insiders overcome the obstacles posed by the war to gain the cooperation of those outside the army and party? Just as it motivated party members, patriotism, and political ideals, working separately or as mutual reinforcements also made some civilians prone to help the New Fourth Army or underground workers who asked for assistance. Conversely, cadres seeking assistance sought out those known or expected to be ideologically sympathetic. Given the opportunity, some civilians seem to have relished the chance to do something to aid the New Fourth Army and Communists in fighting the Japanese.

Cheng Helin was this sort of person. Late in the war when the New Fourth Army decided to push into southern and eastern Zhejiang from central Jiangsu, it needed to establish covert supply linkages from Shanghai to the new Jiangsu-Zhejiang district of the base. To operate a line between the city and the base, a secondary transfer point was required inside Wuxi. Chen Xingsheng, a member of the Shanghai underground, was involved with opening the new route. Chen approached Cheng Helin, an old school mate (*tongchuang*), and asked to use his Wuxi home as the transfer and storage station. Cheng, as his Communist classmate knew, had had a progressive education and been inclined toward revolutionary ideology, yet he was passing the war as a Wuxi restaurateur. Cheng

---

[21] Wu Mingyi and Fang Guofeng, 114–116.

[22] Zhang Jin'gen, "Hai shang mimi yunshu xian" [A Clandestine Sea Transport Line], 365.

agreed to his classmate's request, saying he wanted to help defeat Japan and do something for the revolution. Soon, he was also running a store near the railroad station where contraband was stored before transport to the countryside.[23] For civilian Cheng Helin and CCP member Chen Xingsheng, patriotic and political ideologies were the points of connection that brought the classmates together to participate in covert work.

We saw how Liu Yanru turned to the Helpful Friend Society to locate people necessary to his work. Liu was not the only one to use the Helpful Friend Society and other organizations like it to fulfill wartime goals. Social bonds developed through national salvation work were sometimes strong enough to serve as the foundation for small and large requests for assistance. People active with the Helpful Friend Society were often recruited to both the New Fourth Army and the underground. When Cao Da was trying to recruit medical workers to go to the base in May 1945, friends made through the society introduced him to others they considered patriotic, and these contacts in turn talked to their friends about working for the army.[24] If someone was believed a patriot and had also participated in progressive social activities in the city, an initial fount of trust was confirmed.

It is not surprising that ideology, particularly nationalism, served as a channel for linking party activists with ordinary citizens in the wartime environment. There was, however, another means of gaining assistance. Cadres refer to the exchange of money for assistance about twice as often as they mention patriotism and politics combined. Monetary transactions structured the urban-rural relationship as party agents routinely paid for both goods and services. Since the Communists' purchases were mostly goods subject to the Japanese-imposed laws controlling trade, especially those goods that fell under the material control polices during 1942–1945, their agents and their civilian counterparts were engaged in smuggling and black market transactions. If "the scope and importance of a black market stand in inverse proportion to the power of the state," then the Communists' ability to continually locate, purchase, and transport a broad variety of contraband reveals inadequacies in the Japanese and collaborating regimes' state control over occupied Shanghai.[25] The army and party, engaged not only in a war against Japan but also in the construction of secure and legitimate power centers from which they could wage revolution, found openings in the blockade that separated their bases in the hinterland from China's economic heartland. Money eased the way.

[23] Wu Mingyi and Fang Guofeng, 109–110.
[24] Cao Da, 502–507.
[25] Mark Mazower, *Inside Hitler's Greece: The Experience of Occupation, 1941–44*, 53.

Jiang Jianzhong, a print shop worker who joined the party in 1938, put the party's money to good use after he began posing as a businessperson in Shanghai in 1941. Over time, he bought books, printing paper for currency, printing presses, ink, lathes, tools, medicine, and medical equipment in the city for the New Fourth Army. When looking to buy printing presses, he knew to find brokers in teahouses. Jiang was also part of an arrangement to buy dynamite at a high price from a match manufacturer. When it was time to pay and receive the goods, the parties completed the transaction without ever meeting face-to-face. The seller left the dynamite in an alley for the buyers to pick up. They later packaged it into separate, small, bleached cloth bags so that it looked like English sugar and had small-time peddlers who regularly crossed the Huangpu River carry it out of the city.[26]

Money paved the way for even the enemy to lend its support to the New Fourth Army. Although illicit dealings between the Japanese and New Fourth Army do not appear to have neared the level of Guomindang-Japanese transactions, the Japanese opposition was not immune to dealing with the Communists for a price. Liu Yanru used a ship that had been commandeered by the Japanese navy to move goods up the Yangzi River, and he paid the ship's Japanese captain for its use. The Japanese military police could also be bribed. Along the strategically important Japanese-controlled Hu-Ning Railroad line connecting Shanghai with Nanjing, a New Fourth Army cadre carrying a suitcase filled with vacuum tubes was stopped on one trip by a Japanese police officer at an inspection station. He was prepared for this and immediately handed the officer a bribe and was allowed to pass through unsearched.[27]

Cases of New Fourth Army agents doing business with Chinese collaborators are far more numerous. They also present an intersection point for economic and patriotic forces. Bribing collaborating troops and military police at inspection stations was considered "easy." In traveling between the city and the countryside to move smuggled goods or to relocate personnel to the base, even fifteen-year-olds making the trip for the first and only time knew that they could hand over money or packs of cigarettes to pass through collaborator

---

[26] Jiang Jianzhong, "Jiang Jianzhong tan Shanghai dao Subei de jiaotong gongzuo" [Jiang Jianzhong Discusses Shanghai to Subei Transport Work], 489–490.

[27] Lloyd Eastman studied smuggling between the Guomindang rear and the Japanese and concluded that illegal trade between the supposed enemies was institutionalized. The "involvement of [Guomindang] military personnel in the trade with occupied areas was evident all along the front." Toward the end of the war, government officials "at all levels" were involved in illicit transactions with the enemy. Eastman concludes that Guomindang-Japanese relations, while not "collusion," were something less than "belligerent." See Eastman, 279–282, 292. Wu Mingyi and Fang Guofeng, 108–109.

inspection points unscathed. Regular transport workers prepared bribe money in advance, wrapping a thick stack of small bills in paper so that the amount of cash appeared larger. Collaborator commanders traded arms with the Communists, helped them move in and out of Japanese-controlled areas on land and along the Yangzi and coast, and became partners with party agents in businesses dealing in contraband and set up explicitly for the New Fourth Army's benefit.[28]

Like ideologies then, money contributed to the operation of the army and party's transport and communication routes. It bought the Communists both human cooperation and war materials, yet on its own, it was useless. Individual connections between buyers and sellers were preconditions to its effective use in fighting the war and building the base area. In the context of the wartime environment, how did the Communists tap these sources of patriotism, progressive ideology, and the need or desire for financial gain? Within the framework of urban-rural interaction, what methods were employed and what relationships called on or created to serve the party's ends?

THE BONDS OF ACTION

A prime resource the Communists relied on in the wartime revolutionary process was social relations or connections (*shehui guanxi* or *shehui lianxi*). The memoir accounts of army and underground members are filled with references to the cultivation of and reliance on social connections, and cadres frequently and explicitly identify connections as a prerequisite to the success of their assignments. Because of the clandestine nature of wartime communication and transport work and the risks it entailed, Communists regularly turned to networks of family, friends, and business and social acquaintances for help. Liu Yanru's experience, for example, illustrates the secure and important role that family could play in sensitive operations. The mortar barrels were cut to army specifications at his nephew's work place. He also stored the steel tubes at his aunt's family home. Other cadres on assignment in Shanghai also recruited family members into active underground work and even into the party. They used family members' homes for meetings or stayed with them while carrying out their assignments. Family also provided introductions to other individuals and to larger social networks.

---

[28] Feng Shaobai, "Kangzhan shiqi si jin dizhanqu jinxing zhencha he cefan deng gongzuo de huiyi" [A Memoir of Four Entries into the Enemy-Occupied Area to Conduct Reconnaissance, Instigate Defection, and Other Work During the Resistance War Period], 54–55; Zhang Jin'gen, 363–365; Interview with Zhang Daping, November 1999; Interview with Qian Junsu, November 1997.

Having family members in the city was often a necessary cover or entrée into the urban community. In both the base and Shanghai, party leaders made a point of inquiring into the social backgrounds and connections of new recruits, which allowed the organization to hand pick candidates appropriate for specific assignments. When the party selected someone for liaison or transport work in Shanghai, it was already aware of the person's family relations or social and business experiences. This bureaucratization of reliance on *guanxi* networks during the war can be seen in a Central Committee directive to the party-army. When the CCP sought to improve its armies' influence and relations with nearby nonparty armies within the context of the United Front, the Central Committee ordered the New Fourth Army to have all its United Front departments cooperate with organization departments to gain a detailed understanding of each party member's social relations and then to utilize appropriate people as liaisons.[29]

Similarly, party leaders questioned Communists already involved in underground work about their backgrounds. When Zheng Yuzhi was working for the Shanghai underground as a liaison between Feng Xuefeng, a leader of the Shanghai underground, and Pan Hannian, then serving as the CCP's public representative in Shanghai, Pan questioned Zheng about her family and their political views and occupations. Months later when the party needed to provide a safe house in the city for leaders requiring medical treatment, Pan knew that one of Zheng's sisters worked for a foreign firm. Pan instructed Zheng to get her sister to serve as the guarantor in renting the safe house. Only then did Zheng understand why Pan had so thoroughly interviewed her about her family situation.[30]

Feng Shaobai's work in Shanghai offers an example of the army-party utilizing urban family structures to build the rural base. In December 1941, Feng was a section chief in the Staff Officer Department in the New Fourth Army headquarters at Yancheng in northern Jiangsu. New Fourth Army Commander Chen Yi assigned Feng to enter the city and use his connections with family and friends (*qinqi pengyou guanxi*) to collect contributions for the army, buy medicine, and reconnoiter the enemy. For specific work instructions, Feng was sent to see Liu Shaoqi, then working with the army and heading the Central Plains Bureau.[31] Liu began by asking Feng to detail his social relations (*shehui guanxi qingkuang*) in the city. Feng's aunt, Jiang Dongrong, was from a prominent family. Her father, Jiang Baiqi, had been chief of staff for Sun Yat-sen, and after

---

[29] Zhongyang, "Zhongyang guanyu kuoda jiao pengyou gongzuo de zhishi" [Central Committee Directive on Extending the Work of Making Friends], vol. 2, 31–32.

[30] Zheng Yuzhi, 13–15.

[31] Many army agents sent into Shanghai received their urban work assignments from the army's highest-ranking leaders, demonstrating the importance of these projects.

Sun's death he had refused to work for Chiang Kai-shek. Chiang threw him into jail, leaving Jiang Dongrong with a deep animosity toward the Generalissimo. Jiang's mother's brother, Wu Qiding, had been head of the Guomindang's tax bureau in Shanghai when the war broke out. After Wu left the city with the Guomindang government, he handed over the tax bureau chief's job to Jiang Dongrong's husband, Shao Shijun. Eventually, Shao headed the tax office for the Wang Jingwei regime.[32]

Feng went to Shanghai carrying a letter from Commander Chen Yi to Shao Shijun that thanked Shao for the 30,000 yuan *fabi* he had already contributed to the New Fourth Army and asked him to continue to aid the anti-Japan effort. Getting more money from Shao was one of Feng's assigned goals. He was also to ask Shao for an introduction to the collaborating forces in northern Jiangsu province and to help the New Fourth Army get military materials by arranging for the collaborating armies to do business with the CCP's forces in that region. Feng did not meet with Shao Shijun during this ten-day visit but communicated with him through another relative, Jiang Dawei, who worked as a secretary at the tax bureau. Jiang Dawei was Feng's adopted younger brother, and Feng stayed with him in Shanghai.

Responding through the intermediary, Shao claimed that he did not have any intimate friends connected with the collaborators in northern Jiangsu and therefore could not provide an introduction. As for arms trading with the collaborators there, Shao said that he feared the dangers involved and could not respond to the request. He was, however, willing to again contribute several 10,000 yuan to the army, and Feng carried this money back to the New Fourth Army leaders. Through Shao Shijun, Feng was also able to transport a shipment of medicine and medical equipment back to the base. The medical supplies were from a shipment that Song Qingling's Hong Kong–based Protect China Alliance (Baowei Zhongguo datongmeng) had sent into Shanghai. The Japanese had confiscated the shipment and sealed it in a warehouse. Shao made it possible for Feng to purchase ten crates of supplies from this warehouse.

Outside of family ties, other particularistic relationships also shaped the army agent's operating procedures. Native-place (*tongxiang*) ties, for instance, were a frequent boon to underground work. Shen Youchu was able to open sea routes that moved large quantities of goods and people from Shanghai to the New Fourth Army troops in eastern Zhejiang through his hometown (*laojia*) connections. He returned to his native place in Nanhui County, located on the tip of the Jiangnan delta outside Shanghai, to open a store as a front for secret transport

---

[32] The narrative that follows is based on Feng Shaobai's memoir, "Kangzhan shiqi si jin dizhanqu jinxing zhencha he cefan deng gongzuo de huiyi" 52–63.

work. Because it was his hometown, he knew most of the county's merchant ship owners, and they took on his business of transporting military supplies to Communist guerrillas along the heavily patrolled and guarded Zhejiang coast. Shen's contacts in the area were so extensive (*liyong ge zhong guanxi, sanjiao-jiuliu*) that he was also able to send goods from his store over land to the bases in northern Jiangsu and Shandong.[33] School ties (*tongxue* or *tongchuang*) also lent themselves to relationships that army and party cadre felt they could trust. They turned to classmates for help, as we saw when a member of the Shanghai underground got a former classmate to first offer his home in Wuxi as a transfer station and then later to run a store for the same purpose.

Cadres also mention connections made in a variety of associational organizations as a source of support for their missions. In addition to the New Fourth Army agents who called on people they had met in the Helpful Friend Society, another case is seen in Cao Da's recruiting of intellectuals to the base. Cao used his connections in the pharmaceutical industry to recruit a pharmacist named Wen Yutang. The two men had both belonged to the Shanghai Pharmaceutical Students Friendship Society (Shanghai yaojisheng lianyihui) and the Vocational Circles National Salvation Association (Zhiye jiu jiuguo hui). Wen Yutang ended up not only working actively for the Communists but also sending his son into the New Fourth Army.[34]

As Cao Da and Wen Yutang's relationship suggests, many associational connections were based on contacts made in the course of one's work. Party agents in the city frequently turned to people they knew because of their own, usually prewar, occupations. When we add these associational and occupational ties to the examples of cadre relying on the more personal connections of family and friends, the tie between Shanghai's social and economic structures is visible. With the war not only disrupting normal business channels but also elevating the army agent's need for secrecy to an absolute necessity, the use of trustworthy personal connections to smooth clandestine arrangements and market transactions can only have increased in importance during the war years.[35]

---

[33] Shen Youchu, "Kaipi hai shang jiaotong xian, zhiyuan Zhedong Xinsijun" [Opening a Sea Lane, Aiding the New Fourth Army in Eastern Zhejiang], in *Shanghai renmin yu Xinsijun*, 368–369.

[34] Cao Da, 501–502.

[35] In her study of the art of social relations (*guanxixue*) in contemporary urban China, Mayfair Yang explains the importance of the idea of familiarity when relying on social connections (*guanxi*). Familiarity incorporates notions of mutual trust and obligation, which support the operation of *guanxi*. Family ties are the most familiar, with *tong* (same or shared) relations, such as a shared native-place, school, or workplace, following. "Friendship, kinship, classmates, and so forth are not coextensive with *guanxi*, but serve as bases or potential sites for *guanxi* practice." Mayfair Mei-hui Yang, *Gifts, Favors, and Banquets: The Art of Social Relationships in China,* 111. On the operation of *guanxi* in contemporary rural China, see Yunxiang Yan, *The*

When cadre assignments demanded a contact outside their own social or economic circles, they were forced to work through intermediaries. In situations that necessitated outside introductions, army and party agents often speak of turning to "all sorts of complicated connections" (*tongguo fuza de guanxi*) or "every kind of connections" (*ge zhong guanxi*). References to reliance on these more ambiguous types of connections are as frequent as those to family and friends, and they expose a party willing to deal with social groups outside the standard United Front categories of patriotic capitalists or enlightened local elites. For example, "making friends with all types of people" included those of ill repute. Just as Liu Yanru's assignment called for dealing with a Shanghai gangster, Huang Aidi became a disciple of a collaborating bandit chief, Zhang Aliu, for the benefit of the New Fourth Army. With Zhang as his master, Huang was able to run a ship along a secure sea route from Shanghai to eastern Zhejiang.[36]

As army agents ran the traffic lines that traversed and linked the space between countryside and city, they worked with people in all social and economic strata. The Communists associated with the Central China Base and the Shanghai underground worked with those who could help them achieve their wartime goals, regardless of class or political affiliation. The ability to capitalize on wide-ranging social connections emphasizes the flexibility of the cadres on the ground, as well as that of the party in pursuing its goals. The party-assigned army cadres and the civilians who worked with them were well versed in the social and cultural practices of doing business in the city and along the routes that linked Shanghai to its hinterland. They were able to make the necessary contacts, open up stores, cut deals with capitalists, and make transport arrangements in an economy and society wracked by war. Most of the transactions described in this chapter involve professionals, small business owners, self-employed tradespeople, and skilled industrial workers. Outside urban factory workers, clerical staff, shop clerks, and railway workers, these are not the social classes typically described as drawn to the party for its ideology or socioeconomic programs. Yet they are precisely the people that party agents recruited into their trafficking work through social connections and customary business practices such as introductions and mutually agreed upon fees for services.

Flow of Gifts: Reciprocity and Social Networks in a Chinese Village, and Andrew B. Kipnis, *Producing Guanxi: Sentiment, Self, and Subculture in a North China Village*.

    For more on the New Fourth Army and the use of social relations in penetrating "local society along particularistic ties," see Benton, *New Fourth Army*, 168–188.

[36] Shen Youchu, 366–367. Zhang Aliu also traded arms with the New Fourth Army. See also Wu Chengfang, "Zai geming gongzuo zhong yunyong banghui guanxi de pianduan ziliao" [Snatches of Material on Using Secret Society Connections in Revolutionary Work].

In the market transactions and other arrangements of their missions, social connections were a key resource for the New Fourth Army and the Shanghai underground. One former transport worker attributes the success of the urban-rural relationship to reliance on the masses, the Shanghai underground, and social connections. He described the *guanxi* that he and others counted on as "unfathomable" (*shen buke ci*). "When I recruited (*fazhan*) one person, he or she could recruit ten more. Then they all recruited ten and [the *guanxi* network] became hundreds."[37] With the success of purchase, transport, and intelligence missions so closely tied to the successful use of social connections, cultural norms become central to understanding how individuals went about the process of making the revolution. As the patterns of human interaction unfold along the urban-rural routes, the strength of long-standing cultural values and practices during the war is evident. The bonds of family and friendship and the rules that governed social and economic transactions were not invented by cadres as they went about their work. Rather, their skill and flexibility in getting the job done depended on their ability to make shared and familiar cultural norms and social structures serve their base-building purposes in an environment conditioned by war.[38]

CONCLUSION

Gregor Benton's work on the New Fourth Army has established its importance in the making of Chinese communism. To advance the officially sanctioned view of the revolution that centered on the role of Mao Zedong in the north, the New Fourth Army and the revolutionary movement in southern China was downplayed and denied. Benton has compared the New Fourth Army with its glorified elder brother, the Eighth Route Army, and has found that proportionately, the New Fourth Army and its influence on local society grew at the same rate as the Eighth Route Army's in the north. The less than 10,000 guerrillas

[37] Interview with Xin Yuanxi, November 1997.

[38] Andrew Kipnis's work applying Pierre Bourdieu's theory of practice and Michel Foucault's work on subjectification to the study of *guanxi* relations in rural contemporary China leads to the conclusion here that when cadres exploited social connections, they were also recreating *guanxi* practices as well as themselves. Further research on *guanxi* in the wartime setting and across urban and rural spaces is needed to answer questions such as what did a cadre owe to a Shanghai business owner or wealthy relative in return for their wartime help to the party? Did contributing to the war effort overcome the obligations of social relations or leave party members indebted after the war? When cadres were assigned to serve the war and revolution by engaging in urban commercial and social exchanges, where did they place themselves in the making of Chinese communism? How did the reliance on urban relational networks shape developing political institutions and cultural norms within the rural base areas? Kipnis, 7–11.

who had come down from the mountains to form the army in 1937 grew into a force of over 300,000 that controlled over 34 million people and nearly 250,000 square kilometers in land by the war's end.[39]

In this growth and development of the army and the Central China Base, Shanghai played an important role. Gregor Benton also argues that Shanghai's modern industrial and commercial classes were reflected in the army's composition and thereby made it unique. Because of the Shanghai link, the New Fourth Army "had a greater proportion of workers, students, intellectuals, and women than any other Chinese army, including the Eighth Route Army, which was rapidly cut off by the war from a steady supply of urban recruits." It was the nation's best educated and most modern army, and it was more broadly representative of Chinese society than any other wartime force.[40]

The relationship between Shanghai and the New Fourth Army's base areas reveals that a flow of goods, people, money, and information was maintained between the countryside and the city throughout the War of Resistance. Quantifying this flow precisely is not possible. In building the Central China Base, however, Shanghai's relationship with the New Fourth Army was significant to its success. When we view the wartime revolutionary process from the vantage point of the underground army cadre and cooperating civilians working in Shanghai and along the rural-urban routes they created and used, the historical image of the countryside surrounding the city only in the civil war period after 1945 begins to fall away. Although the image of the wartime Communists making revolution in the rural periphery remains valid, we also see them acting in China's foremost urban center and in the spaces in between. Because of its relationship with Shanghai, the Central China Base gains a commercial quality and a cultural and social sophistication not usually associated with the Communists' rural revolution but long associated with the Jiangnan region.

In thinking of the revolutionary movement between 1937 and 1945, creating a sharp dichotomy between the countryside and the city oversimplifies the complex reality of how army activists and Shanghai urbanites experienced the war. Although the Japanese occupied Shanghai, controlled the region's rail and water lines, and carried out intense mop-up and pacification campaigns around Shanghai and throughout the lower Yangzi region after 1940, the military and base leadership purposefully and simultaneously exploited and depended on the people and products of the metropolis throughout the war. The Communists in the countryside not only relied on the people of Shanghai to give existence and meaning to the rural revolution but to staff and supply it as well. Adding

[39] Benton, *New Fourth Army*, 713.
[40] Ibid., 722–723, 50–76.

Shanghai into the picture of wartime base development reveals the Central China Base as both an urban and rural creation.

As other chapters in this volume show, Shanghai's economy during the war was ultimately a declining one. The New Fourth Army's trafficking lines demonstrate that the war made trade difficult and complex. Yet the continuous movement across the lines that divided the city and the countryside show that the wartime urban-rural relationship was significant not only for urban businesses eager to continue marketing goods in wartime but also for the rural Communist base eager for urban supplies and talents. Even though the "lonely island" is still in many circumstances an apt portrayal of Shanghai in the period before the city's total occupation, the representation of the city as completely cut off from the interior, especially after 1941, is only partially accurate. Shanghai's natural relationship with its hinterland was disrupted by the contingency of war, but the city was simultaneously a continuing and active influence in the Communists' base-building project in central China.

BIBLIOGRAPHY

Benton, Gregor. *Mountain Fires: The Red Army's Three-Year War in South China, 1934–1938*. Berkeley: University of California Press, 1992.
——— *New Fourth Army: Communist Resistance along the Yangtze and the Huai, 1938–1941*. Berkeley: University of California Press, 1999.
Caizhengbu caizheng kexue yanjiusuo and Xinsijun yanjiuhui Shanghai gaoxiao zhuantizu, eds. *Shanghai dixiadang zhiyuan Huazhong kangRi genjudi* [Shanghai Underground Party Support for the Central China Anti-Japan Base Area]. Shanghai: Huadong Shifan Daxue chubanshe, 1987.
Cao, Da. "KangRi shenghuo zaji" [Notes on Living the Resistance War]. In *KangRi fengyun lu* [A Record of the Anti-Japanese Storm], vol. 2. Edited by Zhongguo renmin zhengzhi xieshang huiyi Shanghai shi weiyuanhui and Wenshi ziliao gongzuo weiyuanhui. Shanghai: Shanghai renmin chubanshe, 1985.
Chen, Yung-fa. *Making Revolution: The Communist Movement in Eastern and Central China, 1937–1945*. Berkeley: University of California Press, 1986.
Eastman, Lloyd E. "Facets of an Ambivalent Relationship: Smuggling, Puppets, and Atrocities During the War, 1937–1945." In *The Chinese and the Japanese: Essays in Political and Cultural Interactions*. Edited by Akira Iriye. Princeton: Princeton University Press, 1980.
Esherick, Joseph W. "Deconstructing the Construction of the Party-State: Gulin County in the Shaan-Gan-Ning Border Region." *The China Quarterly*, 140 (December 1994): 1052–1079.
Feng, Shaobai. "Kangzhan shiqi si jin dizhanqu jinxing zhencha he cefan deng gongzuo de huiyi" [A Memoir of Four Entries into the Enemy-Occupied Area to Conduct Reconnaissance, Instigate Defection, and Other Work During the Resistance War Period]. *Dang shi ziliao congkan*, 2 (1980): 52–63.
Jiang, Jianzhong. "Jiang Jianzhong tan Shanghai dao Subei de jiaotong gongzuo" [Jiang Jianzhong Discusses Shanghai to Subei Transport Work]. In *Shanghai dixiadang*

zhiyuan Huazhong kangRi genjudi. Edited by Caizhengbu caizheng kexue yanjiusuo and Xinsijun yanjiuhui Shanghai gaoxiao zhuantizu. Shanghai: Huadong Shifan Daxue chubanshe, 1987.

Kipnis, Andrew B. *Producing Guanxi: Sentiment, Self, and Subculture in a North China Village.* Durham, NC: Duke University Press, 1997.

Li, Wenjie. "Shi qi wan ba qian wu bai yuan de jukuan" [The Huge Sum of 178,500 Yuan]. In *Shanghai renmin yu Xinsijun* [The Shanghai People and the New Fourth Army]. Edited by Zhong Gong Shanghai shiwei dang shi ziliao zhengji weiyuanhui. Shanghai: Zhishi chubanshe, 1989.

Liu, Xiao. "Shanghai dixiadang huifu he chongjian qianhou" [Restoration and Reconstruction of the Shanghai Underground Party from Beginning to End]. In *Shanghai dang shi ziliao congkan* [Collected Materials on Party History] 1 (1979): 32–46.

Liu, Yanru. "Zhandou zai diren de fengsuo xian shang" [The Battle Against the Enemy's Blockade]. *Shanghai wenshi ziliao xuanji* 5 (1979): 134–41.

Zhandou zai dixia yunshu xian shang" [Battle Along Underground Transport Lines]. In *Yiyoushe shi er nian* [Twelve Years of the Helpful Friend Society], vol. 2. Edited by Zhong Gong Shanghai shiwei dang shi ziliao zhengji weiyuanhui and Yiyoushe shiliao zhengjizu. Shanghai: Zhong Gong Shanghai dang shi ziliao xuanji, 1988.

"Yi tiao shusong geming shukan de mimi yunshu xian" [A Clandestine Transport Line for Carrying Revolutionary Books and Periodicals]. In *Shanghai renmin yu Xinsijun* [The Shanghai People and the New Fourth Army]. Edited by Zhong Gong Shanghai shiwei dang shi ziliao zhengji weiyuanhui. Shanghai: Zhishi chubanshe, 1989.

Luo, Suwen. "Xin wang de yanshen: Minguo shiqi Shanghai de Huaren zhiye julebu" [Extending a New Network: Republican Shanghai's Chinese Occupational Clubs]. *Shanghai yanjiu luncong* 12 (January 1998): 99–124.

Ma, Hongwu et al., eds. *Xinsijun he Huazhong kangRi genjudi shiliaoxuan* [Historical Materials on the New Fourth Army and the Central China Anti-Japanese Base Area], 8 vols. Shanghai: Shanghai renmin chubanshe, 1982–1994.

Mazower, Mark. *Inside Hitler's Greece: The Experience of Occupation, 1941–44.* New Haven: Yale University Press, 1993.

Rong, Jiansheng. "Xinsijun she zai Shanghai de mimi banshichu" [The Secret Office Set Up by the New Fourth Army in Shanghai]. *Shanghai dang shi ziliao tongxun* 8 (1987): 1–8.

Shanghai lieshi xiaozhuan [Profiles of Shanghai Martyrs]. Shanghai: Shanghai renmin chubanshe, 1983.

Shanghai shi gonganju gongan shi bangongshi and Luwan, Jing'an gongan fenju gongan shi xiaozu. "Wang wei 'tegong zongbu' mouhai Mao Liying lieshi de jingguo" [The Process of the Wang Collaborator 'Secret Service General Headquarters' Plot to Murder the Martyr Mao Liying]. In *Ming chui qingshi guangzhao houren: Mao Liying lieshi suxiang jiemu jinian ce* [Go Down in History, Illuminate Later Generations: Issue Commemorating the Unveiling of the Statue of the Martyr Mao Liying]. Edited by Shanghai shi Luwan qu renmin zhengfu, Shanghai haiguan, and Shanghai shi di shi er zhongxue. n.p. (Shanghai): n.p., 1990.

Shanghai shi Xinsijun ji Huazhong kangRi genjudi lishisuo yanjiuhui, ed. *Huazhong kangRi douzheng huiyi* [Memoirs on the Anti-Japanese Struggle in Central China].

10 vols. Shanghai: Shanghai Xinsijun he Huazhong kangRi genjudi yanjiuhui and Baijia chubanshe, 1981–1993.

Shen bao. "Zhifu julebu zhuxi Mao Liying zao qiang ji" [Vocational Women's Club Chair Mao Liying Shot Last Night], *Shen bao*, Dec. 13, 1939, 1; "Mao Liying zuo shishi" [Mao Liying Died Yesterday], *Shen bao*, Dec. 16, 1939, 1.

Shen, Youchu. "Kaipi hai shang jiaotong xian, zhiyuan Zhedong Xinsijun" [Opening a Sea Lane, Aiding the New Fourth Army in Eastern Zhejiang]. In *Shanghai renmin yu Xinsijun* [The Shanghai People and the New Fourth Army]. Edited by Zhong Gong Shanghai shiwei dang shi ziliao zhengji weiyuanhui. Shanghai: Zhishi chubanshe, 1989.

Wakeman, Frederic, Jr. *The Shanghai Badlands: Wartime Terrorism and Urban Crime, 1937–1941*. Cambridge: Cambridge University Press, 1996.

Wang, Jihua. "Zhiyejie jiuwang xiehui he Shanghai 'gudao' shiqi de kang di douzheng" [The Professional Circles National Salvation Association and the Struggle to Resist the Enemy in the Shanghai "Gudao" Period]. *Shanghai dang shi ziliao congkan* 2 (1981): 47–54.

Wang, Yaoshan. "Shanghai dixiadang yu Xinsijun" [The Shanghai Underground Party and the New Fourth Army]. In *Xinsijun: Huiyi shiliao* [New Fourth Army: Memoir Materials], vol. 1. Edited by Zhongguo Renmin Jiefangjun lishi ziliao congshu bianshen weiyuanhui. Beijing: Jiefangjun chubanshe, 1990.

Wu, Chengfang. "Zai geming gongzuo zhong yunyong banghui guanxi de pianduan ziliao" [Snatches of Material on Using Secret Society Connections in Revolutionary Work]. *Shanghai wenshi ziliao xuanji* 54 (1986): 21–28.

Wu, Mingyi and Fang Guofeng. "Su-Zhe jiaotong yunshu xian de huiyi" [Recalling the Su-Zhe Communication and Transport Lines]. In *Huazhong kangRi douzheng huiyi* [Memoirs on the Anti-Japanese Struggle in Central China], vol. 4. Edited by Shanghai shi Xinsijun ji Huazhong kangRi genjudi lishisuo yanjiuhui. Shanghai: n.p., 1984.

Yan, Yunxiang. *The Flow of Gifts: Reciprocity and Social Networks in a Chinese Village.* Stanford: Stanford University Press, 1996.

Yang, Mayfair Mei-hui. *Gifts, Favors, and Banquets: The Art of Social Relationships in China.* Ithaca, NY: Cornell University Press, 1994.

Yao, Huiquan. "KangRi jiuwang gongzuo huiyi" [A Memoir of Anti-Japanese Save-the-Nation Work]. In *KangRi fengyun lu* [*A Record of the Anti-Japanese Storm*], vol. 2. Edited by Zhongguo renmin zhengzhi xieshang huiyi Shanghai shi weiyuanhui and Wenshi ziliao gongzuo weiyuanhui. Shanghai: Shanghai renmin chubanshe, 1985.

"Shanghai minzhong yuanzhu Xinsijun de qiangzhi, bupi, jiaoxie" [The Shanghai People's Aid to the New Fourth Army in Firearms, Cloth, and Rubber-Soled Shoes]. In *Shanghai renmin yu Xinsijun* [The Shanghai People and the New Fourth Army]. Edited by Zhong Gong Shanghai shiwei dang shi ziliao zhengji weiyuanhui. Shanghai: Zhishi chubanshe, 1989.

Yeh, Wen-hsin. "Dai Li and the Liu Geqing Affair: Heroism in the Chinese Secret Service During the War of Resistance." *Journal of Asian Studies* 48, 3 (August 1989): 545–562.

Yiyoushe shiliao bianxiezu, ed. "Yiyoushe kaizhan tongzhan gongzuo" [The Helpful Friend Society's Development of United Front Work]. In *Tongzhan gongzuo shiliao zhuanji*, vol. 1 (n.d.): 110–120.

Zhang, Daping. "Huiyi Xinsijun Shanghai banshichu" [Recalling the New Fourth Army Shanghai Office]. *Shanghai dang shi ziliao congkan* 8 (1979): 70–79.

Zhang, Jin'gen. "Hai shang mimi yunshu xian" [A Clandestine Sea Transport Line]. In *Shanghai renmin yu Xinsijun* [The Shanghai People and the New Fourth Army]. Edited by Zhong Gong Shanghai shiwei dang shi ziliao zhengji weiyuanhui. Shanghai: Zhishi chubanshe, 1989.

Zheng, Yuzhi. "Pan Hannian tongzhi dui wo de jiaodao" [Comrade Pan Hannian's Guidance Toward Me]. *Shanghai wenshi ziliao xuanji* 42 (1983): 11–16.

Zhong Gong Shanghai shiwei dang shi ziliao zhengji weiyuanhui, ed. *Shanghai renmin yu Xinsijun* [Shanghai People and the New Fourth Army]. Shanghai: Zhishi chubanshe, 1989.

Zhong Gong Shanghai shiwei dang shi ziliao zhengji weiyuanhui and Yiyoushe shiliao zhengjizu, eds. *Yiyoushe shi er nian* [Twelve Years of the Helpful Friend Society]. 2 vols. Shanghai: Zhong Gong Shanghai dang shi ziliao xuanji, 1985–1988.

Zhongguo Renmin Jiefangjun lishi ziliao congshu bianshen weiyuanhui, ed. *Xinsijun: Huiyi shiliao* [New Fourth Army: Memoir Materials]. 2 vols. Beijing: Jiefangjun chubanshe, 1990.

Zhongguo renmin zhengzhi xieshang huiyi Shanghai shi weiyuanhui and Wenshi ziliao gongzuo weiyuanhui. *KangRi fengyun lu* [A Record of the Anti-Japanese Storm]. 2 vols. Shanghai: Shanghai renmin chubanshe, 1985.

Zhongyang. "Zhongyang guanyu kuoda jiao pengyou gongzuo de zhishi" [Central Committee Directive on Extending the Work of Making Friends], August 19, 1940. In *Xinsijun he Huazhong kangRi genjudi shiliao xuan* [Historical Materials on the New Fourth Army and the Central China Anti-Japanese Base Area], vol. 2. Edited by Ma Hongwu et al. Shanghai: Shanghai renmin chubanshe, 1984.

Zhongyang. "Zhongyang guanyu Shanghai dang de mimi gongzuo de zhishi" [Central Committee Directive Concerning the Secret Work of the Shanghai Party], December 16, 1940. In *Shanghai renmin yu Xinsijun* [The Shanghai People and the New Fourth Army]. Edited by Zhong Gong Shanghai shiwei dang shi ziliao zhengji weiyuanhui. Shanghai: Zhishi chubanshe, 1989.

Zhongyang. "Zhongyang guanyu shenru xuanchuan junwei 'guanyu Wannan shibian de fayan' deng wenti gei Liu Xiao tongzhi de zhishi" [Central Committee Directive to Comrade Liu Xiao on Thoroughly Publicizing the CCP CC Military Commission's "Statement on the Wannan Incident" and Other Issues], February 14, 1941. In *Shanghai renmin yu Xinsijun* [The Shanghai People and the New Fourth Army]. Edited by Zhong Gong Shanghai shiwei dang shi ziliao zhengji weiyuanhui. Shanghai: Zhishi chubanshe, 1989.

Chapter 5

Shanghai Smuggling

FREDERIC WAKEMAN, JR.

Wartime resistance presents its own myths of national unity and common purpose. A standard history of the Chinese response to the Japanese Occupation
is filled with accounts of heroic efforts unified and led by either or both of the
leading political parties against a backdrop of collective sacrifice and popular
cooperation.

There was a certain degree of truth to these myths, of course, and heroic
sacrifices aplenty. But their setting was mainly rural: the land of base areas,
guerrilla camps, red army detachments, and Nationalist do-or-die troops prepared to lay down their lives for the fatherland. In urban China, and especially
in the beleaguered metropolis of Shanghai, occupation brought initial division
and discord[1] – not only because of the assassins' wars of the period of the
"solitary island" (*gudao*), but also because of the sheer fight for physical survival as the deprivation of wartime food supplies after 1941 became a daily
struggle for existence.[2]

The competition for subsistence in turn became an index of treachery. Cor-
pulence was a pictorial symbol of collaboration. The arch *hanjian* ("traitors" –
often a man and a woman sporting together) were cartooned as fat and well-fed:
representations of selfishness and the *sauve-qui-peut* atmosphere of war profiteering and consorting with the enemy. Integrity was leanness: the refusal to
make political compromises in order to ensure personal comfort and survival.

---

[1] Si Yi, "Gudao de yinxiang" [Impressions of the solitary island], 269.

[2] Frederic Wakeman, Jr. *The Shanghai Badlands: Political Terrorism and Urban Crime, 1937–
1941.* Fang Xianting, "Lun liangshi tongzhi" [Food controls], 68–69. Under the policy of "using
war to nourish war" (*yi zhan yang zhan* or *isen yosen*), the Japanese established a Grain Control
Commission (Miliang tongzhi weiyuanhui), or "Mitonghui," that was eventually amalgamated
with Wang Jingwei-regime organs to supervise the requisition and purchase of grain in the
Yangzi delta. Tang Zhenchang and Shen Hengchun, eds., *Shanghai shi* [History of Shanghai],
836.

6. Fleeing the city: Native-place associations organize the transportation of their fellow members back to the village. Source: Courtesy of the Fabre Family.

Both caricatures were, oddly enough, served by the wide array of wartime smugglers who either made profiteering possible or guaranteed enough food (and especially Shanghai's staple, rice) to see the rest of the citizenry through to liberation. The story of contraband, then, was decent survival at the private level, and profane profit-taking in a more public domain where governments and armies on all sides took their due portion of the proceeds and shared in ill-gotten gains.

THE ENCLOSED CITY

The wartime occupation of Shanghai, from the Chinese residents' perspective, was divided into three distinct periods. The first was the period of Fu Xiaoan's mayoralty, when there was almost no impact on the Chinese living in the foreign concessions. The second phase was after Wang Jingwei took power, when there was a terrifying spate of kidnapping and killing in the International Settlement. The third stage was after the Japanese attacked Pearl Harbor and declared war against England. Even though many expected the Wang Jingwei government to extend its authority to the concessions, the Japanese continued to occupy them and maintained complete security over the area, imposing their control system as they wished.[3]

During this period of direct Japanese occupation of what had formerly been the foreign sectors of Shanghai, the city's middle-class dwellers rarely went out, spending most of their time at home during the evenings, when the city fell dark and gloomy.[4] Communications were guarded, "like having a drum muffled," and even when people used the telephone they were extremely cautious for fear of being overheard. There was a rumor at the time that four friends were playing cards, and after the game was over, the winner called one of the losers and promised him a chance for a "counter-attack" (*fangong*). The winner supposedly got into terrible trouble over this remark because it was monitored by the authorities and mistaken as a conspiracy to mount a resistance against the Japanese Occupation.[5]

News was correspondingly hard to come by, especially since the authorities had closed down all anti-Japanese newspapers and had confiscated all short-wave radios.[6] Rumors abounded, of course, but Shanghai's urbanites mainly felt psychologically oppressed as they constantly avoided discussing topics that might get them into trouble.[7] Starved for information, they welcomed newcomers into the city from the surrounding suburbs of Shanghai simply because the outsiders brought news with them.[8]

Needless to say, it was not easy to get into the city, as the Japanese Military Police guarded all the entrances. This had already been a fully devised system of market controls by the time the Japanese occupied Shanghai.[9] Throughout Occupied China, market town gates and major highways were guarded by special units of the Kokyogun (Imperial Cooperation Army) assigned to ensure that all freight shipments carried permits issued by the special services office (*tokubetsuho*) of that particular military zone.[10] In the suburbs of Shanghai

---

[3] Chen Cunren, *Kangzhan shidai shenghuo shi* [A history of life during the war of resistance], 200; Mabel Waln Smith, *Springtime in Shanghai*, 92.

[4] *Shanghai chunqiu* [Spring and autumn annals of Shanghai], 76; Chen Cunren, *Kangzhan shidai shenghuo shi*, 204.

[5] Chen Cunren, *Kangzhan shidai shenghuo shi*, 204.

[6] Ibid., 248–249.

[7] Even short-wave radio broadcasts offered only limited information. That is why, toward the end of the War of Resistance, it was the "traitors" (*hanjian*) themselves, with access to outside resources, who learned of the extent of the American bombing of the Japanese home islands and realized the way the wind was blowing much sooner than ordinary Shanghai urbanites. Ibid., 222–223.

[8] Ibid., 204.

[9] Lin Meili, "Kangzhan shidai de zousi huodong yu zousi shizhen" [Smuggling activities and smuggling towns during the War of Resistance], 15.

[10] Ibid., 4.

these guard posts were usually manned by puppet troops backed up by Japanese Military Police. When rural folk came through the barbed wire and sandbagged checkpoints they were forced to remove their hats and bow to the authorities, and they were also often searched. If they had English or American brands of cigarettes in their pockets, then the Japanese sentries would slap them, whereas Chinese brands like Dalianzhu or Golden Rat went unchallenged.[11] Travel around the city was also difficult, or at the very least trying, during daylight hours. When Shanghainese went across the Northern Sichuan Road bridge they had to dismount from their vehicles and bow to the Japanese Military Police on sentry duty. These controls gradually loosened so that Shanghainese could cross the bridge on a rickshaw instead of proceeding afoot (they still had to doff their hats and pay respect to the guards), but they were maintained vis-à-vis foreigners by way of humiliating them and gaining favor with the Chinese as fellow Asians opposed to white domination.[12]

On one occasion, for instance, a European rode across the bridge on a rickshaw and simply bowed his head politely at the sentry. One of the Japanese military policemen became furious, shouted in rage, and forced him to take off his hat and bow. He then gave the European a tremendous slap on the face, ordered him to prostrate himself on the sidewalk, and stomped on the Westerner's body before he would let the man go. On another occasion the Japanese gendarme ordered the foreigner out of the rickshaw, ushered the Chinese puller into the seat, and, to the delight of Chinese onlookers, had the European haul the rickshaw instead.[13]

RICE

Japanese travel restrictions and checkpoints were more than an affront to the dignity of Shanghai urbanites, Chinese and Westerners alike. They represented the occupiers' alimentary stranglehold upon the city, which needed at least 500,000,000 pounds (ca. four million *dan*) of rice per year to feed its population.[14] After the Battle of Shanghai broke out, and the Japanese troops drew closer and closer to the city, it began to dawn upon the Shanghainese that China was going to be fighting a protracted war and that

---

[11] Chen Cunren, *Kangzhan shidai shenghuo shi*, 200–201.

[12] Frederic Wakeman, Jr., "The Craigie-Arita Talks and the Struggle Over the Tientsin Concessions," 11–15; *Xin shenbao yebao* 1/4/42, 1.

[13] Chen Cunren, *Kangzhan shidai shenghuo shi*, 201.

[14] Hanchao Lu, "Away from Nanjing Road: Small Stores and Neighborhood Life in Modern Shanghai," personal communication from Professor Christian Henriot.

provisions would soon grow sparse.[15] The influx of refugees[16] further reinforced the determination of the citizenry to amass enough food supplies
(though even machine-dried rice eventually spoiled) to fill a household servant's
room.[17]

The problem was finding a supplier. The ordinary Shanghai resident frequented a retail rice store (*midian*) for daily or weekly supplies of grain.[18]
Individual rice stores were generally quite small (65 percent only had about
$200 worth of capital), though they were sometimes attached to a larger
rice company (*mihang*) specializing in grain from certain provinces or countries (Jiangxi or Thailand, for example). Most of the 1,544 members of the
Shanghai rice guild operated out of the front living rooms of their small homes
(*lilong shikumen*), which contained about 5–10 days' worth of sales for the
2,000 or so customers serviced by each establishment. The available supplies,
consequently, were quickly exhausted by hoarders who were trying to store
up rice for the hard times ahead and who at the same time drove up the
price by exhausting inventories of the grain in response to this accelerated
demand.[19]

In honor of the solar New Year's day, the occupation authorities announced
on January 1, 1942, that there would be a special sale of 20,000 bags of rice.
At the same time, however, the Shanghai Municipal Council decreed that rice
stores within the foreign concession would have their hours of sale restricted
from 8:00 in the morning to 4:00 in the afternoon, and close down all together
on Wednesdays and Sundays.[20] These restrictions were relaxed when the additional supply of rice did not completely sell out, and there was a momentary
sense of relief on the eve of the lunar new year's festival.[21] But when *guonian*
actually arrived and the time had come to settle the year's debts, there was a
sudden increase in prices on the black market for gold, bonds, stocks, and cotton
futures.[22] Along with this inflation, the price of rice on the free market rose to

---

[15] Hu Liuzhang, "Kangzhan huiyi ji duanpian zhi huixiang" [An extremely brief recollection of
memories of the War of Resistance], 52.

[16] Chen Cunren, *Kangzhan shidai shenghuo shi*, 225.

[17] Ibid., 60–61, 225; *Shanghai chunqiu*, vol. 1, 77.

[18] Before April 1942 there were about 450 rice and flour stores in the International Settlement.
The SMC closed 250 in April in order to have rice distributed through a smaller and therefore
more easily controlled number of shops. *Shenbao* 9/1/42, 5. According to Christian Henriot,
there were more than 400 shops in the French settlement before 1939.

[19] Lu, "Away from Nanjing Road," 99–100.

[20] *Shenbao* 1/1/42, 6.

[21] Ibid., 5/1/42, 5.

[22] Chen Cunren, *Kangzhan shidai shenghuo shi*, 208.

Table 5.1 *Goods Imported into Fuzhou and Fujian Ports from Occupied China, July 1, 1943 – June 1, 1944*

Items	Amount (kg)	Value (CRB$)
Gasoline, diesel oil, and other machine oils	354	29,120
Machine tools, apparatus, and spare parts	450	168,427
Metals	12,797	1,745,930
Machinery, electrical apparatus, and spare parts	2,493	1,843,261
Signaling apparatus and spare parts	72	46,408
Vehicles and spare parts	7,863	7,897,010
Drugs and medical appliances	139,309	33,475,316
Chemicals	85,492	53,249,868
Alcohol, etc.	12,500	50,000
Cotton goods	763,093	313,577,695
Woolen goods	825	6,254,274
Rice, cereals, flour	11,651	1,126,481
Paper	3,728	6,167,570
Leather	11	27,000
Grand total	1,040,635	425,658,360

Source: Office of Strategic Services, Research and Analysis Branch, R&A #2121 East China Coast, Nov. 1, 1944 (OSS reel no. 2, document no. 8), pp. 250–251.

280 yuan for one picul or *dan* and there were long lines for regulated grain, coal, and cooking oil.[23]

The authorities attempted to repeat the same solution, announcing a public sale by the Rice Management Bureau (Miliang banshichu) of 20,000 bags of rice on February 4, 1942.[24] However, on March 9 the price of black market rice rose again to over 300 yuan per picul. Afraid that such high prices would jeopardize their rule, the Japanese authorities issued an order temporarily freezing rice sales, followed on March 14 by another fiat designed to stifle the black market in grain by prohibiting domestic "national rice" (*guomi*) from entering the foreign concession. The very opposite happened, of course. That same afternoon, in a matter of moments, the price of a picul of rice went up to 400 yuan, and by evening it was over 500 yuan a *dan*. The following day, March 15, 1942, each picul cost 600 yuan, and rumors had it that in the city of Fuzhou [Foochow] the price of rice had soared to over 1,000 yuan per *dan* (for 1943–1944 figures, see Table 5.1). Hoarding was endemic.[25]

---

[23] Tao Juyin, *Tianliang qian de gudao* [The isolated island before daybreak], 63, 65; *Shanghai chunqiu*, vol. 1, 78. See also *Shanghai jiefang qianhou wujia ziliao huibian* [Compilation of materials on prices in Shanghai before and after the liberation], 18.

[24] *Xin shenbao yebao* 4/2/42, 2. The sale of grain in Western Shanghai (Huxi) was carried out, quite unsatisfactorily, following the arrangement of *baojia*. Ibid., 6/2/42, 2.

[25] *Shanghai jiefang qianhou wujia ziliao huibian*, 64.

The authorities responded by again restricting the sale of rice to certain days, curtailing vendors altogether on Wednesdays and Sundays. By September 1942 it was obvious that sales restrictions only increased black marketeering, so – still trying to keep a relatively open "white" market based solely upon price and cost – the authorities announced that "normal" sales hours would resume around the time of the Chinese New Year on January 12, 1943. The resumption was to be carried out under a system of rotation (*lunliu*) store-by-store.[26]

By then, however, the supplies of rice in shops were already becoming depleted, so that gaining access to the staple became an absolute obsession. At first many Shanghai urbanites tried in person to get through the barbed wire stockade around the city and into the suburban villages where they could buy rice on their own. But they stood out too visibly to smuggle the food back into the city. The Japanese sentries on guard used trained police dogs to patrol the barricades and beat, wounded, or killed these amateur smugglers, who were quickly replaced by professional rice-runners better capable of evading arrest.[27]

There were about three thousand small-scale professional smugglers "working" the Shanghai suburbs, which they usually plied by train.[28] Their main outgoing contraband, to be indirectly exchanged for incoming rice, were cigarettes manufactured in Shanghai and selling in the hinterland for about three times the price of purchase. Professionals and amateurs alike would take the train to Suzhou and back: a round-trip run that could be made two or three times a day. The Japanese authorities estimated that if each person carried thirty cartons (that is, 15,000 cigarettes) on the average trip, then, after subtracting the ticket and bribery costs, he or she could earn at least 50 or 60 yuan per day, which could be doubled by smuggling rice back into the city on the return trip.[29] The lure of such profits in tobacco aside, cigarettes were also a form of near-money that provided relatively effective short-term insurance against inflation.

INFLATION

As prices increased several times over during 1940–1941, wages simply could not keep up.[30] The basic wage doubled between 1936 and 1940, but the cost of

---

[26] *Shenbao* 11/1/42, 5.

[27] Tao Juyin, *Tianliang qian de gudao*, 64–65; Chen Cunren, *Kangzhan shidai shenghuo shi*, 196.

[28] Lin Meili, "Kangzhan shiqi de zousi huodong yu zousi shizhen," 16.

[29] Ibid., 15–16.

[30] Yu Maochun, "American Intelligence: The OSS (Office of Strategic Services) in China," 67; Lawrence K. Rosinger, *China's Wartime Politics, 1937–1944*, 38.

living quadrupled over that same course of time.[31] Consequently, spontaneous strike activity, especially in the transportation industry, increased dramatically. During the year-long period from the summer of 1940 to the summer of 1941, an average of 10,000 to 50,000 strikers went out on the picket lines each month.[32]

The puppet administration and the Japanese authorities initially backed this strike activity, partly to undercut Western (and especially British) industrial leadership. On December 1, 1940, the Minister of Social Affairs, Ding Mocun, who had also been a co-founder of the nefarious puppet secret service at 76 Jessfield Road, convened a Social Movement Steering Committee (Shehui yundong zhidao weiyuanhui) which led twenty-nine strikes involving 52,000 workers between December 1940 and September 1941. After the attack on Pearl Harbor, however, the puppet administration's Bureau of Social Affairs became quiescent and Wang Jingwei's secret police began cracking down on the labor movement instead of supporting it.[33] There were a few strikes in the public transportation sector, but labor demands were halfhearted as inflation and unemployment forced workers to work at second jobs or rely on the firms themselves to set up tontines, savings and loan societies, and consumer cooperatives to supplement the native place associations and brotherhoods that held the world of Shanghai labor together during these hard times of rising prices and scarce supplies.[34]

And the times were hard indeed.[35] One of the primary causes of unemployment was simple lack of energy. As the Japanese commandeered coal, the electricity supply declined. By December 1943, less than 40 percent of the textile industry and only 27 percent of Shanghai's flour mills were still in operation (see Table 5.2); domestic electricity was approximately 70 percent of the amount consumed in 1941. Individuals were only permitted to use 25 units of light and 8 units of power per month. Trams stopped running at 8:30 in the evening. Eggs cost $5.50 apiece, rice was $2,500 a picul, there was no coal, and firewood was selling for $500 per hundred catties.[36]

Yet many flourished economically. Wartime Shanghai saw an increasing gap between the very poor and the very rich, who had access to or control over goods

---

[31] Alain Roux, "The Guomindang and the Workers of Shanghai (1938–1948): The Rent in the Fabric," 8.

[32] Ibid., 9.

[33] Ibid., 7–8.

[34] Ibid., 16–17.

[35] Tao Juyin, *Tianliang qian de gudao*, 63.

[36] China Intelligence Wing Report No. C-35-83, 26 April 1944, in FO371/41680, BFOR.

Table 5.2 *Prewar Flour Mills in Jiangsu*

Location	Number of Mills	Annual Capacity (49-lb. Bags)	Annual Output (39-lb. Bags)
Zhenjiang	1	700,000	600,000
Nanjing	3	2,900,000	2,380,000
Nantong	1	1,800,000	1,500,000
Shanghai	11	22,810,000	15,014,000
Taixian	1	1,000,000	900,000
Wujin	1	576,000	435,000
Huaiyin	4	5,000,000	3,700,000
Donghai	1	700,000	600,000
Dongshan	1	600,000	479,000
TOTAL	25	37,286,000	25,629,000

Source: Office of Strategic Services, Research and Analysis Branch, R&A #2121 East China Coast, Nov. 1, 1944 (OSS reel no. 2, document no. 8), pp. 65–66.

that they sold off day by day as prices rose.[37] This "new aristocracy" (*xingui*) stood apart thanks to their flashy Western clothes and expensive consumer habits. It was for them and their Japanese overlords that restaurateurs like Zhong Biao opened a chain of new cafés such as the Xinya da jiudian and the Hongjin jiujia, where only the best Cantonese dishes were served with obsessively spotless implements on sparkling clean plates designed to please the most finicky of well-heeled guests.[38]

Meanwhile, just outside these fancy establishments ordinary urbanites (*shimin*) meekly surrendered their sidewalk-bought dumplings and crullers – their *mantou* and *youtiao* – to the army of homeless beggars camped on Shanghai's city streets.[39]

CURRENCY REFORM

The collaborationist government, under the direction of Zhou Fohai, had initially hoped that the issuance of "new" puppet currency would help stabilize prices and hence keep down wages. However, within the foreign concessions, the "old" currency issued by the Nationalists' former central banks continued to prevail.[40] On December 8, the day of their occupation of the International Settlement,

[37] Xu Rihong, "Shanghai de touji" [Shanghai profiteers], 3.
[38] Chen Cunren, *Kangzhan shidai shenghuo shi*, 223–225.
[39] Ibid., 224.
[40] Chen Cunren, *Kangzhan shidai shenghuo shi*, 61.

the Japanese announced a new policy of *huafen xin jiu bi* (dividing the new and old currency), which forced purveyors to accept the puppet banknotes as payment for the occupiers' military expenses and which outlawed the "old" currency under eventual threat of arrest.[41] This caused a tremendous stir on the stock, bond, and futures markets of Shanghai; and even retail outlets were affected, with shops changing their counter prices to adjust to this draconian change.[42]

One immediate effect of the enforced imposition of the "new" scrip after the March 9 currency reform was an increase in the price of gold, which in three days rose from 14,000 yuan to 20,000 yuan per bar. Another was slowly to increase the value of puppet currency. Even though patriotically minded Shanghainese continued to hold on to the old *fabi*, they gradually shifted over to the new currency after March 14, 1942, when they were allowed to exchange up to 300 yuan of the old official banknotes for puppet notes. The puppet currency consequently began to ascend up to 20 percent in relative value, and all at once long lines began to queue up in front of the puppet banks where the exchanges were taking place. Still, there was such a continuing lack of confidence in the stability of the new currency that the value of the puppet tender only rose slightly relative to the growing inflation, which was further fueled by a corresponding rise in the price of goods – goods such as linen fabric, powdered milk, British cigarettes, blank newsprint, and sugar that were in themselves hedges against inflation.[43] That in turn exacerbated the smuggling problem because Japanese officials were privately able to take the turned-over *fabi* into the nonoccupied areas and spend the money there for goods which were brought back into Shanghai to meet the increasing demand for a better shelter from rising prices.[44]

In the meantime, Shanghai was more than ever dependent upon rice imported from Southeast Asia and its own hinterland for its citizens' survival (see Table 5.3).[45] During the early years of the Pacific War the former was all the more essential because there appeared to have been a drop in food production in

[41] Tao Juyin, *Tianliang qian de gudao*, 66.

[42] Ibid., 66–67. *Fabi* continued to circulate nonetheless, rated now at 5 to 1.

[43] "Trade between Occupied China and Free China," Situation report #6, Office of Strategic Services, Research and Analysis Branch, Far Eastern Section, R & A 553, June 16, 1942, 5; Chen Cunren, *Kangzhan shidai shenghuo shi*, 206–207.

[44] Tao Juyin, *Tianliang qian de gudao*, 67; Kathryn Meyers and Terry Parsinnen *Power and Profit*, ii; R. Keith Schoppa, "The Structure, Dynamics, and Impacts of the Shanghai-Coastal Zhejiang Trading System, 1938–1944," 25.

[45] "Current Food, Coal, and Transportation Situation Prevailing in China," R & A No. 3433, Department of State Interim Research and Intelligence Service, 2 January 1946, Appendix Two, 4.

Table 5.3 *Shanghai: Average Imports and Exports of Cereals, Beans, and Wheat Flour, 1934–1937 (in thousands of metric tons)*

Kind	Imports	Exports	Net Imports	Net Exports
Rice	220	94	126	
Wheat and flour	210	186	24	
Other cereals	3	6		3
Beans	106	30		76

Source: Office of Strategic Services, Research and Analysis Branch, R&A #2121 East China Coast, Nov. 1, 1944 (OSS reel no. 2, document no. 8), p. 46.

the Yangzi Valley owing to the heavy fighting and devastating guerrilla warfare of 1937–1938.[46] The 1939 and 1940 rice crops were normal or slightly above normal, but the Japanese (who stored large stocks of sugar and rice for their own use in Shanghai) annually exported at least 5 percent of the area's rice and wheat to Japan for consumption.[47] They would have purchased or requisitioned more to send back to the home territories, but their methods of taxation and grain collection were inefficient.[48]

Insofar as it was made good, the Shanghai deficit was supplemented legally with imports from Indochina and illegally with Yangzi Valley grain smuggled into the city.[49] To supply the former, the government-general of French Indochina was required to provide 583,000 tons of rice to the Japanese in 1941, 937,000 tons in 1942, and 1,008,000 tons in 1943.[50] Forced cultivation of jute, incidentally, along with a policy that compelled Vietnamese peasants to sell rice to the Japanese at prices lower than market levels, eventually brought about a famine in Indochina that cost several million lives (about 10 percent of the population) during 1944–1945.[51]

---

[46] Office of Strategic Services, Research and Analysis Branch, RNA # 2121 East China Coast, Nov. 1, 1944 (OSS reel no. 2, document no. 8), 46. Shanghai, because of its huge population, had long outgrown the capacity of its hinterland to supply essential foods, even though it did export food because of the concentration of flour mills within its precincts. Ningbo also experienced a shortage in food supplies. Ibid., 38, 47. Contemporary scholars question the reliability of these OSS sources.

[47] Ibid., 38, 45–47, 49.

[48] Ibid., 47.

[49] Although he was vilified as a profiteer for shipping rice in from Southeast Asia, Yu Xiaqing deserved credit for maintaining the food supplies of the city. Chen Cunren, *Kangzhan shidai shenghuo shi*, 61. Yu also "reflagged" the "New Ningshao" as the "Mohlenhoff," registered with the German consulate to ship goods between Shanghai and Ningbo, which was taken over by the Japanese military in April 1941. Schoppa, "Structure, Dynamics, and Impacts," 5.

[50] Bùi Minh Dũng, "Japan's Role in the Vietnamese Starvation of 1944–45," 597.

[51] Ibid., 591–593, 607, 611–618.

In order to maintain public order in Shanghai under these conditions, the Japanese and puppet authorities organized a "household rice" (*hukoumi*) distribution system of food stations that handed out rationed allotments of the staple to each registered household at controlled prices.[52] "Public order" was supposedly maintained in a dual sense. First, by keeping the price of rice down, the occupation authorities hoped to prevent rice riots and other forms of urban dissent. Second, the use of rice rationing, along with the regime's command of access to fuel and other necessities, was part of a controlled economy (*tongzhi jingji*) that was directly linked with the *baojia* mutual responsibility system based upon household membership.[53] In other words, you could not get basic rations in Shanghai without showing an identity card that identified the household or *hu* to which you belonged.[54]

LIFE IN THE LINE

Securing rice in this fashion was "life in the line" – a shopping habit to which Shanghainese were already quite accustomed.[55] At first each household had only to send a single member to claim the entire family's ration. But the accounting for this was too cumbersome, and after July 1942 the authorities insisted that each individual (*kou*) come in person to claim his or her own ration.[56]

People would line up in the early hours of the morning before daybreak to collect their allotments; and though sometimes numbers would actually be painted on the back of each to mark their place in line, others would jump the queue causing fights that threatened to turn into riots. When this happened the police who were overseeing the process (which, as one wag put it, was supposed to teach a proper respect for *zhixu* or "order," as in Japan's New Order in East Asia) lay about them with their batons, applying "discipline" (*jilü*) to beat people back into line. Urbanites consequently looked upon the entire procedure of getting their rice rations as a tremendously hazardous venture, throwing together the middle classes and the hoi polloi in an unseemly and dangerous

---

[52] The rice was of uneven quality, sometimes very good but often very poor. Chen Cunren, *Kangzhan shidai shenghuo shi*, 196.

[53] Fang Xianting, "Lun liangshi tongzhi," 68–69. On December 10, 1941, the Japanese announced to the residents of the foreign concessions that if there were any terrorist incidents, representatives of the households of that particular district would be taken to the military police for severe interrogation. Tao Juyin, *Tianliang qian de gudao*, 15–16.

[54] Zhang Jishun, "Shi kong yi wei: zhanshi Shanghai de baojia zhidu" [A traditional institution in a modern context: the *baojia* system in wartime Shanghai], 4.

[55] Zhao Yan, "Ga piao ji" [Notes on jumping the ration lines]," 88–89.

[56] Zhang Jishun, "Shi kong yi wei," 4.

way. Yet there was not a thing to be done but stand in line for what seemed to be interminable periods.[57]

Waiting in line was particularly trying when the weather turned cold and it rained or snowed. Even those wearing much-coveted padded coats were daily exposed to others in the line who had colds, and winter flu was quite common.[58] More threatening by far was the threat of fleas in the summer and of lice in the winter. Both transmitted typhus. As one's friends grew ill and feverish, often dying within seven or eight days of the onset of the illness, social intercourse was further curtailed or at the very least conducted by nervous visitors wearing long-sleeved clothing to protect against contagion.[59]

It was physically safer, in short, to eschew the rice lines and – if one could afford it – buy one's rice in the privacy of one's home. The rice was originally purchased at the source by petty merchants who "traveled around trading on one's own" (*pao danbang*) by scouring the villages on all sides of Shanghai for a variety of foodstuffs.[60] The goods were exchanged in equivocal zones along the front between Free China and the Japanese-occupied territory where *yin-yang* marketing areas ("not quite free nor exactly occupied") enabled people and goods (cotton, medicine, weapons, rubber tires, food) to move back and forth (see Table 5.4).[61] "Well might the Japanese soldiers look the other way so great were the sums that changed hands.[62] Was it or was it not smuggling? It was hard to say. Whatever it was, it brought Chinese and Japanese together in profitable collusion and called thriving market towns into being where none had existed before."[63]

miel topie

NATIONAL SMUGGLING NETWORKS

Smuggling entrepôts were not unique to the Shanghai hinterland alone, though they had a remarkably similar quality throughout the country.[64] The entire

---

[57] Zhao Yan, "Ga piao ji," 89–99; Chen Cunren, *Kangzhan shidai shenghuo shi*, 197.

[58] At that time, people wearing padded coats and other decent clothing had to avoid dark alleys lest they be set upon and have their garments stripped away. This was called *bo zhu* (shearing the pig). Chen Cunren, *Kangzhan shidai shenghuo shi*, 224.

[59] Ibid., 197–198.

[60] Hanchao Lu, "The Workers and Neighborhoods of Modern Shanghai, 1911–1949," 130–131.

[61] Lloyd E. Eastman, "Facets of an Ambivalent Relationship: Smuggling, Puppets, and Atrocities During the War, 1937–1945," 276–277. See also Joyce Ann Madancy, "Propaganda vs. Practice: Official Involvement in the Opium Trade in China, 1927–1945," 35.

[62] "Trade between Occupied China and Free China," 5; Lin Meili, "Kangzhan shiqi de zousi huodong yu zousi shizhen," 24.

[63] Lynn Pan, *Tracing It Home: A Chinese Family's Journey from Shanghai*, 3–4.

[64] Hsi-sheng Ch'i, *Nationalist China at War: Military Defeats and Political Collapse, 1937–45*, 171.

Table 5.4 *Principal Items of Trade, Free and Occupied China (Quantities indicated where known)*

Exports from Free China to Occupied China	Legitimate or Contraband	Imports into Free China from Occupied China	Legitimate or Contraband
Rice (estimated 3,000 per month)	Contraband	Cotton piece goods	Legitimate
Wood-oil (several hundred tons per month)	Contraband	Cotton yarn	Legitimate
Alum (500 to 1,000 tons per month)	Contraband	Foreign style medicines	Legitimate
Antimony (appreciable quantities)	Contraband	Dyes	Legitimate
Tungsten (appreciable quantities)	Contraband	Sundry light manufactures	Legitimate
Other minerals (some; details unknown)	Contraband	Opium (large quantities)	Contraband
Timber (large quantities in 1943; less in 1944)	Contraband	Foreign style paper	Contraband
Charcoal (large quantities)	Contraband		
Sugar (large quantities)	Contraband		
Chinese medicines (large quantities)	Legitimate		
Tea (large quantities)	Legitimate		
Paper (large quantities)	Contraband		

Source: Office of Strategic Services, Research and Analysis Branch, R&A #2121 East China Coast, Nov. 1, 1944 (OSS reel no. 2, document no. 8), p. 249.

system depended, after all, upon price discrepancies from district to district. These differentials were openly advertised in local newspapers: for example, in Changxing one could buy a picul of rice for 3.8 yuan, then sell that same picul for 10 yuan in Wuxing. The same was true for other commodities, such as tea (western Zhejiang leaves commanded twice the original price elsewhere) or livestock (one 40–50 yuan pig from the hinterland sold for 200 yuan in Hangzhou). In some cases, prices might be sixfold higher on either side of the boundary between Free and Occupied China, so that one had only to make two trips out of six successfully in order to gain a handsome profit.[65]

Moreover, warfare as such abetted smuggling; it turned contrabandage into a career. The first smugglers in this regard were refugees fleeing the hostilities who brought along goods they hoped to sell once they reached a safe zone.[66] They were succeeded by petty merchants who began to invest in the traffic as a form of speculation. "Opportunistic merchants, treacherous merchants (*jianshang*),

[65] Lin Meili, "Kangzhan shiqi de zousi huodong yu zousi shizhen," 124–125.
[66] Yin Yixuan, *Guofang yu liangshi wenti* [National defense and the question of grain supplies], 87; Zhu Tongjiu, *Zhanshi liangshi wenti* [The problem of wartime grain supplies], 63.

enemy agents, public service personnel, assistant officials, intelligence agents, prostitutes, reporters," down to and including seventy-year-old women and young children, all engaged in the illegal trade.[67] Because of the erstwhile Japanese blockade, Free China military units in the guerrilla zones could not be resupplied from behind and had to look for supplies across enemy lines. At the same time residents of the "gray" boundary zones recognized the huge degree of food spoilage taking place with traditional marketing hierarchies momentarily severed, and thus flocked to the smuggling entrepôts that linked central places with their own economic hinterlands.[68]

Jiezhou was just such a place at the junction of Henan and Anhui provinces, where the blockade lines were so long that the Japanese found them impossible to patrol thoroughly with the number of soldiers at their command.[69] "This was the frontier, but it did not feel like life under the guns of the enemy. The place bristled with men bent on making what money they could while they could: profiteers such as could only be seen in a country at war. Every other man you met there seemed to be a dealer or an agent for something. People came from the coast, from the inland regions across the Yellow River and the Yangzi. The town was unbelievably prosperous."[70] Transaction costs were high after 1941 (bribes of "road money" [*maluqian*] sometimes came to 40 percent of the total cost of the product), but this favored the better capitalized merchants who made considerable profits off of the system.[71]

Elsewhere, in the cotton areas of the North for example, raw textile materials were exchanged for manufactured goods from occupied China, such as radio tubes and other necessities.[72] This kind of smuggling long preceded the outright invasion of China by Japan in 1937. That is, after the Manchurian Railway Incident of September 18, 1931, an elaborate contraband network was woven between the northeastern ports of Dalian and Yingkou across the Bohai Gulf, and the shallow shores of the Shandong coast. Once the He-Umezu Agreement was signed in May 1935, establishing a "special political regime" (*teshu zhengzhi*) in Jidong, Eastern Hebei became the scene of enormous smuggling operations, centered on the narcotics trade.[73]

---

[67] Lin Meili, "Kangzhan shiqi de zousi huodong yu zousi shizhen," 14.

[68] Ibid., 5–7.

[69] Ibid., 8.

[70] Lynn Pan, *Tracing It Home, 85.*

[71] Lin Meili, "Kangzhan shiqi de zousi huodong yu zousi shizhen," 8–9.

[72] Report of an American Who Escaped from Peking on May 21, 1943, dated 31/7/43. General William J. Donovan. Selected OSS Documents, 1941–1945. Microfilm, Record Group 226. [File no. 62.]

[73] Li Zhenghua, "'Jiu yiba shibian' zhi 'qi qi shibian' qi jian Riben zai Huabei zousi shulue" [A brief account of smuggling when the Japanese were in Hebei from the "September Eighteenth

Opium and other narcotics were transported into the area from Manchukuo [Manzhouguo] and Chahar [Rehe] where the cultivation of poppies was encouraged by Japanese authorities. The trafficking was in the hands of Japanese and Korean *rōnin* (hoodlums) who became an offensive addition to the local scene after 1935. Smuggling silver out of China through East Hopei [Hebei] reached such levels that it seriously undermined the efforts of the Nanking government to stabilize its monetary system.[74] In addition, to deny the Nanking government the revenues that it desperately needed and in order to bolster Japan's own sagging export market, Japanese authorities connived with the Tongchou [Tongzhou] authorities to look the other way as a veritable flood of goods funneled from Japan through East Hopei to markets in North China untaxed and unregulated.[75] When goods did pass through the customs barriers established by the East Hopei authorities, they were taxed at rates far below those charged by the China Maritime Customs. Reliable statistics are difficult to obtain,[76] but some indication of the scale of the smuggling can be seen in the strong protests delivered to Japan by countries whose loans and indemnities were secured by Chinese customs receipts.[77]

The networks were truly national in scope, though regionally diversified.[78] Just as Jiezhou linked Anhui and Henan, so did Yichang, at the foot of the Yangzi gorges, connect Sichuan with Hunan and other down river provinces that could supply the former with the medicine, cotton thread, and dyes that were otherwise unavailable upstream. The same was true for up river ports such as Wanxian and Badong which funneled salt, wood oil, bristles, and Chinese herbs downstream to be exchanged for cotton yarn, piece goods, sewing materials, and household hardware items.[79]

Jiangxi was an especially important point of origin because in addition to rich and rare mineral supplies (wolfram, antimony, tin, manganese, molybdenum, and silver), it produced a surplus of rice and other agricultural products

---

Incident" to the "July Seventh Incident"], 55–56; OSS Documents R&A No. 2121, Chapter 10, "People and Government in East Asia (A Survey of Conditions in Fuchien, Chekiang, and Kiangsu)." 1 November 1944 (OSS Reel 2, document no. 7), 56. See also Eastman, "Facets of an Ambivalent Relationship," 277–278.

[74] Arthur N. Young, *China's Wartime Finance and Inflation, 1937–1945*, 3–4.

[75] Oliver J. Caldwell, *A Secret War: Americans in China, 1944–1945*, 102.

[76] Lin Meili, "Kangzhan shiqi de zousi huodong yu zousi shizhen," 10; Madancy, "Propaganda vs. Practice," 35; Eastman, "Facets of an Ambivalent Relationship," 278–279; "Trade between Occupied China and Free China," 1; Office of Strategic Services, Research and Analysis Branch, RNA # 2121 East China Coast, Nov. 1, 1944 (OSS reel no. 2, document no. 8), 47.

[77] John Hunter Boyle, *China and Japan at War, 1937–1945: The Politics of Collaboration*, 40.

[78] Lin Meili, "Kangzhan shiqi de zousi huodong yu zousi shizhen," 24 ff.

[79] "Trade between Occupied China and Free China," 1–2.

(tea, ramie fiber, rape seed oil) along with luxury porcelains from the former imperial kilns at Jingdezhen, which the Japanese army occupied.[80] In addition to serving as overseas entrepôts for Jiangxi goods, Zhejiang coastal cities such as Ningbo and Wenzhou ("Little Shanghai") shipped inland large quantities of transportation goods (motor cars, trucks, tires, tools, and gasoline) while less bulky goods came down into southeastern China from the Northwest via Baotou, Lanzhou, and Shaanxi by freight cars of the Beiping-Suiyuan Railway.[81] Smuggled fuel especially attracted Shanghai consumers, where, after Pearl Harbor, there was hardly a drop of gasoline to be found in spite of the Shanghainese's love affair with the automobile. Although many cars' engines quickly were adapted for wood and charcoal combustion, many gasoline burners remained, so that the "new aristocrats" (*xingui*) who had buried gasoline-filled jerry cans in their back gardens were able to make tremendous black market profits.[82]

THE SMUGGLING POLICE

Major Guomindang officials became profiteers through the various trading companies (*maoyi gongsi*) that were set up as fronts for the goods transport offices controlled by Chinese intelligence.[83] That is, wartime bureaucratic capitalism led to private gains while simultaneously affording China's spy masters – and especially General Dai Li, head of military intelligence – ample opportunities to build a huge illicit empire that stretched from Burma and Assam to Yunnan, Guangdong, and Fujian; and that employed over a half million men solely engaged in smuggling gasoline into Free China.[84]

---

[80] Ibid., 3.

[81] Ibid., 1. For other smuggling routes, see Eastman, "Facets of an Ambivalent Relationship," 279–282.

[82] Chen Cunren, *Kangzhan shidai shenghuo shi*, 308.

[83] Lin Meili, "Kangzhan shiqi de zousi huodong yu zousi shizhen," 20–21.

[84] "Trade between Occupied China and Free China," 3–4; Office of Strategic Services, Research and Analysis Branch, RNA # 2121 East China Coast, 1/11/44, (OSS Reel 2, document no. 8), 246–247, 250; OSS XL13558, "China's Intelligence Activities in India," 10/7/45, 2. The coastal smuggling trade was conducted mainly by pirates sailing out of Shenjiamen on Zhoushan Island. Some of these were "puppet pirates" licensed by the Japanese to promote the lucrative opium traffic into Free China and obtain goods such as wood, rice, tung oil, paper, and gold to be sold in the Occupied Zone. On the side they also conveyed passengers from Shanghai to and from ports in Zhejiang, Fujian, and Guangdong. Office of Strategic Services, Research and Analysis Branch, RNA # 2121 East China Coast, "People and Government in East Asia (A Survey of Conditions in Fuchien, Chekiang, and Kiangsu)," 1/11/44, (OSS Reel 2, document no. 7), 41, 58. For Nationalist military involvement in smuggling, see also Eastman, "Facets of an Ambivalent Relationship," 281–282.

Dai Li's smuggling empire was built upon a system of revenue collection enforcement that went back to the formation of a taxation police force during the early 1930s.[85] When Song Ziwen (T. V. Soong) was minister of finance in the winter of 1931–1932, the Nationalist regime had established a Tax Police Force (Shuijing zongtuan).[86] The Tax Police's major rival was the army's Communications Inspection Bureau (Jiaotong jiancha ju), which was then under the thumb of Feng Ti, commander of the Nationalist garrison at Changsha. On October 15, 1938, a disastrous fire broke out at Changsha, disgracing Feng Ti and provoking Chiang Kai-shek to order Feng's execution by a firing squad. The dead officer's Communications Inspection Bureau was immediately taken over by Dai Li, who less than two years later prompted the formation of the Wartime Goods Transport Management Bureau (Zhanshi huoyun guanli ju), also known as the Transport Control Bureau (Yunshu tongzhi ju). General He Yingqin was made chief of the bureau while Dai Li took charge of the Supervisory Office (Jiancha chu) that actually wielded power within the unit by means of more than eighty inspection control points (*jiancha suozhan*) scattered throughout Free China.[87]

This office was covertly designated to conduct the smuggling trade with the enemy and provide another source of financial support for the Bureau of Military Statistics (Juntong). Dai Li's agents established in each of the provinces goods transport management offices (*huoyun guanli chu*), and these offices in turn oversaw a network of goods transport management stations (*huoyun guanli zhan*) that operated under the cover of local businesses (the Xinglong zhuang, Zhenxing zhuang, Xiechang zhuang, and so forth) in collusion with Chinese puppet firms run by the Japanese special services organs.[88] Smuggling, an end in itself, thereby gave the Nationalist resistance apparatus an opportunity to put practically every puppet policeman in Occupied China on General Dai Li's "black" payroll.[89] Moreover, Dai Li's Juntong, which was supplied with

---

[85] C. Lester Walker, "China's Master Spy," 165; *Dai Li zhi si* [The death of Dai Li]. Hong Kong: Xianggang qunzhong chubanshe, n.d., 1.

[86] Song Ziwen originally ordered Zeng Xigui, a West Point graduate, to train the Tax Police regiment. It was said that Chiang Kai-shek took this to be a sign that Song was plotting to seize political power, and so deprived him of command of the Tax Police while appointing H. H. Kong (Kong Xiangxi) minister of finance in Song's stead. Zhu Shikang, "Guanyu Guomindang guanliao ziben de jianwen" [Information about Guomindang bureaucratic capital], 74.

[87] "This bureau has 350 control units and three score inspection units. Tai [Dai] Li issues the permits for the moving of supplies. Transport of people and commodities by road, by railroad, or by airline is under his authority." Adeline Gray, "China's Number Two Man," 15. The chief secretary was Wang Fuzhou, who was later replaced by Lou Guowei. Zhang Weihan,"Dai Li yu 'Juntong ju'," 117; Lin Meili, "Kangzhan shiqi de zousi huodong yu zousi shizhen," 16.

[88] Lin Meili, "Kangzhan shidai de zousi huodong yu zousi shizhen," 16–17.

[89] *Dai Li zhi si*, 2.

Thompson submachine guns and Smith & Wesson revolvers by the OSS-administered Sino-American Cooperative Organization (Zhong-Mei hezuo suo, or SACO), was able to provide its most affluent merchant clients with weapons to give to local police and peace preservation corps in lieu of regular money bribes – further strengthening the Nationalist secret service's clandestine control over territory bound to be contested with the Communists should Civil War ever come.[90]

To that extent, smuggling – which came close to state-controlled trade – was really in the hands of Chinese military authorities such as Generals Dai Li and Tang Enbo, even though civil administrators used American printing presses owned by the Central Bank to counterfeit Northern Japanese military scrip and Wang Jingwei-regime notes to buy goods in Occupied China.[91] For, the goods themselves were eventually smuggled back into the interior by units of the Loyal and Patriotic Army, along with employees of the various military transport management stations, who sold the commodities to the citizens of Free China at a huge profit.[92]

SMUGGLING PREVENTION

The Transport Goods Control Office was an army unit, answering ultimately to the Military Affairs Commission of Chiang Kai-shek's government. But what about the civilian organs charged with restricting and seizing contraband, which was after all such a potentially lucrative source of revenue for the Ministry of Finance? During 1940–1941, British advisers had counseled the Generalissimo to increase the government's income by establishing better smuggling controls.[93]

Chiang Kai-shek accordingly inaugurated a Smuggling Prevention Office (Jisi shu) under the Ministry of Finance employing 60,000 men and directed by Dai Li, himself the biggest smuggler in wartime China.[94] Offices to Control Smuggling were set up in each of the districts ruled by the Guomindang, and these offices in turn supervised inspection and control guard posts (*chaji*

---

[90] Lin Meili, "Kangzhan shidai de zousi huodong yu zousi shizhen," 16, 23.

[91] Dai Li was quite proud of his and Tang Enbo's success as smuggling czars, and he was resentful of the way in which "Kong Caishen [i.e., Kong the God of Finance] . . . looked down upon me as this old Dai Li" because H. H. Kong did not think the secret police chief was capable of making money. Dai Li later unabashedly boasted of his newfound financial skills directly to the *lao touzi* (Chiang Kai-shek) himself. Ibid., 16–17.

[92] Zhang Weihan,"Dai Li yu 'Juntong ju'," 117.

[93] Ibid., 112; Huang Kangyong, "Wo suo zhidao de Dai Li" [The Dai Li that I Knew], 156; Zhang Weihan,"Dai Li yu 'Juntong ju'," 117.

[94] Eastman, "Facets of an Ambivalent Relationship," 277.

suoshao).[95] For the time being this gave Dai Li complete control of the national government's clandestine smuggling apparatus.[96]

> Smuggling control in China (apart from levying of duties, which was done by Customs) was vested in the secret police under Dai Li. In practice, Dai's organization came to "control" a large part of the growing trade with the enemy as its own monopoly, other operators only being allowed to participate if they paid a cut. While many Dai men got rich, the organization itself collected hundreds of millions of dollars, which it used to finance and extend its sinister network. The "trade" became its chief source of funds, which were so great that in 1944 it was estimated that Dai had 500,000 officers, agents, and informers on his payroll.[97]

Dai Li's control over the Smuggling Prevention Office did not go unchallenged. His primary agent assigned to take over the office was Jin Runsheng, who was put in command of the Inspection Unit (Dianyan tuan) and of the Command Unit (Zongtuan) of the Tax Police (Shuijing). However, Sun Liren was unwilling to forfeit his own authority over this key office, and maneuvered to have the unit placed under the Eighth Army, which Sun led. Dai Li responded by establishing a countervailing organization in the first unit of the Tax Police, which was then garrisoned in Sichuan and which was expanded to form a new headquarters along with four separate major brigades (*zongtuan*) under Dai Li's appointees.[98]

An even more telling – and in the end more damaging – challenge came from Chiang Kai-shek's in-laws whose own private engagement in wartime smuggling was exposed to the Generalissimo by Dai Li's Smuggling Prevention Office. Particularly egregious were the contraband activities of David Kong, the son of H. H. Kong who was indicted by Dai Li for smuggling tires and luxury goods across the Burma Road into Free China. At his father's urging, David Kong turned to his aunt, Madame Chiang Kai-shek (Song Meiling), for protection. Dai Li thus found himself up against the entire array of Kongs and Songs, who insisted that the Generalissimo settle the episode in their favor. Chiang Kai-shek therefore was caught between familial claims (the private ✓ interests of the "bureaucratic capitalists" represented in the public's eyes by the Four Great Families) and General Dai's representation of the issue as an affront to the authority of the military regime that now oversaw what had originally

[95] Zhang Weihan, "Dai Li yu 'Juntong ju'," 114–115.
[96] Xu Zongyao, "Zuzhi Juntong Beiping zhan heping qiyi de qianqian houhou," *Wenshi ziliao xuanji* 68.3, 206. See also Roy Stratton, "Navy Guerrilla," 85.
[97] Israel Epstein, *The Unfinished Revolution in China*. 238.
[98] Zhang Weihan, "Dai Li yu 'Juntong ju'," 115.

been under the authority of T. V. Soong and H. H. Kong as Nationalist ministers of finance.[99]

Chiang Kai-shek came down on the side of family, especially since the frequently estranged Songs and Kongs were now united by their common enemy, Dai Li. The Generalissimo first accused General Dai of overstepping his authority by acting out of resentment, and then in July 1943 removed Dai from his command of the Jisi shu (Smuggling Prevention Office), which was turned over to Xuan Tiewu, one of H. H. Kong's men. At the same time, the leadership of the office's provincial control bureaus was shifted and all Juntong (Military Statistics Bureau) personnel were dismissed.[100]

Dai Li's removal from the directorship of the Jisi shu (Smuggling Prevention Office) was misinterpreted by China's American allies as a much broader attack against the excesses of the Military Statistics Bureau. The U.S. embassy in Chongqing reported to the Secretary of State that it was widely believed that "the notorious Tai [Dai] Li, head of the Generalissimo's principal secret political and military police and intelligence organization" had been relieved of his post as a result of: first, "the accumulative effect of arbitrary kidnappings, executions, etc., of agents and employees of highly placed persons, including the execution in the autumn of 1942 of Ling Hsu Liang [Lin Shiliang], head of the Transportation Department of the Central Trust, who instead of using his trucks to evacuate Government supplies from Burma to China, allegedly employed them to bring in 'luxury' goods for high placed persons"; second, conflict with the "corrupt interests" of "high placed persons" arriving from the "organization's corrupt 'smuggling prevention' activities"; third, "bitter rivalry engendered in the Kuomintang's [Guomindang's] secret police, whose main function is the overlapping field of 'dangerous thoughts'; fourth, the breakdown of Dai Li's intelligence organization in the Occupation zone due to successful Japanese counterespionage; and fifth, criticism of Dai Li and his "Gestapo," which Madame Chiang had heard on tour in the United States and which gave her the impression that "Americans believed that Tai [Dai] Li rather than Gissimo actually controlled China through his ruthless utilization of Nazi and Japanese political police methods."[101]

But the loss of control over the Smuggling Prevention Office to civilian authorities hardly crimped Dai Li's operations. For one, he quickly made sure that

---

[99] Ibid.; Huang Kangyong, "Wo suo zhidao de Dai Li," 156–157.

[100] Zhang Weihan, "Dai Li yu 'Juntong ju'," 115–116; Huang Kangyong, "Wo suo zhidao de Dai Li," 156–157.

[101] Atcheson to Secretary of State, Chongqing, 10 Sept. 1943, *Foreign Relations of the United States. Diplomatic Papers, 1943, China*. Washington, D.C.: Government Printing Office, 1957, 112–113.

his trump card – military exigency – would prevail over Kong's reliance upon civilian Ministry of Finance supervision of wartime smuggling. During that same month, July 1943, General Dai placed the headquarters of the Tax Police directly under the Military Affairs Commission and had it renamed the Special Action Army (Biedong jun), which formed eleven special services files or columns (*zongdui*) distributed among each of the war zones of the Guomindang-controlled areas of Free China and assigned especially to supervise and route all ground transportation.[102]

Second, Dai Li reorganized the transportation and communications arms of the Nationalist military into a single unified command responsible for ground patrols, regional inspection stations, radio and postal links, and even aircraft communications. That same July the Military Affairs Commission's Inspection Bureau of the Bureau of Transport Control (Yunshu tongzhi ju jiancha ju) was first revamped as the Water and Land Communications Unified Inspection Office (Shuilu jiaotong tongyi jiancha chu) and then reorganized as the MAC's Communications Inspectorate (Jiaotong xuncha chu) under a Dai Li man, Lieutenant General Ji Zhangjian. Later, in 1945, the Communications Inspectorate was expanded to cover telecommunications (the purview of the former Third Section of Dai Li's Juntong) and air traffic under a special Postal and Aviation Inspection Office (Youhang jiancha chu) directed by Lieutenant General Liu Fan.[103]

Finally, Dai Li shored up his defenses against H. H. Kong and the civilians eager to take over the supervision of smuggling "prevention" by expanding the activities of the Sino-American Cooperative Organization *within* the Ministry of Finance. During 1944 the head of the transportation office in the Wartime Freight Transportation Bureau of the Ministry of Finance was Huang Ronghua. Huang, who had lived for many years in the United States as an overseas Chinese, was also simultaneously head of the communications and transport section of SACO. His job was to look after the fleet of approximately one thousand trucks then in operation all over south China conveying weapons to the guerrillas at the front and returning loaded down with goods purchased from puppet firms in Occupied China.[104]

By 1944–1945 the lading of these vehicles was completely at the discretion of Dai Li, who actually held the position of director of the Freight Transportation

---

[102] Zhang Weihan, "Dai Li yu 'Juntong ju'," 102–103.

[103] Ibid., 113.

[104] Shen Zui, *Juntong neimu* [The inside story of the Military Statistics (Bureau)], 243; Lin Meili, "Kangzhan shiqi de zousi huodong yu zousi shizhen," 16.

Bureau in the Ministry of Finance at the time.[105] As Captain Miles, the deputy head of SACO, explained it:

> Every motor truck had to have a bill of lading showing exactly what was being carried, and, at every barrier, the bill of lading had to be shown and the truck inspected. Hitchhiking was such a prevalent form of graft for truck drivers that it was referred to as "transporting yellow fish" – an expensive delicacy – and General Dai himself was responsible for the controls that were supposed to prevent – and which certainly limited – smuggling and spying.[106]

PUDONG SMUGGLERS

Dai Li's control of smuggling activities in the Shanghai hinterland was closely linked to the activities of the Loyal and Patriotic Army units operating in the area along with other Nationalist guerrillas infiltrated into this region – the Third War Zone – by General Gu Shutong.[107]

After the Battle of Shanghai there had been approximately 13,000 miscellaneous mobile units in this region: 4,000 around Lake Tai under the command of Wang Wei;[108] 7,000 in the immediate vicinity of Shanghai headed by Ge Sen; and 2,500 roaming along both sides of the Nanjing-Shanghai Railroad under Shen Junsheng. This was a hodge-podge force, "not totally devoid of patriotic and heroic elements," but also composed "mainly [of] loafers and brigands with few scruples [who] do not hesitate when the opportunity offers to benefit their own personal ends."[109] Many of these guerrilla fighters, in fact, had been recruited out of the ranks of Du Yuesheng's Green Gang, and were mainly accountable to Dai Li.[110]

---

[105] Walker, "China's Master Spy," 162.

[106] Milton E. Miles, *A Different Kind of War: The Little-Known Story of the Combined Guerrilla Forces Created in China by the U.S. Navy and the Chinese during World War II*, 37. See also "Talk by Admiral Miles before the Conference of the New York State Association of Police Chiefs, Schenectady, New York, July 24, 1957," in Milton E. Miles, Personal Papers, Hoover Archives. Stanford, California, Box 3.

[107] Yung-fa Chen, *Making Revolution: The Communist Movement in Eastern and Central China, 1937–1945*, 37; Chen Cunren, *Kangzhan shidai shenghuo shi*, 328.

[108] "Po Hang Sheng," OSS XL 13215, 19/7/45, Office of Strategic Services, U.S. Army. U.S. National Archives, Military Reference Division.

[109] Enclosure in Shanghai dispatch to His Majesty's Ambassador, no. 632, 22/11/39, F1005, FO371–24682, BFOR.

[110] Marshall, "Opium and the Politics of Gangsterism in Nationalist China," 41. The majority of these guerrilla units – called *youji dui*, "roving strike forces" – were described in the cliché of the times as "roving without striking" (*you er bu ji*). Chen Cunren, *Kangzhan shidai shenghuo shi*, 328.

Separate from these but of equal or greater importance when it came to smuggling goods in and out of Shanghai was the Nationalist guerrilla apparatus in wartime Pudong, across the river from Shanghai proper. The leader of the second brigade (*er dadui*) of the Loyal and Patriotic Army (LPA) for eastern Pudong was, as mentioned above, Lieutenant Colonel Zhang Junliang, a fifty-five-year-old native of the region who had been an illiterate petty merchant before the war. According to an American OSS informant who spent four months with the brigade:

> The major part of Pootung [Pudong] is controlled by Lt. Col. Chang [Zhang]. He controls east Pootung which is the area fronting the Pacific Ocean. West of the railway in Pootung is controlled by the Japs and the south by a Nanking puppet head who, however, is in an "understanding" with Lt. Col. Chang.[111] There are no Japs in the guerilla [sic] area [in] E. Pootung and it is recognized by them as an "uncooperative" area.[112]

Initially there had been numerous armed clashes between the Nationalist guerrillas and the Japanese and puppets, who only exercised full control over a thin coastal strip in western Pudong where they located their food warehouses and prisoner-of-war camps near the major ferry crossings.[113] Further inland, Pudong guerrillas had managed to wipe out an entire detachment of Nanjing-regime police and a Japanese gendarme commander in early July 1941; they conducted mass attacks on a number of villages in the area thereafter.[114] But after Japanese regulars "pacified" the area, which was mainly devoted to truck farming, open warfare dissipated. On the side of the occupiers, village clan heads replaced Nationalist magistrates and local peace preservation corps units were reformed as village police units, ostensibly loyal to the puppet administration in downtown Shanghai.[115]

As far as the LPA guerrillas were concerned, however, these newly recognized village leaders only nominally acknowledged the rule of the Japanese and of the Nanjing regime.[116] Not only did Lieutenant Colonel Zhang Junliang have an "understanding" with the puppet commander in southern Pudong that the LPA would receive advance notice of Japanese military raids; the local police chiefs in western and eastern Pudong agreed never to assail Zhang's bases along the

---

[111] For lack of troops, the Japanese were only able to exercise effective control over the thin strip of land in western Pudong facing on to the Huangpu River. Ibid., 328.

[112] Gray, "The Loyal Patriotic Army," 21.

[113] Chen Cunren, *Kangzhan shidai shenghuo shi*, 328.

[114] *The China Weekly Review* 19/7/41, 221.

[115] Gray, "The Loyal Patriotic Army," 21.

[116] Ibid., 26–27.

seacoast.[117] He had, in effect, his own clandestine local government: "Chang has a radio station; he is in charge of the local schools using Chungking textbooks; he dispenses justice to robbers and criminals – they are shot if guilty as Chang has no time to bother with prisons."[118]

The main purpose of the eastern Pudong LPA, however, was not to protect Colonel Zhang's guerrilla (some might say "bandit") government.[119] Its wartime goal was to keep smuggling and communications routes open between Shanghai and Zhejiang, which was now the main passageway to inland China. Although the Japanese did not realize it, the LPA directed virtually all of the junks traversing Hangzhou Bay. Twelve of these were ocean-going junks that crossed the bay to Yuyao (near Ningbo), typically leaving the Pudong coast at midnight and reaching the mouth of the Qiantang River by daylight. Yuyao, where the LPA had a radio station, was a harbor filled with unused junks among which the smugglers could easily anchor themselves without attracting Japanese attention. Some of the junks were even licensed by the Japanese as merchant vessels permitted to transport harmless commodities but forbidden to ship rice.[120] Licensed junks were most often used to transport papers or guerrilla heads; if searched, the master threw the papers aboard and the guerrillas posed as harmless boatmen.[121]

Before the attack on Pearl Harbor, Colonel Zhang had used American-owned boats to ship gasoline to Zhejiang.[122] The fuel was supplied by an American oil firm supposedly wishing to help Free China. The LPA junks also shipped rubber tires and rice for the Nationalist forces. After December 8, 1941, tires and gasoline were nearly impossible to obtain; Zhang was able to get rice at some risk from Songjiang. That, plus the seizure by the Japanese of the newly reopened East China trade route up the Qiantang River to Jinhua in the spring of 1942,

---

[117] The Japanese only made three raids during the time that Gray was in the area. Col. Zhang had to move from place to place on his motorcycle, constantly changing his headquarters for fear of being betrayed to his enemies by a spy; but for six years he was never taken into custody and the Wang Jingwei regime was totally unable to collect taxes in his domain. Ibid., 21, 24.

[118] Ibid., 25.

[119] OSS Documents R&A No. 2121, Chapter 10, "People and Government in East Asia (A Survey of Conditions in Fuchien, Chekiang, and Kiangsu)," 1/11/44, (OSS Reel 2, doc. no. 7), 56.

[120] A traveling merchant had to have the approval of one's *baojia* head, a guarantee from a merchant company, and along with i.d. card and smallpox vaccination certificate a travel document purchased from the Japanese military. The registered wooden sailboats that dominated the Zhejiang coastal trade had to follow routes regulated by the Japanese navy, which burned and sank stragglers. In addition, trading vessels had to pay off the pirates controlling the coastal zone by purchasing their chiefs' namecards for "free" passage. Schoppa, "Structure, Dynamics, and Impacts," 11, 19–20.

[121] Gray, "Loyal Patriotic Army," 23.

[122] Schoppa, "Structure, Dynamics, and Impacts," 14.

hampered the Zhang brothers' work considerably.[123] Even more constraining, however, were the controls governing egress into Shanghai proper, imposed by the Japanese and puppet troops in charge of establishing a cordon of "peace zones" around the city.[124]

MODEL PEACE ZONES

In November 1940 the deputy chief of staff of the imperial headquarters in Tokyo, Lieutenant General Sawada Shigeru, had been transferred to eastern China to command the Thirteenth Army. Wang Jingwei's puppet troops were still unable to control the countryside. General Sawada was eager to pacify Shanghai's hinterland, and so turned to Lieutenant Colonel Haruke Yoshitane, a counter-insurgency specialist on Major General Kagesa Sadaaki's staff, for a pacification plan. Colonel Haruke had closely studied Zeng Guofan and Chiang Kai-shek's suppression campaigns, and he proposed the establishment of "model peace zones" (*mohanteki wahei chiku*) with the help of Chinese collaborators who would build a primary or grassroots-level political system based upon "self-government" (*jichi*), "self-defense" (*jiei*), and "economic self-improvement" (*jisei*). The model peace zone would be created, after Japanese mop-up operations, by walling off the subjugated area with bamboo palisades, electrified barbed wire, and watch towers.[125] Within the zone, there would be created *baojia* with Chinese collaborators, a police system, a secret service system, and a self-defense corps.[126]

The first model peace zone – which came under the aegis of *qingxiang yundong* (clearing the villages movement) – was to comprise the five counties of Changshu, Jiangyin, Kunshan, Wuxi, and Taicang, just west of Greater Shanghai. Although this plan received the support of General Hata Shunroku, China Theater Commander, the Wang Jingwei regime wavered. Puppet Shanghai officials preferred free smuggling to the seizure of food and goods by the Japanese army; they also feared reassignment to the countryside.[127] A rural pacification committee was not formed until May 22, 1941, by which time initiative for the venture had slipped into the hands of Police Minister Li

---

[123] See, for the Jinhua trade route through Zhejiang to Jiangxi: Lin Meili, "Kangzhan shidai de zousi huodong yu zousi shizhen," 26–27; and Schoppa, "Structure, Dynamics, and Impacts," 20.

[124] Schoppa, "Structure, Dynamics, and Impacts," 22, 29.

[125] John W. Dower, *War without Mercy: Race and Power in the Pacific War*, 43.

[126] Chen, *Making Revolution*, 81–82.

[127] Ibid., 95.

Shiqun, who had masterminded the assassination wars in Shanghai between his notorious henchmen at 76 Jessfield Road and the agents of Dai Li.[128]

Working under Colonel Haruke, who installed an office in Suzhou, Li Shiqun brought in some of his agents from Shanghai to form an intelligence network and trained five thousand cadres and police, most of whom came down from North China to collaborate with Li Shiqun and puppet governor Gao Guanwu. With the help of Japanese soldiers, the puppet police and cadres suppressed most of the Guomindang LPA and at least one-quarter of the Communist New Fourth Army units in the zone.[129] Households were registered under the *baojia* system, and all males between ages fourteen and forty-five were enrolled in a self-defense corps, which was not, however, allowed to carry guns on patrol.[130] In the end, as Japanese military fortunes tumbled elsewhere, the local collaborators who were crucial to the system ceased cooperating, but at least until late 1942 the model peace zone system constituted a rural prototype for parallel control mechanisms in urban centers such as Shanghai.[131]

By early September 1941, in fact, the Japanese had succeeded in bringing order to most parts of the delta pacification area, even though they had to cope with the poor discipline of puppet troops whom the Japanese called "half-reformed bandits."[132] The puppet forces requisitioned grain, looted in disguise, extorted bribes at checkpoints, conspired with Nationalist guerrillas, illegally confiscated travelers' goods, and connived at smuggling – for a price.[133]

DEMON GATES

Precisely because of the hazards of smuggling and the constant need to bribe the sentries who guarded the "demon gates" at the various barbed wire search points surrounding the city, the price of peddlers' rice was continually mounting. If the hucksters were spotted or recognized by the Japanese or puppet police, then

---

[128] Wen-hsin Yeh, "Dai Li and the Liu Geqing Affair: Heroism in the Chinese Secret Service During the War of Resistance," 553; Shi Yuanhua, "Li Shiqun," 436–441.

[129] Li Shiqun also extended their counter-insurgency *qingxiang* (cleaning up the villages) activities north to Baoshan and across the Yangzi into Jiangbei. *Baoshan xianzhi* [Baoshan county gazetteer]. Compiled by Shanghai shi Baoshan qu difangzhi bianzuan weiyuanhui. Shanghai: Shanghai renmin chubanshe, 1992, 22:721.

[130] Chen, *Making Revolution*, 83–88.

[131] Ibid., 97.

[132] Ibid., 94–95.

[133] Ibid., 89–90; Zhang Yuexiang, Lu Kangchang, Li Yijun, "Shanghai jinjiao nongmin kang-Ri douzheng pianduan" [Episodes of the peasants' anti-Japanese struggle in Shanghai suburbs] in People's Political Consultative Conference, Shanghai Municipal Committee, Wenshi Ziliao Working Committee, ed., *Kang-Ri feng yun lu* [Record of the anti-Japanese storm]. Shanghai: Shanghai renmin chubanshe, 1985, 29–30.

they had to pay "taxes" to the patrols or constables, who thereby earned a "new livelihood" through the illegal trade. Often, the bravest rice smugglers, when it came to facing the sentries and barbed wire, were young women who were frequently mauled by the Alsatian police dogs guarding the "gate."[134]

Once inside Shanghai's boundaries, the rice smugglers had to hawk their wares clandestinely through the streets and lanes of the city in order to avoid being arrested. When householders wanted to buy grain, they would invite the grain peddlers into their houses and lock the doors behind them. After they settled on a price, the hucksters, over half of whom were women, would turn their backs, fish around in their drawers, and pull out a secret pocket or bag or even a kind of money belt or waistcoat worn under a woman's gown, which were carrying places for the rice. Then the grain would change hands for money and the smugglers would be on their way.[135]

Back in the model peace zone, native residents still had to have a citizen identification card in order to get through the Japanese and puppet checkpoints. To ship goods in and out meant getting elaborate approvals from the Japanese special services organization, among other agencies, in each district. The overall effect of this clampdown was to depress trade as peasants fell back upon economic self-sufficiency. At the same time, Japanese and puppet merchants used their own privileges to depress the price of blockaded grains and cotton. The cost of imported fertilizers, machines, and irrigation pumps became correspondingly dearer; the result was autarky. Resorting to barter and homespun, peasants used incense instead of matches, and made their own soy sauce, rice wine, and cooking oil.[136]

RICE WORMS

The Japanese used rice as a weapon to dominate Shanghai much as Hitler used the control of food supplies to subjugate Europe.[137] That is, Chinese rice grown

---

[134] Chen, *Making Revolution*, 61, 196–197; Tao Juyin, *Tianliang qian de gudao*, 65.
[135] Tao Juyin, *Tianliang qian de gudao*, 65–66.
[136] Chen, *Making Revolution*, 90.
[137] *Relief and Rehabilitation in China*. Government of the Republic of China. Document No. R&R-1, Sept. 1944, 1; Ernest G. Heppner, *Shanghai Refuge: A Memoir of the World War II Jewish Ghetto*, 77, 114; Christopher Simpson, *Blowback: America's Recruitment of Nazis and its Effects on the Cold War*, 14. Let me hasten to point out, however, that so far there is scanty evidence to substantiate such a conscious overall Japanese plan, as Professor Henriot has pointed out to me. The Japanese preyed on the lower Yangzi area, but mostly out of concern for the supply of their own troops in China and, to a lesser extent, for Japan's own population. The most direct impact of Japanese food control policies after 1941 was to force many residents to leave. In Professor Henriot's words, this was domination over an increasingly empty shell.

in the provinces was used to feed the Japanese army or the civilian population in Japan. Cities such as Tianjin and Shanghai, therefore, had been living on rice imported from Indochina, so that "when Japan secured control of Indochina's entire output of nearly six million tons, she naturally came into possession of a weapon with which to force 'cooperation' upon Occupied China."[138] This weapon was explicitly deployed as a means of social control.[139] For example, there were five cases of Japanese being shot between September 29 and October 18, 1940. In retaliation, the Japanese Military Police sealed off the lanes of suspected areas, and "subjected [them] to a vigorous blockade, which in some sections was sustained long enough, according to current reports, to cause several deaths through starvation."[140]

Little wonder, then, that puppet rice brokers were regarded as parasites – "grain boring worms" (*zhu mi chong*) who fed off of the trade in food. Two of the most despised figures during the Occupation were Hou Dachun, head of the Grain Guild (Miye gonghui) and provincial Grain Bureau (Liangshi ju); and Hu Zheng, director of the food purchasing office for Suzhou, Changzhou, Songjiang, and Taicang districts.[141] Before the War of Resistance broke out, Hou Dachun had been one of the top leaders of the Commercial Press in Shanghai. Hu Zheng, who was married to Hou's sister-in-law Wu Yiqing, had gone to work for the puppet Water Management Bureau (Shui chan guanli ju) of the Bureau of Grain (Liangshi ju). The two men used their wives' connections to forge alliances with the Wang Jingwei regime once the puppets took power.[142]

Hou Dachun's wife, Wu Yunqing, for example, was a sworn sister to She Aizhen, the spouse of secret service head Li Shiqun. Hu Zheng's wife, Wu Yiqing, had a family relationship with Zhou Naiwen, deputy department chief (*bucizhang*) of the Grain Bureau. Using these ties, Hou Dachun secured his own reappointment as an editor at the Commercial Press. Then, at the recommendation of the puppet minister of education, Li Shengwu, Hou was quickly

[138] Vanya Oakes, *White Man's Folly*, 360.

[139] Professor Henriot has wisely noted that the Japanese did seal off areas and force the population to starvation – but only in reprisals to acts of terrorism. That is, he does not believe that the Japanese used the disbursement of food as a general tool of control. In his words, "this was a punishment to dissuade the population to help or support terrorists, but this cannot be presented as a systematic policy that applied to the population at large."

[140] FO371/24663, BFOR.

[141] Hou Dachun was also a major figure in the Shanghai Nationalist Party branch between 1927–1937. He had rebelled against the "CC" clique-dominated GMD apparatus and was active in the struggles for the control of trade unions during the 1931–1932 interlude. (My thanks to Professor Henriot for this information.)

[142] Chen Cunren, *Kangzhan shidai shenghuo shi*, 61; Ji Xilin and Zhao Tianyi, "Yi jiu si san nian 'liangshi tanwu an' zhenxiang" [The inside story about the 1943 'Grain Corruption Case'], 289.

promoted to the post of bureau chief (*juzhang*) of the Jiangsu Provincial Grain Bureau. Before long Hu Zheng was put in charge of the Grain and Vegetable Purchasing Office (Mi liang cai gou bai banshichu) of Suzhou, Changzhou, Songjiang, and Taicang districts.[143]

Needless to say, Hou Dachun took advantage of his newly won position to profit from the rice trade.[144] As a purchasing agent for the Japanese army he was able both to connive illicitly with corrupt grain brokers and to force peasants to sell their produce at a lower-than-market price.[145] Then, when he delivered the staple to the Japanese quartermasters and found them short of currency, he was quick to accept partial repayment in the form of cigarettes, coal, and other black market items that he in turn put out for sale through the merchants with whom he and Hu Zheng came into daily contact. Commercial transactions were always colored, in this regard, by the fact that the two men were backed up by the Japanese special service groups and by 76 Jessfield Road. In April 1943, for example, Hou Dachun engaged in proxy hoarding by buying one thousand piculs (*shi*, or about 150,000 pounds) of brown rice at the current market price from Shi Kaitan, a major grain merchant from Qingpu county. Hou refused to pay for or take delivery of the grain on the spot, however, preferring to have the merchant hold on to the rice himself. When the grain rose in price the following month, Hou paid Shi off at the previous rate, sold at market prices, and pocketed the 400,000 yuan in profits for himself. Knowing who stood behind Hou Dachun, the Qingpu merchant dared not question the deal.[146]

Hou Dachun enjoyed a host of similar arrangements with other "treacherous merchants" (*jianshang*), and he gradually built up his own chain of warehouses in which to store the hoarded grain. Enraged by his exploitation, local rice growers bided their time until Hou's luck ran out with the defeat of the Japanese. Then they reported him to the Nationalist authorities, who discovered Hou's many warehouses full of unreported white rice. When he was arrested and interrogated, Hou revealed a smuggling and black market network of even vaster scope, implicating dozens of colleagues including the highly respected and well thought of Songjiang figure, Geng Jizhi, who turned a pistol on himself before he could be seized.[147] Hou Dachun was eventually tried by the Central Special Court (Zhongyang tebie fating) and then executed by a Nationalist

---

[143] Ji Xilin and Zhao Tianyi, "Yi jiu si san nian 'liangshi tanwu an' zhenxiang," 289.
[144] Chen Cunren, *Kangzhan shidai shenguo shi*, 250–251.
[145] Ji Xilin and Zhao Tianyi, "Yi jiu si san nian 'liangshi tanwu an' zhenxiang," 290.
[146] Ibid., 289–290.
[147] Geng had served as French language secretary of the Shanghai Municipal Government. Chen Cunren, *Kangzhan shidai shenghuo shi*, 152.

shooting squad at the Jade Flower Terrace (Yuhuatai) killing ground outside of Nanjing.[148]

PARADOXICAL UNITY

During the summer of 1944, the southeastern coastal provinces of China continued to experience food deficiencies, but, even though the puppet government's grain purchasing system was a relative failure, Jiangsu as a whole actually enjoyed surpluses (see Table 5.5).[149] Partly as a result of the Japanese capture of Hunan with its grain supplies, the monthly adult rice ration in Shanghai was raised to 4.3 kilograms or 9.5 pounds.[150] Since a moderate daily allowance was one pound per day per individual, and since the population of Shanghai was estimated in 1944 to number 3.5 to 5 million people, there was still a tremendous discrepancy between the normal daily requirement and the amount of rice actually available.[151] In fact, during January 1943 there was considerable discussion of the need to inaugurate, in the place of "universal rationing" (*fuhen haikyu*), a system of "priority rationing" (*jutenshugi haikyu*) that would allot rations differentially according to place of residence, occupation, status, age, and gender.[152] By August 1944, the food control authorities had held a series of meetings to discuss ways of increasing their control over the supply of wartime staples.[153]

These meetings were convened in part because of severe inundations in the Changzhou and Luxi area in the lower Yangzi delta. The flooding, together with a marked reduction in the supply of fertilizers, had led to a 10 percent drop below the normal grain harvest, which in Jiangsu usually amounted to

---

[148] Ji Xilin and Zhao Tianyi, "Yi jiu si san nian 'liangshi tanwu an' zhenxiang," 289.

[149] Tang Zhenchang and Shen Hengchun, eds., *Shanghai shi*, 836.

[150] Office of Strategic Services, Research and Analysis Branch, RNA #2121 East China Coast, 1/11/44 (OSS reel no. 2, document no. 8), 38.

[151] Ibid., 47–48. According to military reports, the population of Shanghai had returned to prewar levels by December 1943. Ibid., 49. These estimates of food need based upon population were not very reliable. See, e.g., "Current Food, Coal, and Transportation Situation Prevailing in China," R & A No. 3433, Department of State Interim Research and Intelligence Service, 2 January 1946, Appendix 2, 4.

[152] "Shanghai shokuryo haikyu seido no jutenshugi ka ni kansuru iken to kengi" [Opinions and suggestions about the priority systematization of Shanghai's food rationing system], in *Chugoku seikei* [Chinese political economy], vol. 5. Shanghai: *Chugoku seiji keizai kenkyujo kan* [Publication of the research institute on Chinese politics and economy], March 1943, 111–116, 119. The benchmark for the system would have been a basic monthly allotment of 1 *dou* and 5 *sheng* of rice, which would nearly have met the average monthly need of 1 *dou* and 6–7 *sheng* of rice per capita.

[153] *Shenbao* 16/8/44, 2, and 28/8/44, 2.

Table 5.5 *Estimated Food Surpluses and Deficiencies – Three East Coast Provinces*

Food	Fujian (estimated population 11,755,000)		Zhejiang (estimated population 16,093,000)		Jiangsu (estimated population 37,000,000)	
	Surplus or deficiency (in metric tons)	Percent of production	Surplus or deficiency (in metric tons)	Percent of production	Surplus or deficiency (in metric tons)	Percent of production
Rice	−28,800	−1	+64,500	+3	+400,000	+10
Wheat	−69,450	−14	−130,650	−22	+841,000	+33.6
Barley	−15,800	−9	−5,500	−1	+318,500	+27.7
Corn	−100	−5	−2,850	−5	+38,800	+6.0
Gaoliang (sorghum)	0	0	−150	−5	+239,700	+51.6
Millet	−50	−0.5	−50	−0.4	0	0
Sweet potatoes	+78,300	+5	+11,530	+8	+449,00	+27.2
Soy beans	−18,100	−26	−11,100	−18	+168,900	+26.0
Total (expressed in rice equivalent)	−166,200				+2,160,400	

Source: Office of Strategic Services, Research and Analysis Branch, R&A #2121 East China Coast, Nov. 1, 1944 (OSS reel no. 2, document no. 8), p. 55.

3,579,000 tons of rice and 2,500,000 tons of wheat.[154] Still, by 1945 the popular perception was that the rice crisis was at least momentarily over.[155] "As for the Shanghainese eating rice, even though there was always some confusion over drawing household rations, by this time the grain market had settled down despite occasional fluctuations in price."[156]

Paradoxically, as some admitted at the time, the "treacherous" speculators and war profiteers had positively stabilized the Shanghai grain market precisely because of the ability of the much-despised "grain boring worms" to smuggle food into the city.[157] In one sense, therefore, despite the city's initial divisions, the "new aristocrats" had unified the metropolis with its hinterland beyond the Japanese barbed wire fences and the nightly patrols of the puppet Peace Preservation Corps.[158] We are left, therefore, not only with a depiction of Shanghai smuggling that underscores the rifts between the new rich and old poor, between active collaborators and passive resistants, between the well-fed and the poorly clothed; but a representation that also affirms the unity of collective urban identity, of shared victimhood under foreign occupation, and of common deprivation when all but the most favored had to make do with brown rice and oatmeal wine, hand-me-downs and patched coats.[159]

We are left as well with many more questions than this essay can possibly answer. How massive was the transfer of the coastal urban population to the Southwest, and how did this wartime migration affect the "black economy" that flourished in order to feed and clothe the refugees of Free China while sustaining the subsistence of Shanghai's own swollen refugee population? Did the rise of a prodigious contraband trade that obviously fattened the purses of the armies of the night – Juntong secret agents, Japanese military policemen, Sichuan trading company entrepreneurs, Yokohama speculators – also stimulate growth in several critical sectors of the national economy?[160] How did the

---

[154] Office of Strategic Services, Research and Analysis Branch, RNA # 2121 East China Coast, 1/11/44 (OSS reel no. 2, document no. 8), 38, 47.

[155] Office of Strategic Services, U.S. Army. U.S. National Archives, Military Reference Division. Document 2 in Reel 3, no title, no date; Appendix 2, 7.

[156] Chen Cunren, *Kangzhan shidai shenghuo shi*, 228; "Current Food, Coal, and Transportation Situation Prevailing in China," R & A No. 3433, Department of State Interim Research and Intelligence Service, 2 January 1946, Appendix 2, 4.

[157] Chen Cunren, *Kangzhan shidai shenghuo shi*, 61; Tao Juyin, *Tianliang qian de gudao*, 65.

[158] "War transformed the Shanghai system of space, making proximate areas in reality 'hinterland' and distant areas 'near.' War destroyed the natural regional urban hierarchy, making small fishing villages more essential to Shanghai and the continuation of the system than cities and county seats, making Wenzhou closer and more essential to Shanghai than Ningbo, that longtime commercial partner." Schoppa, "Structure, Dynamics, and Impacts," 32.

[159] Si Yi, "Gudao de yinxiang," 269; Chen Cunren, *Kangzhan shidai shenghuo shi*, 223–224.

[160] Lin Meili, "Kangzhan shiqi de zousi huodong yu zousi shizhen," 9.

burgeoning of these clandestine empires affect China and Japan once the War of Resistance was over? Was the fundamental commercial and financial centrality of prewar Shanghai so displaced by the new trading and smuggling networks as to prefigure the relatively passive economic role assigned to the city by Chairman Mao and the Communist Party after May 1949? That is to say, was the wartime "enclosure" of Shanghai by the Japanese Imperial Army the beginning of the end of the city's paramountcy as the metropolitan center of China's national culture – an outcome that was not just politically determined by the Communists' peasant armies in 1949, but economically and culturally fashioned much earlier as prewar commercial networks yielded to new trading channels, and Shanghai "Modern" gave way to rural nativism with its strong anti-urban bias?

And, finally, was not the thrill of national victory over the invading enemy tempered – if not compromised – by the awareness that the Japanese had brought a fair degree of law and order to Shanghai after all? As Chen Cunren remarked in his wartime memoir:

> After the Japanese occupied the International Settlement, public order was absolutely excellent. There's no need to mention the absence of robbery and looting; even petty thieves kept silent and lay low. The murderous activities of [the puppet secret police at] Number 76, which the city people had come to detest in ordinary times, ceased now in the International Settlement with [the secret police] lowering their flags and silencing their drums. Because of these advantages [of the Japanese Occupation], city folk felt much more at peace.[161]

Like the recovery of Chinese national sovereignty over the concessions, or reflections upon the comparative advantages and disadvantages of wholesale smuggling, the momentary abatement of social disorder under Japanese rule left the citizens of the city with nothing but mixed feelings. They had outlasted the conquerors from abroad, but carpetbaggers from inland Chongqing were soon to arrive, filled with self-righteous disdain for the Shanghai survivors compelled to stay behind.

BIBLIOGRAPHY

John Hunter Boyle, *China and Japan at War, 1937–1945: The Politics of Collaboration.* Stanford: Stanford University Press, 1972.
BFOR – British Foreign Office Records. London: Her Majesty's Public Record Office.

---

[161] Chen Cunren, *Kangzhan shidai shenghuo shi*, 248.

Oliver J. Caldwell, *A Secret War: Americans in China, 1944–1945.* Carbondale and Edwardsville: Southern Illinois University Press, 1984.

Lau Kit-ching Chan, *China, Britain and Hong Kong, 1895–1945.* Shatin, Hong Kong: Chinese University of Hong Kong, 1990.

Chen Cunren, *Kangzhan shidai shenghuo shi* [A history of life during the War of Resistance]. Hong Kong: Changxing shuju, n.d. [preface dated 1975].

Yung-fa Chen, *Making Revolution: The Communist Movement in Eastern and Central China, 1937–1945.* Berkeley, Los Angeles, London: University of California Press, 1986.

Hsi-sheng Ch'i, *Nationalist China at War: Military Defeats and Political Collapse, 1937–45.* Ann Arbor: University of Michigan Press, 1982.

China Weekly Review.

Dagong bao (L'Impartiel). ca. 1914–.

Dai Li zhi si [The death of Dai Li], edited by Xianggang qunzhong chubanshe. Hong Kong: Xianggang qunzhong chubanshe, n.d.

General William J. Donovan, Selected OSS Documents, 1941–1945. Microfilm, Record Group 226.

John W. Dower, *War without Mercy: Race and Power in the Pacific War.* New York: Pantheon Books, 1986.

Bùi Minh Dûng, "Japan's Role in the Vietnamese Starvation of 1944–45," *Modern Asian Studies* 29.3: 573–618 (1995).

Lloyd E. Eastman, "Facets of an Ambivalent Relationship: Smuggling, Puppets, and Atrocities During the War, 1937–1945," in Akira Iriye, ed., *The Chinese and the Japanese: Essays in Political and Cultural Interactions.* Princeton: Princeton University Press, 1980, 275–303.

Israel Epstein, *The Unfinished Revolution in China.* Boston: Little, Brown, 1947.

Fang Xianting, "Lun liangshi tongzhi" [Food controls], in Fang Xianting, ed., *Zhanshi Zhongguo jingji yanjiu* [Studies on the Chinese wartime economy]. Chongqing: Shangwu yinshu guan, 1941, 68–72.

Foreign Relations of the United States. Diplomatic Papers, 1943, China. Washington, D.C.: Government Printing Office, 1957.

Poshek Fu, "Struggle to Entertain: The Political Ambivalence of Shanghai's Film Industry Under the Japanese Occupation, 1941–45," in Law Kar, ed., *Cinema of Two Cities: Hong Kong – Shanghai.* Hong Kong: Urban Council, 1994, 39–62.

Adeline Gray, "China's Number Two Man," RG226, entry 139, box 183, folder 2449, OSS Files, National Archives, Washington, D.C.

Adeline Gray, "The Loyal Patriotic Army: A Guerilla [sic] Organization Under Tai Li," RG226, entry 139, box 183, folder 2449, OSS Files, National Archives, Washington D.C., pp. 18–29.

Ernest G. Heppner, *Shanghai Refuge: A Memoir of the World War II Jewish Ghetto.* Lincoln: University of Nebraska Press, 1993.

Hu Liuzhang, "Kangzhan huiyi ji duanpian zhi huixiang" [An extremely brief recollection of memories of the War of Resistance], *Zhuanji wenxue* [Biographical literature], 76.4 (1986): 52.

Huang Kangyong, "Wo suo zhidao de Dai Li" [The Dai Li that I Knew], in Wenshi ziliao yanjiu weiyuanhui, eds., *Zhejiang wenshi ziliao xuanji*, no. 23, pp. 152–170. *Neibu* publication. Zhejiang: Renmin chubanshe, 1982.

Ji Xilin and Zhao Tianyi, "Yi jiu si san nian 'liangshi tanwu an' zhenxiang" [The inside story about the 1943 'Grain Corruption Case'], in *Wang wei zhengquan neimu* [The inside story of the Wang puppet regime]. Jiangsu wenshi ziliao, fascicle 29. Nanjing: Jiangsu wenshi ziliao, 1989, pp. 289–295.

Li Jilin, comp., *Kangzhan wenxue qikan xuanji* [Compilation of literary periodicals from the War of Resistance]. Nangong, Hebei: Shumu wenxian chubanshe, n.d., vol. 1.

Li Zhenghua, "'Jiu yiba shibian' zhi 'qi qi shibian' qi jian Riben zai Huabei zousi shulue" [A brief account of smuggling when the Japanese were in Hebei from the "September Eighteenth Incident" to the "July Seventh Incident"], *Yunnan jiaoyu xueyuan xuebao* [Journal of the Yunnan Teachers College], 1: 55–60 (1991).

Lin Meili, "Kangzhan shidai de zousi huodong yu zousi shizhen" [Smuggling activities and smuggling towns during the War of Resistance]. Paper presented at the Symposium on the Sixtieth Anniversary of the July Seven War of Resistance (Jinian qiqi kangzhan liushi zhounian xueshu yantaohui), Academia Sinica, Taiwan, July 18–20, 1997.

Albert T. Lu, "The Unabated Smuggling Situation in North China," *Information Bulletin* 1.11: 1–30 (Aug. 21, 1936), published by the Council of International Affairs, Nanking, China.

Hanchao Lu, "The Workers and Neighborhoods of Modern Shanghai, 1911–1949." Ph.D. thesis, University of California, Los Angeles, 1991.

Hanchao Lu, "Away from Nanjing Road: Small Stores and Neighborhood Life in Modern Shanghai," *Journal of Asian Studies*, 54.1: 93–123 (February 1995).

Joyce Ann Madancy, "Propaganda vs. Practice: Official Involvement in the Opium Trade in China, 1927–1945." M.A. thesis, Cornell University, 1983.

Jonathan Marshall, "Opium and the Politics of Gangsterism in Nationalist China, 1927–1945," *Bulletin of the Committee of Concerned Asian Scholars* 8.3: 19–48 (July–Sept. 1977).

Brian G. Martin, "Resistance and Cooperation: Du Yuesheng and the Politics of the Shanghai United Committee, 1940–1945." Paper prepared for the conference "Wartime Shanghai (1937–1945)," Lyon, France, October 15–17, 1997.

Kathryn Meyers and Terry Parsinnen, *Power and Profit*. Unpublished manuscript, Lafayette College, 1997.

Milton E. Miles, *A Different Kind of War: The Little-Known Story of the Combined Guerrilla Forces Created in China by the U.S. Navy and the Chinese during World War II*. Garden City, NY: Doubleday, 1967.

Milton E. Miles, personal papers, Hoover Archives. Stanford, California.

Nanjing shi dang'anguan, eds., *Shenxun Wang wei hanjian bilu* [Records of the trials of the Wang (Jingwei) puppet traitors]. Yangzhou: Jiangsu guji chubanshe, 1992. 2 volumes.

Vanya Oakes, *White Man's Folly*. Boston: Houghton Mifflin, 1943.

Office of Strategic Services, Research and Analysis Branch, RNA # 2121 East China Coast, November 1, 1944 (OSS reel no. 2, document no. 8).

Office of Strategic Services, U.S. Army. U.S. National Archives, Military Reference Division.

OSS Documents R&A No. 2121, Chapter 10, "People and Government in East Asia (A Survey of Conditions in Fuchien, Chekiang, and Kiangsu). November 1, 1944 (OSS Reel 2, document no. 7), pp. 54–66.

Lynn Pan, *Tracing It Home: A Chinese Family's Journey from Shanghai.* Tokyo: Kodansha International, 1992.

Relief and Rehabilitation in China. Government of the Republic of China. Document No. R&R-1, September 1944.

Laurence K. Rosinger, *China's Wartime Politics, 1937–1944.* Princeton: Princeton University Press, 1944.

Alain Roux, "The Guomindang and the Workers of Shanghai (1938–1948): The Rent in the Fabric." Paper presented at the conference on China's Mid-century Transitions, Harvard, September 8–11, 1994.

R. Keith Schoppa, "The Structure, Dynamics, and Impacts of the Shanghai-Coastal Zhejiang Trading System, 1938–1944." Paper prepared for the conference on Wartime Shanghai, Lyon, France, October 15–17, 1997.

Shanghai chunqiu [Spring and autumn annals of Shanghai]. Hong Kong: Zhongguo tushu bianyi guan, 1968. Two vols.

Shanghai jiefang qianhou wujia ziliao huibian [Compilation of materials on prices in Shanghai before and after the liberation], comp. Shanghai Institute of Economics, Chinese Academy of Sciences. Shanghai: Shanghai renmin chubanshe, 1958.

"Shanghai shokuryo haikyu seido no jutenshugi ka ni kansuru iken to kengi" [Opinions and suggestions about the priority systematization of Shanghai's food rationing system," in *Chugoku seikei* [Chinese political economy], vol. 5. Shanghai: *Chugoku seiji keizai kenkyujo kan* [Publication of the research institute on Chinese politics and economy], March 1943, 110–140.

Shenbao.

Shen Zui, *Juntong neimu* [The inside story of the Military Statistics (Bureau)]. Beijing: Wenshi ziliao chubanshe, 1984.

Shi Yuanhua, "Li Shiqun," in Huang Meizhen, ed., *Wang wei shi hanjian* [Ten Wang puppet traitors]. Shanghai: Shanghai renmin chubanshe, 1986, 429–475.

Si Yi, "Gudao de yinxiang" [Impressions of the solitary island], pt. 2, in Li Jilin, comp., *Kangzhan wenxue qikan xuanji* [Compilation of literary periodicals from the War of Resistance]. Nangong, Hebei: Shumu wenxian chubanshe, n.d., vol. 1, 269–270.

Christopher Simpson, *Blowback: America's Recruitment of Nazis and its Effects on the Cold War.* New York: Weidenfeld and Nicolson, 1988.

Mabel Waln Smith, *Springtime in Shanghai.* London: George G. Harrap and Co., 1957.

Roy Stratton, "Navy Guerrilla," *United States Naval Institute Proceedings,* July 1963, pp. 83–87.

Tang Zhenchang and Shen Hengchun, eds., *Shanghai shi* [History of Shanghai]. Shanghai: Shanghai renmin chubanshe, 1989.

Tao Juyin, *Tianliang qian de gudao* [The isolated island before daybreak]. Shanghai Zhonghua shuju, 1947.

U.S. Military Intelligence Reports, China, 1911–1941.

Frederic Wakeman, Jr., "The Craigie-Arita Talks and the Struggle Over the Tientsin Concessions." Unpublished paper, Berkeley, California, 1962.

Frederic Wakeman, Jr., *The Shanghai Badlands: Political Terrorism and Urban Crime, 1937–1941.* Cambridge: Cambridge University Press, 1996.

C. Lester Walker, "China's Master Spy." *Harper's* 193: 162–169 (August 1946).

Xin shenbao yebao [The new Shenbao evening newspaper].

Xu Rihong, "Shanghai de touji" [Shanghai profiteers]. Part 1, *Dagong bao*, November 28, 1942, p. 3; Part 2, *Dagong bao*, November 29, 1942, p. 3.

Xu Zongyao, "Zuzhi Juntong Beiping zhan heping qiyi de qianqian houhou," *Wenshi ziliao xuanji*, no. 68, pp. 126–151. Beijing: Zhonghua shuju, 1980.

Wen-hsin Yeh, "Dai Li and the Liu Geqing Affair: Heroism in the Chinese Secret Service During the War of Resistance," *Journal of Asian Studies* 48.3: 545–562 (1989).

Yin Yixuan, *Guofang yu liangshi wenti* [National defense and the question of grain supplies]. Shanghai: Zhengzhong shuju, 1936.

Arthur N. Young, *China's Wartime Finance and Inflation, 1937–1945.* Cambridge: Harvard University Press, 1965.

Maochun Yu, "American Intelligence: The OSS (Office of Strategic Services) in China." Ph.D. thesis, University of California, Berkeley, 1994.

Zhang Jishun, "Shanghai lilong" [Neighborhood lanes], transl. Ma Xiaohe. Unpublished paper, Center for Chinese Studies, University of California, Berkeley, 1994.

Zhang Jishun, "Shi kong yi wei: zhanshi Shanghai de baojia zhidu" [A traditional institution in a modern context: the *baojia* system in wartime Shanghai]. Paper presented at the Seminar on Urban Culture and Social Modernization of Twentieth-century Shanghai, "Wartime Shanghai," Center for Chinese Studies, University of California, Berkeley, December 2–3, 1994.

Zhang Weihan, "Dai Li yu 'Juntong ju'" [Dai Li and the Military Statistics Bureau], in Wenshi ziliao yanjiu weiyuanhui, eds., *Zhejiang wenshi ziliao xuanji*, no. 23, pp. 79–151. *Neibu* publication. Zhejiang: Renmin chubanshe, 1982.

Zhao Yan, "Ga piao ji" [Notes on jumping the ration lines]," *Zazhi* [Magazine] 15.5: 88–95 (August 10, 1945).

Zhu Shikang, "Guanyu Guomindang guanliao ziben de jianwen" [Information about Guomindang bureaucratic capital], in Chinese People's Political Consultative Conference National Committee, Wenshi ziliao yanjiu weiyuanhui, eds., *Wenshi ziliao xuanji* [Selections of historical materials], fascicle 11, pp. 72–88. Beijing: Zhonghua shuju, November 1960.

Zhu Tongjiu, *Zhanshi liangshi wenti* [The problem of wartime grain supplies]. Chongqing: Duli chubanshe, 1939.

Part II

Chapter 6

The Great Way Government of Shanghai

TIMOTHY BROOK

The Great Way Government (*Dadao zhengfu*) constitutes one of the shorter and more obscure chapters in the political history of wartime Shanghai. Inaugurated on December 5, 1937, under Japanese patronage, this municipal administration consisted at first of nothing more than an office in Pudong, the suburb across the Huangpu River from the International Settlement. The regime was a creature of the Japanese army, and as such had difficulty attracting local politicians of any reputation, mounting an effective administration of the city of Shanghai, or establishing its authority over the larger Shanghai region. Within less than five months, the Great Way Government was reconfigured as a regular municipal administration subordinate to a new occupation regime based in Nanjing.

Given its ignominious birth and hurried demise, it is no surprise that the Great Way Government is almost unheard of. Our ignorance stems in part from the not unreasonable impression that this administration had little impact on the history of Shanghai; this chapter will not substantially challenge that impression. The obscurity of the Great Way Government is due as well to the scantiness of documentary evidence of its functioning, at least prior to the opening of the Shanghai Municipal Archives,[1] though even there the dispersed and unsystematic materials dealing with the regime's interactions with other organs and agencies do not provide a complete picture of how it was created, who served it, or what they were trying to do. But the greatest reason for the

---

[1] The Shanghai Municipal Archives [Shanghai shi dang'anguan] is the principal repository of documentary materials on the Great Way Government. Some of the documents are reprinted in its *Ri-wei Shanghai shi zhengfu* (Japanese-puppet Shanghai municipal governments) (Shanghai: Dang'an chubanshe, 1986), pp. 1–16, 135–148, 431–443, 791–810. Although the Great Way was a creature of the Japanese Army, I found nothing on it in the Archives of the Self-Defense Research Institute or the Foreign Ministry Archives in Tokyo. *Ri-wei Shanghai shi zhengfu* will hereafter be referred to as *RSZ*, Shanghai Municipal Archives, as *SMA*.

scholarly neglect of the Great Way Government may be its unattractive substance. Unlike some later Japanese-sponsored regimes that assembled vaguely plausible ideologies of national renewal and recruited men with some public reputation, the Great Way Government was a sorry sight of unknown politicians who were whisked in from outside and enjoyed no toehold on any high ground of morality or efficiency. If this regime has one unique claim on the attention of those interested in more than the history of Shanghai, it is as the first self-styled regional Chinese "government" that the Japanese army sponsored to administer occupied China. Obliged to devise its own arrangements without the benefit of prior example, it was beset by the sorts of failures that often dog first attempts, but it was the first rung in a long ladder of organizations and ideologies up which Chinese collaborators climbed during the war in search of a workable relationship with their occupiers, one they never found.

ORIGINS

The Japanese takeover of Shanghai and its vicinity was more or less completed by November 12, 1937. During that month, what remained of the Guomindang administration of the city sought refuge in the International Settlement and the French Concession. The areas outside the foreign enclave were left without administrative or police functioning except where it was imposed by the Central China Area Army (CCAA, *Naka Shina hōmengun*), the invading Japanese force. Japan had launched the invasions of north China in July and Shanghai in August as punitive measures to force a political change on the Chinese government, but it became clear through the fall of 1937 that the maneuver of invasion was not going to yield the desired political outcome and that an occupation would be necessary. Tokyo was not keen to allow its expeditionary forces to engage in the sort of political experiment that the Guandong Army had launched in Manchuria in 1931, yet early in September the North China Area Army (NCAA, *Kita Shina hōmengun*) was entertaining the idea of a puppet state based in Beijing, and by early November arguing for it in Cabinet. Reluctant to commit the resources needed for a China war, the Army General Staff in Tokyo pressured the Konoe Cabinet for a diplomatic closure to the "China Incident." As the area armies pressed forward without forcing Jiang to capitulate, the mood in Cabinet shifted toward the idea of a comprehensive solution: giving up hope of bringing Jiang's regime into negotiation and working on replacing it with another regime more sympathetic to Japan. On December 1, the Supreme Command in Tokyo authorized the NCAA to form a Chinese regional government in Beijing, which it did two weeks later. On the same day, it authorized the CCAA to capture Nanjing without, however, granting it similar permission to set up a regional regime in its newly conquered territory. The CCAA would have to make do for the moment with a series of local administrations.

The task of reestablishing civil order in the areas through which the CCAA passed was handled by its Special Service Department (Tokumubu). The first step was usually for the army to recruit Chinese to form a "peace maintenance committee" (PMC, *zhian weichihui*) which took over local administration as Nationalist officials fled their posts. Within a matter of weeks, the Special Service would send down half a dozen agents – demobilized officers, former employees of the South Manchurian Railway Company (Mantetsu), or other Japanese with first-hand knowledge of China and an ability to speak Chinese – to form a "pacification team" (*senbuhan*). Among their first tasks was regularizing the often hastily assembled PMC into a "self-government committee" (SGC, *zizhi weiyuanhui*). The goal was to get the SGC staffed by more respectable and influential elites than those who had climbed aboard the PMC, a better class of local residents who, it was hoped, could run an administration that worked with the Japanese but enjoyed some credit with the local people.

As the Shanghai region fell under the control of the CCAA, localities within the region were brought one by one into the pacification process. A Mantetsu report of March 1938 on pacification in central China shows that Shanghai was divided up among thirteen pacification teams, most of which had three to five members.[2] The first was set up in Baoshan as soon as that town fell in October. The largest was the eleven-member pacification team in the South City (Nanshi) formed on November 15.[3] The other sections of urban Shanghai to which pacification teams were assigned were Pudong and the Western District (Huxi).[4]

---

[2] The thirteen teams were located in the South City, Pudong, Jiading, Baoshan, Chongming, Zhenru, Kunshan, Taicang, Qingpu, the Western District, Chuansha, Nanhui, and Fengxian; Mantetsu Shanhai Jimusho, "Naka Shina senryū chiku ni okeru senbu kōsaku gaiyō" (March 1938), reprinted in Inoue Hisashi, ed., *Kachū senbu kōsaku shiryō*, pp. 48, 50.

[3] In addition to its eleven members, the South City Pacification Team had another four security personnel to handle the thousands of war refugees who had gathered there. The co-functioning of the pacification team and the military police in the South City is mentioned in Mantetsu Shanhai Jimusho, "Naka Shina hōmen senbu kōsaku jōkyō," p. 3, and Mantetsu Shanhai Jimusho, "Naka Shina senryūchi ni okeru nanmin no jōkyō narabi busshi jōkyō," p. 2, both reprinted in Inoue, *Kachū senbu kōsaku shiryō*, pp. 23, 26.

[4] The Western District pacification team was set up shortly after Shanghai fell at 94 Jessfield Road, where it was joined by the district detachment of the Japanese Military Police. According to the "Report on the Situation in the Western District" (January 30, 1939), p. 5 (Shanghai Municipal Police Files, hereafter referred to as SMP, File 9114[c]), "One Mr. Sakurai was then chief of the [pacification] section. It cooperated closely with the Japanese Military Police from the very

These scattered committees were linked upward to a central pacification office within the Special Service Department, but they lacked the horizontal integration needed to provide Shanghai with a unified administration. To achieve that, an overall municipal office would have to be installed. The question of what sort of body should administer Shanghai was not a purely technical question, however. It became tangled up with the military interservice issue of whether the NCAA in Beijing was being granted powers of political control that the CCAA in Shanghai wanted but was being denied. The CCAA would get its chance to create a central China regime, the Reformed Government (*Weixin zhengfu*), which would be inaugurated on March 28, 1938. But that development still lay in an undefined future, and something had to be done in the present if the CCAA hoped to stake its claim on the future political shape of occupied China. What it did was to set up a "government" (*zhengfu*) rather than a more modestly titled "self-government committee" to take over the administration of Shanghai. The Great Way Government thus emerged as a municipal administration in the guise of a state regime.[5]

The regime appeared suddenly under the leadership of a political unknown named Su Xiwen (his first official portrait appears in Photo 7). Su had been in Shanghai since October, presumably to take part in planning for a collaborationist regime well before Shanghai was under Japanese occupation.[6] The CCAA judged that the moment for launching a Shanghai-based collaborationist regime was ripe once Tokyo committed itself to a long-term occupation on December 1. Four days later, Shanghai's new government was founded, though at that point the only personnel it had signed on were the chief of police and the head of the police accounting department (their service with the Great Way Government officially began on December 3). Chief of Police Zhu Yuzhen was not a local man but, like many in the Shanghai police force, hailed from Shandong province. A graduate of the prestigious Baoding Military Academy, Zhu since 1923 had pursued a policing career in Fujian and had not worked in

outset in tracing the anti-Japanese elements and organizations as well as the property of Chinese officials. In this connection, large numbers of Chinese agents recruited from the loafer class were employed to assist the Japanese in such secret activities." The pacification team was replaced by a Special Service unit in June 1938.

[5] A Great Way Self-Government Committee was organized in December 1937. Its membership was distinct from that of the Great Way Government, consisting entirely of Pudong businessmen; "Zizhihui jianzhang," SMA File R1-1-152 (the text is undated but was filed on December 28, the same day that most of the other documents pertaining to the founding of the regime, including its manifesto, were filed). It was a local Pudong body organized under the aegis of the Great Way Government. To avoid confusion I shall refer to it in this chapter as the Pudong Self-Government Committee.

[6] *RSZ*, p. 13; Mōgi Kikuo, *Shanhai shi daidō seifu shisaku hōkoku, ryakureki*.

Shanghai prior to his December 3 appointment. The head of accounting was similarly brought in from outside Shanghai.[7] No other appointments predating December 5 appear in the surviving personnel documents of the Great Way Government, suggesting that not much was in place by the founding date. The only other early police appointment, dated to inauguration day, was the head of the administrative section, a man whose education and prior career had been entirely in Manchuria. Another ten days passed before two other section heads were appointed, both again outsiders to Shanghai. Only as of December 18 were office staff and secretaries at lower levels being appointed, drawn mostly from the large pool of unemployed Shanghai police and civic personnel. The regime thus started out with a skeletal upper management re-cruited from outside Shanghai and slowly assembled its personnel from local applicants thereafter.

Su Xiwen, the head of the new regime, was of ambiguous background. He appears to have been born in Amoy in 1892, though nothing about the man's history is beyond question. According to a Hong Kong newspaper report, his original name was Su Junying, but he changed it to Su Songzhi, and later to Su Youxiang.[8] He had other identities as well, for a Japanese magazine in January 1938 referred to him as Su Jixiao.[9] His family dealt in tobacco and sugar, and as Amoy became a major trading partner with Japan after 1895, it is likely that the Su family was involved in and enriched by this trade. Su studied political economy at Waseda University in Tokyo, returning to China to hold a series of mid-level posts in the Fujian and Guangdong administrations beginning in 1916. He joined the GMD faction around Hu Hanmin, but broke with the party as Hu's faction shifted to the left. After a decade in government service, Su became a professor at Chizhi College, a Shanghai university of middle rank. At this time, according to his Japanese biography, Su began to draw on Daoist and Buddhist ideas to develop a religious philosophy that he called the "Great Way spirit" (*dadao jingshen*), which advocated the unity of all peoples and the common origin of all creeds (*tianxia yijia, wanfa guiyi*; "the realm is one family, all doctrines form a unity"). His Buddhist affiliation apparently caused him to change his name yet again, this time to Su Xiwen,[10] and to become drawn into politics, allegedly to apply his allusively heterodox ideas in the cause of

---

[7] "Shanghai shi dadao zhengfu jingcha ju zhiyuan lülibiao," SMA File R1-1-93.

[8] *Xingdao ribao* (Hong Kong), November 22, 1939, p. 4; Mōgi, *Shanhai shi daidō seifu shisaku hōkoku, ryakureki.*

[9] *Shina jihen gahō* 11 (January 27, 1938), p. 31.

[10] The etymology of Xiwen is puzzling. *Xi* ("tin") could refer to the ceremonial metal staff (*xizhang*) of a Buddhist abbot, with its allusion to the notion of sweeping away evil, but I am unable to construe its meaning in collocation with *wen* ("writings").

agitating for transparency in government. This may have been why the GMD issued a warrant for his arrest, although it may have had to do with espionage for the Japanese. In any case, Su fled north in 1936 to take up a position in a Japanese "development company" and work for what a Japanese source calls the "peasant self-government movement," which was a Japanese scheme to mobilize rural support in the northeast in order to undercut Chinese control in the region between Mukden and Beiping. Two months after the Japanese army opened its offensive in Shanghai, Su returned, and in December surfaced from obscurity to become the new "mayor."

To ask who Su Xiwen was is a less useful way to approach this odd figure than to ask with whom he was connected. The available biographical fragments in Japanese sources depict someone with regional, business, and educational ties to Japan, through which he was drawn into Japanese schemes to enlarge its economic and political presence in China. He is presented as having both intellectual and lay-religious credentials, along with a commitment to resist the corruption of the GMD regime. More important, it would seem, are the social and political connections that his religious avocation provided him. According to a newspaper article published in July 1938 after the assassination of Su's nominee for chief prosecutor, both Su and the candidate (the latter characterized as "a devout Buddhist as well as a zealous Daoist") were members of the China Mutual Aid Association, a Daoist "spirit sand writing altar" on Weihaiwei Road. This building was the site of constant comings and goings among the association's members and was large enough to house some of them in times of political difficulty.[11] The reference suggests a sort of Chinese freemasonry that provided Su with a network of contacts through which he could maintain links with sympathizers and recruit supporters. An outsider in Shanghai needed such a network to assemble an administration for the Japanese, and one that stood entirely apart from the sorts of networks upon which the former GMD administration had relied. The collaborators under Su Xiwen would thus come from a completely different sector of the city's lesser elite, one that had been unsuccessful previously in gaining access to political office.

Su Xiwen announced the formation of the Great Way Government at a public gathering on December 5, 1937 (see photo 7) and issued a set of documents to communicate the regime's legitimacy and authority: a manifesto, a declaration of his assumption of mayoral authority, a provisional organizational outline, a telegram to other governmental bodies announcing his regime's formation, an

---

[11] *Eastern Times*, July 22, 1938, in SMP File D-8636. Both Su and the nominee were Fujian natives who knew each other prior to coming to Shanghai, which may indicate that native-place networks were intertwined with the China Mutual Aid Association.

7. Su Xiwen announcing the founding of the Great Way Government, December 5, 1937. Source: Mogi Kikuo, *Shanhai shi daido seifu shisatsu hokoku* (Investigative report on the Great Way Government of Shanghai), 1938.

announcement to the powerful Bankers' Guild and the Chamber of Commerce, and a notice to former municipal employees that they had seven days within which to report back to work.[12] Of these, the manifesto and the telegram provide the clearest statements of ideology and policy. Copies of both were sent to all Shanghai newspapers along with a cover letter demanding immediate publication (the dilatory received a followup letter the next day repeating this order in curter terms).

In none of these documents does Japan's role in creating this regime appear as more than a shadow. Clearly an effort was being made to give the Great Way Government an appearance of integrity and autonomy, not only in Great Way declarations but even in Japanese documents. Other than one internal Japanese account of January 31, 1938, which notes that the regime was formed "with the help of the Imperial Army,"[13] this body of documents is silent as to the work the Japanese side did to bring the regime into existence. In the same spirit, a propaganda booklet on the regime published in Tokyo insists that "there are

[12] These documents are reprinted in *RSZ*, pp. 1–9. Internal correspondence concerning the last announcement may be found in SMA File R1-1-97.

[13] *RSZ*, p. 11.

only two Japanese officials in this government,"[14] even though the January 31 account names no less than thirty-four pacification agents assigned full time to the Great Way Government. Despite the imposition of pacification staff, to say nothing of the overt presence of the Japanese occupation forces in Shanghai, the collaborators had to project the appearance that the regime was a purely Chinese creation, constructed around Chinese ideals and devoted to serving Chinese interests, while operating an administration that satisfied the security and material needs of the occupiers. A tension between indigenous and foreign claims is not something unfamiliar in the history of Shanghai administration, of course. In this case, however, the split between an overt Chinese claim to administrative authority and a covert foreign demand for control was of an intensity more extreme that anything Shanghai had ever experienced.

Reconstructing an administrative entity this odd and this brief is not easy. The Great Way Government does not appear to have done much, but even more troublesome, much of what it did or planned to do is simply not documented and can be traced only indirectly through linked archival materials. This lack of direct documentation means that we can learn only certain things about this regime, four of which constitute the next four headings in this chapter: ideology, jurisdiction, police, and revenue. Ideology is the aspect of the regime that was most exposed to public view at the time, since the Great Way had to publicize itself. It made great claims for what it stood for, though what it claimed was always more than what it actually represented. Within the internal documents that circulated within the Shanghai region during early 1938 and survive in the municipal archives, the issue of jurisdictional control is prominent, given the Great Way's keen desire, and general inability, to dominate competing agencies. As the police were the main agents for asserting this control, the documents concerning jurisdiction often reveal aspects of their functioning. Finally, the regime's desperate need to overcome its financial viability left paper trails of its searches for revenue, though not of what it actually collected. Here too, as we shall see, the police were key agents in trying to assert claims to revenue.

IDEOLOGY

When a regime collaborates with an occupying military force, it cannot celebrate capitulation to foreign interests as its raison d'être, but must work to make foreign military domination disappear by fashioning an appropriately native appearance. Regimes of this sort have tended to go on the ideological

---

[14] Mōgi, *Shanhai shi daidō seifu shisaku hōkoku*, p. 8.

offensive against the more persuasive forces that claim to represent the nation, and to sound a conservative call for cultural renovation.[15] The Great Way regime did just that, challenging GMD modernism and staking its own legitimacy with a conservative Chinese brand of renovationist ideology it called the "Great Way" (*dadao*). The term did double duty in naming this regime. It provided an easy-to-grasp ideological label; at the same time, it exuded a moral resonance greater than what one would expect from a municipal operation slapped together merely for the purpose of keeping things running. A city was in the foreground, but a phantom nation lay behind it. All this was more than Su Xiwen could have dreamed up, as we shall see.

In the manifesto and the telegram that the Great Way Government released to other governmental bodies on inauguration day, it alludes to state formation and carefully avoids reference to Shanghai or the usual tasks of urban administration. In these texts, it identifies the nation as the end point in the reconstruction process that the Great Way Government saw itself initiating: "changing the flag with the aspiration of rescuing the people from disaster and bringing this generation into the realm of Great Unity (*datong*)," in the words of the manifesto. The process of nation-building follows the building-block logic of moral transformation in the Confucian classic, *The Doctrine of the Mean*, by "organizing every village, county, province, and nation into one Great Family." The difficulty is seen to lie not in the integration of the units but in their initial formation as moral communities. Once the family is morally ordered, the higher social levels will follow suit and a Great Way nation will emerge.

The reason that the nation needs to be rebuilt is not the Japanese invasion, states the manifesto, but the political infighting and armed conflict unleashed by warlordism and the "Party dictatorship" of the Guomindang. Not only has the Guomindang created a "hell on earth," but it has damaged the viability of genuine political life by making it "impossible to select the wise and capable," that is, by excluding non-Party members. Japan enters the story at this point in the manifesto with the oblique comment that "internationally it has not been possible to speak of trust or cultivate closeness." The telegram to other government bodies acknowledges that the object of this sentence is Japan when it pictures the invasion as a stroke of good luck for the Chinese people: "Fortunately the Japanese Imperial Army has brought its presence to the Central Region (*zhongtu*) and has cut out the evil and obstinate on our behalf." The manifesto adopts a more oblique rhetoric of "rooting out the warlords and the Nationalist and Communist parties on behalf of the people of our nation." Japan is

---

[15] On the appeal of conservative renovation to collaboration regimes, see Timothy Brook, "Collaborationist Nationalism in Occupied Wartime China."

thus pictured not as an external element, but as a neighborly force of renovation whose intervention internal conditions have made necessary. Between
Japan and China there is assumed to be a convergence of moral values and
interests that in China had been submerged by Guomindang self-interest: a
mutual reliance and respect based on the Confucian schoolboy morality of
the Five Bonds and the Eight Virtues, and a joint commitment to achieve,
in the increasingly conspicuous language of Japanese regional hegemony,
"peace."

The Great Way (*dadao*), according to the manifesto, is the means for realizing
peace on a universal plane:

> Throughout human history there has been no one who does not love peace.
> Peace is the gate to good fortune; without peace there can be none. Ac-
> cordingly, only when people as well as nations carry out the Great Way
> in their relations with each other can they achieve true peace. Otherwise,
> regardless of what laws restrain them, if they do not act in accordance with
> the Great Way, then certainly one cannot speak of true peace. This is an
> unalterable truth.[16]

Endowed with transcendent value and existing purely in the realm of truth,
dadao serves to lubricate interpersonal and international relations. Its actual
content remains vague in these documents, although certain capacities are attributed to it. "The Great Way does not consist in setting oneself above or apart"
from others, declares the manifesto; it is "the nature that heaven has bestowed."
Given that it finds its clearest expression in the natural bond of kinship, it is
"bestowed on all people" without distinction of nationality. It is not merely a
personal virtue, however, but manifests itself through national bodies to the
extent that they trust and are close to each other. Thus the manifesto on the
one hand stresses the universality of the Great Way, which is accessible to "all
people" and is animated through "the natural virtues of all humankind," while
on the other regarding it as inseparable from the moral tasks of nations tied
together in a larger regional system.

The notion of a seamless combination of the individual-in-his-family and the
nation-in-the-world goes back two millennia to the *The Classic of Rites* (*Li ji*)
of the Han dynasty. This text is the locus classicus for *dadao*, which James
Legge translated as the Grand Course:

> When the Grand Course was pursued, a public and common spirit ruled
> all under the sky; they chose men of talent, virtue, and ability; their words

---

[16] *RSZ*, p. 1.

were sincere and what they cultivated was harmony. Thus men did not love their parents only, nor treat as children only their sons.[17]

The Great Way is described in this classic not as a reality currently in existence, but as a remembered state, a nostalgia for an earlier and purer age. It was a nostalgia regularly revived by Confucian moralists of the Chinese state throughout the imperial era, and resuscitated for what would be the last time by Su Xiwen and his group toward the end of 1937. By declaring their goal to be the renewed pursuit of a lost classical ideal, the little clutch of politicians who emerged in Pudong as a government on December 5 were declaring their alignment with an old official moral tradition. That the Great Way of the classics would be realized in China through foreign occupation may have struck the few who noticed this ideological construction as at least ironic.

The regime intended that the Great Way take on the full burden of political ideology – which is to say that it should not just justify policies but guide practice. Nine days later Su Xiwen announced that "all administrative policies are to be maintained according to the Great Way." He explains that at a general level this means promoting "Great Unity" and cherishing "love and peace," and at a local level, "preserving security and order."[18] As specified in the charter of the Peace Maintenance Committee for Shanghai county, which lay up river from the city, the practice of "the Great Way of humankind" meant "organizing as one family to establish a politics of self-government and condemning Party-state politics and Communistic thinking."[19]

The Great Way had the imprimateur of the classics, yet stylistic peculiarities in all the texts I have quoted describing the concept suggest that we need to ask with whom they originated. The charter of the Shanghai County PMC makes extensive use of the copula *shi*, repeatedly uses the pronoun *ci* ("this"), and tends to position verbs at the end of sentences, all of which hint at Japanese authorship.[20] The occasionally awkward language of the manifesto, notably the extensive use of pronouns and copulas as well as the adverb *dai* (J. *hotondo*), similarly have the feel of Japanese constructions. And indeed they were. The real author of the Great Way ideology was not Su Xiwen at all, but Nishimura Tenzō, the head of the Special Service unit attached to the Great Way Government. Clues to his role are not difficult to pick up, for they appear in a Japanese

---

[17] James Legge, trans., *Li Ki*, vol. 27 of the Sacred Books of the East, ed. Max Müller (1885), pp. 364–365.
[18] *RSZ*, p. 135.
[19] "Shanghai xian zhian weichihui zhangcheng," SMA File R1-1-4.
[20] Noriko Kamachi has kindly confirmed my suspicion that this text was probably written by a Japanese.

propaganda booklet on the Great Way Government published in Tokyo early in February.[21] Opposite the first page of the text is a photograph of Nishimura and Su standing on either side of a large calligraphic scroll that reads "the man of benevolence has no enemies" (the text opposite echoes this theme by using the phrase "no enemies under heaven" to describe the military power of the Japanese army in China). More revealing is an advertisement on the inside of the back cover for two short books by Nishimura. One is a newly published set of two essays, "On the Fundamental Unity of Religions" and "The China Affair and Japan's Mission," the former sounding suspiciously like the sort of philosophical interest that Japanese biographies allege Su Xiwen to have held (and thus may well not have). The other advertised book is Nishimura's *Sekai kensetsu no daidō* (The Great Way of World Reconstruction), then in its eighth edition. An advertisement thus exposes the origin of the Great Way ideology, for Nishimura Tenzō was using this language seven editions before the Shanghai regime emerged as an Asian expression of the single great truth that East Asia must embrace its Japanese destiny of unity and peace. The occupation of Shanghai gave him the opportunity to mobilize his Confucianistic scheme of moral rearmament to postulate a conservative regional hegemony for Japan.

One has to wonder whether Su Xiwen had anything at all to do with the Great Way spirit his Japanese biographers attributed to him. Even if he didn't, this prefabricated ideology suited his purpose, which was to launch what some might take as a plausible vision of China within an East Asia dominated by Japan. A universal value transcending the separate interests of particular nations would suit the burden of collaborationist ideology, which is to permit nationalism to retain its moral traction, but only as a lesser vehicle on the path to universal salvation. Appealing to universal truth in order to deflate an intensely nationalistic cause like anti-Japanese resistance posed grave difficulties for propagandists in Shanghai, who had to persuade an unsympathetic populace that allegiance to an occupying military power was morally superior to continuing support for a routed Chinese government. Success in this claim required the contradictory assertion that the decision to form and serve a collaborating regime had been entirely Chinese. This point is made, among other places, in an article that the secretariat of the Great Way Government planted in the Manchurian paper *Shanhaiguan News* in March. The article rounded out the list of the regime's achievements by saying that "all this has been a matter of our nationals (*guoren*) dealing with the affairs of their own nation, without there being [anyone else]

---

[21] Mōgi, *Shanhai shi daidō seifu shisaku hōkoku.*

in the background."[22] Although straining all credulity, the euphemization of Chinese as "nationals" rather than as "Chinese" was necessary to avoid having thereby to name those who had displaced Chinese from running their own nation. Su Xiwen continued to use this euphemism long after the Great Way Government was gone. In a text issued on the first anniversary of the Shanghai Municipal Government on October 1, 1939, he speaks of Chinese as *guoren* and *bangren* ("people of the country").[23] These expressions allow him to euphemize the Japanese as "our neighbors" when he concedes the legitimacy of their use of force against Guomindang militarism without having to pose China and Japan as mutually exclusive categories. As long as the *guo* was morally subordinate to a Great Unity, it had no occasion for challenging another *guo*. If distinctions were to be made, they should be not between nations but between those who embraced the Great Way and those who fell short of its ideal of universal harmony.

Rewriting the all-under-heaven claim of the Chinese throne in the *Classic of Rites* into a moral justification for Japanese hegemony in East Asia, which he did when he provided Su Xiwen with the name for his regime, was Nishimura Tenzō's contribution to collaborationist ideology. Drawing on the classics was part of a larger cultural move on the part of the Japanese in those early days of occupation to manufacture moral legitimacy for their collaborators. By reconstituting the language of imperial rule (though without reinvesting China with the centrality that that language implied), the Special Service hoped to mark a plausible break with Guomindang practices – to appear more "Chinese" than the Republic – and thereby mobilize popular dissatisfaction with its threatening and despised modernism.

One device used to this end was the calendar. The documents issued on the regime's emergence declare it to have been founded not on December 5, 1937, but on the third day of the eleventh month of the *dingchou* year. Reference to the old lunar calendar was not only a restoration of past practice; a return to the sixty-year cycle also served to get around having to use the year designation that had by 1937 become conventional, and that was to identify it as "the twenty-sixth year of the Chinese Republic." Using a dating system that lingered on only in rural usage might have given pleasure to cultural conservatives, who disliked having to take on signs of Westernization, but it generated confusion within the administration – especially as the Japanese themselves employed the Western calendar. This little touch of self-Orientalizing archaism

---

[22] "Dadao zhengfu mishuchu wei touji xuanchuan xinwengao zhi *Shanhaiguan gongbao* han" (March 8, 1938), *RSZ*, p. 796.
[23] *Shanghai tebieshi zhengfu chuzhou jinian tekan*, p. 22.

was abandoned for external communications on February 21, 1938, and disappeared when the Great Way Government was disbanded two months later.[24] The cultural authenticity was unconvincing when arrayed against the shock of military occupation, no matter how distasteful a Western modernity might have seemed.

JURISDICTION

As an unknown entity over in Pudong, the Great Way Government had to establish authority where none existed, and it had to do so as a consequence of conditions that its patron had imposed in the first place. This double burden left the Great Way Government with the appearance of being opportunistic and powerless at the same time. The heads of other administrative entities within the boundaries of its jurisdiction freely used this situation to their advantage by playing Great Way and Japanese personnel against each other whenever doing so would strengthen their hand in local affairs. And the Japanese were not averse to playing the same sort of game. Asserting regional authority thus became the Great Way Government's particular nightmare.

Within the city of Shanghai, the Great Way Government assumed nominal jurisdiction over six of the seven urban districts: Pudong, the South City (Nanshi), the Western District (Huxi), Zhabei, Zhenru (including Dachang and Nanxiang), and the Central District (Jiangwan). The seventh, Wusong, was a Japanese military zone and out of reach. Intended to be as regionally expansive as the former municipal government, the regime sought to extend its control north, east, and south to the seven adjoining counties of Beiqiao (formerly Shanghai county), Jiading, Baoshan, Fengxian, Nanhui, Chuansha, and Chongming.[25] The staffing commitments of the Special Service personnel working for the Great Way Government indicate that Beiqiao was the only suburban district brought under Great Way administration. Baoshan was absorbed into a subsequent municipal administration,[26] but the rest, although they may have submitted periodic reports to Shanghai, continued to remain beyond its grasp until much later.

To assert its jurisdiction, the Great Way Government had to work with the numerous PMCs and SGCs that by December 1937 were dotting the suburban

---

[24] *RSZ*, pp. 15–16. There was a brief attempt to supersede year designations by the Republic once the new Reformed Government was installed in Nanjing, for in April the designation "first year of Reform" (*weixin yinian*) was occasionally used, but this innovation was quickly abandoned.

[25] The jurisdictional plan for the regime is outlined in Japanese documents reprinted in *RSZ*, pp. 12–13.

[26] *RSZ*, pp. 14–15.

landscape. These committees might oversee only a single town (*zhen*) or canton (*xiang*), or might claim authority at the district (*qu*) or county (*xian*) level. Some had emerged under Japanese army direction, others through the independent efforts of local individuals. The common theme of the statements they released announcing their formation was the need to bring back order, as we read in the founding manifesto of the Pudong SGC:

> In the wake of the military devastation, the area has been chaotic, bandits have arisen in a swarm, and residents have seen their homes destroyed and have fled. They have been left uprooted with nothing on which to depend. This disaster is entirely the responsibility of the Party Army, which has driven the people to this suffering. Troubled by what we have seen, we have set up a self-government committee to stabilize the area and encourage businesses to return in order that the markets may flourish again. By so doing, we are laying the foundation for the Great Way Government and affirming our close friendship with Great Japan. As a result, good people can live in peace, take pleasure in their work, and be permitted to enjoy happiness.[27]

For the Great Way Government, the prospect of working with these committees was not as cheerful as this statement of approaching good order might suggest. It faced the task of identifying, ratifying (or annulling), and eventually reorganizing these quasi-independent bodies into better subordinated administrative units that did what was demanded of them.

Su Xiwen went on the offensive in early January by issuing "Great Way Government Announcement No. 8." In this text, Su conceded that the PMCs had played a valuable role in managing local affairs as the fighting moved west. Now, however, it was necessary to reverse that judgment:

> The PMCs emerged at an appropriate moment, but not all on these committees were good. Some members used them to expand their own power, coming up with ingenious excuses to collect taxes, making outrageous assertions, and allowing corrupt practices to flourish. Not only were they unable to restrain themselves and work for the public good and extend benefits through the countryside; quite the contrary, they used the occasion to profit from and harm their local areas. What started out as well-meaning has ended up as evil. If they are not dissolved right away, who knows how deep the damage these committees are doing to their local areas will go? Now that the various organs of this government are being established and

---

[27] "Bingxian zhi hou," SMA File R1-1-152.

police authority has already been restored, the tasks [of administration are being met by] those responsible for them and there is no need for parallel organs. In addition to ordering the bureau of police to have its stations determine whether [the committees] within their areas are speedily dissolved, this order is promulgated so that merchants and people alike all know of this.[28]

The dissolution order was issued to the police on January 4.

Some local elites found this assessment of the PMCs and SGCs as dubious entities suitable to their own purposes, and used similar statements to appeal to municipal authorities to dissolve committees with which they were in conflict, or from which they had been excluded. This was a problem in the Western District, although it only surfaces in the archival record a year later on January 14, 1939, when a self-styled "representative of the people" of the Western District sent a detailed letter to the Shanghai Special Municipality. Writing on behalf of 118 members of the Huangpu West Fellow Residents' Association (*Puxi tongrenhui*), the author observes that when it still belonged to Shanghai county prior to the arrival of Guomindang authority, the Western District was well governed by locally respected administrators. He says that the area was more or less able to weather the disorder of Guomindang reorganization, when it was absorbed into Shanghai municipality and its police force incorporated into the Shanghai police. But when the war of resistance moved west, good administration disappeared, to disastrous consequences:

> Hoodlums (*liumang*) living here and there [in the district] rushed forward to take over, wielding power and running an administration under the guise of "maintenance." They treated their locality as though it were a profit-making business, imposing levies and accumulating wealth. There was nothing they would not do and no evil they would not commit, with the result that good people vanished without a trace and bandits arose in great number, committing several murders and rapes every day. The exactions they imposed on small businesses, the names for which always changed, were too numerous to count.[29]

The author of the letter explains that the local elite of merchants and teachers, men such as himself, refused to have anything to do with the disreputable types who controlled the PMCs that popped up in the Western District. They gathered privately to discuss the most pressing problems that needed immediate attention

---

[28] "Dadao zhengfu bugao 8" (draft), SMA File R1-1-154.
[29] "Cheng wei luchen Huxi qu yiwang zhenggou qingxing," SMA File R18-126.

and drew up their own program of action. Not being a legally constituted administrative organ, however, they realized that they had to wait until a thorough municipal reorganization got rid of the "monstrous maintenance committees and all other illegal organizations" that had come into existence in the early days of the occupation.[30]

As this complaint indicates, the newly formed self-government committees assumed the right to exercise policing and taxing powers, making their decisions on these matters, at least initially, without clearance or reference to a higher authority. For example, the Pudong SGC declared in its regulations the right to investigate anyone undermining local order, and established three detective offices for the purpose. The other spheres of responsibility it acknowledged were facilitating the work of the Japanese army (guiding army units, providing interpretation, and explaining unfamiliar local customs), engaging in relief and medical work, and ensuring the circulation of commodities. The priority of security and economic functioning in the work of the SGCs fits with the membership of the Pudong group. Of the sixteen local residents, who were between the ages of twenty-six and fifty-nine (with a median age of just thirty-eight), half were owners or managers of small businesses or members of the Pudong Chamber of Commerce. Of the other half, five worked for the fire and ambulance services (one was a member of the Pudong Red Cross Association) and another three were identified as local constables. In Pudong, the local representatives of the new order thus consisted of small-time businessmen assisted by a smattering of former state security personnel. This pattern can be found repeated in most of the local bodies formed in the occupied Shanghai region.[31]

---

[30] The characterization of the former SGC personnel as "hoodlums" probably obscures a distinction more of class and wealth than of public conduct, and is consistent with the assessment of a police report from the International Settlement that the Chinese who worked with the Japanese agencies in the Western District were from "the loafer class," the standard Shanghai Municipal Police translation for *liumang* (see note 4). The association's nominee for public office was a lawyer, Chen Xishun. The municipal government was not about to elevate Chen to the leadership of a district office that already had a head, but it did recommend that the office consider him for the headship of one of the town offices under the district office. Chen was soon appointed to be head of the town office of Longcao, and in that position attended a meeting of town heads on February 7, 1938 at which Kitaoka Tatsuo, the Japanese adviser to the Western District office, explained organizational processes and ordered them to implement *baojia* registration. Shortly after that meeting, Chen decided to resign. Kitaoka approved as his replacement the head of the Caojin District Maintenance Committee, who had served previously as the head of the secretariat of the former South City SGC; "Cheng wei chengbao ge zhenzhang yi jiuzhi," SMA File R18-126.

[31] "Huiyuan mingdan," SMA File R1-1-152. By way of comparison, the town council of Guzhen in Chuansha county was composed of eighteen members ranging in age from twenty-six to fifty-one, with a median age of forty-two. The head of the town council had been the head before the occupation, and the assistant head, the local constable. Those for whom occupations are given were all businessmen; report of Chuansha xian Guzhen daili zhenzhang, SMA File R1-1-152. In

Of course, while restoring security and reviving the economy were endpoints in which most interests converged, establishing a tolerable working relationship with the Japanese had to be the first item on every committee's agenda, whether it chose to place it there or not – though most did. The SGC in the town of Tangqiao, Pudong, for instance, prioritized "the language barrier" and "misunderstandings" before "reviving the market" as the three issues its members saw themselves having to resolve quickly.[32] By implication, both had given rise to conflict with the occupation force. By further implication, these tasks had nothing to do with the Great Way Government. The latter was simply not an element in this aspect of local affairs.

Su Xiwen tried to push the process of bringing these autonomous bodies throughout the Shanghai region under his control by ordering the police on January 21 to submit a list of the names of elected leaders in every town, village, and neighborhood in the region within ten days. This task proved to be impossible. Ten days later Chief of Police Zhu Yuzhen told Su that local police had reported to him that, "given the difficulties in holding elections," they needed another week to complete the assignment. Even that postponement was optimistic. As late as March 19, police in both the South City and the Central District were still reporting that "local circumstances" – meaning the power of these committees to refuse giving information about their memberships – made it impossible to forward the names as requested. Three days later both the Baoshan and Gaoqiao police filed similar excuses. All that Zhu Yuzhen could counsel was patience: "Local administration will hereafter gradually be carried out," he assured Su. "When it is, matters will eventually improve."[33] The Great Way grip over these areas was next to nil, and no alternative procedure presented itself. All the regime could do was to continue pressing for regularization by demanding that, when a local SGC was formed, it, or the district SGC to which it reported, provide updated lists of committee members and service personnel.[34]

Those lower-level jurisdictions that came under the purview of the Great Way Government were ordered to change their names so as to convey an impression of a unified administration. District and town committees were required to drop their original designations of PMC or SGC in favor of "administrative affairs

the town of Tangqiao, seven of the nine members of the town office (which served as a suboffice of the Tangqiao SGC) were businessmen; the other two were farmers. They varied in age from thirty-six to fifty-nine, with a high median age of fifty; petition of Tangqiao zizhihui Tangqiao zhen banshichu, SMA File R1-1-153.

[32] Report from Tangqiao zizhihui Tangqiao zhen banshichu, SMA File R1-1-153.

[33] SMA File R1-1-155.

[34] "Wubao qu fenju xiajing zizhi weiyuanhui zhiyuan mingbiao," SMA File R1-1-152.

office" (*zhengwushu*) and "town affairs committee" (*zhenwuhui*).[35] Renaming may have been conceived as the beginning of a process designed to co-opt or reduce the power of these bodies, but that process in many places did not go much further. Evidence of the resilience of the early SGCs is reflected in the apparent success with which SGC personnel from the opening months of the occupation were able to hang onto their posts through subsequent reorganizations. Personnel files from the Western District Office from 1940 attest to this success. To offer a clutch of examples: three of the six tax offices in the Western District were overseen by men who had been SGC personnel; three of the four staffers at the Xinhua Town Office were original members of the Xinhua SGC, and their head had been vice-chair of another SGC in the area; two of the three officials at the Hongqiao Town Office had been employees of the Hongqiao SGC, and the third had worked for the nearby Qibao SGC; and two of the four staff members at the Longcao Town Office had been employees of the Zaojin SGC (one as an interpreter), while the other two had been with the South City SGC.[36] This high rate of survival suggests that the SGCs were successful in resisting central control in at least some jurisdictions, and not just in 1938 but through subsequent reorganizations.

The Great Way Government was not the only actor in the drama of gaining recognition. Several groups actually approached the Great Way Government for its ratification, presumably to swing local contests for power. It is in this context that two representatives of the fishing population on the coastal islands belonging to the former counties of Baoshan and Chuansha petitioned the Great Way to form a PMC. They were emphatic in their denunciation of the Guomindang's "Party military government," which "never once sent an official to direct an organization for us, but only knew how to levy the fish tax, which was a heavy burden on the people." The petitioners claimed that the islanders were ecstatic about the founding of a new regime, which will "rescue the people from disaster," and responded by recommending some local people to organize a provisional PMC.[37] Everything in the petition lines up smoothly with Great Way rhetoric. Unfortunately, no response is included in the file in the Shanghai

---

[35] "Gaoqiao zhen zhenwuhui huize," SMA File R1-1-152; "Shanghai tebieshi shizheng xunling di 532 hao," SMA File R18-126. In some places the local SGCs were able to resist taking on the designations *zhengwushu* and *zhenwuhui* until the fall of 1938. They were uniformly changed to *gongshu* and *gongsuo* ("office") in January 1939.

[36] "Shanghai tebieshi Huxi qu Hongqiao zhen zhengongsuo zhiyuan yilan biao" and "zhenzhang lüli biao," "Shanghai tebieshi Huxi qu Xinhua zhen zhengongsuo zhiyuan yilan biao" and "zhenzhang lüli biao," "Shanghai tebieshi Huxi qu Longcao zhengongsuo zhiyuan yilan biao," SSD File R18–275.

[37] Petition submitted by Wang Zhenjiang and Wu Zhenya, SMA File R1-1-153.

Municipal Archives in which this petition is preserved, and no other evidence indicates whether the petitioners were given the recognition to go ahead. But the Great Way Government was not prepared to rubber-stamp every request for recognition. When three companies in Chuansha applied in January for official recognition of an SGC under its leadership, they were told that they had no authority to do so.[38]

The Chuansha petitioners sought to bolster their case by noting that they were seeking permission as well from the local Japanese military commander – neglecting to note that the Japanese army had already appointed someone else to run local affairs, someone who acknowledged some measure of Great Way authority.[39] If invoking the army was a subtle pressuring device, it backfired. The Japanese army did at times act locally to bolster Great Way authority. For example, when a Special Service unit discovered buried weapons and ammunition in Nanzhen in Gaoxing District, it did not confiscate these items but handed them over to the town SGC for transmission to the Great Way Government.[40] On the other hand, it may well be that the latter was regarded as powerless when it did not have the blessing of the former. When an association of Suzhou natives living in Shanghai petitioned for permission to set up a peace maintenance committee in Suzhou under the leadership of two of their members, they addressed it simultaneously to both agencies.[41] The double addressing of the petition could be construed as indicating equal authority; more likely it signified that one could not act without the express agreement of the other.

Sometimes the inequality of the relationship breaks into view, as it does in the case of the Tangqiao SGC. The Great Way Government discovered in January that this committee was operating without its authorization and ordered the Pudong police to investigate. The police report pointed out that this SGC was working closely with the army unit stationed there, and that the prior PMC in Tangqiao had been formed by the local garrison after it had taken over (and completely destroyed) the town. The garrison had reported this arrangement to the North Pudong Garrison Command, and that agency had approved the body and provided passes to assist its members in their work. When the PMC was made over into an SGC on January 16, provisional regulations were drawn up that are explicit regarding the SGC's primary dependence on the Japanese army.

---

[38] "Cheng wei zuzhi Chuansha zizhihui qingqiu," SMA File R1-1-152.

[39] "Chuansha shangmin zizhihui wei baogao shi," China Number Two Historical Archives, Record Group 2001(2), File 19.

[40] Report of the Gaoxing qu Gaoxing Nanzhen shangmin zizhihui, SMA File R1-1-152.

[41] Petition of Wuxian (Suzhou) binan tongxianghui, SMA File R1-1-152.

The first regulation notes that this body was set up by order of the local army unit; the second, that it was charged with working to resolve misunderstandings between Japanese soldiers and the local people; the fifth, that all important issues be reported to the army; the eleventh, that all SGC decisions be ratified by the army; and the thirteenth, that the regulations themselves had to have army approval (they were in fact duly submitted to the local army unit).[42] These regulations reveal that the Tangqiao SGC, even though it operated within Pudong, was entirely indifferent to the existence of the Great Way Government and related exclusively to the authority of the Japanese army. The Great Way might order an investigation, as indeed it did, but it could do nothing more. Only after the demise of the Great Way Government would the Japanese army begin to relinquish hands-on control of local administration.

POLICE

The most active agency of the Great Way Government, and at times the sole sign of its functioning, was its police force. When a Japanese pictorial magazine wanted to publish a picture in late January showing that Shanghai was now under the Great Way Government, all it had was a photograph of a policeman standing in front of the Pudong office. Without the police, especially in the opening months, the new administration had no hope of imposing real jurisdiction or enforcing security. The police were thus the first department to be staffed, as already noted, and Great Way police posts were set up where possible in the city and suburbs during December and January. This initiative did not necessarily mean that those areas came under anything more than nominal Great Way control, but the posts were at least steps toward realizing that objective. The elevation of lower-level police posts in outlying areas into full stations in March and April are evidence of an increasingly successful centralization of police authority.[43]

Police authority often had to be asserted in competition with another security authority, as happened in the Western District. An independent police bureau was established there following a meeting the Japanese Military Police convened in the Kung Dah Cotton Mill on December 13. Chinese shop owners and Japanese residents gathered to discuss measures for maintaining law and order, then passed a resolution to set up a police bureau headed by a Chinese who had the strong support of Japanese mill owners. The new bureau was stationed at 94 Jessfield Road, which was the headquarters of the Japanese pacification

---

[42] "Wei cheng fuchi jucha bao Tangqiao zizhihui zuzhi jingguo," SMA File R1-1-152.

[43] E.g., report on Zhoupu police station (April 4, 1938); SMA File R1-1-4.

team and the Military Police (Kempeitai), strong indication that it operated under Japanese direction. It functioned for seven weeks until February 5, when police authority was finally transferred to the Great Way regime. Only after this transfer was it possible for the Great Way Government to claim jurisdiction in the area and set up other administrative offices in the Japanese-dominated areas of the Western District.[44]

Similar tugs of war over police authority were played out in other parts of Shanghai. As in the Western District, Chinese police units were formed and operated under Japanese control, and the Great Way police were often powerless to do anything other than place them and the committees to which they reported under surveillance.[45] One attempt to enhance Great Way presence, especially in rural areas dominated by the Japanese army, was the formation in April of a Youth Corps. The initial proposal suggests an entity that was really more a paramilitary corps than a Boy Scout troop, for it cites the need to use this corps to exert increased vigilance against "bad elements," a conveniently loose term that could designate anyone the regime did not like. Regulations drawn up in May narrowed the range of targets by declaring that the corps was to supplement the bandit-suppression work of the Japanese army and the police.[46] Still, a centrally controlled paramilitary body could either augment or neutralize the security forces already there, depending on local conditions, thereby strengthening the hand of the Shanghai administration over units that were less than fully cooperative, and that may have been so by virtue of being able to hide behind Japanese military patrons. The fact that the regime was under the domination of a single invader did not mean that that invader administered the areas under its control in a unified way. Nor would it mean that those who came forward to collaborate would agree to submit to a centralized hierarchy that placed them farther down the pyramid than they would have liked.

The conditions of occupation placed before Great Way security agencies problems peculiar to those conditions: resolving conflicts between Chinese and Japanese,[47] protecting regime personnel from assassination, and countering

---

[44] "Report on the Situation in the Western District" (January 30, 1939), pp. 2–3, SMP File 9114(c).

[45] Surveillance of police: report of Zhu Yuzhen (April 8, 1938), SMA File R1-1-105; surveillance of a chamber of commerce replacing a PMC: report of Zhu Yuzhen (January 22, 1938), order of January 28, 1938, SMA File R1-1-4.

[46] "Shanghai Great Way Government Announcement No. 19," SMA File R1-1-126; "Outline Regulations" submitted by Zhang Shangyi (May 6, 1938), SMA File R1-2-221.

[47] E.g., the police had to step in when a Japanese soldier took his watch to be repaired at a watch shop in Gaoqiao and struck the watchmaker with his bayonet when he couldn't make himself understood; report of Hu Zhenggu (January 28, 1938), SMA File R1-1-103.

insurgency. Within the city, the second of these concerns was paramount. A report in early January from the head detective of the Great Way police indicates that he had a good sense of the two main threats. One was GMD security chief Dai Li's organization, consisting largely of Blue Shirts and former Communist agents and located in the International Settlement. The other was labor boss Zhu Xuefan's Green Gang organization in the French Concession, which mobilized routed soldiers and the urban unemployed to engage in attacks on pro-Japanese personnel. Both groups moved their headquarters among restaurants and foreign-owned buildings every two or three days, effectively preventing detection.[48] Su Xiwen was the primary target for the assassination squads that these entities organized, though he managed to escape from every attack unscathed. The burden on the police was extraordinary, and proved to be more than Police Chief Zhu Yuzhen could handle. When a morning meeting that Su Xiwen attended on April 15 was bombed, Su collected Zhu's resignation three days later for the breach in security.[49] The pressure of terrorist attack did not daunt Su, but it was sufficient to discourage people from being recruited into the Great Way administration. Those who did take office often resigned within weeks of accepting their appointments.[50]

The spectacular threat of assassination inside the city was paralleled by a simmering insurgency in the surrounding rural areas. The Great Way Government ordered that the traditional system of mutual surety groups known as the *baojia* be instituted, that *baojia* captains be appointed throughout the region to assist with stabilizing the countryside, and also that censuses be done so that every person be identified and vouched for.[51] But these projects were slow to be carried out and left insurgents untouched. Late in January, the town of Chuansha was invaded by four to five hundred guerrillas demanding material

---

[48] Report of Hu Zhenggu (January 10, 1938), SMA File R1-1-72. There are many more such reports in this file. These two organizations are discussed in Frederic Wakeman, *Policing Shanghai*, pp. 283–287. It is worth noting that the Great Way police also placed pro-Japanese counterinsurgency bodies such as the East Asian Anti-Communist League under surveillance as well; police report to Su Xiwen (February 16, 1938), SMA File R1-1-71.

[49] Report of Zhu Yuzhen (April 18, 1938), SMA File R1-1-2.

[50] The headship of the municipal bureau of finances proved difficult to fill, probably because of its high profile. Ren Baoan had taken the post but resigned it at the end of February. His replacement, He Jiayou, took up the job only to resign six weeks later "because of a weak constitution and ill health"; letter of He Jiayou (accepted March 18, 1938), SMA File R1-1-2; report of Ren Baoan (March 1, 1938), SMA File R1-1-3. From one document in the archives on which Ren Baoan has written a note dated April 16, it appears that Ren returned briefly in mid-April to fill in for He Jiayou as head of finances prior to Su Xiwen's assuming the post on April 20; report from Songjiang PMC (April 8, 1938), SMA File R1-1-5.

[51] The imposition of *baojia* is noted in the report of the Gaoxing qu Gaoxing Nanzhen shangmin zizhihui, SSD File R1-1-152.

support for the resistance. Another group of twenty hit the nearby town of Xiaowan the next day, requisitioning goods and demanding donations to their cause. The merchants of Chuansha, many of whom had only recently returned and reopened their businesses, responded by declaring a strike. A desperate acting town head appealed for military protection, not just because these raids made it "impossible for the people to live in peace and take pleasure in their work," but because it interfered with the operation of the economy,[52] the issue to which I now turn.

REVENUE

The success of his collaborationist regime, as Su Xiwen surely realized, would be judged by the degree to which the economy was restored and the regime able thereby to become self-supporting. Su Xiwen was not immediately under pressure to raise revenue. According to a Japanese source published at the time, he received a contribution of a million yen from an unnamed "friend" in Tianjin to get the regime going.[53] The Great Way Government announced on December 15 that no taxes would be collected within the areas damaged by fighting until January.[54] The tax holiday was intended to relieve local businesses, as well as to lure others across the Huangpu River to Pudong, but it could only be temporary. At the end of December, Su issued his "Sixth Directive" to his police and finance bureaus, stating that as businesses were reopening all over the city, they should be expected to assist the regime in meeting the heavy expenses of rebuilding Shanghai, and that agents of the finance bureau would be sent out in the company of policemen to Pudong, the Western District, the South City, and Zhabei to begin collecting business taxes starting on the first day of the lunar year (January 31, 1938).[55]

The more immediate source of revenue was traffic, of goods in transit and of people on ferries. The earliest such levy appears to have been on the eight ferries crossing the Wusong River. The Great Way Government began collecting a ferry tax cooperatively with the Wusong SGC on January 2. This was followed by a levy on vegetables brought into the Western District starting on January 11. In both cases, Japanese Special Service personnel were involved, which could put them in some conflict with the Great Way police. In fact, two days before the

---

[52] Report from Tao Rukan (January 30, 1938), "Diaocha biedongdui," SMA File R1-1-72.
[53] Mōgi, *Shanhai shi daidō seifu shisatsu hōkoku,* p. 7.
[54] *RSZ,* p. 431.
[55] "Shanghai shi dadao zhengfu xunling zidi liuhao" (December 30, 1937), SMA File 1-1-147. The month's delay did not apply to Gaoqiao, Dongyu, and Xidu on the grounds that they had suffered no damage.

new tax regime was to begin on January 31, Zhu Yuzhen warned Su Xiwen that the Japanese appeared not to have understood that as of that date, all taxes were to be collected by agents of the municipal government and not by themselves.[56]

One of the toughest and most successful competitors for revenue was the South City SGC. The South City was the core of the old Chinese city and economically the most vibrant part of the occupied parts of Shanghai. The self-government committee that a Japanese pacification agent established there in mid-January was remarkably resistant to municipal pressure. The Great Way Government kept sending policemen over to investigate what the SGC was doing. As they discovered, it was doing a great deal to stimulate the revival of the South City economy and assist the large numbers of refugees who collected there or just across the boundary with the French Concession. Its ability to control rice, which both fed the refugees and generated revenue, was the key to its success. By late February, the South City SGC had achieved control of the rice market by placing the dozen rice shops within the refugee zone under the supervision of its Office to Sell Confiscated Materials. This office had seven or eight outlets in Jiumudi and two or three in Dongjiadu, which in the opinion of an official from the Great Way Social Affairs Bureau were charging monopolistic prices (second-class *yangxian* rice was being sold by the *dan* for 13.2 yuan, over 3 yuan higher than the price in Pudong, and at an even higher rate when sold in smaller amounts). The Great Way official who prepared a report on rice sales in the South City accused the SGC of driving up food prices by its excessive taxes and thereby intensifying instability, which he then contrasted with the "benevolent administration" of the Great Way Government.[57]

The South City SGC had its own Finance Bureau, which raised revenue by levying a fee on vegetable stalls in the markets at Jiumudi and Xiaopudu, both of which flourished under the stimulus of high demand for food. It managed to gain access into the world of wealthier merchants through the South City Chamber of Commerce. The Chamber, which predated the occupation, was particularly prosperous because of an agreement with the French authorities allowing its members to operate in the Concession freely. The SGC replaced the chamber with its own Commercial and Industrial Bureau and most members registered, though the Chamber seems to have continued a shadow existence, carrying out its liturgical functions and levying the fees necessary to keep the markets running. Despite the complaints of some merchants that the new bureau was exacting excessive taxes (a situation which obliged Japanese pacification

---

[56] Reports of Zhu Yuzhen (January 7, January 12, January 29, 1938), SMA File R1-1-147.
[57] "Jin jiang gongli eryue ershiliu ri fu," SMA File R1-1-157.

agents to step in and negotiate between the merchants and the SGC),[58] the SGC was able to continue running South City affairs until a more powerful municipal administration than the Great Way Government had the support of the Japanese authorities to shut it down in July. Despite its attempts to intervene, the Great Way Government was left out of these profitable goings-on, as a police report on South City commercial affairs in March or April makes plain:

> We find that the various organs of the South City Self-Government Committee have arrogated all power in this area and have taken over every aspect of its administration, taxing at will. The South City is under the formal aegis of the city government, yet it has set up its own banner and has placed all manner of obstacles in the way of the administrative powers of the Great Way Government.[59]

The Great Way Government was powerless to wrest control from the South City SGC. It reported this situation to Nishimura's pacification office in Pudong, but was unable to secure the support it needed to oust the local body and replace it with officials willing to cooperate in building a unified regime that would extend across both Pudong and the South City.

As the South City example indicates, raising revenue was not only a matter of collecting taxes. The shattered economy had to be stimulated to a level such that goods were once again being moved publicly and so could be taxed. The inhibitor here was the Japanese military restriction on boat traffic. Unless the functioning of the inland waterways was restored, goods could not go in and out of the city, to the detriment of both urban and rural commerce. As a group of petitioners from Tangqiao wailed, "If we do not speedily find a way to allow commerce to flourish, we won't have the means to maintain our locality." The implied consequences were more than economic, "maintain" being a code-word for "peace maintenance," and the Tangqiao SGC attached its name to the petition out of concern that schools in Tangqiao needed police protection, which had to be paid for. The petitioners were asking for assistance to allow commercial boats to move without hindrance on the inland waterways. One petitioner asked that the route between Tangqiao and Zhangjiabang be opened to allow supplies of rice and firewood to come in from the villages in Songjiang farther west. Two other merchants asked that the route from Tangqiao into the concessions be opened so that they could transport dyed cloth and liquor. One

[58] Report of Social Affairs Bureau (April 27, 1938), SMA File R1-2-160.
[59] "Cheng wei chengbao shi an," SMA File R1-1-153; "Shanghai Nanshi shangjie lianhehui tonggao" (March 1938), SMA File R1-1-154.

farmer needed to get to his source of supply for lime in Yexie Town. Another wanted permission to transport vegetables to the South City.[60] Requests to re-open waterways gave the Great Way Government a point of fiscal leverage, for the traffic a local committee was asking to resume would have to allow itself to be taxed. But each side could and did see this differently, and conflicts over who controlled transit revenues arose between Shanghai and the outlying towns.[61]

Revenue issues could also pit the Great Way Government against the Japanese army. This competition was not entirely economic, as the army was not yet seeking to monopolize revenues. The problem was not simply that the merchant who moved his goods over waterways was indistinguishable from a guerrilla quartermaster moving supplies and ammunition, but rather that he operated on a landscape that was as familiar to him as it was foreign to those who claimed to represent the occupation state. The Great Way Government was thus caught between opposing pressures. To get the support of urban and rural commercial interests, it had to link Shanghai as fully to the surrounding region as it had been before the war. It is for this reason that the propaganda article on the restoration of order in Shanghai, which the regime secretariat planted in the *Shanhaiguan News* in March 1938, made a point of declaring: "All boats on the waterways, so long as they first register, are permitted to operate."[62] On the other hand, in many places the regime was obliged to respect Japanese security measures and not contest the cordon that its army placed around Shanghai. As long as security was high on the CCAA's agenda, the Great Way regime could only work within the conditions it imposed.

RECONFIGURATION

The Great Way Government lasted less than five months. It was replaced on April 28, 1938 by an entity more purely municipal in name as well as ambition, the Shanghai Municipal Commission (*Duban Shanghai shi gongshu*).[63] Several factors militated in favor of abandoning the "government" of Su Xiwen. There was, first of all, the contradiction caused by the formation of the Reformed

---

[60] Petition of Tangqiao zizhihui Tangqiao zhen banshichu, SMA File R1-1-153.

[61] As it did, for example, on the boat route from Jiading county into Shanghai in March 1938; "Katei senbuhan kiroku" (April 1938), p. 7, in Inoue, Kachū senbu kōsaku shiryō.

[62] "Dadao zhengfu mishuchu wei touji xuanchuan xinwengao zhi *Shanhaiguan gongbao* han" (March 8, 1938), *RSZ*, p. 795.

[63] The neutral *gongshu* ("office") was used for government offices in the late-imperial era; e.g., *Qiongzhou fuzhi* (1619), 3.84a. The use of this term suggests a conscious attempt to normalize administrative terminology into pre-Republican usage. It was superseded later that year when the Municipal Commission was renamed using the Republican category of Special Municipality.

Government in Nanjing at the end of March. Two "governments" could not coexist in the lower Yangzi; Su Xiwen's regime had to be reduced to something less. This adjustment took a full month to carry out, suggesting some resistance somewhere within the occupation system. In its outcome, though, the reconfiguration caused little rupture, for Su was able to continue in roughly the same capacity under the new title of director-general.

A second aspect of the downgrading of the Great Way Government appears to have had something to do with the interservice rivalry between the Japanese army and navy. The Reformed Government was very much an army project, as the Great Way Government had been. The navy was unhappy with both arrangements, largely because it feared Japan being drawn into another Manchuria. A whiff of this problem comes to light in a British intelligence report for October 1938 coming out of the consulate general in Shanghai. On the 16th of that month, the municipal commission was reconfigured for a second time into a special municipality. Su was passed over for the new position of mayor, however, in favor of the more eminent former chairman of the Shanghai Chamber of Commerce, Fu Xiaoan (1871–1940). As secretary general of the municipal secretariat, Su was second in command. He served as acting mayor in the autumn of 1940 following Fu's assassination, but he lost that position after six weeks to Chen Gongbo (1892–1946). According to British intelligence, Fu Xiaoan was a client of the navy. His appointment was regarded as "a further move by the Japanese navy in their struggle to retain the lion's share in local influence and control, as against attempted encroachment by the Japanese military." The reorganization was understood to be an attack on the army in the figure of Su Xiwen, "who now occupies the post of Secretary-General to the new Administration and is carrying on an obstructionist campaign with the aid of members of the Japanese Special Service Section against Fu Siao-an and the Japanese naval landing party, who support the new mayor." The report speculates, wrongly as it turns out, that Su "may shortly be removed from the Shanghai area, leaving Fu Siao-an in complete control."[64] Apparently the army was strong enough to keep their client on the scene, if only in second place.

A third element to the collapse of the Great Way Government may have been the perception that it failed to meet the goals set for it. The British consulate general was not impressed with what it could discern of its performance, commenting in its April 1938 intelligence report that "there are few signs of any organised municipal administration in the area nominally controlled by

---

[64] British Consulate General (Shanghai), "China Summary," 1938, no. 10, para. 14–15; National Archives of Canada, File 6045-40c.

the mayor."[65] This judgment could just as easily reflect an incapacity to see beneath the surface of things in areas under Japanese military occupation, as it does failure, yet let us suppose it is true. Certainly this chapter has supplied ample evidence that this regime did not make impressive headway. It was unable to impose a unified authority over the Shanghai region, variously facing local and Japanese resistance to its claims. It may also have been plagued by its own ineptitude and ill-planning, though the documents in the municipal archives give the impression of a regime hard at work to do something. One signal of its weakness, or at least of its poor connections to powerful people, is that Great Way personnel tend not to appear on the personnel lists of subsequent municipal regimes.[66]

Despite its limits to its achievements, there is no clear evidence that the Japanese army scrapped the regime because it regarded it as a failure. The judgment of failure came rather from the Chinese audience to which the regime had had to play. The political tenor and hack Confucian ideology of the Great Way Government, with its archaic slogans calling for "using the Way of the Sun-and-Moon to establish the nation" and its ingenuous declarations that "all men are brothers and the world is a Great Unity,"[67] were hopelessly out of touch with the temper of the times in a modernizing, and occupied, city. Shanghai residents had heard much about "the nation" since the 1910s, but would any have recognized "Sun-and-Moon" as a metaphor that one of Confucius's disciples applied to the Master? So too they were under constant reminder that they lived in a larger world, but would they have wanted to use that awareness to restage the Confucian piety about brotherhood with the Japanese soldiers who occupied their city? In the end, most Shanghainese were probably indifferent to the regime's ideological posture, preferring to go about the business of surviving despite the insecurity that invasion brings and work back to some measure of normalcy as conditions improved. The sole legacy of the Great Way Government after mid-1938 was its name, which continued in popular use as the name of the Shanghai municipal government for several years after the Great Way had been reconfigured out of existence. The persistence of this language may reveal

---

[65] British Consulate General (Shanghai), "China Summary," 1938, no. 4, para. 6; National Archives of Canada, File 6045-40c.

[66] For example, in the 1940 personnel lists for the Western District Office, only one of forty-six local officials is noted as having served in the Great Way Government, although half a dozen had held positions in self-government committees operating during the Great Way period; "Shanghai tebieshi Huxi qu . . . zhiyuan yilan," SMA File R18-275. Fu Xiaoan on November 1, 1938 confirmed the right of Great Way personnel to continue in their posts under his administration; *RSZ*, p. 49.

[67] These are among the official slogans published for Japanese consumption in Mōgi, *Shanghai shi daidō seifu shisatsu hōkoku*, p. 10.

that all forms of collaboration at the municipal level would be tarred with the same brush of contempt and indifference until the occupation was over and this scoundrel time came to a close.

BIBLIOGRAPHY

Brook, Timothy. "Collaborationist Nationalism in Occupied Wartime China." In *Nation Work: Asian Elites and National Identities*, edited by Timothy Brook and Andre Schmid, pp. 159–190. Ann Arbor: University of Michigan Press, 2000.

Inoue Hisashi, ed. *Kachū senbu kōsaku shiryō* [Materials on pacification work in central China]. Tokyo: Fuji Shuppan, 1989.

Mōgi Kikuo, ed. *Shanhai shi daidō seifu shisaku hōkoku* [Report on the Great Way Government of Shanghai municipality]. Tokyo: Kinzensha, 1938.

Shanghai shi dang'anguan [Shanghai municipal archives], ed. *Ri-wei Shanghai shi zhengfu* [Japanese-puppet Shanghai municipal governments]. Shanghai: Dang'an chubanshe, 1986.

Shanghai tebieshi zhengfu [Shanghai special municipality], ed. *Shanghai tebieshi zhengfu chuzhou jinian tekan* [Commemorative volume for the first anniversary of the Shanghai Special Muncipality]. Shanghai, 1940.

Wakeman, Frederic, Jr. *Policing Shanghai*. Berkeley: University of California Press, 1995.

Chapter 7

Resistance and Cooperation

Du Yuesheng and the Politics of the
Shanghai United Committee, 1940–1945

BRIAN G. MARTIN

In the 1930s the Nanjing Government's compact with the Green Gang boss Du Yuesheng was a fundamental relationship which buttressed its control over Shanghai, China's largest city and its financial and commercial center. The Green Gang, indeed, was an integral part of the corporatist system of power which Jiang Jieshi's Guomindang fashioned after 1932.[1] The outbreak of war and the subsequent Japanese occupation of Shanghai and its hinterland destroyed this system, but the Guomindang-Green Gang relationship endured and was given fresh impetus by the exigencies of war.[2]

Banished to the remote western province of Sichuan, Jiang's Government needed to maintain some presence in its former heartland – the Shanghai-Nanjing region – in order to contest the legitimacy of the Japanese-sponsored puppet regimes and to prevent the communists from monopolizing national salvation activities in this key region. So the links with Du Yuesheng's Green Gang became one means by which the Chongqing Government sought to maintain an underground presence in Shanghai. For Du Yuesheng, living in effective exile in Hong Kong, his relations with Chongqing were important to bolster his prestige and to assist him in maintaining his authority within the Shanghai Green Gang. This mutual dependence received institutional expression in the Shanghai United Committee (*Shanghai Shi Tongyi Weiyuanhui* – SUC) which was the instrument for coordinating the Guomindang's underground resistance after 1940.

---

[1] Brian G. Martin, *The Shanghai Green Gang: Politics and Organized Crime, 1919–1937*. Berkeley: University of California Press, 1996, Chapters 7 and 8.

[2] For a discussion of the Shanghai Green Gang during the early part of the war, see Brian G. Martin, "Resistance and Collaboration: The Green Gang and Shanghai's 'Isolated Island' (*gudao*), 1937–1941." Paper presented at the colloquium *Shanghai: Culture et Histoire (1843–1949)*, INALCO, Paris, January 27–29, 1997. See also Frederic Wakeman, Jr., *The Shanghai Badlands: Wartime Terrorism and Urban Crime, 1937–1941*. Cambridge: Cambridge University Press, 1996, passim.

But the political and economic implications for the Chongqing Government of the long military stalemate after the outbreak of the Pacific War subtly changed the objectives of the SUC. From an instrument of resistance it became a vehicle for tacit cooperation between the Chongqing Government and the puppet Nanjing regime within the context of Japanese-sponsored peace initiatives in 1943–1944. By 1944, indeed, the SUC as an organization for marshaling underground resistance forces in the occupied areas had become largely moribund, although an attempt was made to revive it in mid-1945 in the context of preparing for landings by U.S. Marines on the East China coast. The present chapter discusses how this transformation occurred and what it reveals of Guomindang-Green Gang collaboration under wartime conditions.

STIMULUS: THE CHALLENGE OF THE WANG JINGWEI REGIME

The emergence of the Wang Jingwei peace movement in May 1939 posed a real threat to the Chongqing Guomindang Government. The existing puppet governments, such as the Reformed Government in Nanjing, had little legitimacy. They were mainly composed of opportunistic politicians associated with long-gone warlord regimes which had been overthrown in the process of national reunification by the new revolutionary regime of the Guomindang in the late 1920s. The Wang Jingwei peace movement, however, was different. Wang Jingwei himself was a national figure who had been an early member of Sun Yat-sen's revolutionary organization and, perhaps, was the closest Guomindang leader to Sun at the time of the latter's death in 1925. From the late 1920s through the 1930s, Wang was the major civilian political rival to Jiang Jieshi, asserting that he was the true political and ideological heir of Sun. The majority of Wang's followers were long-standing members of the Guomindang, and some, like his two senior lieutenants, Chen Gongbo and Zhou Fohai, had also been members of the Communist Party early in their political careers. The Wang Jingwei peace movement, therefore, could appeal to shared progressive party values as well as to a nascent war weariness. Wang's pessimism about China's ability to defeat Japan was not limited to his immediate followers, but was widely held at senior levels of the Guomindang regime. When Wang Jingwei finally established his "National" Government in Nanjing on March 30, 1940, therefore, it posed a genuine challenge to the Chongqing Government, which the latter could not ignore.

At the time that Wang Jingwei publicly launched his peace movement, the pressures of underground work had begun to take their toll on the Guomindang's organization in Shanghai. Before the outbreak of the Sino-Japanese War in 1937, the Shanghai party apparatus was controlled by the CC Clique – one of the most powerful factions within the Guomindang.[3] The CC Clique derived its name from the two brothers, Chen Guofu and Chen Lifu, who set it up; they were both key supporters of Jiang Jieshi and successively ran the Guomindang's powerful Organization Department. After the fall of Chinese Shanghai, the CC Clique continued to control the party's underground work in the city. In late 1938, however, the leadership of the Shanghai Party Branch became the subject of serious conflict within the CC Clique, with attempts to replace the existing Shanghai Party branch head, Tong Xingbai. The belief that Tong had connived in the arrests by the Japanese Kempeitai (military police) in May 1939 of three members of the opposing faction in the CC Clique intensified criticism of Tong. Tong, however, appealed for support to his factional leader, Wu Kaixian, and to his Green Gang mentor, Du Yuesheng. Both Wu and Du held discussions with Chen Lifu, who finally agreed to retain Tong as director of the Shanghai Party Branch and to transfer his nominated replacement, Zheng Yitong, to another post.[4]

This struggle over the leadership of the Shanghai Party Branch had a corrosive effect on the morale of the local members of the CC Clique. Some were thus predisposed to listen to the overtures from the Wang Jingwei peace movement. Wang Jingwei's convening of the so-called "Sixth National Congress of the Guomindang" in Shanghai in August 1939 was the signal for numerous defections among local Guomindang party members and labor organizers, nearly all of them affiliated with the CC Clique. They included two leading members of the Shanghai Party Branch's standing committee, Cai Hongtian and Wang Manyun, who took with them the branch's official seal and most of its personnel files, together with Huang Xianggu, Zhang Yingzeng, and Miss Jin Guangmei of the local party branch, and the Guomindang labor organizer, Zhang Kechang, who had played a leading role in the prewar Shanghai Postal Workers' Union.[5] These defections seriously jeopardized the Guomindang Government's position in Shanghai, and by September 1939, the SMP Special Branch described pro-Chongqing organizations in Shanghai as "moribund."[6] One of the casualties

---

[3] For information on the CC Clique and its involvement in Shanghai politics in the 1930s, see Martin (1996), pp. 163–168. See also Hung-mao Tien, *Government and Politics in Kuomintang China, 1927–1937*. Stanford, Calif.: Stanford University Press, 1972, pp. 47–52.

[4] Shanghai Municipal Police Files (SMP) (May 11, 1939) D9194; SMP Files (May 11, 1939) D9194/1; SMP Files (May 11, 1939) D9194/2; SMP Files (May 22, 1939) D9194; SMP Files (May 26, 1939) D9194; SMP Files (June 20, 1939) D9194; SMP Files (June 26, 1939) D9194.

[5] SMP Files (May 29, 1940) D8615; Wu Shaoshu, "Ji Shanghai Tongyi Weiyuanhui" (A Record of the Shanghai United Committee), *Wenshi Ziliao Xuanji*, 29, 1962, p. 79; Qin Shou'ou, "Tanhua yixiande Shanghai Tongyi Weiyuanhui" (The brief flowering of the Shanghai United Committee), in *KangRi Fengyun Lu* (A Record of the Anti-Japanese Tempest). 2 vols. Shanghai: Shanghai Renmin Chubanshe, 1985, vol. 1, p. 228; Martin (1996), p. 171.

[6] SMP Files (September 22, 1939) D8615.

189

of this disaster was Tong Xingbai, who was recalled to Chongqing in October 1939.[7]

The erosion of the power of the CC Clique in Shanghai also had a negative effect on Du Yuesheng's power base in Shanghai. Du's political influence in Shanghai was intimately bound up with his relations with the CC Clique, as his involvement in the resolution of the crisis over Tong Xingbai's leadership early in 1939 demonstrated. Many of the CC Clique defectors to Wang Jingwei were also followers of Du Yuesheng. These included Cai Hongtian, Wang Manyun, Huang Xianggu, and Geng Jiaji. The labor boss, Zhang Kechang, had also been an important member of Du's Endurance Club, and he had played an important role in ensuring Du's control of the key Postal Workers' Union. Zhang's defection, therefore, threatened Du's control of the Shanghai labor movement, as well as that of the Guomindang. The defections of local CC Clique members had effectively split Du's own followers. Many of his gangster followers, such as Xie Baosheng and Gao Xinbao, went over to the Wang regime. By the second half of 1939, therefore, both the Guomindang CC Clique and Du Yuesheng's organization were thrown into a serious crisis by the advent of the Wang Jingwei peace movement.

THE CREATION OF THE SHANGHAI UNITED COMMITTEE, JANUARY–APRIL 1940

The defections of senior Guomindang figures to the Wang Jingwei peace movement and the virtual collapse of the Guomindang's underground political organization in Shanghai infuriated Jiang Jieshi. He blamed Chen Lifu for this disaster and ordered him to reconstruct the Guomindang's Shanghai organization forthwith. Chen did not need such prompting. The Shanghai defections had seriously compromised the CC Clique and weakened its position in the factional politics of the Chongqing Government, given the importance of its control of the Shanghai underground to its overall strength in Guomindang politics.[8]

Chen turned to Wu Kaixian, the deputy head of the Guomindang's Organization Department and leader of the dominant Shanghai subfaction of the CC Clique, to remedy the situation. Wu, however, quickly realized that the CC

---

[7] SMP Files (May 29, 1939) D8615.

[8] *Da Liumang Du Yuesheng* (Big Gangster Du Yuesheng). Edited by Shanghai Shehui Kexue Yuan Zhengzhi Falu Yanjiusuo Shehui Wenti Zu (The Social Issues Section of the Political and Legal Institute of the Shanghai Academy of Social Sciences). Beijing: Qunzhong Chubanshe, 1965, p. 73; SMP Files (September 18, 1939) D9555(c); Sidney H. Chang and Ramon H. Myers, eds., *The Storm Clouds Clear Over China: The Memoir of Ch'en Li-fu, 1900–1993*. Stanford, Calif.: Hoover Institution Press, 1994, pp. 139–140.

Clique alone could not reinvigorate the Guomindang's underground activities in Shanghai, and that it would need the cooperation of other major factions, such as the Huangpu Clique and the Three People's Principles Youth Corps (*Sanminzhuyi Qingniantuan*). He therefore saw the need to develop a single organization which would commit all the major Guomindang factions to a common effort to reconstruct party, political, military, and educational activities in Shanghai, but one in which the CC Clique would be predominant.[9]

Despite his activities, however, Wu Kaixian was not the preponderant influence in the creation of the SUC. The key roles were played, in fact, by the Executive Yuan – of which Jiang was President – and Du Yuesheng. Writing in January 1940, Zhang Qun, then Vice-President of the Executive Yuan, observed that the idea for the SUC, together with its draft program and organizational structure, was the result of discussions that were held in Hong Kong in December 1939 between Huang Yanpei, the Executive Yuan's representative, and Du Yuesheng.[10] These proposals were approved by the Executive Yuan in late February 1940 with only minor changes.[11] The Chongqing Government considered the creation of the SUC to be a matter of urgency in the prosecution of the war against Japan, so it was made directly subordinate to the Executive Yuan. Composed of twenty-four prominent individuals drawn from Shanghai's political, industrial, financial, commercial, educational, and labor circles, the SUC was controlled by a five-man Standing Committee. Within this Standing Committee the key figures were Wu Kaixian, the Shanghai CC Clique leader who also doubled as SUC Secretary, Dai Li, the head of Guomindang Military Intelligence (Juntong), and Du Yuesheng.[12]

The SUC had four main objectives: to "stabilize" the Shanghai situation and to control all local national salvation work, primarily by supporting the local

---

[9] Wu Shaoshu (1962), pp. 79–80; SMP Files (May 29, 1940) D8615. On the main Guomindang factions during the war years, see T'ien-wei Wu, "Contending political forces during the War of Resistance," in James C. Hsiung and Steven I. Levine, eds., *China's Bitter Victory: The War With Japan, 1937–1945*. Armonk, N.Y.: M. E. Sharpe, 1992, pp. 52–58. On the Youth Corps, see Lloyd E. Eastman, *The Seeds of Destruction: Nationalist China in War and Revolution, 1937–1949*. Stanford, Calif.: Stanford University Press, 1984, pp. 89–107.

[10] *Executive Yuan Archives:* Letter from Zhang Qun to Wei Daoming, January 10, 1940, in *Minguo Banghui Yaolu* (Essential Documents on Secret Societies in the Republican Period). Edited by the Chinese Second Historical Archives. Beijing: Dang'an Chubanshe, 1993, p. 313.

[11] *Executive Yuan Archives* in *Minguo Banghui Yaolu* (1993), p. 316.

[12] The other two members of the Standing Committee were Jiang Bocheng, another senior member of the CC Clique, and Yu Hongjun, the Mayor of Shanghai. *Executive Yuan Archives*: Letter from Zhang Qun to Wei Daoming, January 10, 1940 in *Minguo Banghui Yaolu* (1993), pp. 313, 315; *Executive Yuan Archives*: Memorial to Jiang Jieshi, President of the Executive Yuan, from the SUC Standing Committee, April 23, 1940 in *Minguo Banghui Yaolu* (1993), pp. 319–320.

Guomindang party and government organs in Shanghai and ensuring Guomindang control over local capitalists' and workers' organizations; promoting a broad-based anti-Wang Jingwei movement which would carry the fight to the puppet organizations; strengthening propaganda in support of Jiang Jieshi as the leader of a united Chinese resistance movement; and undertaking any task required of it by the Executive Yuan.[13] To achieve these objectives the SUC established nine sections (*zu*) responsible for national salvation work in the fields of culture, education, industry and commerce, labor, foreign affairs, and relief. It also set up two committees to mobilize native place associations and to promote defections from collaborationist organizations. These sections and committees were to operate in complete secrecy, and an office was set up in the French Concession to coordinate their work, under the control of Wu Kaixian and Jiang Bocheng who were responsible for SUC underground activities in Shanghai. The SUC headquarters was established in Hong Kong under the direction of Du Yuesheng.[14]

The SUC's finances came from a variety of sources, and, given the high degree of secrecy enveloping the organization, they were not subject to standard auditing procedures. The SUC's finances could not even be referred to by name, but were entered into the Executive Yuan's account books under the rubric "Shanghai and Hong Kong wartime special services expenses."[15] So it is not surprising that few questions were asked about the way in which the committee spent its funds. The original set-up expenses of Ch$50,000 and the regular running costs of the Shanghai and Hong Kong offices (which totaled Ch$294,700 and HK$72,710 respectively for the period March to December 1940) were furnished by the Executive Yuan.[16] In addition to these regular expenses, the Executive Yuan also met the SUC's extraordinary

---

[13] *Executive Yuan Archives*: Memorial to Jiang Jieshi, President of the Executive Yuan, from the SUC Standing Committee, April 14, 1940 in *Minguo Banghui Yaolu* (1993), pp. 317–319; *Executive Yuan Archives*: Order No. 868 approving the SUC organization and system, April 26, 1940 in *Minguo Banghui Yaolu* (1993), p. 320; Wu Shaoshu (1962), p. 83; Qin Shou'ou (1985), pp. 229–230.

[14] *Executive Yuan Archives*: Memorial to Jiang Jieshi, President of the Executive Yuan, from the SUC Standing Committee, April 14, 1940 in *Minguo Banghui Yaolu* (1993), pp. 317–319; *Executive Yuan Archives*: Order No. 867 endorsing SUC funding request, April 26, 1940 in *Minguo Banghui Yaolu* (1993), pp. 323–324.

[15] *Executive Yuan Archives*: Letter from the Executive Yuan to the Secretariat of the Supreme Defence Council, January 25, 1942 in *Minguo Banghui Yaolu* (1993), p. 327.

[16] *Executive Yuan Archives*: Order No. 867 approving SUC funding request, April 26, 1940 in *Minguo Banghui Yaolu* (1993), pp. 323–324; *Executive Yuan Archives*: Statement by the SUC Standing Committee Secretary, Wu Kaixian, to the President and Vice-President of the Executive Yuan on the SUC's expenses for 1940, July 10, 1941 in *Minguo Banghui Yaolu* (1993), pp. 325–326.

expenses. In January 1942, for example, it wrote to the Secretariat of the Supreme Defense Council (*Guofang Zuigao Weiyuanhui*) seeking its approval for a secret payment of Ch$964,110.64 to the SUC to meet extra-budgetary expenditures for 1941.[17] Through his association with the Chongqing Government's Central Relief Commission (*Zhongyang Zhenji Weiyuanhui*, CRC) – he headed up the CRC's Ninth Area Relief Office in Hong Kong – Du Yuesheng also had access to relief funds which he channeled into the coffers of the SUC. In November 1940, for example, Xu Shiying, CRC Chairman, wrote to Kong Xiangxi (H. H. Kung), Vice-President of the Executive Yuan, explaining that the CRC had in the course of 1940 made three separate payments to the SUC totaling Ch$700,000, and that he was now seeking Kong's approval to pay Du a further Ch$300,000 on behalf of the SUC.[18]

Du Yuesheng's influence within the SUC was pervasive. Its members included his fellow Green Gang boss, Huang Jinrong; his followers Lu Jingshi, Zhu Xuefan, and Huang Renzhi; his secretary Yang Wei; business associates Wang Xiaolai, Qian Xinzhi, Zhou Weilong, and Lin Kanghou; as well as cronies of long standing, such as Yang Hu. Du, moreover, enjoyed sworn brother relations with Dai Li, while Wu Kaixian became a "disciple" (*dizi*) of Du's. Du also appointed leading members of his personal organization, the Endurance Club (*Heng She*), Guo Lanxin and Wang Shaozhai, to the SUC secretariat.[19] In Shanghai, liaison work on behalf of the SUC was carried out by Du's followers, Xu Caicheng, Wan Molin, and Zhang Jixian (head of the Shanghai Bureau of the French news agency, Havas). When Wu Kaixian and Jiang Bocheng went to Shanghai to set up the SUC coordinating office and commence underground activities, it was Du Yuesheng, through his intermediary Xu Caicheng, who arranged meetings with the leading Shanghai Green Gang bosses, Huang Jinrong and Jin Tingsun. Both Huang and Jin introduced Wu to the local Chinese capitalists who had been active in support of the Chinese military during the battle for Shanghai from August to November 1937. These contacts were crucial for the success of SUC efforts in reviving Guomindang underground activities in Shanghai.[20]

---

[17] *Executive Yuan Archives*: Letter from the Executive Yuan to the Secretariat of the Supreme Defence Council, January 25, 1942 in *Minguo Banghui Yaolu* (1993), pp. 326–327.

[18] *Executive Yuan Archives*: Letter from Xu Shiying to Kong Xiangxi, November 16, 1940 in *Minguo Banghui Yaolu* (1993), p. 325; *Executive Yuan Archives*: Order No. 1022 approving the CRC's request, November 22, 1940 in *Minguo Banghui Yaolu* (1993), p. 325; *Da Liumang Du Yuesheng* (1965), pp. 70–71.

[19] *Da Liumang Du Yuesheng* (1965), pp. 74–75.

[20] *Da Liumang Du Yuesheng* (1965), pp. 75–76; Wu Shaoshu (1962), p. 82; SMP Files (October 27, 1939) D8615; SMP Files (October 30, 1939) D8586(c); SMP Files (May 29, 1940) D8615.

THE SUC'S ACTIVITIES 1940–1941

One of the first actions by Wu Kaixian in Shanghai was to restore secure radio communication with Chongqing. He put Wan Molin in charge of communications and provided him with the services of two members of the Zhongtong (the Guomindang party intelligence service which was controlled by the CC Clique), who were specialist communicators and who had charge of the telegraphic codes. Wu also brought with him a large amount of cash which he used to try to buy over those who had defected and others who had adopted a wait-and-see attitude to the war, to pay for propaganda articles published in the Shanghai press, and to provide relief to unemployed youths and students.[21]

An important aspect of Wu's activities was to organize the work of the various SUC sections. Particularly important was the work of the cultural, educational, financial, industrial, and labor sections.[22] The cultural section sought to promote the Chongqing Government's national salvation propaganda in the media, theater, and the movies, and to counter Japanese and collaborationist propaganda; while the education section sought to strengthen Guomindang cells in primary, middle, and vocational schools and within universities in order to stimulate students' patriotism. A key part of this work was to gain control over those educational establishments with communist affiliations. At the SUC's inaugural meeting, for example, Wu approached the representative of the communist-affiliated China Vocational Education Society (*Zhonghua Zhiye Jiaoyu She*), one Yao Huiquan, to persuade him to agree to a number of Wu's "students" working within the continuing education schools operated by the society; but Yao succeeded in deflecting this request.[23]

Wu Kaixian could be quite direct. He would frequently telephone the Shanghai news agencies to instruct them on the type of news they could or could not publish. Jin Xiongbai, a collaborationist journalist and confidant of Zhou Fohai, recounts an incident where the *Shen Bao* and the *Xinwen Bao*, two leading Shanghai papers, were about to publish an advertisement for the opening of the Shanghai branch of the Nanjing Government's Central Savings Bank, when Wu telephoned the editors of both newspapers and told them not to print the advertisement. It did not appear.[24] The financial section pursued

---

[21] *Da Liumang Du Yuesheng* (1965), p. 76.

[22] *Executive Yuan Archives*: Letter from Zhang Qun to Wei Daoming, January 10, 1940: Enclosure in *Minguo Banghui Yaolu* (1993), p. 314.

[23] Yao Huiquan, "Genzhe dang chengpo hei'an moxiang guangming (With the party breaking through the darkness toward the light)," *Wenshi Ziliao Xuanji*, 104, 1985, pp. 169–170.

[24] Jin Xiongbai, *Wang Zhengquan de Kaichang yu Shouchang* (The Rise and Fall of the Wang Jingwei Regime), 3 vols. Taibei: Li Ao Chubanshe, 1988, vol. 1, p. 166.

policies in support of stabilizing the Chongqing Government's currency, the *fabi*, and targeted those who circulated the currency of the Nanjing regime; while the industrial and commercial section sought to undermine economic support for the Japanese and create economic confusion in the areas controlled by the Wang government. And the workers' section focused its activities on the estimated 300,000 who had been organized into the Guomindang's Lianyihui and the Shanghai General Labor Union (*Shanghai Shi Zonggonghui*). It sought to increase their national consciousness, reduce the control over them exercised by the Japanese and the Nanjing authorities, and counter communist agitation. Wu's activities on behalf of the SUC in Shanghai quickly brought him to the attention of the Wang Jingwei special service organization and its head, Ding Mocun, offered a Ch$50,000 reward for Wu's removal.[25]

Even before the SUC was fully organized, those involved with its establishment achieved their most spectacular coup by engineering the defection of two close aides of Wang Jingwei, Gao Zongwu and Tao Xisheng, together with a copy of the draft treaty between the Japanese and Wang Jingwei, at the end of 1939 and the beginning of 1940.[26] Du Yuesheng played a key role in the coup's success. Under pressure from Jiang Jieshi, Dai Li approached Du Yuesheng through the chief of the Juntong's South China Area in Hong Kong, Wang Xinheng, to help him engineer the defection of leading followers of Wang Jingwei. Through a mutual friend Du made contact with a refugee Shanghai capitalist, Huang Suchu, who was close to both Gao Zongwu, Wang's special diplomatic representative, and Tao Xisheng, Wang's chief publicist. Du then made two trips to Chongqing to discuss with Dai Li the possibility of trying to get Gao and Tao to defect. With Jiang Jieshi's agreement, it was decided that Huang visit Shanghai and sound both men out on their preparedness to defect. On his return to Hong Kong, Huang told Du that both Gao and Tao had seen a draft treaty between Wang Jingwei and the Japanese that made them regret their association with Wang. The only thing holding them back was their fear of being punished as traitors. Du immediately informed Chongqing, and it was

[25] SMP Files (October 30, 1939) D8586(c). Other SUC members also had prices on their heads. Ding Mocun had also offered a reward of Ch$ 30,000 for the apprehension of Wu Shaoshu, dead or alive. SMP Files (May 29, 1940) D8615.

[26] The following is based on the first-hand account of Wang Xinheng, the chief of the Juntong's Hong Kong operations, as told to Guo Xu, in Guo Xu, "Du Yuesheng yu Dai Li ji Juntong de guanxi (Du Yuesheng's relations with Dai Li and the Juntong)" in *Jiu Shanghai de Banghui* (1986), pp. 328–330. See also SMP Files (May 29, 1940) D8615; John Hunter Boyle, *China and Japan at War, 1937–1945: The Politics of Collaboration*. Stanford, Calif.: Stanford University Press, 1972, pp. 277–280; Xie Yongguang, *Xianggang KangRi Fengyun Lu* (The Record of the Storm of Hong Kong's Resistance to Japan). Hong Kong: Tiandi, 1995, pp. 130–138; and *Da Liumang Du Yuesheng* (1965), pp. 83–84.

agreed that Huang should return to Shanghai with Jiang's promise that there would be no reprisals, a sum of Ch$100,000 for "expenses," and Du's assurance that he personally guaranteed the offer. In January 1940, Huang returned to Hong Kong with both Gao and Tao, and a few days later the terms of the draft treaty were published in the Hong Kong press. The propaganda effect of these defections and the treaty disclosures was devastating and greatly boosted the stocks of the Chongqing Government. True to the deal brokered by Du, Gao was allowed to go to the United States with a sum of US$50,000, and Tao flew to Chongqing where he became one of Jiang Jieshi's personal aides.

The SUC also succeeded in thwarting the Wang Jingwei regime's attempts to win over the Chinese capitalist Yu Xiaqing. Yu was the leading member of the powerful Ningbo commercial group and the doyen of Chinese business in Shanghai. His defection to the puppet regime, therefore, would not only boost its legitimacy; it would also deal a perhaps fatal blow to the SUC's efforts to gain the active support of Shanghai's Chinese business circles. After the loss of Chinese Shanghai to the Japanese in November 1937, Yu Xiaqing had succeeded in fending off Japanese overtures while devoting his energies to rebuilding his war-shattered San Bei Steam Navigation Company by reflagging his remaining vessels with foreign flags of convenience and shipping Southeast Asian rice from Saigon and Rangoon to Shanghai. Locally grown Chinese rice was almost impossible to obtain due to the Japanese military's confiscatory purchases of rice in Central China, and the population became increasingly dependent on imported rice. Yu thus made a small fortune – estimated at Ch$5 million – through his rice import operations.[27]

Throughout 1940 Wu Kaixian, together with Jiang Bocheng and Xu Caicheng, exerted a great deal of effort trying to persuade Yu to leave Shanghai. But Yu procrastinated – he was an old man in his eighties and he was reluctant to let go of his lucrative wartime rice import business. So Wu had recourse to a ruse. He showed Yu a telegram purporting to come from Wu Tiecheng, the Guomindang Governor of Guangdong and former Mayor of Shanghai, conveying Jiang Jieshi's order that Yu immediately come to Chongqing. Faced with this telegram Yu hastily left Shanghai at the end of March 1941.[28] Hearing of Yu's imminent departure, the Japanese authorities unsuccessfully tried to forestall it by sending to Shanghai a very old Japanese friend of Yu's to persuade him to remain.[29]

---

[27] Ding Richu and Du Xuncheng, "Yu Xiaqing jianlun (A brief discussion of Yu Xiaqing)," *Lishi Yanjiu*, 3 (1981), pp. 164–165; Robert W. Barnett, *Economic Shanghai: Hostage to Politics, 1937–1941*. New York: Institute of Pacific Relations, 1941, pp. 56–60.

[28] *Da Liumang Du Yuesheng* (1965), p. 76; Wu Shaoshu (1962), pp. 86–88.

[29] Ding Richu and Du Xuncheng (1981), p. 165.

The SUC also supervised the resumption of the assassinations of high-profile collaborators. One of these was the Green Gang boss Zhang Xiaolin, who had long been in the sights of Juntong assassination squads, but had to a degree been protected by his past relations with Du Yuesheng. At the end of 1939, however, the Chongqing Government learned that Japanese military intelligence wanted to appoint Zhang as the puppet governor of Zhejiang, and so a decision was made to assassinate him. An attempt on January 15, 1940, however, was bungled and one of Zhang's associates, Yu Fengjian, was killed by mistake. Later that year Zhang survived another attempt on his life while he was sitting in his car at a traffic light on the Avenue Foch. Finally the Juntong bribed Zhang's personal bodyguard, Lin Huaibu, to murder him. On August 14, 1940, while Zhang was engaged in conversation with Wu Jingguan, a member of the Zhejiang puppet government, at his home on the Rue Wagner, Lin seized the opportunity to shoot and kill him.[30] Two months later the Juntong assassinated Wang Jingwei's Mayor of Shanghai, Fu Xiao'an. Fu was hacked to death in his sleep on the night of October 10–11, 1940 with a vegetable chopper wielded by his cook, Zhu Shengyuan, who had been bribed by the Juntong. Zhu was never caught.[31]

Despite the successes of the SUC, the Wang Jingwei regime nevertheless was able to consolidate itself in the course of 1940. Wang's Government was proclaimed at the end of March and eight months later Japan extended it full diplomatic recognition with the signing of the Basic Treaty in Nanjing on November 30, 1940. After Fu's assassination, Wang Jingwei appointed the head of his government's Executive Yuan, Chen Gongbo, as Mayor of Shanghai on November 20, 1940, which greatly strengthened the connections between Wang's Nanjing regime and Shanghai.[32] At the same time, the foreign settlements became a less secure haven for Guomindang operatives as the Japanese increased the pressure on the foreign authorities throughout 1940. On January 6, an attempt was made on the life of the SMC Secretary, Godfrey

[30] Zhu Jianliang and Xu Weizhi, "Zhang Xiaolin de yisheng (Zhang Xiaolin: A life) in *Jiu Shanghai de Banghui* (1986), p. 346; Chen Gongshu, *Lanyishe Neimu* (The Inside Story of the Blue Shirts). Shanghai: Guomin Xinwen, 1943, pp. 100–105.

[31] Wang Renze, "Fu Xiao'an" in *Minguo Renwu Zhuan* (Biographies of Leading Personalities of the Republic), vol. 4. Beijing: Zhonghua Shuju, 1984, p. 158; *Su Xiwen's Report to the Executive Yuan on Fu Xiao'an's Murder, October 19, 1940* in Shanghai Shi Dang'an Guan (The Shanghai Municipal Archives), ed., *RiWei Shanghai Shi Zhengfu* (The Japanese Puppet Shanghai Municipal Governments). Beijing: Dang'an Chubanshe, 1986, pp. 64–65.

[32] Barnett (1941), p. 21; Howard L. Boorman, ed., *Biographical Dictionary of Republican China*, vol. 1. New York: Columbia University Press, 1967, p. 201; Frederic Wakeman, Jr., "Political terrorism during the War of Resistance," *Centennial Symposium on Sun Yat-sen's Founding of the Kuomintang for Revolution*. Taipei, Taiwan, November 19–23, 1994, p. 17.

Phillips, and in the following month the SMC agreed to hand over the policing of the extra-Settlement Roads to a specially constituted force controlled by the Wang Jingwei regime.[33] The situation deteriorated further with the turn of events in the European war – the German victories over the Anglo-French forces and the fall of France in June. All British land forces were withdrawn from Shanghai in August. The arrival of de Margerie as the new French Consul General brought the Concession under the control of the Vichy regime, and on November 7, a Franco-Japanese accord allowed the Wang Jingwei regime to install judges in the Chinese courts located in the French Concession.[34] Police of the Wang Jingwei regime patrolled the streets of Xujiahui and Wang's special service agents operated freely within the Concession.

CRISIS: THE OUTBREAK OF THE PACIFIC WAR AND
THE ARREST OF WU KAIXIAN

With the outbreak of the Pacific War in December 1941 and the Japanese occupation of the Shanghai International Settlement and Hong Kong, the SUC lost any secure base from which to conduct its underground operations. The Japanese Kempeitai now operated at will throughout Shanghai, which led to a marked increase in the arrests of Chongqing agents and the subsequent defections of a number of them. Among the latter was Chen Gongshu, the head of the Juntong's Shanghai operations. He provided the Japanese with details of all the Chongqing government's underground organizations and agents in Shanghai, including the SUC and its senior agents Wu Kaixian and Jiang Bocheng. As a result, the Kempeitai launched an intensive dragnet to find these agents, and, having located his hideaway in the French Concession, they arrested Wu Kaixian on March 18, 1942.[35] The Kempeitai turned Wu over to the Wang Jingwei regime's special service organization, known colloquially as "Number 76" from its address on Jessfield Road in the Western District, for interrogation. Although Wu's interrogators, who included Chen Gongshu himself, tried to persuade him to work for the Wang Jingwei government, Wu refused and twice tried to commit suicide, once by taking poison and on another occasion by jumping from the second floor of the building where he was detained. The Japanese wanted to execute Wu, but he was protected by his former CC Clique colleagues who had

---

[33] J. V. Davidson-Houston, *Yellow Creek: The Story of Shanghai*. London: Putnam, 1962, pp. 163–164.

[34] Barnett (1941), pp. 21,40; SMP Files (November 13, 1940) D8593.

[35] *Da Liumang Du Yuesheng* (1965), p. 84; Jin Xiongbai, vol. 1, p. 166; Wu Shaoshu (1962), p. 90; Boyle (1972), p. 284.

defected, such as Wang Manyun and Cai Hongtian, as well as by Zhou Fohai himself, who had an emotional meeting with Wu about three weeks after his arrest.[36]

The loss of its bases in Hong Kong and Shanghai and especially the arrest of Wu Kaixian threw the SUC into confusion. Obtaining Wu's release became the SUC's overriding objective in 1942. Du Yuesheng sought to use the connections which his Shanghai agent, Xu Caicheng, had developed with Japanese intelligence to secure Wu's release, and he kept in regular radio communication with Xu. Jiang Bocheng, who had returned to Shanghai in mid-May to resume the SUC's underground work, also sought means to rescue Wu. But neither attempt met with success; the Japanese, who regarded Wu as a valuable prisoner, kept him under close guard.[37]

These events also prompted a reorganization of the SUC which greatly strengthened Du Yuesheng's position within the organization. A new position of chairman of the SUC Standing Committee was created and offered to Du. As chairman, Du was the most powerful figure in the revamped SUC; he had the authority to oversee all aspects of the SUC's activities, to call Standing Committee meetings and to resolve differences among Standing Committee members. The SUC established a new headquarters in Chongqing and a new forward operations base in the Shanghai suburbs.[38] In Chongqing, Du Yuesheng needed to establish new secure routes of communication with Shanghai, and given the vagaries of the military frontlines, these routes had to go through Northwest China. So in October 1942 Du undertook a trip to the cities of the northwest where he established branches of the Commercial Bank of China (which he controlled) as well as branches of the Endurance Club, and also developed his relations with the local Guomindang military commander, Hu Zongnan, and local secret societies. In this way he not only extended his influence into this region but also ensured safe physical communications with Shanghai and the Japanese-occupied zones for the conduct of SUC operations.[39]

[36] Jin Xiongbai, vol. 1, pp. 167–169; *Executive Yuan Archives*: Report by Du Yuesheng to the Executive Yuan on SUC activities, March 13, 1943 in *Minguo Banghui Yaolu* (1993), pp. 327–328; Cai Dejin, ed., *Zhou Fohai Riji* (Zhou Fohai's Diaries), 2 vols. Beijing: Zhongguo Shehui Kexue Chubanshe, 1986, vol. 2, p. 669.

[37] *Da Liumang Du Yuesheng* (1965), p. 84; *Executive Yuan Archives*: Report by Du Yuesheng to the Executive Yuan on SUC activities, March 13, 1943, pp. 327–328.

[38] *Executive Yuan Archives*: Memorial to the President and Vice–President of the Executive Yuan by the SUC Standing Committee on SUC reorganization, May 5, 1942 in *Minguo Banghui Yaolu* (1993), pp. 320–322; *Executive Yuan Archives*: Order No.1533 approving SUC reorganization, May 27, 1942 in *Minguo Banghui Yaolu* (1993), p. 323.

[39] *Da Liumang Du Yuesheng* (1965), pp. 81–82.

In late 1942 the Japanese sought to use Wu Kaixian as an emissary for their peace initiative which they were then developing as part of a strategy to exploit the widespread demoralization within the Chongqing Government and to take it out of the war or at least neutralize it. By the end of 1942 the mood in Chongqing was bleak. Early hopes of a speedy Allied victory had been replaced with a discouraging assessment that the Allied strategy of first defeating Germany meant that it would probably be at least four years before Japan could be defeated. It was felt that China could not maintain its military resistance for such a period and there was a growing view in some official circles that China should look out for itself.[40] So there was a disposition among some sections of the Chongqing Government to be receptive to these overtures.

Zhou Fohai raised the issue in terms of the need for the Wang Jingwei Nanjing Government and the Chongqing Government to work together to find a solution to "the national crisis" during his first meeting with Wu Kaixian on April 4, 1942.[41] But it was not until the end of October 1942 that Zhou began to seriously press the issue. Zhou had three meetings with Wu – on October 25 and 26, and November 12 – in which they discussed Jiang Jieshi's attitude toward Zhou, the need for both Guomindang regimes to deal with the growing communist threat, and the possibility of the "unification" of the Nanjing and Chongqing governments.[42] At the same time, Zhou sent a special emissary to Chongqing to sound out prominent individuals, including Du Yuesheng and his business associate Qian Xinzhi, about the Chongqing Government's preparedness to seek peace. Although none of these dared raise the peace issue with Jiang Jieshi, Zhou nevertheless pursued the contacts and in early January 1943 he sent his emissary, Chen Baohua, back to Chongqing with confidential communications for prominent Guomindang leaders – Kong Xiangxi, Chen Guofu, Chen Lifu, and Chen Bulei – as well as for Du Yuesheng and Qian Xinzhi.[43] Convinced that there was sufficient interest in Chongqing to pursue the initiative, on March 5, 1943 Zhou informed Wu Kaixian that he would be released in order to convey peace proposals to Chongqing.[44] These proposals, allegedly including a

---

[40] *Dept. of State. Chinese Newspaperman's Concern Regarding Present Situation in China, May 25, 1943 893.00/15048*, in Joseph W. Esherick, ed., *Lost Chance in China: The World War II Despatches of John S. Service*. New York: Vintage, 1975, p. 102.

[41] *Zhou Fohai Riji* (1986), vol. 1, pp. 166–167.

[42] *Zhou Fohai Riji* (1986), vol. 2, p. 759; vol. 2, pp. 766–767.

[43] *Zhou Fohai Riji* (1986), vol. 2, p. 769; vol. 2, p. 791.

[44] *Zhou Fohai Riji* (1986), vol. 2, p. 821; Jin Xiongbai, vol. 1, pp. 169–171. Informed contemporaries believed that the circumstances of Wu's release made it highly likely that he conveyed peace proposals from the Japanese. See *Dept. of State. Chinese Newspaperman's Concern Regarding Present Situation in China, May 25, 1943 893.00/15048*, in Esherick, ed., *Lost Chance in China*, pp. 103–105.

Japanese offer to return to the status quo prior to the Marco Polo Bridge Incident, were the subject of serious discussions among some members of the Chongqing Government.[45]

By mid-1943, therefore, the SUC became caught up in the politics of peace discussions. But its middle-man role in facilitating contacts between the Nanjing and Chongqing governments appears to have divided its leadership. This seems to have reflected a power struggle within the SUC itself which had been gathering momentum since early 1942, and which pitted Du Yuesheng and Wu Kaixian against Wu Shaoshu, a senior SUC member, and Jiang Bocheng. On his return to Chongqing, Wu Kaixian was feted by Du Yuesheng, Dai Li, and Chen Lifu. Wu Shaoshu, who had given a noncommittal response to separate Japanese overtures, however, set about undermining Wu Kaixian by publicizing the radio contact between Chongqing and Nanjing. This revelation prompted certain members of the People's Political Council (*Canzhenghui*) to begin impeachment proceedings against Wu Kaixian. Jiang Jieshi had been prepared to allow these clandestine contacts to continue; but he quickly lost interest once news of the Allied victories in North Africa reached Chongqing and he ordered the clandestine transmissions to be suspended.[46]

The controversy over the abortive secret peace discussions had badly fractured the SUC leadership, and its organization had effectively ceased to function as an agency for conducting clandestine operations in Shanghai by mid-1943. This was underscored by the arrest of Wu Kaixian's successor as resistance coordinator, Jiang Bocheng, in 1944.[47] Some SUC leaders, notably Du Yuesheng, sought a new role for the organization. They found it in the context of the "strategic" trade in cotton between the occupied and unoccupied zones, and they, therefore, sought to use the SUC's networks as a means of facilitating economic relations between Chongqing and Nanjing.

TRADING WITH THE ENEMY: THE TONGJI AND MINHUA COMPANIES 1943–1944

By 1943, with the front lines more or less stabilized, goods were traded in large quantities between the unoccupied and occupied zones. As Lloyd Eastman has observed, the 2,000-mile "front" running from Shanxi in the north to Guangdong in the south was almost impossible for either side to guard

---

[45] Lawrence K. Rosinger, *China's Crisis*. New York: Alfred A. Knopf, 1945, p. 99.

[46] Wu Shaoshu (1962), pp. 91–92; Esherick (1975), pp. 103–105. Rosinger notes that on August 10, 1943, reference to these peace proposals was made in the officially controlled Chongqing press. Rosinger (1945), p. 99.

[47] Jin Xiongbai (1988), vol. 1, pp. 171–174; *Zhou Fohai Riji* (1986), vol. 2, p. 1087.

effectively, and in fact proved to be highly porous, allowing a more or less steady flow of people and goods to pass from one side to the other.[48] In the first years of the war, Jiang Jieshi's government had proscribed this trade with the occupied zones on the grounds that it strengthened the enemy's sinews of war. But with the passage of years and as a military stalemate settled over the China theatre, the Chongqing Government gradually relaxed this proscription. Cut off from China's industrial heartland, it needed access to those manufactured goods which its own refugee industries could not produce in order to help counter endemic inflation – whose pace quickened after the outbreak of the Pacific War – and so ensure a degree of social stability in the cities and towns of "free" China.[49] This cross-zone trade quickly became an important source of revenue for the Chongqing Government, and Dai Li was given command of the Ministry of Finance's Anti-Smuggling Bureau (*Caizhengbu Jisishu*) in order to protect this important part of the government's tax base. Dai Li's control of the Anti-Smuggling Bureau was also an important source of extra-budgetary revenue for the Juntong, which quickly developed a stake in the cross-zone trade.[50]

Du Yuesheng himself had been heavily involved in this cross-zone trade since 1942, and even earlier if his narcotics trafficking out of Hong Kong is taken into account.[51] In March of that year he set up the China Industry and Commerce Trust Company (*Zhonghua Shiye Xintuo Gongsi* – CICTC) whose specific business was to purchase goods in the occupied zone and transport them to the interior. The CICTC brought together Du Yuesheng's Green Gang lieutenants, such as Gu Jiatang, with senior Endurance Club members, such as Lu Jingshi and Luo Qinghua, long-standing business associates, like Qian Xinzhi, and Sichuanese financiers, like Kang Xinru and Liu Hangshen. The CICTC was able to make its purchases in the occupied zone through Du's Shanghai agent, Xu Caicheng. Goods were shipped from Shanghai to border zones, such as Hengyang in Hunan, and from there the CICTC brought them to Chongqing.[52] In moving these goods Du needed the cooperation of Dai Li, which he ensured by giving Dai a share of the profits and by judiciously providing interest-free loans to the Juntong – a total of four separate loans

---

[48] Lloyd E. Eastman, "Facets of an ambivalent relationship: Smuggling, puppets, and atrocities during the War, 1937–1945," in Akira Iriye, ed., *The Chinese and the Japanese: Essays in Political and Cultural Interactions.* Princeton, N.J.: Princeton University Press, 1980, p. 275.

[49] Chiang Kia-ngau, *The Inflationary Spiral: The Experience in China, 1939–1950.* Cambridge, Mass.: MIT Press, 1958, pp. 43–58.

[50] Eastman (1980), p. 277; Guo Xu (1986), p. 330; *Da Liumang Du Yuesheng* (1965), p. 80.

[51] On Du's trafficking in narcotics during his Hong Kong period, see Martin (1997), p. 11.

[52] *Da Liumang Du Yuesheng* (1965), pp. 79–80.

between December 1941 and June 1944.[53] Du made substantial profits through the CICTC's commercial activities and this helped to consolidate his position in Chongqing business circles.

In early 1943, Zhu Huiqing of the Freight Transport Regulation Office (*Huoyun Guanliju*) persuaded Dai Li of the need to address the serious shortages in cotton yarn and cloth in "free" China by setting up an agency to purchase the necessary cloth in Shanghai. Dai Li brought in Du Yuesheng, who had the required experience in running such an agency through the activities of the CICTC, as well as having his own interests in the cotton industry – he was the major shareholder in the Shashi Cotton Mill and he was on the board of the government's Cotton Yarn and Cloth Regulation Bureau (*Shabu Guanliju*).[54] The new cotton purchasing agency, the Tongji Company (*Tongji Gongsi*), was established in mid-1943 as a "joint official-merchant enterprise" under the control of the Executive Yuan.[55] Du headed the "private" investors and provided one-third, later increased to one-half, of the company's capitalization of Ch$100 million, and the bulk of the balance was paid up by the key "official" investors, the four national banks – the Central Bank of China, the Bank of China, the Bank of Communications, and the Farmers' Bank, together with the Post Office Savings Bank. The company's key personnel were a mix of Du's Green Gang coterie and Endurance Club members, Juntong members to look after Dai Li's interests, and agents of the Cotton Yarn and Cloth Regulation Bureau answering to Kong Xiangxi. The company was effectively controlled by Du Yuesheng, who was responsible for the purchasing operations, and Dai Li, who controlled the transportation system. Branches were set up in Chongqing and at Shangqiu and Jieshou on the Henan/Jiangsu border where the occupied and unoccupied zones met. Shangqiu and Jieshou were the major entrepôts until they were overrun at the beginning of the Japanese offensive, "Operation Number One (*Ichigo*)," in April 1944. From then until the end of the war, the major entrepôt was transferred to Chun'an in Zhejiang.[56]

The company's Shanghai branch was managed by Du's agent, Xu Caicheng, and was formally a separate company, the Minhua Company (*Minhua Gongsi*). Xu used his connections with Japanese military intelligence to help get the

---

[53] Guo Xu (1986), pp. 330–331.

[54] *Da Liumang Du Yuesheng* (1965), p. 79.

[55] Although cotton was the principal commodity traded by the Tongji Company, according to Jin Xiongbai it also traded in other strategic goods such as medicines and rubber goods. Jin Xiongbai (1988), vol. 1, p. 139.

[56] Guo Xu (1986), pp. 331–332; Wu Shaoshu (1962), p. 93; *Da Liumang Du Yuesheng* (1965), pp. 85–86; Guo Lanxin, "Du Yuesheng yu Heng She" (Du Yuesheng and the Endurance Club), in *Jiu Shanghai di Banghui* (1986), p. 314.

company started, and, according to what Xu told Wang Manyun, it was Japanese intelligence that provided its initial capitalization of Ch$300 million in puppet currency.[57] Although the Japanese were interested in obtaining minerals and opium from the regions under Chongqing's control, they saw the Minhua Company principally as another means to promote their "peace initiative" with the Chongqing Government, or, at the very least, as a vehicle for maintaining some sort of political contact with it.[58] So they persuaded Zhou Fohai to become involved, and he, together with Xu Caicheng, launched the company at a banquet on September 4, 1943.[59] The Minhua Company had fourteen directors who, in addition to political figures like Wang Manyun, also included leading Shanghai businessmen such as Lin Kanghou, Yuan Lideng, and Wen Lanting.[60] Zhou Fohai's representatives on the board of directors were Duan Hongguang, the second son of the former Anfu Clique Chief Executive Duan Qirui, and his confidant, the journalist Jin Xiongbai.[61] Zhou maintained general oversight of the company, while Xu managed its day-to-day operations.

During the last phase of the war the Tongji/Minhua Company purchased two major consignments of cotton cloth in Shanghai and transported them to Chongqing. The first was in December 1943 and consisted of 3,000 "pieces" (*jian*) of cloth. The Minhua Company made the purchases in Shanghai and the consignment was shipped to Shangqiu on the Henan/Jiangsu border under the supervision of Xu Caicheng's son-in-law and a Japanese interpreter. At Shangqiu the consignment was handed over to the Tongji Company's local agent, Wang Yaokui, who used the services of Dai Li's Freight Transport Bureau Regulation Office to ship it on to Xi'an and Chongqing. Once in Chongqing the consignment was handed over to the Cotton Yarn and Cloth Regulation Bureau, which then paid the Tongji Company Ch$80 million for the transaction.[62]

The second consignment for 500 pieces (*jian*) of cotton cloth was shipped in June 1944 to Chun'an, Zhejiang, the new entrepôt for interzone trade. The

---

[57] *Da Liumang Du Yuesheng* (1965), p. 86. Xu Caicheng's contact in Japanese intelligence was one Kawamoto with whom the Japanese-speaking Xu had established a relationship of trust; see Jin Xiongbai (1988), vol. 1, p. 139.

[58] According to Jin Xiongbai, the Japanese never received any minerals or opium in exchange for the cotton cloth, medicines, and rubber goods traded by the Minhua Company. Jin Xiongbai (1988), vol. 1, pp. 139–140.

[59] *Zhou Fohai Riji* (1986), vol. 2, pp. 912, 916.

[60] According to Jin Xiongbai, the names of the directors were sent to Chongqing for approval by the Chongqing Government's Military Affairs Commission, in other words Jiang Jieshi. Jin Xiongbai (1988), vol. 1, p. 139.

[61] *Da Liumang Du Yuesheng* (1986), p. 86.

[62] *Zhou Fohai Riji* (1986), vol. 2, p. 961; Guo Xu (1986), p. 333; Guo Lanxin (1986), p. 314; *Da Liumang Du Yuesheng* (1965), p. 86.

consignment was routed through the Guomindang's Third War Zone and while in transit it was seized by Gu Zhutong, the Third War Zone commander, for use by his own troops. The Tongji Company's embarassment was compounded by the fact that its agent accompanying the consignment, Xu Ziwei, was kidnapped by guerrilla/bandits and was only released after Ch$70,000 ransom was paid. Gu's action led to a furious exchange of letters with Dai Li and the standoff was only finally resolved with Jiang Jieshi's personal intervention. Jiang approved the transfer of the consignment to the Third War Zone command for its use and instructed the Ministry of Finance to pay the Tongji Company Ch$20,600,000.[63] Although there were no further cotton consignments, the Minhua Company continued to ship medicines and rubber goods until the Japanese surrender.[64] With the end of the war, the Minhua Company was merged with the Tongji Company on August 13, 1945 and the Tongji Company moved its headquarters to Shanghai. It continued to operate throughout the civil war period with Xu Caicheng as its general manager and in close cooperation with the Security Bureau of the Ministry of National Defense (*Guofangbu Baomiju*) – the successor to the Juntong – under its new head Zheng Jiemin.[65]

PREPARING FOR AN ALLIED INVASION: THE REACTIVATION OF THE LOYAL AND PATRIOTIC NATIONAL SALVATION ARMY 1945

In the last months of the war, with the approach of Allied victory, the Chongqing Government sought to revive the resistance functions of the SUC. In particular, it wanted to activate the pro-Chongqing guerrillas of the Loyal and Patriotic National Salvation Army (*Zhongyi Jiuguo Jun* – LPNSA) to assist with planned landings of U.S. forces on China's southeast coast. The LPNSA operated in the Jiangnan hinterland of Shanghai, and had been particularly active in the Lake Tai and Pudong regions. Its origins lay in the mobilization by Dai Li and Du Yuesheng during the battle for Shanghai in 1937 of local secret societies (the Green Gang and the Triads) as irregular forces in support of Chinese troops.[66] After the fall of Shanghai and the Jiangnan region to the Japanese, the LPNSA operated as guerrilla bands behind enemy lines with Du Yuesheng in Hong Kong exercising a general supervisory role over their activities. But the attitude of the LPNSA guerrilla bands toward the Japanese and the collaborationist authorities

---

[63] *Zhou Fohai Riji* (1986), vol. 2, p. 1037; Guo Xu (1986), p. 333; Guo Lanxin (1986), p. 314.
[64] Jin Xiongbai (1988), vol. 1, p. 140.
[65] Guo Xu (1986), pp. 333–334; *Da Liumang Du Yuesheng* (1986), p. 87.
[66] On the LPNSA, see Wakeman (1996), pp. 19–24; Martin (1997), pp. 2–3; Yung-fa Chen, *Making Revolution: The Communist Movement in Eastern and Central China, 1937–1945*. Berkeley: University of California Press, 1986, pp. 481–482.

was ambiguous, an ambiguity that was compounded by the Chongqing Government's hostility to the activities of communist forces in the Jiangnan. Dai Li and Du Yuesheng, therefore, had difficulty controlling the actions of individual LPNSA commanders and defection to the puppet forces was a chronic problem.[67]

After the outbreak of the Pacific War, LPNSA activities were subsumed into the general guerrilla operations managed by the newly created Sino-American intelligence organization, SACO (Sino-American Cooperative Organization), which brought together Dai Li's Juntong and the Office of Strategic Services under the command of U.S. Navy Commander Milton E. Miles.[68] Training camps were set up for LPNSA units in the unoccupied zone and American officers were seconded to train these units in guerrilla and intelligence-gathering techniques with mixed success. In preparation for the Allied landings, Dai Li, Milton Miles, and Du Yuesheng undertook an inspection tour of SACO training camps in the Jiangnan in June 1945.[69]

The destination of the inspection group was Chun'an, Zhejiang, the interzone entrepot, where they set up their headquarters. An LPNSA training unit was established – the Workers Loyal and Patriotic National Salvation Army Training Squad (*Gongren Zhongyi Jiuguo Jun Xunlianban*) – and Du's chief lieutenant, Lu Jingshi, was sent to Shanghai to recruit workers for this squad. Du also made contact with a number of LPNSA commanders who operated in the environs of Shanghai, such as Ma Bosheng and Ding Xishan, and instructed them to coordinate their activities in preparation for the American landings. At the same time, Du wanted to revive his own networks in the Jiangnan and so opened a branch of his Endurance Club in Chun'an and began recruiting members. Japan's unconditional surrender on August 15 preempted these plans and the revived LPNSA was never used against the Japanese.[70]

CONCLUSION

The SUC was the primary means by which the Chongqing Government coordinated its underground resistance in Shanghai in the early 1940s. Its origins lay in the crisis in the pro-Chongqing Guomindang underground provoked by the arrival of the Wang Jingwei peace movement and its success in encouraging the

---

[67] Martin (1997), p. 9.

[68] Milton E. Miles, *A Different Kind of War*. New York: Doubleday, 1967, pp. 377–403.

[69] Guo Xu (1986), p. 327.

[70] Guo Lanxin (1986), pp. 314–315; *Da Liumang Du Yuesheng* (1965), pp. 89–91; Guo Xu (1986), p. 327; Miles (1967), pp. 507–521.

defections of numerous Shanghai party cadres. So great was this success that Chongqing's underground resistance organizations were reduced to shambles.

The SUC, therefore, was designed to shore up pro-Chongqing sentiment in Shanghai and the surrounding Jiangnan region. Its principal role in its early days was to promote the destabilization of the socioeconomic structures in order to contest the attempts of the Wang Jingwei regime to assert its legitimacy as the "genuine" Guomindang Government. To do this effectively, all pro-Chongqing factions with interests in the Shanghai region needed to be brought into the one organization in order that their operations could be better coordinated. The SUC, therefore, resembled a broad coalition composed of elements from the CC Clique, the Three People's Principles Youth Corps, the Juntong, and the Green Gang. Within this coalition Du Yuesheng's Green Gang organization played a particularly important role. The crisis in the pro-Chongqing resistance had the effect of reaffirming for both the Chongqing Government and Du Yuesheng their respective need for one another, and the creation of the SUC provided an institutional framework for this revitalized cooperation.

But the success of a reconstituted resistance movement also depended on victories in the field which would sustain and give credibility to the underground struggle. However, the long period of military stalemate after the outbreak of the Pacific War and Chongqing's disappointment at the relatively minor role assigned it in the United States' global military strategy put new pressure on the underground resistance which emphasized its inherent ambiguities. In the course of their underground activities, SUC agents found it necessary to develop relations with puppet officials, and this was particularly important where they were seeking to encourage defections. Relations were assisted by the fact that many SUC operatives and Shanghai puppet officials knew one another personally, they had all been members of the Guomindang, and many had belonged to the same faction – the CC Clique – before 1939. But such personal networks, while facilitating contacts, could also blur the distinction between personal friendship and professional responsibilities. And as the war dragged on with no clear outcome, the ambiguities became more pronounced. The equivocal nature of relations between Chongqing agents and puppet officials was enhanced by the fact that these agents had a second charge, to circumscribe as best they could the activities of the communists and ensure that they did not appropriate the standard of the national salvation movement in Shanghai. This shared anticommunism, therefore, increased the scope for some form of tactical accommodation between the Guomindang underground and the puppet authorities.

The Wang Jingwei Government and Japanese authorities sought to exploit these ambiguities in the interests of promoting their "peace" initiatives, and their attempts to develop indirect channels to the Chongqing Government were greatly assisted by the arrest of the SUC's senior agent in Shanghai, Wu Kaixian. With Wu's cooperation the SUC's role was subtly transformed from one of fostering resistance to one of facilitating contacts between the Nanjing and Chongqing governments. This change in function also coincided with the increased authority exercised by Du Yuesheng over the SUC. Du was an enthusiastic supporter of the policy of tactical cooperation with the Nanjing puppet government, which greatly assisted the development of his own economic interests in both Chongqing and Shanghai. Du used the SUC's networks to further economic relations with the occupied zone through the operations of the Tongji/Minhua companies. By early 1944, therefore, the SUC had virtually ceased to be an agency for the coordination of resistance activities and had become one channel through which increasingly intimate political and economic contacts were maintained between Chongqing and Nanjing. The attempts in the last couple of months of the war to reactivate the SUC's networks only served to demonstrate how attenuated these had become for the purposes of resistance.

Chapter 8

From Revenge to Treason

Political Ambivalence among Wang Jingwei's Labor Union Supporters

ALAIN ROUX

A lot of new information from Chinese sources is now pouring out of China and is renewing many historical issues about the war of resistance against Japan (*kangRi zhanzheng*). My purpose in this chapter is to take stock of what we already know on the pro-Japanese and "collaborationist" labor movement in Shanghai during the first years of that war (1937–1941) and start a quick exploration of some new tracks. After Pearl Harbor, the takeover of the International Settlement by the Japanese changed the general situation in Shanghai so radically that investigating it would require a separate essay.

In this preliminary study, I shall first recall the general trends of pro-Japanese Trade Unions in Shanghai. Then I shall present the main features of the pro-Wang General Labor Union of Shanghai West, which was then the only union that did not serve as a mere façade for Japanese secret agents or Chinese hoodlums, crooks, and scabs.

More precisely, I shall try to examine the practical behavior of these questionable unionists during the more serious strike of the time, in which they were involved. It occurred at the French Company of Electricity and Streetcars (Compagnie Française des tramways et de l'électricité – hereafter CFTE) in the autumn of 1940.

Some conclusions can be drawn from this analysis of those troubled years on the difficult relations between Shanghai workers and politics.

THE PRO-JAPANESE TRADE-UNIONISTS IN SHANGHAI: COOLIES AT PUPPETS' SHOW

The study of Shanghai trade unions during the war calls for several reminders. I chose four that were more relevant to my topic.

1. The machinery of Guomindang (hereafter GMD) control over Shanghai workers under Jiang Jieshi. GMD control of the workers rested on a tripod: the

Shanghai General Labor Union (*zong gonghui* – hereafter GLU), under Lu Jingshi and Zhu Xuefan, the Shanghai GMD (*Dangbu*) under Wu Kaixian, Lu Jingshi, and the CC Clique, and the Bureau of Social Affairs of the Shanghai Special Municipality (*Shanghai tebieshi shehuiju* – hereafter BSA),[1] under Pan Gongzhan and the CC Clique. Behind this construction there was Du Yuesheng's *Qing Bang* (Green Gang) and inside it Du Yuesheng's followers, labor bosses, and "big sticks" (*gong gunzi*).[2]

This machinery, which remained loyal to the Wuhan, then the Chongqing Nationalist government, tried to survive in the foreign settlements, under Zhou Xuexiang[3] (Tobacco Workers Union of Yangshupu), Hu Menglin (Zhou's lieutenant), Fan Caizong (Postal Employees union), and Shao Shubai (Yangzi Steamers Cabin Boys' Union), after the Japanese occupation of all the districts of Shanghai under Chinese administration (*Shanghai tebieshi*). They turned to intelligence and terrorism under the guidance of Dai Li's *juntong*,[4] but were

---

[1] Henriot, Christian: *Shanghai 1927–1937: Elites Locales et Modernisation dans la Chine Nationaliste.* Paris. Éditions de l'École des Hautes Etudes en Sciences Sociales. 1991. [*Shanghai, 1927–1937: Municipal Power and Modernization in Nationalist China.* Berkeley: University of California Press. 1993.]

[2] See Roux, Alain: *Ouvriers et ouvrières de Shanghai à l'époque du Guomindang, 1927–1949.* Thèse de doctorat d'Etat. Université de Paris 1- Sorbonne. 1991. Manuscrit. 1,990 pages (hereafter Roux 91), chapter IX: "La perte du contrôle GMD, 1937–1945," pp. 1185–1435. For more details on the GMD labor control see Roux, Alain: *Grèves et politique à Shanghai: les désillusions. 1927–1932.* Paris: Éditions de l'École des Hautes Études en Sciences Sociales. 1995 (hereafter Roux 95), pp. 257–298. On Du Yuesheng and the Shanghai workers, see Martin, Brian: *The Shanghai Green Gang: Politics and Organized Crime, 1919–1937.* Berkeley: University of California Press. 1996 (hereafter Martin).

On the general situation, three classic books are useful: Barnett, Robert W.: *Economic Shanghai: Hostage to Politics, 1937–1945.* New York: Institute of Pacific Relations. 1941. Hinder, Eleanor: *Social and Industrial Problems of Shanghai, with Special Reference to the Administration and Regulation Work of the Shanghai Municipal Council.* New York: Institute of Pacific Relations. 1942; Hinder, E.: *Life and Labor in Shanghai: A Decade of Labor and Social Administration in the International Settlement.* New York: Institute of Pacific Relations. 1944. Two new books provide fresh analysis and more precise data: Yeh, Wen-hsin, ed.: *Wartime Shanghai.* London: Routledge. 1998 (hereafter Yeh 98); Tao, Juyin: *Gudao jianwen: kangzhan shiqi de Shanghai* [Things seen and heard in the lone islet: Shanghai during the War of Resistance]. Shanghai: Renmin chubanshe. 1979 (hereafter Tao). (This is a reprint of a book first published just after World War II.)

[3] The biographies of most of these trade unionists and labor politicians can be found in Bianco, Lucien and Chevrier, Yves, eds.: *Dictionnaire biographique du mouvement ouvrier international: la Chine.* Paris: Les Editions Ouvrières/ Presses de la Fondation Nationale des Sciences Politiques. 1985 (hereafter Bianco). See also Chang, Kai, ed.: *Zhongguo gongyunshi cidian* (Historical dictionary of the Chinese workers movement). Beijing: Laodong renshi chubanshe. 1990. pp. 687–831.

[4] *Juntong* was the abbreviation for *junshi weiyuanhui tongji diaocha ju* (Board of Inquiries and Statistics of the Committee for Military Affairs), the most famous secret political police of Jiang Jieshi. Stimulating new insights on this frightening organization can be found in Yeh, Wen-hsin: "Dai Li and the Liu Geqing Affair: Heroism in the Chinese Secret Service during

210

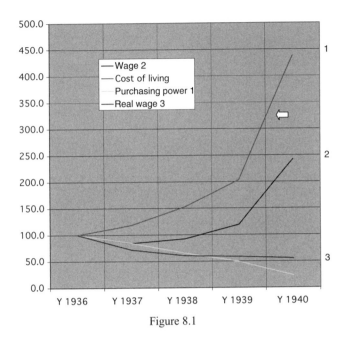

Figure 8.1

beaten at their game by Doihara Kenji's Japanese special service and Wang Jingwei's agents Li Shiqun and Ding Mocun.[5] During the winter of 1939, it ended in a complete disaster, after Shao Shubai's assassination (December 1, 1939) and Wang Tianmu's treason.[6]

Jiang Jieshi's tripod, although it had been destroyed, left to the "genuine GMD," now in Nanking under Wang Jingwei, a pattern of labor control, which it tried to rebuild without success.

2. The revival of labor militancy. In the fall of 1939, the rapid deterioration of workers' living conditions spurred them to protest. The index of the cost of living for workers which was set at 100 in July 1937 climbed to 118.15 at the end of 1937, 152.9 at the end of 1938, and 203.25 at the end of 1939, after a brutal surge of prices after August and rice riots in December, and 438.2 at the end of 1940[7] (see Figure 8.1). Data for 1941 are incomplete, but the situation

---

the War of Resistance." *Journal of Asian Studies.* 43, no. 3 (August 1989): 545–562, and Yeh, Wen-hsin: "Urban Warfare and Underground Resistance," in Yeh 98, pp. 133–156.

[5] Wakeman, Frederic, Jr.: *The Shanghai Badlands: Wartime Terrorism and Urban Crime, 1937–1941.* New York: Cambridge University Press. 1996 (hereafter Wakeman 96), and Wakeman: "Urban Control in Wartime Shanghai," in Yeh 98, pp. 133–156.

[6] Wang Tianmu was Dai Li's main agent in Shanghai.

[7] American Diplomatic Archives (hereafter USDS) 850.1 American General Consulate in Shanghai: *Shanghai Prices Index Numbers (Cost of living for Chinese Workers): 1937 to 1939.*

kept worsening: The monthly expenditures of an ordinary worker's family in October 1940 amounted to 104.15 yuan. It needed 208.33 yuan in October 1941, according to the Industrial Section of the Shanghai Municipal Council. Although basic wages doubled between 1936 and 1941,[8] the cost of living quadrupled.

For two years, there was no significant labor reaction: workers were, like other Chinese, knocked out by China's military disasters. But strikes started during the winter 1939–1940[9] and came into full swing between the summer of 1940 and the summer of 1941 (see Figure 8.2). The number of labor strikes in Shanghai reached the highest level ever since the strike wave of the May 30th movement (*wusa yundong*) in 1925 and the Northern Expedition (*beifa*) in 1927.[10]

3. *The impotence of the Chinese Communist Party (hereafter CCP)*. The CCP had very little to do with this revival of the workers' action, even if it tried, with little success, to take advantage of the second united front concluded with Jiang Jieshi after the Xi'an Incident, to rebuild its demolished organizations in winter 1937–1938, under the leadership of the "five Lius" (Liu Xiao, Liu Changsheng, Liu Ningyi, Liu Shaowen . . . and Wang Yaoshan or Sha Wenhao).[11] Any real effort should have required some kind of cooperation between communists and GMD underground agents, something Wang Ming (Shen Shaoyü) proposed in 1938, but Mao Zedong refused. And Mao's view prevailed. On the other side, the GMD underground agents were the CC Clique or followers of the Green Gang,

---

In 1940 and 1941, the indices were printed in the *Shanghai Municipal Gazette* under the responsibility of the Industrial Section of the Shanghai Municipal Council (Eleanor Hinder). Most of the data are missing between February and October 1941.

[8] Indexes of real salaries from the same sources. 1936: 100; 1937: 71.8; 1938: 60.41; 1939: 58.59; 1940: 55.3.

[9] The paradoxical economic boom of 1938–1939 in the Shanghai settlements ended during the summer of 1939–1940, when the Japanese military closed off shipping between Shanghai and upper Yangzi ports. Shanghai was then isolated (*Gudao Shanghai*; see Tao, p. 12). See Coble, Parks M.: "Chinese Capitalists and the Japanese: Collaboration and Resistance in the Shanghai Area, 1937–1945," in Yeh 98, p. 75.

[10] Sources. Shanghai Municipal Annual Report. Industrial Section. For 1938, 34 strikes, 17,027 strikers, 58,382 workdays lost. For 1939: 117 strikes (96 in International Settlement, 6 in French Concession, 5 in both), with 33,314 strikers, 607,357 workdays lost. For 1940: 289 strikes (201 in International. Settlement, 30 in French Concession, 25 in both), with 114,230 strikers, 658,484 days lost. For 1941, 329 strikes, 137,628 strikers, 1,189,441 days lost.

By comparison, during the May 30 movement, there were 156,000 strikers in the first week of June, and perhaps 3 million days lost before the end of the general strike. From March 21–23, 1927, there were 800,000 strikers during three days of general strike, and 2,400,000 days lost. In 1928, there were 148 strikes, with 215,958 strikers and 2,048,826 days lost.

[11] The fifth "Liu" is often said to be Liu Shaoqi. But at the time, he was first in Tianjin, then in Yan'an.

Strikers

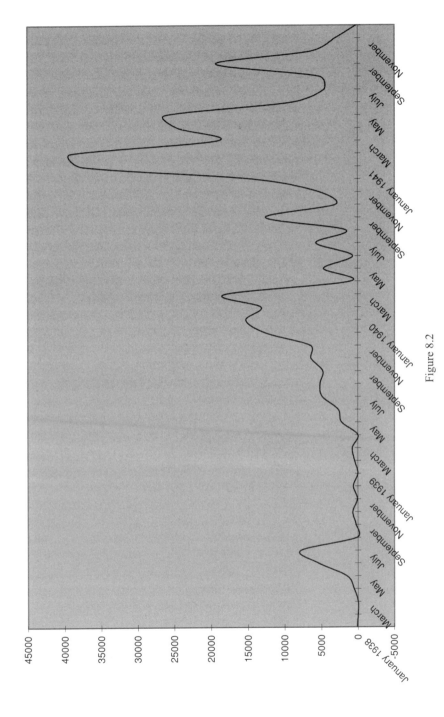

Figure 8.2

Lost Workdays

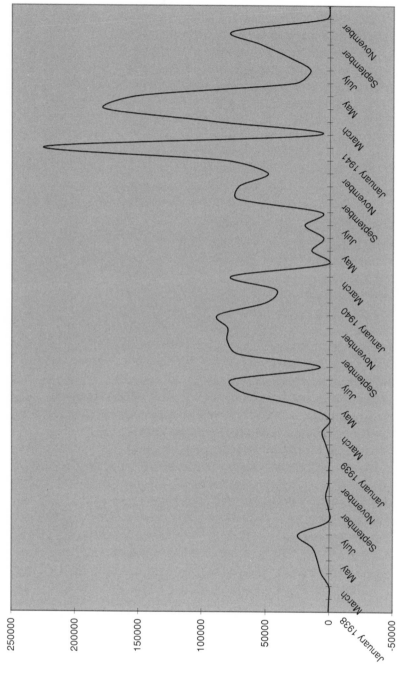

Figure 8.2 (*continued*)

that is, the more eager anticommunists in the whole GMD. Is cooperation between cats and dogs conceivable?[12]

In any case, genuine communist work among Shanghai workers was almost nil. If we read *Zhenli* (Truth), a periodical published by the CCP in Shanghai from December 9, 1937 to July 15, 1938, the first article on the labor movement in Shanghai appeared in issue no.14 (May 20, 1938). It contains no information at all. There is only one other article by Jin Yan (?) in the last issue of the magazine on "how to act among Shanghai workers": It explains that underground communists have to follow the united front line and "to be in touch with veterans and skilled workers." In another communist underground magazine, *Dangde shenghuo* (Party Life), published in Shanghai from March 20, 1939 to March 4, 1940, there is an article that explains how to prepare a Red First May and another one on how to organize political work in the mills owned by enemies: the best way for an underground agent to act is to use the contradictions opposing Chinese traitors and never reveal his own political opinions. Actually, the best publication by the CCP in Shanghai at that time was a disguised book, published in 1939 with a false address in Hong Kong, *Shanghai chanye yu Shanghai zhigong*[13] (Shanghai Industries and Shanghai Workers), written by former communist red unionists[14] and concerned sociologists. It is a book full of nostalgia about past labor waves. These communists were clearly out of touch with the workers' actual struggles.

4. The Japanese labor strategy. Before 1940, the Imperial Navy tried to use the economic discontent of the working class to destabilize the European authorities of the International Settlement and of the French Concession.[15] For this purpose, the Navy set up an Association for Worker Welfare (*Fuyihui*) in October 1938 in Pudong and East Shanghai (Yangshupu), using the traditional hoodlums of the area. A *ronin* from Taiwan, named Lin Zijiong, and a Japanese *yakuza* named Okuba headed the Association, a grouping of fifty trade unions

---

[12] There is a lot of new information on the situation of the CCP in Shanghai on the eve of the Japanese attack in Stranahan, Patricia: *Underground: The Shanghai Communist Party and the Politics of Survival, 1927–1937.* Lanham, Md.: Rowman and Littlefield. 1998. See pp. 202–228 (on the "five Liu" activities).

[13] The book was reprinted in 1984 by the Shanghai renmin chubanshe, with a foreword by labor veteran Zhang Qi. The names of the authors, Zhu Bangxing, Hu Linge, and Xu Sheng, are pseudonyms for Liu Ningyi, Liu Changsheng, and Zhang Yongzong.

[14] For instance, the good and lively chapter on the CFTE strikes is said to have been written by Xu Amei. Source: my interview with Zhang Qi, May 1984, in Shanghai. Zhang Qi told me that, as Xu Amei was semi-illiterate, he spoke and somebody wrote. This kind of rewriting process explains why the chapter on the CFTE is more vivid than the other chapters of the book.

[15] Boyle, John Hunter: *China and Japan at War: The Politics of Collaboration: 1937–1945.* Stanford: Stanford University Press. 1972 (hereafter Boyle).

with a supposed membership of 44,000 in October 1938 and 105,549 in January 1939. The two leaders had close relations with the *Daminhui* (Great People's Association) and other anti-British and pro-Japanese Associations. They provided financial support to a police detective of the Dadao (Great Way) Municipality (collaborationist) in Pudong called Zhu Yuzhen, to establish a Workers' League of the Chinese Republic (*Zhonghua minguo gongren tongmenghui*). On May 20, 1939 the League began a long strike, with the incident (the murder on June 6 of a British overseer, Richard Maurice Tinkler, by Japanese soldiers) at the British China Printing and Finishing Mill (*Lunchang*), which employed 3,200 workers in two mills at Pudong.[16]

The strike lasted six months, and nearly 400,000 workdays were lost, before an agreement was reached on November 17. Workers had been out of the mill since the beginning, actually out from an action that was supposed to be theirs: In fact, a strike committee in charge of the movement decided everything by itself and met in the building of the Dadao Municipality. Workers had no meetings to discuss with their self-declared leaders and were only summoned from time to time to shout in the streets, or in a movie theater, anti-British slogans, for which they received some money. The picket lines were composed of local gangsters who behaved very aggressively. As soon as the mill was reopened, this would-be League vanished. The East Shanghai *Fuyihui* still existed, but it was involved in selling drugs, passes for the International Settlements, and badges protecting against Japanese soldiers' bullying.[17] It never tried to become an ordinary trade union. Its aim was not to protect labor interests, but to stir up anti-British trouble among workers.

The *Fuyihui* was again behind the November 1939 strike at the British shipyards, the New Engineering and Shipbuilding Works (*Ruirong*), which employed 1,000 workers at Yangshupu, and 500 on the opposite bank in Pudong. A detective from the Shanghai Municipal Police wrote detailed reports on the meetings of some of the leaders of the strike committee with Kuboda and Lin Zijiong and with other people from the Japanese General Consulate.[18] Once

[16] Roux 91, pp. 1271–1283. A heavy file in the Public Record Office (hereafter PRO), Archives of the British Foreign Office: FO 371/12728 from May to December 1939. On Tinkler see Robert Bickers: "Who Were the Shanghai Municipal Police and Why Were They There? The British Recruits of 1919," in Bickers, Robert and Henriot, Christian, eds.: *New Frontiers: Imperialism's New Communities in East Asia, 1842–1953*. Manchester: Manchester University Press. 2000, pp. 178–191.

[17] Barnett, *Economic Shanghai*, p. 68. PRO. FO 371 c) 6449; Police Report November 6, 1939.

[18] Shanghai Municipal Police (hereafter SMP) 263 D Dossier 8941 A1. Shanghai Dockyards Ltd Strike. Special Branch reports: November 20, 22, 25, 27, 1939 and December 1, 28. Police Interrogation by D. S MacKeown of Zhang Desheng: November 23–25.

again, as soon as the strike ended, with a rather favorable agreement, nothing was left behind: The Japanese did not want to sponsor a genuine labor movement.

Let us follow, for instance, the activities of a certain Zhang Desheng, a simple coolie hired by the day, who had emigrated to Shanghai in 1925. This thirty-eight-year-old family man, a native from Xuzhou (Jiangbei or *kompo* in the Shanghai dialect) was one of a group of thirty workers fired on November 22 for "laziness." Out of despair, Zhang set out to find someone to recommend him to one of the organizations that recruited along the wharves. In the early 1930s, he would have met some low-ranking follower of Du Yuesheng. By then, he was received by the same Lin Zijiong who asked him to persuade his fellow co-workers to join the *Fuyihui*. On that condition, Lin Zijiong would look after him. Zhang was one of the workers' delegates to a meeting between the strikers of the British-owned New Engineering and Shipbuilding Works and the Japanese consulate. His behavior is devoid of any patriotism. It is no more than a cry for help and elementary clientelism. Such an attitude was not rare among coolies from the depressed Subei or Jiangbei (*Kompo*) area, who were often despised by Shanghai sojourners from Jiangnan as unpatriotic people.[19] These Japanese-sponsored workers' unions were fake unions and true Japanese secret agencies. Not a single pre-1937 union official is to be found among these strange new unionists.[20] They did not last long: When an agreement was reached with the company, Zhang Desheng was fired with a meager compensation of CH\$ 60: He had been used and could be dispensed with.

There was hardly any difference with the General Labor Union of the Shanghai Special Municipality (*Shanghai tebieshi zonggonghui*),[21] created on August 26, 1940. Basically it was also Japanese controlled, with Hu Shaochen and a bunch of riff-raffs as its nominal leaders. Hu and his supporters were natives from Huangpi, near Wuhan, a place of ill repute which provided cart-pullers and longshoremen to the triple city. Yet 38 percent of the union officials

---

[19] Honig, Emily: *Creating Chinese Ethnicity: Subei People in Shanghai. 1850–1980*. New Haven: Yale University Press. 1993.

[20] Shen Yixing, Jiang Peinan, and Zheng Qingsheng: *Shanghai gongren yundong shi* (A History of the Labor Movement in Shanghai). Shenyang. Liaoning chubanshe. vol. xia. 1996, pp. 262–278 ("Appearance and Disappearance of Puppet Trade-Unions during the Japanese Occupation") (hereafter Shen Yixing). Washington, DC: Modern Military Room at the National Archives. SMP, 263/D 9601. General labor unrest from February 15 to November 14, 1940. USDS, 850 D4: Labor. From April 15 to August 1, 1940. "Difficulties of the Chinese Laborers' Welfare Association." PRO. FO 371/ 24 657 folio 1530: Intelligence Report from British general consul George, March 31, 1940.

[21] Memento (*gaikuang*) of 158 pages kept in Shanghai Municipal Archives. Printed December 1940. Roux 91, pp. 1315–1327.

had been union officials before 1937. Most of them belonged to the *gongtong*,[22] the terrorist organization which replaced the red GLU after the April 12, 1927 Jiang Jieshi "coup." One of these officials, Chen Xiupu, had been the chairman of the silk reeling union of Yangshupu in 1933 and member of the supervision committee of the Shanghai GLU in 1934, under Zhu Xuefan. All had close relations with the pro-Japanese *Daminhui* and with Dadao Municipality under Mayor Fu Xiao'an. The Shanghai GLU of 1940 was called the GLU of Nanshi, because all of its thirty-one trade unions were located in the southern district of Shanghai (the "Chinese Bund"), in Pudong and in the French Concession. The southern GLU was not a mere political frame. It had some social substance.

The reasons for that rather small, but significant, difference with the *Fuyihui* was related to some change in Japan's China policy. The war was more difficult than had been expected, and the United States obviously was supporting Jiang Jieshi's government in Chongqing: The risk of an extension of the military conflict to the whole Pacific area was increasing day by day. So Japan could not content itself with its disreputed Chinese agents as those *Fuyihui* people. It needed some substantial Chinese friends, with deep roots among the Chinese workers. But, at the same time, Japan did not have complete trust in its declared Chinese friends. That contradiction in Japan's policy toward China was illustrated by the political crisis that developed then, as shown by the Japanese diktat on Wang Jingwei during the Yuyuan Road Conference at the end of 1939, Tao Xisheng's flight to Hong Kong on January 4, 1940, and the establishment of a national government in Nanking under Wang Jingwei on March 30, 1940.[23] The southern GLU was created a few weeks after the founding by a score of genuine union leaders of Wang Jingwei's Shanghai GLU, on June 23, 1940, which in this way was restricted to West Shanghai and could not be extended to Shanghai South or to Pudong, and came to be known only as the West Shanghai GLU. As the Japanese also kept alive their flimsy East Shanghai *Fuyihui*, they did not allow Wang Jingwei to have full control of all the Shanghai workers' unions.

THE WEST SHANGHAI GENERAL LABOR UNION: A DECEPTIVE REVENGE

The short history of the West Shanghai GLU is a history of an unsuccessful attempt, in four tries, to change the deal made by a few genuine unionists who

---

[22] Abbreviation for *Shanghai gonghui zuzhi tongyi weiyuanhui*, Committee for the Unification of the Labor Organizations. See Roux 95, pp. 69–76.
[23] Boyle, pp. 256–276.

had been supporting Wang Jingwei since the early 1930s and sought revenge on Jiang Jieshi and his followers in the social movement. Their collaborationist turn was not intentional or ideological. Having strong roots for many years among workers, they were efficient unionists but reluctant collaborationists.

1. The first to act was Zhang Kechang and his Association for the Chinese Labor Movement. Since winter 1939, the Japanese-sponsored *Fuyihui* had been supplanted during most labor conflicts in West Shanghai by a new Association for the Chinese Labor Movement (*Zhongguo gongren yundong xiehui*)[24] under Zhang Kechang, a post office clerk. Zhang was one of the eleven unionists who had reorganized the famous Post Office Employees' Union with Lu Jingshi and Zhu Xuefan, after the elimination of communist elements in April–May 1927. Zhang Kechang had sympathies for Wang Jingwei and Chen Gongbo in 1928–1930. He led a strike in October 1928 which Jiang Jieshi did not appreciate at all. On May 19, 1932, he took the lead of a delegation from the Postal Employees' Union which met Mayor Wu Ticheng and negotiated the end of a new, unpleasant strike. He had been, along with Zhu Xuefan and Lu Jingshi, one of the founders in 1933 of the *Hengshe*, a proxy organization for Du Yuesheng. In 1937 he was still one of the leaders of the Postal Union, where he was head of a semi-secret club, called *Chang She*, with 200–300 followers. Under the umbrella of his association, Zhang Kechang developed a federation of communication, electricity, and water companies' employees. The general secretary was Xu Amei, a former communist at the CFTE, who was very popular after leading a victorious strike against French management in the summer of 1930.[25]

The illusion of revenge on foreign bosses and Jiang Jieshi's harsh control over the labor movement since the early 1930s gave some popularity and efficiency to Zhang Kechang's Association. Many former trade unionists joined Zhang Kechang when he supported Wang Jingwei in a public statement on March 19, 1940, on the eve of the founding of the Nanking government. Among the

---

[24] Roux 95, pp. 300–316. Shen Yixing, pp. 265–272. SMP 263/N 276.c) Secret Police Special Branch October 17, 1940. SMP 263/D 6449 A. Secret Police. October 28, 1940. D 9601: General labor unrest, February 1940 to January 1941. Biographies of Zhang Kechang and Fan Yifeng in Bianco.

[25] On this fascinating labor activist, see my paper in *Etudes Chinoises*. vol. 15, no.1–2. Spring 1996. "Patrons français et ouvriers chinois, dans la Chine du Guomindang: Xu Amei ou le dilemme d'un syndicaliste révolutionnaire," pp. 33–70. Expelled from the CCP in June 1930 for refusing the Li Lisan line, Xu Amei was arrested by French police (with Du Yuesheng's assistance) and jailed from 1931 to 1937 for communist activities. In 1937 he was again in touch with Zhang Qi, a communist underground agent, but was spotted by Wang Jingwei's secret police and killed. His collaboration with Zhang Kechang clearly was revenge against the French bosses of the CFTE and Jiang Jieshi's agents in the labor movement. Strongly nationalist, Xu Amei organized workers' squads to help Chinese soldiers during the Shanghai battle in August–September 1937 and was not at all a collaborationist.

110 unions represented, some were inconsistent, but most were real unions and many had followed the "South Federation of Trade Unions" during the political crisis of December 1931, which welcomed in Shanghai the Cantonese-fighting Jiang Jieshi and his "North Federation of Trade Unions," and belonged to the "reorganizationist" faction of the GMD led by Wang Jingwei and Chen Gongbo. It was their revenge, as it was the revenge of those Seven Big Unions, which tried in 1928–1930 to create a kind of semiautonomous labor movement in Shanghai and had been stiffled by the CC Clique and Du Yuesheng's followers.[26] So, the foundation of the West Shanghai GLU resulted from the convergence of this revanchist mood among unionists and of the labor miltancy revived by the economic crisis.

2. The Ministry of Social Affairs of Wang Jingwei's "genuine" GMD, which had difficult relations with the Dadao Municipality of Shanghai, had first set up a Steering Committee of Social Movement (*Shehui yundong zhidao weiyuanhui*) at 75 Jessfield Road, under Wang Manyun, of the pre-1937 *Dangbu*. Wang Manyun was replaced afterward by Sun Mingqi, who also had been a member of the former GMD *Dangbu*. Both were working with the famous archmurderer Ding Mocun, in front, at 76 Jessfield Road. On June 23, 1940, the Committee organized the meeting to found the new Shanghai GLU, at 95 Edinburgh Street, a half mile farther west. Sun Mingqi was still the president, with Zhang Kechang as vice-president. Seventy-eight percent of the officials had been labor officials in the 1930s (as were Zhang Kechang and Fan Yifeng of the Chinese omnibus company in Zhabei) or members of the *Dangbu* executive organs (as was Yu Yaoqiu) – twice more than in the southern GLU. Some had led strikes and militant unions. There were thirty-four active trade unions under the West Shanghai GLU. One of them was the BAT union (now named *Yizhong*), under Lou Jingguan with one mill in Yangshupu and the other in Pudong . . . and none in Shanghai West. Chief of the Shaoxing brotherhood in the Pudong mill, Lou had been one of the leaders of the BAT great strike of 1927–1928 and sided with Zhu Xuefan, then one of Du Yuesheng's main followers in the GLU, when he opposed Chen Peide,[27] in

---

[26] Roux, Alain: "Réévaluation du rôle des syndicats officiels dans le Shanghai du Guomindang," in Alleton, Viviane and Volkov, Alexei: "Notions et perceptions du changement," in *Mémoires de l'Institut des Hautes Etudes Chinoises* (Collège de France), vol. 36, 1995, pp. 119–132. Those Seven Big (*qi da*) were the BAT Tobacco union, Nanyang Tobacco union, the two Commercial Press unions (printing and mailing), the Postal union, the Chinese Nandao streetcars union, and the News Vendors' union. The CFTE union sided with the Big Seven, but never formally joined them when they published common statements.

[27] A coolie from Subei, who became chairman of the BAT union in December 1927 and led the victorious strike of those tobacco workers. He was popular, but belonged to the *Hong Bang* (Red Gang or Triad). So he was independent from the CC Clique network which controlled the

1933–1934. There were also Postal, Shanghai Power, British Streetcars, British Buses, and CFTE unions. Most of them were unions of skilled workers, and most of those unions had supported Wang Jingwei in the late 1920s and early 1930s. During its year of existence, the West Shanghai GLU was engaged in 254 strikes, with 94,199 strikers. Twenty of these strikes were large, mainly in the autumn of 1940 among workers of public utility companies in the foreign settlements, where a general strike of transportation employees was avoided at the last minute. Of course, the Japanese were eager to create disturbances in the two territories under the control of "white imperialists," thanks to these labor conflicts. Nevertheless, these strikes led by revengeful union leaders were basically motivated by real economic difficulties and enjoyed broad support among the poverty-stricken workers. These movements were caused by the revival of the labor militancy and reinforced it as well. The Japanese occupiers benefited from the well-documented capacity for defensive protest by Shanghai workers undercut by recent history and wartime circumstances. In 1940 there was an eclipse of the patriotic feelings of hopeless Shanghai workers.

3. But those would-be avengers were compelled by their Japanese masters to become ordinary traitors (*hanjian*).[28] Most of them accepted their fate and gradually turned into discredited puppets: By the winter of 1940, the GLU had lost its original mobilizing power. Perhaps this explains why Ding Mocun decided on December 1, 1940 to restore the control over the labor movement by the Steering Committee of Social Movement.[29] The three labor federations were now useless and could even serve as a cover for some hidden subversive elements. On February 1, 1941, the two GLU (South and West) and the *Fuyihui* (East) were dissolved. The Steering Committee under Sun Mingqi, Zhang Kechang, and Lin Saiwen (an obscure bureaucrat) was again in charge of all union activities. On September 16, 1941 a Committee for Popular Movements (*minzhong*) was established in the International Settlement under Zhou Fohai

Shanghai labor movement in the 1930s and lost his chairmanship in 1934 when a new strike failed. See his biography in Bianco.

[28] The change in the Japanese policy toward Wang Jingwei was decided in December 1942, when it became clear that the war would last and that occupied China had to be revived in order to support the needs of the Japanese military on the continent. The decision was made to allow some autonomy to the Nanking Government. See Coble, Parks: "Chinese capitalists," in Yeh 98, pp. 66–67. In December 1940, the Japanese secret services, in charge of the Shanghai labor movement, still preferred complete control of the Nanking Regime. Ding Mocun and Li Shiqun were required to submit daily intelligence reports on the social movement to the Japanese colonel Haruke Sadaaki's military secret unit, the Plum Blossom Agency (*Ume kikan*). See Wakeman, "Urban controls," in Yeh 98, p. 140.

[29] SMP 263 D 6449, A General Labor Situation. November 7, 1940. D 9601 (c) General Labor Union. December 14, 1940. Shen Yixing, xia, pp. 272–278.

and Ding Mocun, with Sun Mingqi, Fan Yifeng, and Yu Yaoqiu. There was no room for workers' activities outside of Japanese control.

4. Many strikes still took place in 1941, most of them wildcat strikes. Labor unions had nearly disappeared. Strikes were spontaneous and the workers were mobilized through their traditional network of native-place associations (*tongxianghui*), brotherhoods, semireligious sects, and secret societies. The roots of the social movement were strong, but its split structure, which favored horizontal conflicts over vertical ones and opposed workers of different origins and status, hindered any extension of the movement. There were hundreds of strikes but no strike wave. Those who had thought of seeking revenge after 1937 on the CC Clique and GMD bureaucrats who had suppressed them in the early 1930s were at a loss. They had dreamed of being avengers. But now they were only trapped into becoming ordinary traitors.

THE JESSFIELD PARK STRIKE (*ZHAOFENG GONGYUAN DA BAGONG*) OF THE CFTE EMPLOYEES:[30] THE DILEMMA OF THE WORKERS[31]

The impossibility of turning the West Shanghai GLU away from becoming a political tool for the Japanese (and Wang Jingwei's administration) and making it an organization embodying some genuine unions for the promotion of workers' protests will be illustrated by the strike led by the CFTE[32] union in the autumn of 1940.

Xu Amei's Last Performance

We have already seen how Wang Jingwei's labor faction had tried in the late 1930s to use the authority of Xu Amei, the celebrated leader (and ex-communist)

---

[30] From September 25 to October 22, 1940.

[31] Many sources on that strike: French Consular Archives from Shanghai. Ministère des Affaires Etrangères. Nantes. A 116, 33 vols. December 6, 1940. A file of 400 pages, including a "secret" police report by Moret and Fabre no. 5217/S, September 23, 1940 (hereafter MAE). *Minguo dang'an*, Taibei 1990 no. 1: Report on the Strike by the Steering Committee of the Labor Movement, pp. 41–45 (hereafter Steering). Wang Enzhen, Zhang Haopi, et al.: *Shanghai Fadian yundongshi* (History of the French Company of Streetcars and Electric Lights). Shanghai: Shanghai gongchandangshi chubanshe. 1991 (hereafter *Fadian*).

[32] One thousand seven hundred workers were employed at the CFTE in 1940. Two hundred were employees in the central offices, 600 were workers of the shops (*jiwubu*); 60% were from south Jiangsu (120 were born in Shanghai), 30% from Zhejiang (Shaoxing and Ningbo), and only 10% from the north of the Yangzi (mainly Shandong). Seven hundred drivers and conductors were driving the 60 buses, 100 streetcars, and 38 trolleybuses of the company (*chewuju*). Two-thirds were from the north of the Yangzi (half from north Jiangsu) and one-third from Jiangnan (half from Shanghai); 100 were coolies digging trenches or maintaining the tracks and 100 worked in the electric and water works.

of the CFTE union from 1928 to 1931. When he resumed his work in the CFTE shop as a fitter in 1937, after six years in jail, he was soon again the chairman of a militant union. He gave some impetus and some legitimacy to the undergoing process of Wang Jingwei's new Shanghai GLU. But he was too independent, and was murdered on December 29, 1939 by Wang Jingwei's secret police: He was suspected of again being acquainted with the communist underground. His personal tragedy can be a good illustration of the fate of Wang Jingwei's attempts to build a strong foundation for his government among the Shanghai workers: when a true union was created, the workers tried to use it for their own economic interests and did not support Wang Jingwei's general political orientation or Wang's heavy Japanese connections.

Old and New Unionists at the CFTE

The increase in inflation in 1940 and the high price of rice were inciting workers to protest. At the CFTE, a few conductors, among whom the trade union had always been rather weak while the affiliations to brotherhoods (*dixionghui*), native-place associations (*tongxianghui*), and secret societies were traditionally rather strong, as often with people from the north Yangzi area (Jiangbei), had been fired during the first weeks of September by inspectors who accused them of "squeeze."[33] Bus and streetcar drivers, most of them also from Jiangbei, expressed their solidarity with the conductors. The social tension led to the murder of a Chinese inspector, who was one of the "running dogs" of the company directors, and to two arrests and a dozen dismissals among the conductors. At the same time several stoppages or sit-down strikes (*taigong*) for a cost-of-living bonus were called on the shop floors, where the workers seemed reluctant to launch a general strike that would not displease the Japanese. The drivers and conductors walked out on September 25, 1940, but less than one-third of their co-workers followed suit, and the shops failed to join entirely: The most skilled workers were hesitant to join a strike instigated by people who were on good terms with Japanese agents. The influence of three conflicting union structures can be seen here.

  1. The pre-1937 "old union" had a strong foothold in the shops, where 600 skilled or semiskilled mechanics, mainly from Jiangnan, worked. Several of the leaders of the old union had relations with the Chongqing GMD.[34] Its

---

[33] A conductor "squeezes" the company when he collects only a half fare from a passenger and does not issue him any ticket, keeping the money for himself.

[34] Here we find notably two leaders of this union who were former friends of Xu Amei (Yu Guixiang and Chen Xiaodi) and two others who were longtime disciples of Du Yuesheng (Zhang Fubao and Shi Quanfu).

increasingly disoriented cadres began going over to the West Shanghai General Labor Union, which benefited from the efforts and the funding of the Labor Movement Steering Committee, housed in a villa near Jessfield Park. They were mollified by the presence on the Labor Movement Steering Committee of popular leaders who had been engaged in union work since the late 1920s and early 1930s. Gu Jiwu, the Minister of Social Affairs in Wang Jingwei's cabinet, and his adviser on labor issues, Jiang Zhaoxiang,[35] kept close watch on these activities, but they were initially unable to convince the old union to call the shop workers to go on strike.

2. A group of conductors followed a handful of GMD militants linked with the Blue Shirts, among whom was Fan Yuzhang. They set up a small union at Nanshi, on Dalin Street,[36] which joined the Southern GLU.

3. Conductors and drivers spent more and more time at the Jessfield Park villa.[37] Notwithstanding, those people attracted by the Steering Committee managed to influence only a third of the drivers and conductors, still divided between traditional native-place associations (one-third of them were born in Jiangnan and two-thirds in Jiangbei) and brotherhoods, which were hesitating on the political issues. The foreman Li Linshu's *Lianyishe* brotherhood, which had a strong foothold among the conductors and drivers born in Pudong, challenged the influence of Triad follower Liu Degong's brotherhood, also called *Lianyishe*.[38] The latter was strong among workers from the north Yangzi area and sympathized with Wang Jingwei's agents. On the other hand, Li Linshu's followers refused to strike.

A Hesitating Strike

The rising union was the one that had joined the West Shanghai General Labor Union on September 24, in a theater on Edinburgh Road. Three hundred workers attended the founding meeting, which received Jiang Zhaoxiang's greeting. Among the participants, there were members of the GMD who were hostile to Jiang Jieshi since the early 1930s and fought for revenge. But as the crisis

[35] *Fadian*, p. 152: A conductor, Wang Cuixing, played soccer on the same team as Jiang Zhaoxiang, second in charge of the Labor Movement Steering Committee. The inspector Guo had suspended him for three days for "bad behavior." Wang Cuixing at once ran for help to the villa near Jessfield Park, and asked Jiang Zhaoxiang to protect him.

[36] Near the Recreation Ground at Small Western Gate (Xiao Ximen), where CFTE strikers held their meetings in 1928 and 1930.

[37] The place was more attractive, because it was near the Badlands, which was then the more popular place of entertainment. See Wakeman 1996.

[38] With other Chinese characters.

worsened, former supporters of Chongqing joined the new union, together with former 1930s "strike breakers"[39] and isolated communists. The popular ticket redactor[40] Zhou Guoqiang[41] made the keynote speech. This former friend of Xu Amei and communist had lost contact with the CCP after 1931 and had become Liu Degong's right-hand man in his *Lianyishe*. Another speaker was Gu Jinrong, who in 1929–1930 was president of the Employees' Circle (*julebu*), and had tried to break the 1930 strike. Zhou Guoqiang had been arrested when he attacked that Circle in July 1930! In 1940, they both called for the strike.

Divided along old antagonisms, the movement marked time until a conductor was murdered by an Annamite policeman on September 26, when pickets attacked a streetcar. The strike spread slowly to the shops, where it started only on October 11, while the GMD and the CCP decided separately to support it: Both knew the fighting tradition of Shanghai workers when one of them was killed by "imperialist running dogs." The sixteen initial demands of the workers were reduced to seven. All were very concrete and not political.[42] They included separate grievances from the shop mechanics and from the drivers or conductors. The West Shanghai GLU gave strikers one yuan a day (equal to one-half pay) and five bushels of rice. It was a general strike that could last long: The 800 initial strikers now numbered 1,700. They all knew that the defeated and half-occupied France under Pétain was weak. Difficult negotiations started on October 13 and ended on October 22 with reasonable success – an agreement and a return to work. A collective photo of all the strikers was shot in Jessfield Park, which gave its name to the movement. The workers refused the Nanking government flag. The union had gained recognition, under Zhang Fubao. It was unified and was overseen by the West Shanghai GLU. A labor revival?

---

[39] For instance Gu Jinrong, conductor no. 107, the president of the Employees Club, which was housed in the Company Office, had been an arch-enemy of Xu Amei.

[40] A chief conductor.

[41] Biography in *Fadian*, pp. 403–408, with photograph. After 1949 he was a communist veteran and labor hero. He died in 1979. Born in 1908 at Gaoyou near Yangzhou (*kompo*) into a poor family, he received some elementary education for four years (with many interruptions) and went to Shanghai in 1924, where he was successively a sailor on the Huangpu, a shop assistant, a worker in a knitting factory, then at the Pudong BAT. He became a conductor at the CFTE in 1926 and participated in the March 1927 uprising. He fought at the Gaochangmiao arsenal and joined the CCP when he was in a worker picket at the Sanshan Guild in Nanshi. He was Xu Amei's friend in 1930 and was arrested with 23 other strikers when they attacked Gu Jinrong's Employees Club. He lost his communist connections in the following years, but was very popular among conductors when he organized a "tontine," the *Xinyi chuxinhui*. He was said to be "as loyal as Guanyu." In 1932 he joined foreman Liu Degong's *Lianyishe* brotherhood (which was different from Lin Lishu's!). He became its leader after 1933. He is supposed to have joined the Triad (*Hong men*) only in 1945, "because the party ordered him."

[42] Wounded on September 26, the conductor Zhang Yongkang died on September 29.

A Pyrrhic Victory

In point of fact, though, the existence of the revived union was tenuous and its appearances were rare. The reality for which it provided the façade can be seen through the figure of Zhou Guoqiang. A network of native-place associations structured the community of drivers and conductors: The natives of Jiangbei, the northerners, the natives of Hubei, of Ningbo, of Shanghai, or even of Pudong, formed separate groups. In the shops, which recruited massively in Zhejiang, the cleavages were organized along voluntary "secret societies" and "brotherhoods," among which were the Guanyu brotherhood and the subsidiary networks of the Qing bang and the Hong bang (Triad).

Therefore, the victory of the pro-Wang Jingwei GLU of Shanghai West during the Jessfield Park strike was a Pyrrhic one: It disappeared after a confused action in August 1941, some months after it won.

CONCLUSION: THE MAKING AND UNMAKING OF THE SHANGHAI WORKING CLASS

In his pioneering book on the making of the English working class, Edward P. Thompson[43] explains that "working class" does not exist in a permanent, definitive state, as a "thing," but rather as a "process," made of historical, economic, political relations, which are undergoing a continuous evolution. In Shanghai, this process was accelerated by the political events that took place between 1919 and 1927. During 1928–1929, the class-making process was still operating, despite the political reversal of the GMD White Terror. During the 1930s, however, the CC Clique control of the labor movement and the economic crisis started an opposite process of class-unmaking.

Between the winter of 1939 and the winter of 1942, there was an impressive revival of labor militancy. However, if we compare the number of strikes and strikers during those three troubled years with other periods of labor unrest (May 4, 1919, May 30, 1925, March 1927), we cannot fail to note new characteristics:

1. There was no general strike, as defined by Elizabeth Perry,[44] that is, a large, cross-class strike, extended to a whole city (or county), which is galvanized by public opinion aroused by central political grievances, and stimulated from outside, mainly by intellectuals. The March 1927 Shanghai uprising was

---

[43] Thompson, Edward P.: *The Making of the English Working Class*. London: Victor Gollancz. 1963, pp. 11–13.

[44] Perry, Elizabeth: "Shanghai's Strike Wave of 1957," *The China Quarterly*, 137, March 1994, pp. 1–27.

a general strike. On the other hand, Shanghai workers never went out on strike in 1940–1941 to support Wang Jingwei's policy or to abolish the foreign settlements. Their strikes were related to immediate, narrow, unpolitical economic issues.

2. The powerful 1940–1941 labor movement can hardly be called "a strike wave," in spite of rather impressive statistical data. It was only in the fall 1939 that a strike wave could have happened among the employees of the foreign-owned public transportation companies, but it was avoided at the last moment. Strikes, albeit numerous and sometimes simultaneous, were separate, spontaneous, uncoordinated actions.

3. Workers did not play a major part in Shanghai politics because they were divided and unable to find any satisfying political support. Only the coolies and unskilled workers were in such a distressed state that they accepted any help, even from pro-Japanese unionists. But they could not build real unions. The only workers who had such potential were the skilled workers who enjoyed job security. But they refused to remain for very long in the pro-Wang Jingwei's unions, because it offended their patriotic feelings, as shown in the French Streetcars Company (CFTE) strike. The apparent success of the West Shanghai GLU was only a flash in the pan.

4. However, those skilled workers mastered the art of striking and won some protest power. It was due mainly to the existence in every company of a dense network of brotherhoods, native-place associations, and more-or-less secret societies. The splitting into small groups was quite visible among postal workers, in streetcar repair and maintenance shops, among metal workers and mechanics. The Luban or Guangdi worshipping associations were particularly widespread. This micro associative life might have given rise to internal divisions and horizontal conflicts, but it also facilitated thoroughgoing mobilizations when unions or political groups knew how to rally them. In this case, the internal fragmentation of the work force could become a strength for the protest in the company. This was clear during the 1940 CFTE strike. Perhaps it is an answer to the controversy between Chesneaux and Perry on the issue of the role of secret societies in the Shanghai workers movement.[45] The workers were so divided that they could engage in a strong contest only on cross-class, general,

---

[45] In his *History of the Chinese Labour Movement (1919–1927)*, Paris: Mouton. 1962 (English translation 1968), Jean Chesneaux wrote that the secret societies and brotherhoods were "feudal remnants" that harmed the efficiency of the labor movement. On the other hand, Elizabeth Perry considers, in her *Shanghai on Strike: The Politics of Chinese Labor*. Stanford: Stanford University Press. 1993, that a traditional social network gave strong roots to workers' protests, which can explain, for instance, the paradoxical labor militancy during the "white terror" in the second half of 1927.

patriotic objectives, as in 1919, 1925, and 1927. It was obviously impossible in 1940–1941.

So the determination of the Shanghai workers in 1940, even if Wang Jingwei was then trying to build a network of trade unions loyal to his regime, did not mean that Shanghai workers supported the Nanking government. It was only an autonomous protest movement against their increasing impoverishment. Wang Jingwei's unions were not avengers against Jiang Jieshi's oppression, but willing tools for the Japanese or, sometimes, Noah's mantels hiding the workers' traditional defense associations. As a political project, it ended in complete failure.

Chapter 9

Settlers and Diplomats

The End of British Hegemony in the International Settlement, 1937–1945

ROBERT BICKERS

The biggest change in Shanghai's political landscape between 1937 and 1945 was the formal end of the tripartite division of the city. The nominally international, but British-dominated International Settlement, and the French Concession, were abolished – and the International Settlement was, in a sense, abolished twice for good measure. The January 11, 1943 Sino-British and Sino-American treaties ended extraterritoriality and the treaty ports; while under a July 1943 pact the city was also "extricated" from "Anglo American shackles."[1] Shanghai was always more than the foreign concessions, but in their development after 1842 they had come to hold its financial, industrial, and commercial heart. Who held the International Settlement, held Shanghai.

The end of British hegemony in the International Settlement was not necessarily a bad thing as far as British diplomats – or a prominent section of the British business community – were concerned, nor did it happen just because of the Pacific war. The years between 1937 and 1945 contain the last phase (outside Hong Kong) of the decolonization of the British presence in China. This process was initiated by British diplomats as a result of the foreign policy changes associated with the victory of the Guomindang in 1927. The aim, broadly, was the dismantling of the treaty port system and the accretions which had evolved into a colonial-style presence in Shanghai and Tianjin in particular, and its reshaping into a trading presence grounded in orthodox state-to-state diplomatic relations.[2] However, the treaty port establishment, which reached its fullest form in the early 1920s, was rooted out with greater speed and less fuss than would almost certainly have been the case in peacetime.[3]

[1] *Shanghai Times*, 1 January 1943, 1, 3.

[2] Robert Bickers, *Britain in China: Culture, Community and Colonialism, 1900–49*.

[3] The best survey of the treaty port structure remains Albert Feuerwerker, *The Foreign Establishment in China in the Early Twentieth Century*.

There are two points to remember here. First, "British Shanghai" is a vague term. Operating in Shanghai under the protection of the British state down to December 1941 were: settler Britons, expatriate Britons, British military and diplomatic agents, British-protected Indian, Sephardi Jewish, and Chinese subjects, Eurasians, Dominions subjects, and more. The community commonly described as "British" was fractured: socioeconomic interests, "race," religion, class, employment, loyalty, and identity serve to make the category of "British" awkward as an analytical tool. Two sectors of the community concern us here, settlers and expatriates. Settlers (Shanghailanders) were Britons whose loyalties were primarily local, secondly imperial, and thirdly British, and who fell into one of three employment categories: the treaty port service sector and administration; property ownership and land speculation; small business. Without the treaty port system this sector could not have developed, nor could it be sustained. Settlers formed the majority among British nationals in the city. The Shanghailander identity developed in the decades after the opening of the treaty ports in 1842, and was a coherent, discrete strand in the local identities that developed among overseas Britons in the British diaspora which populated the dominions, empire, and zones of informal influence such as Argentina. Shanghailanders had their own histories, founding legends, argot, taboos, ceremonials, and rituals.[4] "Expatriates" worked for the British transnationals operating in the city (ICI, BAT, Lever Brothers, APC, CPF), or for the bigger China companies (Jardines, Hong Kong and Shanghai Bank, Swires). Shanghai was incidental; they might have been sent anywhere in China, or wherever their employers operated. They distanced themselves from settlers, who they treated as social inferiors, and expatriate interests were much more closely aligned with those of the British government. In wartime, as we shall see, and in crisis, Shanghailanders' British and imperial identities became more pronounced (they were nothing if not pragmatic), but like the French "Shanghaiens" Shanghai was still their home.

The second point is that the Shanghai Municipal Council [SMC], which administered the International Settlement, was itself an actor with a degree of autonomy. It was not a proxy colonial administration under the heel of the British state. As Christine Cornet shows, the French Consul General could usurp the independence of the French Municipal Council, which was done after 1927. However, the Settlement was an internationally run enclave, subject certainly to various degrees of overt and covert influence from foreign (and Chinese) governments, but it was run by the Council, and settlers dominated

---

[4] For a fuller presentation of this thesis, see my "Shanghailanders: The Formation and Identity of the British Settler Community in Shanghai, 1843–1937," 161–211.

8. Reminders of war in a city returned to normalcy. Source: Courtesy of
the Fabre Family.

that Council. The SMC would never have functioned in Shanghai if it had not
been careful to tailor its policies (or absence thereof) to the demands and desires
of the majority Chinese population, and the limits of its governance were set by
the level of their quotidian acceptance of the administration. There is often an
assumption that the relationship between British diplomats and the SMC was
formal, but while there certainly was close cooperation between agencies of the
SMC – notably the Shanghai Municipal Police [SMP] – and British imperial or
metropolitan agencies, these links were ad hoc, contingent, and largely restricted
to specific shared threats. As the crisis of the mid- to late 1920s had showed,
British diplomats could not tell the SMC what to do, and leading settler figures
such as Harry Arnhold, a favorite with the ratepayer electorate, held sway on the
Council itself. When it came to the policies and activities of the SMC, neither
the structure of the International Settlement, as drawn up in the various Land
Regulations, nor the mentality of the Shanghailander, allowed much room for
diplomatic diktat.

It is important to make these points at the start because the wartime period saw
this successful culmination of the British diplomatic offensive to seize control of
the SMC back from the settler interest. The post-1927 period had been marked

by the forcible re-entry of the British state into its zone of informal influence in China generally, and the commencement of the nationalization of the British side of Sino-British relations. British imperial and domestic interests in China were felt to be at risk from the activities and attitudes of the settler establishment. For the British Foreign Office [FO] this process meant at first nudging the SMC into making conciliatory gestures after the disaster of May 30, 1925 when SMP killings of Chinese demonstrators sparked a China-wide anti-British and anti-imperialist movement; then, after 1927, into making substantive reforms in the constitution of the International Settlement, and changes to policies – such as the exclusion of Chinese nationals from the main Settlement parks – which had almost irreparably damaged the international public image of the SMC. Diplomatic pressure was applied in a bid to encourage reforms in the personnel, practices, and policies of the Council, and the long-standing "benign neglect" of the autonomous pretensions of the self-proclaimed "Model Settlement" was abrogated. Benign neglect of the SMC by the British government had occurred because as long as it delivered the goods – a stable base-camp for British trade in China generally – then little local peculiarities and pretensions could be tolerated. May 30 showed that those pretensions were now too dangerous.

The rooting of a major change in Shanghai's political landscape in events dating back to 1927 is necessary. Wartime created arenas of conflict between states, organizations, and individuals, and even within the individual conscience in Shanghai, but the International Settlement was already an arena of conflict between nominal friends, and between friends and enemies. First, there was this attempted disestablishment of settler hegemony, and the settler response, as Shanghailanders defended their very existence. This conflict had spilled over, as the leadership of the SMC was replaced, or shifted its loyalties into line with British diplomats, into conflict between settler Britons and the SMC. As the Council was perceived to be adopting a policy of appeasement toward diplomatic "sell-outs," settler Britons had organized themselves into the Shanghai British Residents' Association in 1931, and mobilized against British diplomats and the oligarchs they felt were abandoning them.[5]

Allied to this was a slowly growing conflict between the SMC and its mostly British foreign personnel. Reform of the administration's priorities exacerbated its financial difficulties, and by the late 1930s the Council was having difficulty meeting the financial commitments it had made to "Foreign" staff. Second, there was Anglo-American conflict over the running of the Council, although by 1937 this mostly settled. Sterling Fessenden's struggle against the British

---

[5] Bickers, *Britain in China*, 146–151.

old Guard had largely been resolved in his favor.[6] Third, there was the conflict over sovereignty generally in the International Settlement, and in particular over the "External/Outside Roads" areas between the SMC and the Municipality of Greater Shanghai – the latter a leftover from the expansionist forward policy of the SMC which had come to a halt in 1925.[7] Fourth, there was Japanese pressure for greater representation on the Council and in the staff of the SMC. The Japanese were not alone among foreign residents of the International Settlement in taking the rhetorical cosmopolitanism of the SMC at face value. But with rather better justification than the White Russians who attempted to talk their way into the International Settlement polity, Japanese business and ratepayer groups argued that their numbers and economic clout in the city more than justified a far greater slice of the SMC cake than the Anglo-American oligarchy allowed them. Consequently, from 1936 onward an at times bitter struggle for greater access was fought, while British interest groups slackened the pace of their own conflicts and worked together against Japanese activity. Last, there was the continuing struggle between the SMC and Chinese residents of the International Settlement, over taxation and representation on the Council itself in particular.

If one key theme in events after Marco Polo bridge was continuity in conflict, the second must be positioning for the postwar settlement, and the sheer necessity of seeing things through. Chinese nationalism was clearly perceived by Britons as the greater long-term threat. So the defining characteristic of the British experience of the eight years of warfare was a concern with survival, and the accommodations that had to be made to ensure survival, and about careful positioning for the sorting out that would follow a peace. Survival involved attempting to regain, or retain, normality, and it meant pragmatism: Settlers had to make themselves useful, to avoid being abandoned by a preoccupied British government. In the meantime, although "the day of the Anglo-Saxon majority may well have disappeared," mused the SMC's British secretary-general in December 1940, "If we lose control, we shall at least leave a going concern in good order."[8]

---

[6] Nicholas R. Clifford, *Spoilt Children of Empire: Westerners in Shanghai and the Chinese Revolution of the 1920s*. The most notable Fessenden victory was the contemporaneous sackings of Police Commissioner E. I. M. Barrett and his rival W. G. Clarke in 1929: Shanghai Municipal Archives [SMA] U 1-3-4062, U 1-3-2791.

[7] Christian Henriot, *Shanghai, 1927–1937: Municipal Power, Locality, and Modernization*; Frederic Wakeman Jr., *Policing Shanghai 1927–1937*; Frederic Wakeman, Jr., *The Shanghai Badlands: Wartime Terrorism and Urban Crime, 1937–1941*.

[8] G. G. Phillips, "Memorandum," 30 December 1940, in F2091/130/10, Great Britain, Public Record Office [PRO], Foreign Office files, FO 371/27631.

WAR, AGAIN

Initially the British treated this like any other war in or near Shanghai, and strove for normality. War had been accounted normal since 1924, in recent memory, while protecting Shanghai from warfare which singed its borders had been a defining motif in the "imagined" history of the International Settlement since the 1854 "Battle of the Muddy Flat." For many foreign residents, who rarely ventured into the Chinese city and suburbs, the International Settlement had always been an island, safe, at heart, from war. The conflict in 1932 had been short and (relatively) contained, and the expectation was that 1937 would be similar.[9] Britons began filing their claims for war damage through the British Consulate-General as they had done routinely before as a result of warlord warfare or banditry, and they attempted to stand up for their treaty rights – especially over the Japanese closure of Hongkou and Yangshupu.[10]

But this was not war as usual. Although the SMC tried to bargain concessions to Japanese demands for fuller and more executive representation in return for the integrity of the Settlement borders, effective power in Shanghai lay with those who had military force. The SMC became a pawn in the wider diplomatic standoff between the British empire and Japan alongside the Burma road, the Tianjin crises, and the Kowloon-Canton railway issue. For the first time, much of the diplomatic exchange over the International Settlement was conducted through the British embassy in Tokyo, rather than in China.[11] The steady and firm application of pressure by the Japanese on two fronts – against the Chongqing presence in the International Settlement, and against the Settlement government itself – left the SMC floundering. Its sovereignty was removed or challenged in the Northern and Eastern districts, and in the Western External Roads area, its police were suborned and its very existence threatened by rumors of Japanese military takeovers.[12] To accompany negotiated struggle there was the destabilizing terrorist campaign undertaken in the Settlement, and the "Badlands" situation in the disputed Western External Roads area. The SMC capitulated almost from the start on a great many issues of principle and practice – especially policing practice – and each concession was accompanied by more pressure.[13] The wonder was, as Council Chairman (and Jardine's

---

[9] Bickers, 'Shanghailanders,' 243–245; Basil Duke (SMP) to family, 30 January 1937, Duke family papers.

[10] See various documents in the file F4880/10, 1937; Shanghai No. 312, 17 May 1940, F3500/3500/10, FO 371/24703, PRO.

[11] See Antony Best, *Britain, Japan and Pearl Harbor: Avoiding War in East Asia, 1936–41*; and B. A. Lee, *Britain and the Sino-Japanese War, 1937–1939*.

[12] See, e.g., Shanghai No. 599, 16 September 1940, F5287/31/10, FO 371/24663, PRO.

[13] Robert W. Barnett, *Economic Shanghai: Hostage to Politics 1937–1941*, 3–41.

director) W. J. "Tony" Keswick noted in January 1941, that the Japanese just did not take over earlier. Economic Shanghai, he thought, was the reason, and fear of confronting the United States.[14]

That the International Settlement was worth more to Japan under the illusion of normality, and under well-ordered, peaceful foreign control, than it would be otherwise, was an unquestioned assumption. In this case the SMC and the British in general might cynically be seen as actively collaborating with the Japanese war machine after 1937 by running the International Settlement on their behalf, especially as they so efficiently assisted the activities of the Japanese security apparatus. In fact there was a precedent for this cooperation with de-facto local authority in the close relationship established between the SMP and the Shanghai Public Security Bureau in anticommunist activities throughout the 1930s.[15] But Shanghai was useful all round. The International Settlement served an important role in the survival strategy of the National Government, and the SMC played on this, even asking Chongqing to order its men to assassinate collaborators outside the Settlement, so as not to destabilize it.[16] The Council was eager to avoid alienating the National Government in the short run, and British diplomats channeled explanations and excuses for its concessions to Japanese demands back to Chongqing.

Like the SMC, British businesses also attempted to carry on as normal after the outbreak of the war, but were forced to look abroad for new sources of supplies and new markets because of Japanese restrictions. They were also faced with little local compromises and deals with the Japanese and the puppets, to keep labor and supplies moving, to end strikes, and to buy peace. The China Printing and Finishing Company's [CPF] large Lunchang mill faced the Yangshupu district across the Huangpu in Pudong. The war restricted the company's supplies of cotton and coal from North and Central China, forcing them to rely on imports.[17] CPF's political sympathies lay firmly with the Chinese, whom they felt would always be the best customers, rather than with British cotton's international rival, Japan. But "it would be wise to keep in mind," as the Chairman remarked in 1939, "that the Japanese [are] in possession."[18] Still, 1938 and 1939 were boom years for many companies in the International

---

[14] W. J. Keswick to B. D. Beith, 6 January 1941, F2091/130/10, FO 371/27631, PRO.

[15] Patricia Stranahan, *Underground: The Shanghai Communist Party and the Politics of Survival, 1927–1937*, 108–118.

[16] See G. G. Phillips to Sir Archibald Clark-Kerr, 29 June 1940, FO 676/435, PRO.

[17] "Report on a visit to the CPF's mills and works at Shanghai, March 1938." Calico Printers' Association archives [hereafter CPA] M 75, Manchester City Library [hereafter MCL]. CPF was the fully owned subsidiary of the Manchester-based Calico Printers' Association.

[18] CPA Minute Book 25, 26 September 1939, MCL.

Settlement, and CPF was no exception. By April 1940 the company was selling in India, Malaysia, Manila, Indonesia, and to Chinese buyers in Hong Kong who were shipping cloth into Southwest China.[19] The ongoing currency crises and restrictions also dictated the search for new markets abroad. CPF needed to earn hard currency to pay for raw materials imports. They were not the only ones. As one British trade official put it in 1939: "Shanghai is becoming an industrial town trading with non-industrial countries, instead of a gateway leading from industrial countries into the rural hinterland of China."[20]

CPF's biggest crisis was the May–December 1939 strike. Beginning in a largely unpremeditated manner over issues relating to the treatment of staff by the plant's security personnel, the dispute was almost immediately hijacked, and the Mill propelled into the political spotlight.[21] Because of its extra-Settlement location, British troops, brought into the plant to protect it from worker activism, had to be replaced by Japanese marines who "guarded" the land entrances. More significantly, the puppet authorities and local Japanese military forces seized control of the strike, which became the vehicle for a fierce and deeply worrying anti-British campaign which coincided with the crisis over the Tianjin British concession, which was blockaded by Japanese forces.[22] There were marches and rallies, and anti-British propaganda leaflets and booklets were published and circulated. The Japanese Special Service Section and the Pudong Branch of the Daminhui were heavily involved in the conflict (which both the workforce and the SMC had attempted to depoliticize at the start).[23] The nerves of the foreign employees were shaken by the violence that accompanied the initial outbreak on May 20, 1939, and subsequent days. One manager died of a heart attack, and the plant's British security chief was killed by Japanese marines in an ugly incident that took place after they had allowed wreckers to break into the compound on June 5.[24]

The Pudong puppet authorities demanded large sums for "Labour Expenses" to end the strike, while violent intimidation kept the workforce away.[25] The strike

---

[19] CPA "Minutes of the 15th AGM," 3 May 1939; Minute Book 25, 2 April 1940, MCL.

[20] R. P. Heppel, minute, 20 April 1939, on Clark Kerr No. 207, 3 March 1939, F3657/3657/10, FO 371/23519, PRO.

[21] Interview with P., Shanghai, April 1997; a full file on the strike can be found in SMP D 6968, NARA. See also *Shanghai fangzhi gongren yundong shi* [History of the Shanghai textile workers' movement], 272–278.

[22] On the Tianjin crisis see Best, *Britain, Japan and Pearl Harbor*, 71–86.

[23] Eleanor Hinder note on China Printing and Finishing Company Strike, 26 May 1939, SMP D 6968, NARA.

[24] Barnett, *Economic Shanghai*, 65–67; Robert Bickers, *Empire Made Me*, chapter 10, passim.

[25] CPA Minute Book 24, 20 June 1939, 11 July 1939, 31 October 1939, MCL.

ended on November 27, but the real victor was the puppet regime: $250,000 was handed over by CPF into a "relief fund" in return for "labour guarantees."[26] CPF was not averse to dealing with the devil if needs must; like other British concerns they realized who called the tune for the moment. CPF, like the SMC, and like the British diplomatic establishment, certainly huffed and puffed and blustered in their dealings with the various overlapping and superseding organs of the puppets and the Japanese, but as John Keswick noted in January 1941: "words" were the "only weapon" left to the British.[27] The start of the war in Europe vastly increased the dangers of their being quietly abandoned by the British government.

Normality in political life was as difficult an illusion to revive as in business. The SMC was forced by the emergency and by Japanese, Chongqing, and British pressure, to extend its activities into whole new areas of quotidian life and thought; from refugee relief to more general food and fuel supplies, to censorship of print media and radio. The political crisis was compounded by the enforced urban migration from the Chinese suburbs and hinterland, and by industrial relocation into the Settlement. The Council reacted to Japanese pressure, to British diplomatic pressure eager to avoid confrontations, and to the promptings of its police. But this encroachment had also been a trend throughout the 1930s as the Council was modernized and cajoled into providing services for the Chinese ratepayers and into confronting more effectively the problems of a modern, urban environment. The ever-expanding activities of Eleanor Hinder's Industrial and Social Section are one good example.[28] Now the SMC really did become a state within a state, and it fell to the Council alone to organize responses to many of the crises affecting the Settlement – importing rice from Indo-China for example. It also took on new financial powers, taxing business premises and cigarette sales.[29]

British businesses were also forced into deeper paternalistic relationships with their workforces. CPF found itself arranging for vegetables to be available for purchase by women operatives in hurriedly arranged hostel accommodations, setting up transports across the Huangpu for staff forced to flee Pudong, stockpiling rice and issuing rice and cost-of-living allowances. The company was forced into a relationship with the workforce that it did not want. The SMC, and the SMP, also found themselves in this situation, taking on *danwei*-like

---

[26] Clark-Kerr to Robert Howe, 6 December 1939, enclosing Shanghai No. 390, 27 November 1939, F1011/31/19, FO 371/24662, PRO; CPF Minutes, 20 December 1939, SMA Q 199-1-1.

[27] W. J. Keswick to B. D. F. Beith, 6 January 1941, F2091/130/10, FO 371/27631, PRO.

[28] E. M. Hinder, *Life and Labour in Shanghai: A Decade of Labour and Social Administration*.

[29] Shanghai No. 881, 26 September 1941, F10067/130/10, FO 371/27634, PRO.

responsibilities for Chinese staff, who were increasingly hard hit by inflation and shortages, and who became more restive and prone to strike.

TAKING BACK THE REINS: THE FO SEEKS CONTROL

As the SMC encroached into the lives of both its foreign and Chinese inhabitants, so the British government extended its legal control over British subjects and their activities in the International Settlement, over broadcasting and newspapers for example, and a stricter watch was kept on those with Axis links or sympathies. Various precautions were taken to try to control Chinese interests that took advantage of British extraterritoriality with the connivance of British friends, or to the financial advantage of those who lent their names.[30]

At the same time, the deteriorating situation saw the extension of the reach of the Foreign Office into the SMC and the culmination of its attempts to gain effective control over its activities. Rice supplies, the municipal elections, the Northern Districts, the composition of the SMP, the Bad Lands, individual murders, and other incidents were all reported to London and discussed in Whitehall. The British military also took a closer interest. Crime in the Western District, and then by extension throughout the International Settlement, became a defense issue for the British forces whose sector this was. The distinctions between a militarized SMP and British troops doing police duties-in-all-but-name, became very fine.[31] British Far Eastern intelligence, which had developed a useful relationship with the SMP on a number of security issues since World War I, seems to have made much more routine use of SMP Special Branch intelligence after 1937. With little in the way of effective resources in place of its own, and with many common problems after the start of the Sino-Japanese war, this coziness comes as no surprise.[32] The exchange of information indicates both the contingent incorporation of the SMP into British imperial security schemes and the SMC's desperate search for a sponsor, and for diplomatic support in the face of Japanese demands. Repeating a familiar pattern of calling on British support when in danger (notably in 1926–1927) the SMC – like individual

---

[30] Shanghai No. 346, 12 July 1939, F10204/84/10, FO 371/23456, PRO. On treason and collaboration see Bernard Wasserstein, *Secret War in Shanghai: Treachery, Subversion and Collaboration in the Second World War.*

[31] War Office to FO, 25 February 1939, F1944/84/10, FO 371/23453; C-in-C Shanghai to Shanghai Consul-General, 23 December 1939 in Shanghai No. 426, 30 December 1939, F1528/162/10, FO 371/24682, PRO.

[32] Richard J. Popplewell, *Intelligence and Imperial Defence: British Intelligence and the Defence of the Indian Empire, 1904–1924*, 268–276; Richard J. Aldrich, *Intelligence and the War against Japan: Britain, America and the Politics of Secret Service.*

Shanghailanders – argued for its importance as a bastion of British interest. When it perceived itself in danger, the SMC temporarily abandoned its autonomous claims in the face of its need for support: This time the FO did not let go.

The diplomats gained their greatest leverage as a result of crises over the composition of the Council and its personnel, and its deteriorating financial position.

In 1936 the Japanese Residents' Association first broached the convention that it would field only two candidates for SMC seats, and that British electors would vote for them first, ensuring their election. Mobilization of British voters through the British Residents' Association defeated this challenge; in 1939 it became clear, however, that the number of Japanese electors was growing at a rapid rate as a result of vote splitting.[33] The SMC itself secretly lobbied the Consulate-General to urge a British response using similar tactics. Diplomatic approval was needed, to support lowering consular fees for the nominal property transfers needed, which were put into effect in time for a bitter municipal election in 1940.[34]

The Anglo-American majority survived the 1940 election, but the diplomats who facilitated the necessary gerrymandering knew that the Japanese actually had a very good case for increased representation in all aspects of Settlement life. British officials worried that such activity might provoke unilateral Japanese action to seize or destabilize the Settlement. Ill feeling stemming from the election partly lay behind the assault on SMC Chairman W. J. Keswick by Hayashi Yukichi, President of the Japanese Residents' Association, in January 1941.[35] With another Council election looming, the Consul-General, British councillors, and SMC Secretary-General Godfrey Phillips met shortly afterward to find ways to avert "the possibility of bloodshed on a serious scale," as the situation was "untenable and unjustifiable."[36] The result was the April 1941 Provisional Council Agreement which suspended the Land Regulations and the electoral process, and introduced a consular-appointed Council. The agreement met Japanese complaints part way by diminishing the overt British presence on the SMC through the appointment of Dutch and Swiss members. It also sealed British consular control of that presence: The autonomy of the SMC was fatally compromised.[37]

---

[33] See, e.g., G. W. Swire to R. G. Howe, 18 April 1939, F3896/84/10, FO 371/23454, PRO.

[34] The evolution of the policy can be viewed in various files in the series F162/10, FO 371/24682-4, PRO.

[35] Ibid., 35–36.

[36] Memorandum in Shanghai No. 17, 11 February 1941, F883/130/10, FO 371/27631, PRO.

[37] Chongqing No. 183, 20 April 1941, F3212/130/10, FO 371/27632, PRO.

British diplomats had secured their long-sought-after control over settler politics, but growing tensions led to the effective abandonment of this policy of overt involvement in the affairs of the International Settlement. As London was bombed, Shanghai's demands for special treatment – for negotiations leading toward the establishment of neutral status in the event of conflict, for example – won little sympathy. "Shanghai have been the spoilt child of this country too long. They will have to stand on their own feet more in future," minuted one London diplomat in March 1941.[38] Why not let the Japanese take over the International Settlement altogether, mused an FO committee the following month, and let it burden them militarily and logistically.[39] Metropolitan priorities no longer lay in combating Japanese encroachment in Shanghai, but in positioning for an expected wider violent conflict in the Pacific. The stricter definition of British imperial interests identified as a result excluded China; Hong Kong became the new front line of the British empire in East Asia, but the cornerstone of imperial defense was Singapore, guardian of communications with the Southwest Pacific. Hong Kong was merely an "outpost"; and Shanghai moved beyond the bounds of empire.[40]

FO support for the SMC and its desire to break the settler hold on the Council were complementary policies. The Japanese invasion of Manchuria in September 1931 had led to the suspension of earlier negotiations about the abolition of extraterritoriality and the return of the International Settlement to Chinese jurisdiction. The draft treaty initialed in June 1931 was shelved when Chiang Kai-shek dropped demands against the British and the United States, in a bid to garner international diplomatic support.[41] But there was every expectation that a final resolution of the Sino-Japanese crisis would precipitate a resolution of treaty port issues. Defending the SMC against the Japanese was a long-term negotiating tactic. Although British prestige was felt to be at stake, the actual aim was to survive, and to preserve the pre-1937 status quo to get as good a deal as possible from the Nationalist government in the inevitable aftermath. Whatever the Japanese acquired, diplomats knew, would not easily, if at all, be returned to British hands after the war.

Diplomatic usurpation of the settler position was effected in partnership with expatriate British businesses. Jardines, Hong Kong Bank, ICI, BAT, CPF, and Swires became involved because they could see that the old Settlement days

---

[38] A. H. Scott minute on Shanghai No. 187, 3 March 1941, F1681/1676/10, FO 371/27707, PRO.

[39] FE Dept Minute, 7 April 1941, F2737/1676/10, FO 371/27707, PRO.

[40] Paul Haggie, *Britannia at Bay: The Defence of the British Empire against Japan, 1931–1941*, 168, 174.

[41] Bickers, *Britain in China*, 148–151.

were finished, and so they also moved to buy time, and position themselves for peace. Shanghailanders lost control of the SMC to this coalition of diplomats and the "British hongs on the Bund" – eight of which alone held 5,127 British votes in February 1941 (out of a total of 12,500 British votes). The local democracy of the self-styled "Model Settlement," where the voice of the smaller treaty port people was often previously loudly heard, became irrelevant.[42]

The Council's financial crisis contributed to its loss of autonomy. "Bad finance" was compounded by the fact that after 1927, when the Council feared that in the long term control would be surrendered to Chinese, the SMC undertook a series of measures to remove public utilities from possible Chinese control. The electricity and water departments were sold off to U.S. and British interests respectively, in a sharing of the spoils. In a bid to safeguard the interests of its own personnel, the SMC had introduced new contracts for "foreign" (British) staff issuing pensions, and making a commitment to part pay pensions in Sterling. The cumulative result of these moves was disastrous – the Council lived off the utility sales which allowed it to prolong artificially low municipal rates and avoid politically troublesome rate rises. The loss of significant revenue-generating districts to Japanese control in the aftermath of the 1937 conflict was another problem, which arose just when the wide-ranging new emergency responsibilities of the SMC forced it into much higher levels of spending. Moreover, the collapse in exchange rates vastly inflated the Sterling commitments to an ever-increasing list of British pensioners.[43]

The squeeze also seriously damaged the SMC's operational efficiency. Salary costs were held down where possible. Most damagingly, Chinese members of the SMP in particular found themselves adrift. A spate of petitions from rank and file constables in August and September 1939, and increases in disciplinary cases for petty corruption, prompted the SMC to move all the men up the pay scale, but the deteriorating situation at the end of November 1940 led men to strike over rice allowances. "We have been trading on the loyalty of our Chinese Police in the interests of economy" complained Commissioner of Police K. M. Bourne in December 1940; similar disturbances were averted in November 1942 by increases in allowances and selective transfers and dismissals. Economic

---

[42] W. J. Keswick to B. D. Beith, 6 January 1941, F2091/130/10, FO 371/27631; Shanghai No. 11, 1 February 1941, F534/130/10, FO 371/27631; Shanghai No. 65, 25 February 1941, F4054/130/10, FO 371/27632, PRO.

[43] Butterfield & Swire, Shanghai, to John Swire & Sons, London, 8 December 1939, in G. W. Swire to R. G. Howe, 29 December 1939, F210/162/10, FO 371/24682, PRO; pensioners rose in number to over 200 by the end of 1941, from 15 in 1925 (SMC, *Annual Reports*, 1925, 1941). See also Barnett, *Economic Shanghai*, 31–36.

disaffection on this scale made Chinese constables much more receptive to the suborning activities of puppet agents.[44]

The first month of the European War was not an auspicious moment for the despatch of the British ambassador's first note to London about the SMC's financial situation, and its request for a loan – or a loan guarantee – of £500,000, but preferably £1 million.[45] In the event, the loan negotiated by the SMC from the Hong Kong and Shanghai Bank in 1940 was brokered by the diplomats and served to highlight again the important role of the Foreign Office. These negotiations, and those concerning the elections and the Provisional Council,[46] drew diplomats and expatriate businessmen closer together and away from the "community" – as they termed the settler interest – which was clearly felt by this new partnership to bear the blame for such problems arising.[47] The European war cemented this relationship as "firms of good repute," such as ICI or CPF, were aided in their efforts to import raw materials from the United States while settler interests were squeezed out. Expatriate businessmen used their close contacts to move smoothly into senior positions in the new wartime organizations formed by the imperial state – Tony Keswick of Jardines, for example, or Valentine St John Killery of ICI, who took on important positions in the Ministry of Economic Warfare and Special Operations Executive. There they worked to fight the Japanese, but also to protect their own business interests in the long term.[48]

Of course, British big business made friends wherever necessary. There were many instances of closer business relations with Chinese elites being sought and established after the conflict began, often in the hope of improving political ties in the long term: Chinese companies were reflagged as British, and prominent individuals were offered directorships. This was also firmly in the traditional mode of treaty port business activity, in the history of flags of convenience and alliances of extraterritorial privilege and Chinese capital. But it was given a different flavor by the fact that, unlike 1932, most Shanghailander sympathies lay with the Chinese by the end of 1937. CPF cultivated Li Ming, and also Du Yuesheng, but it was also forced to cut deals with Pudong puppets. Butterfield & Swire approached their long-term Japanese rivals Mitsui Bussan Kaisha in November 1941 and gained an understanding that the firm would do all it could

---

[44] "Pay of Chinese Constables," parts 1–3, SMA U-102-5-32,33,34.

[45] Clark-Kerr No 1133, 3 December 1939, F10756/84/10, FO 371/23456, PRO.

[46] Memorandum in Shanghai No. 17, 11 February 1941, F883/130/10, FO 371/27631, PRO.

[47] John Swire & Sons, London to Butterfield & Swire, Shanghai, 2 February 1940, Swire Papers, Box 2063, Library, School of Oriental and African Studies (SOAS).

[48] W. J. Keswick to Ashley-Clarke, FO, 19 March 1941, F2254/1676/10, FO 371/27707, PRO; Aldrich, *Intelligence and the War against Japan*, 103–104.

to protect Swire interests in the coming conflict.[49] There was greater fear than ever before over the mass of the Chinese in the Settlement. The worry that the socioeconomic situation would lead to riots and instability was pervasive, and certainly informed the willingness of British individuals to work under the Japanese after Pearl Harbor: Then it was the Japanese alone who had the troops to deal with such problems. Wartime relations in the International Settlement between national communities did not necessarily mirror the political alliances operating worldwide.

ORDINARY PEOPLE

Despite the encroachments of the previous decade on foreign power and privilege, British settler society in Shanghai still had a very strong sense of its own identity: Their vision was local; the SMC was its Council, the SMP its police force. The Shanghailander British failed to see why they should be evacuated from their home, or evicted from their jobs because of difficulties elsewhere. But individual Britons, whatever their occupation or status, found their lives increasingly confined. Their political and economic freedoms were restricted by the British government, the SMP, and by terrorism; and there was the pervasive fear of later retribution at the hands of the Japanese or the Chinese. Private activities also became circumscribed: behavior on the street when walking past, or near, a Japanese sentry, for example. The cantonization of the city by defensive barriers, the sandbagging of buildings, and security procedures to guard against terrorist attack all impinged on Shanghailander normality.

After the Japanese seizure of the Northern Districts life became more physically confined to the area south of the Suzhou Creek, a crowded rump hemmed in by fixed sentry posts, fortifications, and stop and search measures. Of course this directly affected those with business interests in the areas, but it also cut out over half of the Settlement from the normal life of British residents. This fragmentation occurred in a period of enforced urban migration and urbanization accompanied by the relentless standing-to of troops, of the Shanghai Volunteer Corps (SVC, a merchant militia), and of the police on the political anniversaries that peppered the calendar: more barricades at intersections, and inspections of cars, bikes, rickshas, and schoolboys' satchels; there were curfews, search parties at hotels, tea shops, and lodging houses. The searchers were

[49] Butterfield & Swire, Shanghai, to John Swire & Sons, London, 14 April 1941, Butterfield & Swire, Shanghai, to Butterfield & Swire, Tianjin, etc., 20 November 1941, Swire Papers, JSS XII 4/14, SOAS.

ordered to be lenient and unintrusive with non-Chinese, but it still cantonized the atmosphere.[50]

Physically too, there were other infringements. Officials were subject to assassination attempts: Godfrey Phillips, SMC secretary-general, Reginald Yorke, Special Branch chief, and Tony Keswick, Council Chairman, were the most prominent. Other individuals were beaten, arrested, or killed by the Japanese, including members of the CPF staff.[51] The era of routine policing duties for the SMP was supplanted by the era of gun-warfare. The SMP became a paramilitary force, with armored cars, machine guns, and the odd prolonged firefight with the men from "76." This was not the force most of these men had joined, nor was it a force many of them had any desire to be in. It was bad for the nerves and the health. Reginald Yorke, for example, retired in October 1940 to save his own, and his wife's, mental health. Sometimes policemen prominently involved in conflict with the puppets had to be removed from Shanghai. Probationary Sergeant Jock Kinloch was recruited, with diplomatic help, into British colonial police service elsewhere after the August 19, 1939 shooting incident in which two puppet police were killed, after meetings were organized by the Daminhui and others against him.[52]

Still, for all this danger, the diary of seventeen-year-old Joan Mains shows her cycling to school regardless, and most of the 3,000 British women and children evacuated to Hong Kong by August 21, 1937 were back by Christmas. Individuals attempted to perpetuate their prewar normality. The core of Shanghailander identity lay in its claim to be a real community in which people lived and worked, and created and consumed culture. Moves to shut down the Municipal Orchestra in 1938 were defeated, for reasons which clearly indicate the importance to morale of continuing to act as if Shanghai was still a communal home where some compromises to civilized standards just could not be made. The orchestra was re-envisioned and defended as an important cultural asset. Life in the city for Shanghailanders was saturated with such symbolism. Wartime made prominent other strands of Shanghailanders' complex identity, but if they were more conscious of and more demonstrative in their Britishness and imperial citizenry after the onset of the European conflict, they remained Shanghailanders, and this local identity's assumptions

---

[50] "Precautionary measures to be adopted on the anniversary of the outbreak of local hostilities, August 1940," SMP N 297/1, NARA.

[51] For one contemporary list see "Recent cases of assault by Japanese against British subjects," 11 April 1938, F5543/35/10, FO 371/22075, PRO.

[52] R. W. Yorke, Personnel file, U 102-3-1549, SMA; SMP D9391, NARA; Chongqing No. 974, 3 September 1939, F9809/84/10, FO 371/23456, PRO. See also Bickers, *Empire Made Me*, chapter 11, passim.

and demands were to shape their experience of and attitudes toward Japanese occupation.[53]

Morale could not stay high indefinitely after 1937. People did start leaving after the European war began. Army reservists in the SMP resigned to rejoin their units. Others, scenting the wind, resigned, shipped their families to Australia, and joined up. Some men were pulled out by the British Government. To stem the flow the SMC persuaded the FO to instruct its staff to remain at their posts as their contribution to the war effort.[54] Businesses were hit just as badly: Foreign staff morale at CPF was severely dented by the 1939 strike, and by the growing problems of living in the city: the cost of living, uncertainty, crime, and the threat of violence.[55]

CPF provides a good focus for looking at British business on the edge of the Pacific war. It was a prime British moaner as tension mounted. The cotton market generally was bad: Power rationing decreased production by a third, raw cotton prices rose as imports were restricted, and exports became more difficult to place.[56] The bulk of CPF production, the company claimed using figures that the FO thought "highly imaginative," got through to Free China, and their continued production was needed, CPF asserted, to fulfill orders for India and to prevent closing down the plant, throwing their workers out of their jobs, and undermining the social stability of the Settlement.[57] When the American-led blockade came into force in July 1941, they did all they could to evade it; even, in mid-November 1941, proposing a huge barter deal with a Japanese company, swapping Indian cotton for Japanese-produced grey cotton yarns and cloth to sell in the Dutch East Indies.[58] Against the blockade other British firms badgered the Consul General, arguing their case in London for trade to be kept alive. This was seen as special pleading by those who still felt themselves to be exceptional, but it was more a desperate desire to stay useful, and not to be abandoned.

OCCUPATION, 1941–1945

The Shanghai British were unpopular with the diplomats and military long before Pearl Harbor because of such concerted efforts to evade the blockade, and the attempts of this "spoilt child" to have the city declared economically

---

[53] Bickers, "Shanghailanders," passim; SMC, *Annual Report*, 1938, 16.
[54] See Commissioner Bourne's letter to British members of the force (n.d., 1940) in F4117/44/10, FO 371/53598, PRO.
[55] CPA Minute Book 25, 3 February 1940, MCL.
[56] Shanghai No. 954, 22 October 1941, F11294/285/10, FO 371/27673, PRO.
[57] See passim, the files in FO 371/27672-3, PRO.
[58] Shanghai No. 1049, 15 November 1941, F12478/285/10, FO 371/27673, PRO.

and politically neutral in the event of conflict. An official telegram explicitly ordering British Subjects not to "assist the enemy voluntarily in running municipal administrations, public utilities or other essential services" was sent on December 6, 1941, too late to be acted on in Shanghai.[59] News that senior SMC officials were still at their jobs after December 8, "for the welfare of the Settlement,"[60] initially disgusted some Foreign Office observers in London, although Anthony Eden, the Foreign Secretary, minuted in March 1942 that the onus lay on British subjects to decide whether they could "embarrass the enemy war effort most by remaining" in their positions or by resigning them.[61] Looking to the end of the war, the diplomats began to support those who stayed on. Physical danger, and simple economics, led many to make unpleasant choices; private withdrawal or escape were difficult. Also, although the FO had thought that those who could, ought to get out, the bulk of the British community believed that Shanghai was their home, and that the eventual restoration of peace would bring them the restoration of pre-1937 normality. The strength and integrity of this settler mentality must be considered. There were strong financial ties too: for Shanghailanders like their French neighbors abandoning the city meant abandoning jobs, property, savings, superannuation, and pensions. Also, as former Customs official Owen Gander remarked in his diary in April 1942, those still in Shanghai at the end of the war stood a better chance of regaining their old positions.[62] Individuals mirrored the thinking of big business and the diplomats in their deliberations.

Although some British-owned shops and firms were left largely unmolested, larger companies, manufacturing plants, and utilities were taken over by Japanese administrators answering to the Asia Development Board.[63] Many senior managers stayed on in their posts for as long as they could to protect the interests of their staff; only a few refused to serve at all under Japanese supervision. Most Allied business employees were dismissed by the Japanese administrators of their confiscated firms; CPF employees were out by the end of January 1942, although fourteen of them were permitted to occupy flats in the compound until the end of February 1943.[64] Some expressed puzzlement

---

[59] FO No. 1204, 6 December 1941, F13613/130/10, FO 371/27634, PRO.

[60] Notification No. 5676, G. G. Phillips, *Shanghai Municipal Council Gazette* [*SMCG*], 26 December 1941, p. 281.

[61] A. H. Scott minute on Berne No. 702, 27 February 1942, F1959/1494/10, FO 371/31677; Eden minute on Berne No. 499, F1495/1494/10, FO 371/31679, PRO.

[62] Owen Gander Diary, 25 April 1942, Imperial War Museum, Department of Documents [IWM].

[63] Extract from letter from Consul General A. H. George to J. H. Le Rougetel, 1 October 1942, F7057/391/10 in WO 208/378a, PRO.

[64] Q 199-1-53, SMA.

at the turn of events; Owen Gander, dismissed after twenty-seven years of service with the Maritime Customs, wondered why "the position of foreigners in the service should have been affected by the political situation."[65] British and American employees of the SMC actually increased in number as these unemployed people were taken on, ostensibly to assist in the emergency activities of the Council: dealing with food and fuel supplies, transport, or new taxes. In time-honored fashion Shanghailanders used the SMC's revenues to maintain themselves at the expense of the rate-paying Chinese majority. It kept them off the limited doles handled by the national relief organizations but it also revealed, in a sense, their view of the purpose of the Council.[66]

STILL AN INTERNATIONAL SETTLEMENT, 1941–1943

The Japanese takeover of the Council was slow, legalistic, and undertaken with due decorum. In the eyes of the "Japanese authorities" the Provisional Council Agreement was "still in force," according to newly appointed Council Chairman K. Okazaki. Allied councillors resigned in January 1942 ("at the request" of those same "authorities"), but were not replaced. Most in fact continued to serve on the committees which supervised the work of the administrative departments: R. G. MacDonald was still sitting on the Watch Committee in October 1942. The Municipal Advocate stayed at his post until he "retired" in September, but the most senior British personnel were "retired" – one was even allowed to stay on as an adviser until he reached pensionable age – or else resigned in February. Not only did all other SMC personnel still in Shanghai continue serving, but they continued to receive promotions, Long Service Medals, and so on.[67]

Although refusing to involve themselves in the arrests of fellow nationals – as Commissioner of Police K. M. Bourne made clear as early as December 20, 1941 – to all intents and purposes the routine policing of the city by the SMP continued as before. This included assisting the Japanese Gendarmerie in the arrest of Chinese suspects.[68] Testimony from serving officers indicates that relations with Japanese members of the force continued to be good, although new Japanese personnel were drafted into the force – especially as middle-ranking

[65] Owen Gander diary, p. 16, IWM.

[66] J. W. Allan, "Report on the Shanghai Municipal Council," 20 September 1942 [hereafter Allan Report, 1942], in War Office to FO, 4 May 1945, F2717/63/10, FO 371/46191, PRO. On relief activity see W. G. Braidwood, "British Residents' Association of China, December 1941–June 1943" (typed manuscript, c. 1944) in PP MS 47, Papers of A. G. N. Ogden, Box 5, File 32, SOAS.

[67] *SMCG*, 30 January 1942, p. 9; 27 March 1942, p. 34; 30 October 1942, p. 167; Allan Report, 1942.

[68] See, e.g., SMP D 8299/362 and D 8299/364, 12 and 20 December 1941, NARA.

Britons, and those with Army reserve status, were removed from the SMP on July 31, 1942.[69] That still left 160 Britons, including 4 Superintendents.[70] Good relations with Japanese fellow employees seemed to have been maintained across the SMC, and point perhaps to the ongoing strength of the rhetoric of internationalism.[71]

Working under Japanese control posed few problems for the mass of Britons in the SMC. Council Secretary-General G. G. Phillips resigned in February, finding it improper to continue working in such a prominent role in a now–Japanese controlled organization. Isolated from Britain, in a city now controlled by the Japanese, but not interned, and allowed to continue working, it is hardly surprising that Britons remained in their posts. The continued "International" status of the SMC meant that they could rationalize their actions – as some have in retrospect – by virtue of a technicality: They were not working for the Japanese, but for the SMC. Moreover, the need for a continued income, for access to ration and fuel allowances and accommodation, meant that resignation or noncooperation was not an option. Of 2,779 Britons identified in the February 1942 census as living in the International Settlement, over half were women and children: Private responsibilities dictated many public actions.[72]

Reports reaching the Foreign Office indicated that the Japanese did not have the personnel available to take over the running of the city and its services, and that it quite suited them to use enemy nationals.[73] Belief in their own irreplaceability as guardians of "high standards," combined in Shanghailander minds with fear of not only a decline in services (and the security of their incomes), but also of a possible collapse of public order if they no longer served at their posts – especially the SMP, who argued that by staying at their posts they were still obeying FO instructions and preserving British interests.[74] Rumors circulated about disturbing anti-British violence and the collapse of order after the fall of Hong Kong, and Britons worried after Pearl Harbor, as they had worried before, about the Chinese crowd.[75]

---

[69] Interviews with FGW (13 September 1996) and FP (13 March 1996), *SMCG*, 31 July 1942, p. 101.

[70] *SMP Diary 1943* (Shanghai: SMC, 1942).

[71] See, e.g., J. Chadderton memoir, IWM 85/42/1. Chadderton served in the council's Public Health Department.

[72] Allan Report, 1942; *SMCG*, 27 March 1942, p. 34.

[73] Allan Report, 1942; 'Extracts from despatch dated 25th September 1942 from Mr George (formerly HM Consul-General Shanghai) to Mr Le Rougetel (formerly HM Chargé d'Affaires, Shanghai), F7058/391/10, FO 371/31668, PRO.

[74] See also the MI2c report, "Note on Position of British Personnel of Shanghai Municipal Police," February 1943, WO 208/378a, PRO.

[75] Gander diary, 25 April 1942, 26, 32.

The International Settlement remained an "International" Settlement, and in local propaganda much was made of the fact that under the old order the SMC was a British bailiwick, but now indeed it had become truly international and the contributions of the White Russian presence in the SMP, for example, was now to be fully recognized for the first time. (The hapless Russians, meanwhile, previously ordered to learn English, now found themselves taking compulsory Japanese classes.)[76] While the SMC provided due ceremonial when the SVC was formally disbanded in September 1942, and marked the "resignation" of distinguished senior British employees by awarding them generous pension entitlements, it also set about dealing with issues concerning commemorative statues in the Settlement (down came Sir Robert Hart), road names, and the municipal coat of arms.[77]

The Council itself continued to function as such until August 1943. The bureaucratic machine kept working, albeit a little more crankily than before. Searching for precedents for Japanese personnel called up for war service, the administration examined the files for procedures adopted with British personnel during the First World War.[78] The *Annual Reports* for 1941, and for 1942, were published, in Chinese, Japanese, and English – although when the 1942 report appeared in July 1943 its English-language readership was a little restricted.[79] The 1943 budgetary estimates dealt with such wartime matters of the moment as the resurfacing of school basketball courts, providing two-hundred new niches to the columbarium at Bubbling Well Cemetery, and increasing latrine provision throughout the Settlement.[80] English remained the language of internal documents until well into 1943, even in correspondence between Japanese (Japanese became the official language of the SMC in early 1943).[81] The fiction of normality was not only needed by the British. The Axis and neutral personnel who took over the running of the SMC were no keener on its abolition. The principle of maintaining a foreign-run administration in the city was important to Japanese nonmilitary and Axis power interests alike.

Normality, then, included what had become the normality of financial crisis; and this finally put paid to the Orchestra, which was abolished in May 1942.[82]

[76] *Shanghai Times*, 30 January 1942, p. 3; S. D. Ivanoff to Controlling Officer, Russian Auxiliary Detachment, 22 February 1943, U-102-5-5, SMA.
[77] "Disbandment of SVC," U-102-5-5; see SMC Minute, 9 December 1942, in U 1-4-1828, SMA.
[78] SMC Secretary to the Co-ordinating Committee, 19 February 1942, U 1-4-1828, SMA.
[79] *Shanghai Times*, 28 July 1943, p. 3.
[80] Treasurer SMC to Secretary SMC, 8 January 1943, U-102-5-54, SMA.
[81] See, e.g., the 3 November 1942 letter from Commissioner of Police Watari to Council Chairman Teraoka in U-102-5-5, SMA; *Shanghai Times*, 31 January 1943, p. 3.
[82] *SMCG*, 1 May 1942, p. 65; Robert Bickers, "'The Greatest Cultural Asset East of Suez': The History and Politics of the Shanghai Municipal Orchestra and Public Band, 1881–1946."

Expedients adopted before Pearl Harbor were slowly extended afterward: Brothels were explicitly licensed, and other revenue-raising schemes imposed.[83] The excess costs involved in employing non-Chinese personnel (including Japanese) were as great a problem after Pearl Harbor as they had been before. The removal of British and British Indian personnel from all branches of the SMC was as much a financial necessity as it was a political goal.[84] Disaffection over pay in the Chinese branch of the SMP continued as before. By the end of April 1942 there had been significant increases in dismissals for graft, but the situation was such that the SMC found it much more difficult to meet requests for help for his "under-fed and under-paid men" from Chief Deputy Commissioner of Police Yao.[85] "We were under the impression that the discrimination against the Chinese branch in pay would be removed following control of the Settlement by the Japanese," noted one anonymous letter of complaint, but "the treatment given to us by you people is no better than before."[86]

The range of activities considered appropriate also shifted only partially. The SMP Special Branch still busied itself with the collection of information about foreign political activity in the city, even if that activity was sanctioned, or even organized by Japanese agencies – such as reports on the "Independent Australia League."[87] The SMC remained an institution with some operational autonomy, which it attempted to protect (through not withdrawing its financial contribution to the *Baojia* system, for instance),[88] an institution which still needed to search for, and collate information, for its own purposes. The evidence from the archives is that the essential structures of the SMC, and the SMP in particular, remained intact even when the Settlement was nominally subsumed within the Special Municipality. It was the only coherent administrative machine left in the city apart from the Japanese military. The Commissioner-General's 1940 boast that "we shall at least leave a going concern in good order" was partly borne out by events.

ABOLITION

The price of the wartime conflict had already been heavy for Shanghailanders by 1941, and they had lost control of the SMC to an alliance of British multinationals and big China houses, who worked increasingly closely with diplomats

---

[83] *SMCG*, 30 October 1942, 161–162.
[84] See the minutes of the Special Finance Sub-Committee, 18 December 1942, U-102-5-54, SMA.
[85] Yao to Commissioner of Police, 30 September 1942, U-102-5-33/26, SMA.
[86] Anon., 10 November 1942, in U-102-5-33/26, SMA.
[87] File in SMP N 1457(C), NARA.
[88] Minutes of the Special Finance Sub-Committee, 18 December 1942, U-102-5-54, SMA.

in Shanghai and in London. The price of Pearl Harbor was heavier. For the United Kingdom the new alliance with Chongqing meant having to sign away the treaty port system in the February 1943 Sino-British treaty. As the heavier price would have been the loss of the Crown Colony, Hong Kong, the surrender of the International Settlement at Shanghai, the British Concession at Tianjin, and sundry other relics of the foreign establishment was considered to be acceptable.[89] Given the trend of British policy after 1925, the refocusing of Britain's China policy toward a China bridgehead in Hong Kong, which could headquarter a modernized commercial presence throughout China, was perfectly logical. Indeed, Hong Kong's role in the British China trade had been changing slowly throughout the 1930s, as British firms began to rethink their practices and long-term policies in the light of the National Government's company legislation and economic nationalism. The conflict in Shanghai in 1932 had been one foretaste of the possible vulnerability of Shanghai, and the tensions after 1937 saw British firms start to relocate registrations to the apparently more assured security of the British colony.[90]

The great advantage of the treaty's timing was that not only was organized British opinion in China itself under wraps – either under Japanese control or in British uniform – but organized China trade opinion in the UK was hardly in a position to argue for the perpetuation of treaty port privileges in the territory of a new ally. On top of this, British public opinion had been largely pro-Chinese since the beginning of the conflict in 1937. Without benefit of public support, and with those using private channels of access to policy makers in the Foreign Office appearing to lack integrity when they sought to argue for the old order, Shanghailanders stood no chance of preserving their world. Not that, as was commonly claimed, any of them knew about the February treaties until their release at the war's end in 1945 anyway.[91]

Diplomatic feelings, already skewed by Shanghai's pleas for aid as the American embargo had gone into effect in 1941, were further incensed by the apparent indifference Shanghailanders displayed toward matters of treason. The ambiguities of a situation in which the Japanese army had merely marched in and effected a change of ownership were only slowly accepted in London.

---

[89] K. C. Chan, "The Abrogation of British Extraterritoriality in China 1942–43: A Study in Anglo-American-Chinese Relations," 257–291.

[90] Bickers, *Britain in China*, 239.

[91] Interviews with FGW (13 September 1996) and FP (13 March 1996); "When the Americans released us out of the internment camps, we found that *Shanghai had been returned to China* and far from serving 'imperial interests,' we had not only lost our homes, but our jobs had been given away as well." R. E. Hargraves to Foreign Office, 5 April 1946, F5485/44/10, FO 371/53590, PRO.

The catastrophic collapse of British power in Southeast Asia in the face of the Japanese onslaught left little patience in the face of news that British subjects were continuing to work for the now–Japanese-controlled SMC, and public utilities. British prestige, already hammered by its military collapse, would be lowered still further, argued General Wavell, Indian C-in-C, if British subjects in Shanghai worked on as normal.[92]

Indeed, life certainly continued in a quasi-normal fashion for Britons in the pre-internment period. Rates and taxes had to be paid. Joan Mains went to school, and out to tea parties, to eat ice cream and hot dogs. George Cameron went shoplifting (and got caught).[93] Charles Hill and Dorothy Ferguson got married at Holy Trinity Cathedral.[94] Others died of old age. But diaries and reports show a strained, nervous, fearful, crushing boredom, soaked in rumors: of torture at the Kempeitai's Bridge House headquarters, of repatriation, and of the coming of internment. Commodity shortages and price inflation became obsessions. Cars were registered and requisitioned. Housing became a problem as property was requisitioned and as letting companies were instructed not to renew Allied national leases. Lack of communication with the world outside Shanghai was demoralizing. For Westerners at least, although escape to unoccupied China was not difficult for some, "island Shanghai" was exactly that.

Worse still, for many Shanghailanders, were the little disturbances to the old life, which actually inverted the settler world order. Former Council Chairman and settler leader Harry Arnhold found himself having to use a bus to get to work from Hongqiao. The journey was such an "ordeal" that his wife just stayed at home. Shanghailanders complained that Japanese restrictions were specifically designed to humiliate them in the eyes of the Chinese, but for a community always conscious of its prestige, perquisites, and place, wartime generally was one long humiliation. Arnhold and others held on to their servants for as long as possible, although here lifestyle and charity achieved an even mix, but after September 1942 he had to sack his gardener.[95] Reports that Shanghailanders were living life much as usual, however much an Arnhold might disagree with the use of the term, aroused some hostility amongst official observers in blitzed

<hr>

[92] General A. P. Wavell to Chief of Imperial General Staffs, 14 May 1942, WO 208/378a, PRO.
[93] Joan Mains Diary, IWM; SMP N1416, 3 February 1942, NARA.
[94] On 31 January 1942: Holy Trinity Marriage Register 7, Ms.1571, Lambeth Palace Library, London.
[95] H. E. Arnhold, "Shanghai 1941–45," Hoover Institution, Stanford; F. Sullivan letter, "Our Non-Business Pre-Internment Experiences," December 1943, WO 208/378a, PRO.

Britain, and in general the accounts of post–Pearl Harbor life must have done much to undo residual support for the settler establishment among the diplomats whose energies had previously served to support the Shanghailander position.[96] Internment in February–March 1943 affected most Britons (the elderly and infirm aside), and must have come as a relief of sorts, putting an end to some uncertainties. It also firmly placed Britons in an identifiably captive position vis-à-vis the Japanese enemy, unlike the Shanghai French, and helped properly incorporate them into the broader tale of British imperial defeat at the hands of Japan. Internment in that way finally made imperial Britons out of Shanghailanders.[97]

THE END OF BRITISH HEGEMONY

The diplomats won. Wartime and occupation accelerated the demise of the existing British presence in Shanghai. The settler interests that had fought against the diplomats' attempts to ease them out after 1927 were abolished at a stroke. A reduced foreign presence in Shanghai remained after the war, but it was shorn of the physical trappings of a self-styled colonialism – its Council, police, volunteer militia – and also of the mental trappings: names, traditions, rituals, self-confidence, energy. A Liquidation Commission sat to sort out the tricky personnel and property details left over by the wartime abolition of the treaty system and the concessions.[98] Britons continued to live, work, marry, and die in the city, some of them, indeed, because they had nowhere else to go. But their hold on China's real capital city was broken.

Across the front line, during the occupation, other Shanghai British businessmen were having the time of their lives indulging in unfettered and British government-sanctioned free enterprise on the Chinese black markets. Businessmen working for the Special Operations Executive established operation "Remorse," which aimed to purchase quinine and Chinese officials. Networks of distributors and buyers for Indian rupees, watches, diamonds, cigarette paper, and medicines were established in a bid to buy influence, safety, and food for prisoners, and to smooth the British path back into Hong Kong by suborning the Guangxi provincial government. This strange campaign served overall

---

[96] "Conditions of British Subjects in China under Japanese Occupation February 1942–August 1945," WO 208/378a, PRO.

[97] On internment see, for example, Hugh Collar, *Captive in Shanghai* (Hong Kong, Oxford: Oxford University Press, 1990).

[98] And a British presence, of course, remained to be dismantled after 1949: for both see Bickers, *Britain in China*, 234–244.

to "keep the British foot within the China door."[99] "Remorse" was a Shanghai businessman's dream: few rules, and fewer scruples. There was no Council, there were no ratepayers, and no settlers moaning on about their history, birthrights, and orchestra, and getting in the way of efficient business.

Khaki was contagious: CPF's Managing Director visited Chongqing in early 1944. Such was the fear of Guomindang carpet-bagging that he suggested "certain Shanghai businessmen should be given temporary army rank and attached as liaison officers to United Nations troops when they entered Shanghai."[100] That way they could identify British properties in Japanese hands and ensure that they weren't snaffled by the Chinese. The authorities saw little sense in the suggestion, but it stands as a symbol of how far big business and the government had come together during the wartime emergency. CPF got its mill back anyway, but Shanghailanders ceased to exist.

BIBLIOGRAPHY

Archives

Hoover Institution Library and Archives
H. E. Arnhold manuscript, "Shanghai 1941–45"

Imperial War Museum, London
J. Chadderton memoir, IWM 85/42/1.
Owen D. Gander diary
Joan Mains diary

Manchester City Library and Archives
M75, Papers of the Calico Printers' Association [CPA]

National Archives and Records Administration, Washington, D.C.
RG 263, Shanghai Municipal Police Special Branch Files

Public Records Office, Kew

FO 371   Foreign Office General Correspondence, Political
FO 676   Embassy and Consular Archives China, Correspondence Series 2
HS 1   Special Operations Executive: Far East: Registered Files
WO 208   War Office, Directorate of Military Intelligence

---

[99] B/B.3 to D/Fin, 26 June 1944, HS 1/291; on "Remorse" see Robert Bickers, "The business of a secret war: Operation 'Remorse' and SOE salesmanship in wartime China," *Intelligence and National Security* (forthcoming).

[100] Chunking No. 487, 3 May 1944, F2415/2415/10, FO 371/41670, PRO.

School of Oriental and African Studies, Library
John Swire & Sons, Ltd. papers
Papers of Sir A. G. N. Ogden

Shanghai Municipal Archives [SMA]
China Printing and Finishing Company records
Shanghai Municipal Council, Secretariat files, 1919–1930
Shanghai Municipal Police, Personnel files, Administration files

Books

Aldrich, Richard J., *Intelligence and the War against Japan: Britain, America and the Politics of Secret Service* (Cambridge: Cambridge University Press, 2000).

Barnett, Robert W., *Economic Shanghai: Hostage to Politics 1937–1941* (New York: Institute of Pacific Relations, 1941).

Best, Antony, *Britain, Japan and Pearl Harbor: Avoiding War in East Asia, 1936–41* (London: Routledge, 1995).

Bickers, Robert, "Shanghailanders: The Formation and Identity of the British Settler Community in Shanghai, 1843–1937," *Past and Present*, 159 (May 1998), 161-211.

Bickers, Robert, *Britain in China: Community, Culture and Colonialism, 1900–49* (Manchester: Manchester University Press, 1999).

Bickers, Robert, "'The Greatest Cultural Asset East of Suez': The History and Politics of the Shanghai Municipal Orchestra and Public Band, 1881–1946," in Chang Chi-hsiun (ed.), *China and World in the Twentieth Century: Selected Essays* (Taipei: Institute of Modern History, Academia Sinica, 2000).

Bickers, Robert, *Empire Made Me: An Englishman Adrift in Shanghai* (London: Allen Lane, 2003).

Chan, K. C., "The Abrogation of British Extraterritoriality in China 1942–43: A Study in Anglo-American-Chinese Relations," *Modern Asian Studies*, 11 (1977), pp. 257–291.

Clifford, Nicholas R., *Spoilt Children of Empire: Westerners in Shanghai and the Chinese Revolution of the 1920s* (Middlebury: University of New England Press, 1991).

Feuerwerker, Albert, *The Foreign Establishment in China in the Early Twentieth Century* (Michigan Papers in Chinese Studies, no. 29: Ann Arbor, Center for Chinese Studies, University of Michigan, 1976).

Haggie, Paul, *Britannia at Bay: The Defence of the British Empire against Japan, 1931–1941* (Oxford: Clarendon Press, 1981), pp. 168, 174.

Henriot, Christian, *Shanghai, 1927–1937: Municipal Power, Locality, and Modernization* (Berkeley: University of California Press, 1993).

Hinder, E. M., *Life and Labour in Shanghai: A Decade of Labour and Social Administration* (New York: Institute of Pacific Relations, 1944).

Lee, B. A., *Britain and the Sino-Japanese War, 1937–1939* (Stanford: Stanford University Press, 1973).

Popplewell, Richard J., *Intelligence and Imperial Defence: British Intelligence and the Defence of the Indian Empire, 1904–1924* (London: Frank Cass, 1995).

Shanghai fangzhi gongren yundong shi [History of the Shanghai textile workers' movement] (Shanghai: Zhonggong dangshi chubanshe, 1991).

Shanghai Municipal Council, *Annual Report*, 1937–42.
Shanghai Municipal Council Gazette [SMCG], 1941–42.
Shanghai Times
SMP Diary 1943 (Shanghai: SMC, 1942).
Stranahan, Patricia, *Underground: The Shanghai Communist Party and the Politics of Survival, 1927–1937* (Lanham, MD: Rowman and Littlefield, 1998).
Wakeman Jr., Frederic, *Policing Shanghai 1927–1937* (Berkeley: University of California Press, 1995).
Wakeman Jr., Frederic, *The Shanghai Badlands: Wartime Terrorism and Urban Crime, 1937–1941* (Cambridge: Cambridge University Press, 1996).
Wasserstein, Bernard, *Secret War in Shanghai, Treachery, Subversion and Collaboration in the Second World War* (London: Profile Books, 1998).

Chapter 10

The Bumpy End of the French Concession and French Influence in Shanghai, 1937–1946

CHRISTINE CORNET

Between 1937 and 1945 Shanghai entered a new era of hostile environment due to the war and the Japanese occupation, which marked the end of the settlements and of the city's international status. In this context, the foreigners who shared the fruits of Shanghai's economic prosperity in the pre-1937 period had to review their influence by showing their support toward both the Chinese government of Chongqing in Free China and the pro-Japanese government in Nanjing. In France, the arrival of the Vichy regime modified the evolution of the Concession in Shanghai. Then, wartime, occupation, collaboration, and capitulation accelerated the demise of the existing French presence in Shanghai.

For the French nationals established in the largest city of China for nearly a century, if the siege of Shanghai (August–November 1937) was an unprecedented catastrophe for the city, they felt outside of the event because the status of the settlements was preserved. Even after December 1941 when Japanese troops entered the center of the city, the French were spared, because Japan preferred to exercise diplomatic pressure on the Vichy government. In fact, since that management of the French Concession had, from 1940 on, been the responsibility of an administration appointed by the Vichy government, the collaboration between French and Japanese governments postponed the terms of the retrocession and the abolition of the extraterritoriality rights.

The French Concession was abolished twice: on July 30, 1943 and on February 28, 1946. By the end of the war in the Pacific, the French presence in Shanghai was already weak. Under Japanese pressure, and following the example of the British and Americans, France had officially agreed to renounce its extraterritoriality privileges and to restore Chinese sovereignty over its concessions. Then in January 1943, all the western powers officially renounced their treaty rights. In August 1943, Chen Gongbo, the head of the Special

Municipality of Shanghai placed by the government of Nanjing since October 1940, became the mayor of Shanghai reunified under the control of the Japanese.

Following a "declaration of principle" made by the Vichy government on February 24, 1943, an agreement of intent was signed with Nanjing on May 18. On the following July 30, the Shanghai French Concession was returned to the government of Wang Jingwei. But actually the question of extraterritoriality was never resolved prior to the treaty of February 1946.

With the disintegration of the settlements and the context of war, the Shanghai international development system as the doctrine of the open door policy was partly destroyed. The city's economic base was also directly affected. Shanghai turned to itself. Activity in the port declined even if the abundance of both manpower and money stimulated a revival of industrial activity. In order to avoid control by the Japanese, Chinese businessmen moved south and toward the spared French Concession. Chinese refugees swelled the population of the settlements.

Despite this uncertain context, the majority of the French community believed that Shanghai was their home and believed in the eventual restoration of "their" Concession after the end of the war. "Their" Concession in Shanghai consti-tuted a pattern for all concessions in China. Though small in size compared with the British settlers, the French residents in Shanghai, as their neighbors called them "the Shanghainese" ["les Shanghaiens"], appropriated Shanghai for themselves. Then, abandoning Shanghai meant abandoning jobs, property, savings, and in a sense a comfortable life. If the two settlements were equally shaken by the occupation of the Japanese army, the large degree of autonomy of the French Concession before 1940 was affected by the new regime of Vichy, which announced its largest state control and a policy of collaboration. But unlike the International Settlement, the French Concession was never occu-pied and became an isolated island in an isolated Shanghai. Between 1943 and 1945, a large number of the former employees of the Concession worked under Chinese control but in spirit to maintain French influence in Shanghai. Working under this control posed numerous problems, but most of the French accepted this transitional administration while waiting for things to improve. The Japanese and French capitulation raised hopes for the French commu-nity, which did not understand why the French Concession had not returned to the old status quo. After 1945, the French diplomatic representative still con-sidered that the extraterritorial status must continue until such time as it was abolished by a treaty in due and proper form with the Nationalist government. This treaty, signed in February 1946, confirmed the liquidation of the French Concession between two recognized governments. The definitive liquidation was negotiated in a context of vengeance against the collaborationists, and

9. A wounded Chinese soldier supported by a Vietnamese police officer in the French Concession. Source: Courtesy of the Fabre Family.

the French community was largely fractured between ex-collaborationists and pro-Gaullists.[1]

The study of the takeover of the French Concession requires first a brief look at the political background before 1937, which helps us to understand the status of the French Concession, the identity of its community, and the political context before the negotiation of the retrocession under the Vichy regime. Then, the process and the conditions in which the handover of 1943 were negotiated will be explored to identify the actors and the stakes. The transitional period between 1943–1945 showed how the ex-French Concession, the 8th district in the new Chinese municipality, still existed with a fractured community in a context of treachery and jealousy. The fate of the employees was posed since 1942 but not resolved until 1946. The negotiations for the definitive liquidation in 1946 of any French presence in China revealed another stake: The aim of French diplomacy was not the fate of the former concessions in China but the evacuation of the Chinese troops in the north of Indochina where France hoped to reaffirm its sovereignty.

---

[1] For collaboration, see Bergère, MC, "L'épuration à Shanghai (1945–1946): l'affaire Sarly et la fin de la Concession française," in *XX siècle*, pp. 25–41.

A SMALL FRANCE IN SHANGHAI: IDENTITY AND PARTICULARITIES OF
THE FRENCH CONCESSION AND FRENCH MINORITY COMMUNITY

Established in 1849, the French Concession in Shanghai was France's most important possession in China. Its symbolic significance went beyond its actual size and role. Here, we have to identify two particularities. The French community in Shanghai was as fractured as the British community among settlers, diplomats, policemen, officers, expatriates, and businessmen. Under the French consular authorities, the foreigners were numerous: Chinese, Vietnamese, white Russians refugees, Americans, and Europeans. The second point is that the French Municipal Council (FMC) was an actor with a real degree of autonomy before 1940. The Concession developed early as a kind of microstate with its own rules. But, unlike the Shanghai Municipal Council of the International Settlement, the political and administrative local power of the FMC was confiscated in the hands of the only consul-general since 1927. This defect was the result of the social and political troubles of 1927, which weakened the foreign presence in Shanghai but also served to reinforce the personal power of the consul-general. The FMC was suspended because of the Chinese threat. This decision was based on article 8 of the French municipal rules of 1868, completed by the consular order of November 12, 1926 which stipulated that in case of war or civil events threatening the Concession, the consul-general was authorized to suspend the council. Then the FMC was replaced by an appointed administrative municipal temporary commission.[2] From 1927 to 1940, the FMC was never elected by the ratepayers of the Concession. This usurped power created numerous problems in terms of French Concession representativity, particularly during the war and Vichy period. But the main problem was that the French residents were a minority, as Table 10.1 shows.[3]

Actually, since the nineteenth century, the lack of French residents was a constant threat to the existence of the Concession. In 1875, the electoral list included 206 electors, among whom only 72 were French and only 41 had the vote.[4] The mass of Chinese inhabitants was a pressure since the beginning of

[2] French ministry of foreign affairs (MAE), Nantes Diplomatic Archives (ADN) série A noire, Carton N° 106, letters of September 8, 1926 and November 16, 1926, consular order of November 12, 1926.

[3] MAE/ADP, Asie-Chine, vol. 800. ADN, Fonds Beijing Embassy, vol. 255–225 bis. Shanghai Municipal Archives, French Administrative Council, U38/2803-2809. ADN, vol. 256 bis, police 1939–1943. Zou Yiren, *Jiu Shanghai Renkou Bianqian de Yanjiu*, Study of Changes in the Evolution of the Population of Old Shanghai, Shanghai, Shanghai Renmin Chubanshe, 1980, pp. 97–147.

[4] ADN Carton No. 6, Godeaux's letter to foreign ministry, January 31, 1875. Twenty-one were municipality or police employees and did not have the vote.

Table 10.1 *Population of the French Concession in Shanghai*

	Chinese	Germans	Russians	Americans	British	Japanese	French
1910	114.470	148	7	44	314	105	436
1915	146.595	270	41	141	681	218	364
1920	166.667	9	210	549	1044	306	530
1925	289.261	270	1403	1151	2312	176	892
1928	351.453	353	2538	1380			1125
1930	434.807	597	3879	1541	2219	318	1208
1932	462.342	641	6045	1672	2684	275	1367
1934	479.294	725	8260	1792	2630	280	1430
1936	454.231	821	11828	1791	2648	437	2342
1942	824.613	2272	13.997	658	2090	1102	2497
1947							1068
1949							1017

the Concession, then in 1914 and during the 1920s. In 1926 Chinese residents got two appointed advisers with deliberative voices. Then, after the order of October 16, 1926, the FMC was composed of four French advisers elected by French residents, four foreigners elected by foreigners, and finally three Chinese advisers appointed by the consul-general.

Yet, throughout its history and despite its foreign population, the administration of the Concession remained an exclusive preserve of the French residents. The municipality (administrative services: secretariat, public health, public works, education) and the police departments were the main employers of the Concession. Municipality and police employees represented about one-half of the French population in the Concession. Of course, numerous Chinese and Russians were employed in all the French administrative services, with a preference for the police as Table 10.2 shows.[5]

The authorities of the Concession always endeavored to protect its autonomy both vis-à-vis its neighbor, the International Settlement, and the Chinese successive administrations. Adaptation became necessary in the face of successive events in the Nationalist movement in 1926–1927, Japanese imperialism in 1931, and during the war and postwar periods.

In times of political trouble, such as the 1911 revolution, the May 30 incident, or the April 12 coup by Jiang Jieshi, it would close its iron gates and call in military reinforcements to defend the Concession. Obviously, the Japanese

---

[5] Shanghai Municipal Archives, French Administrative Council U38/2803-2809. ADN, vol. 256 bis, police 1939–1943.

Table 10.2 *French Police Force Employees*

Nationality	1935	1936	January 1938	December 1938	1939	1940	1941
French	156	158	148	172	174	166	177
Europeans Other	43	46	46	46	41	46	49
Annamese	481	470	660	783	900	959	1,082
Chinese	1,400	1,434	1,694	1,382	2,074	2,193	2,284
Russians	127	127	376	283	348	353	371
TOTAL	2,207	2,235	2,924	3,116	3,537	3,717	4,014

occupation opened an era of tension and instability in the French-administered territory. With the occupation, the structure of multiple state authority only be-came more complicated, with consequences for the functioning of the economy, as explained by Timothy Brook.[6]

In France, the establishment of the Vichy government in 1940 also had a di-rect impact on Sino-French and Sino-Japanese diplomatic relations. The Vichy government adopted a pro-Japanese policy. The general consul Marcel Baudez, who remained in office until May 1940, was replaced in October by a Vichy appointee, Roland de Margerie. The French government was also represented by the ambassador Henri Cosme. But Cosme was accredited to the government of Jiang Jieshi in Chongqing and had no official relations with Wang Jingwei's government in Nanjing. The French diplomatic representatives tried to protect the long-term existence of the Concession, but the goal of the Vichy regime was more largely the preservation of French business in China and its pres-ence in Indochina. Futhermore, in the 1940s, it was more preoccupied with the European internal situation than the Shanghai context.

VICHY-NANJING-CHONGQING: NEW SINO-FRENCH AND NIPPO-FRENCH DIPLOMATIC RELATIONS

The military conquest of China by the Japanese army and the establishment of a Chinese puppet government in Nanjing in April 1940 destabilized Sino-French relations. Initially, the French government recognized the government of Jiang Jieshi as the legitimate authority. After 1940, the Vichy government officially maintained diplomatic relations with Chongqing where Jiang Jieshi installed his

---

[6] Timothy Brook, "Impact of Japanese Occupation on the Economy of Shanghai," *Wartime Shanghai*, colloquium, Lyon, October 1997.

government, but to placate the susceptibility of the Japanese, it also established a permanent contact with Wang Jingwei in Nanjing. The ambassador, Henri Cosme, advocated a balanced policy of equilibrium between the two contending governments with the hope of preserving good relations with Japan and China and pursuing business in Asia. This created a tricky situation for the Vichy diplomacy and French position in Shanghai. The management of the French Concession was then a complicated affair and the fate of the French employees became uncertain.

After Pearl Harbor, the Asian conflict became international. The Japanese increased their pressure on Vichy, whose policy in East Asia was to bide for time to prepare for the future. The situation in the settlements became increasingly difficult because of the lack of communications between Europe and Shanghai and the economic crisis. Social order in the French Concession was seriously challenged by strike movements in the French companies that employed numerous Chinese workers. In separate telegrams sent to the French general consul in Shanghai, H. Cosme believed that the French government would have to choose between Nanjing and Chongqing. The trend toward collaboration with the Japanese was reinforced by the return of Pierre Laval as foreign minister in the Vichy government. The Asian department of the foreign ministry, however, opposed in principle any collaboration with the Japanese and meticulously prepared the retrocession.

In January 1943, Japan appeared as the first foreign power in China to officially retrocede its concessions in different Chinese cities. In June 1943 the Japanese agreed to allow the Wang Jingwei government to assume administrative control over the International Settlement in Shanghai.[7] At this time, the collaboration between Nanjing and Tokyo was clear. In giving up its concessions to the government of Nanjing, Japan reinforced its influence against the western powers and Wang Jingwei obtained sovereignty in principle and recognition of his government. The Japanese decision posed an immediate threat to all the western powers in China. On February 23, 1943, the Vichy government officially declared its intention to renounce its advantages as obtained under the treaties of the nineteenth century. One important privilege, the thorny issue of extraterritoriality, was referred to in vague terms.[8] This statement followed the British and American agreements signed with the Chongqing government on January 11, 1943. The French acceptance implied a tacit recognition of the

---

[7] John Hunter Boyle, *China and Japan at War 1937–1945: The Politics of Collaboration*, Stanford University Press, Stanford, 1972.
[8] MAE/ADP War 1939–1945, Vichy/Asia, vol. 144, January 1942–May 1944, Vichy, June 17, 1943.

Wang Jingwei government. Nanjing and Tokyo were both very satisfied, even if the details of implementation were not explicit. The French Concessions in Hankou, Canton, and Tianjin were also transferred to the Chinese authorities on May 19.[9] In the case of Shanghai, however, although the issue was raised, no action was actually taken. The following months were marked by an active Japanese policy, under the initiative of Minister to China and later Vice Minister of Foreign Affairs Shigemitsu Mamoru, who hastened the pace of the negotiations between the government of Wang Jingwei and a Vichy delegation. The negotiations for the surrender of the diplomatic legation in Beijing had been led by Salade, consul in Nanjing, in March 1943.

On the following July 30, the Shanghai French Concession was handed back to the government of Wang Jingwei. The consul-general Roland de Margerie presided over the official ceremony. Although present in Shanghai, the French ambassador Henri Cosme did not attend because he was accredited to the government of Jiang Jieshi. The return of the French Concession was thus concluded between two governments – that of Vichy and that of Nanjing, neither of which recognized the other and neither of which existed by the autumn of 1945. The official statement, with regard to French community reactions, seemed to be made in haste. In fact, the fate of the French was locally discussed without a global policy, while the maintenance of French interests in business was clearly prepared by the Asian department of the foreign ministry.

PRINCIPLES OF RETROCESSION: SAVE SOMETHING FROM THE WRECK

The handover marked a watershed in the French communities in China because they were not psychologically prepared; even H. Cosme did not really believe in the takeover and thought that the concessions could be saved until the end of the war.[10] The handover of the concessions in Tianjin, Hankou, and Shamian were quickly negotiated. But retroceding the French Concession in Shanghai constituted a political, diplomatic, and personal stake. The French Concession for both the French community and French diplomacy was the symbol of the French presence in China.

Officially, the aim of Vichy was to preserve the French presence and influence in China. Between February and July 1943, the French foreign ministry (Asia Department) and the French diplomatic authorities in China prepared the retrocession with one goal: Maintain as long as possible the French influence in Shanghai. This aim comported two points: Transform municipality properties

---

[9] ADP-War Vichy-Asia 1939–1945, vol. 144, note of the Shanghai consul-general, September 15, 1945.

[10] ADP/War 1939–1945, Vichy-Asia, vol. 141. Cosme's telegram to MAE, July 9, 1943.

into state property called "the French Center" to exempt them from the negotiations.[11] The principal properties were the French municipal college, the Sino-French school, the Pasteur Institute, the Alliance française, the Bernez Cambot caserne, cemeteries, a radio station, the charitable institutions fund, and the grounds of the Cercle Sportif.[12] Roland de Margerie had excluded them from the negotiations in extremis.

The second point to consider was the fate of the employees of the French Concession: Chinese, Vietnamese, Russians, and French. A few months before the negotiations the actors in the French Concession with the diplomatic authorities thought about the re-employment of their personnel. They agreed to pay an indemnity to all French and foreign personnel based on their terms of service.

The Chinese personnel worked in the municipality and police departments. In 1943, the French municipality employed 2,091 Chinese: 457 agents, 1,530 workers, and 104 firemen. And in 1942, 2,284 were working in the police departments.[13] All these employees incorporated the departments of the puppet Chinese municipality after the retrocession. The Vietnamese came from the Garde Indigène of Indochina. They were dispatched to Shanghai in two batallions (Bataillon Supplétif Tonkinois – BST) during the events of 1925 in order to protect the French Concession. With their families, the Vietnamese community comprised 1,319 persons.[14] For them, the solution was to return to Indochina, but because of the lack of commitments, they were connected to the French military authority of BMICC, "Bataillon mixte d'infanterie coloniale de Chine," in waiting for their repatriation. Lieutenant-Colonel Artigue, headquarters chief who controlled it, was favored by the Vietnamese and Japanese. The French Ministry of Colonies supported their salaries and then discharged the municipality. Russians were immedaitely laid off because the Chinese did not want to incorporate them into their departments. They also received an indemnity based on the duration of their service.[15] Some of them worked in the French schools, army, and orchestra.

---

[11] ADN, Peking Embassy, telegrams between Cosme and de Margerie, March 28, 1943 to July 1944.

[12] Ibid.; telegrams of May 29 and June 2, 1943. The charitable institutions fund, "caisse des oeuvres," was a special account nourished by the profits made on the auditorium and Canidrome tax. It was created in December 16, 1927 in order to develop the French-Chinese charitable and educational institutions.

[13] ADN vol. 181, Chinese in the French police. Chinese policemen letter to the French consul-general in Shanghai, May 23, 1946.

[14] ADN vol. 261, Fonds Peking Embassy, telegrams between Cosme and de Margerie from March 28, 1943 to May 1944. Among them 908 soldiers and 60 noncommissioned officers (NCO).

[15] In June 1943, Cosme and de Margerie agreed to pay the Russians an indemnity of 3 months plus one-third of salary month by years worked; 1 month plus one-third of salary month by years

For the French personnel the situation was more complicated because of the different status between those who were employed in the municipality services and those who were employed in the police departments. And within these two categories there existed subcategories. The employment situation was as follows: The French municipal agents were directly employed by the consul-general. They signed a five-year contract and received nine months of paid holidays after five years of service. The policemen were almost all soldiers and they were incorporated into the police force. They did not have a contract but the internal police rules were based on the same terms: They enlisted for five years.[16] For those who taught in the French municipal college or the Sino-French college, the negotiators decided to place them under the responsibility of the French state before the retrocession. All the employees of the municipal properties transformed into state properties were immediately re-employed. They became civil servants as personnel of the embassy or consulate. A case-by-case treatment functioned for a minority of individuals before the retrocession. The well-known Sarly was appointed general inspector of the Chinese police, Valentin became deputy chief of the inspectorate, four other policemen changed rank, Jourdan and Bougon were directly appointed to Indochina services. This discriminatory treatment became a matter of jealousy and contributed to the division of the French community.[17]

From March 1943 to July 1943, de Margerie and Cosme elaborated on two previous principles to open the negotiations: At first, the Chinese authorities attempted to employ in their municipal services all French personnel until re-establishment of connections with France. The French authorities undertook to repatriate their personnel. Then, the Chinese authorities paid the layoff in-demnity and paid holidays for the duration of their "Chinese" service. The idea was that the French personnel changed their boss, not their job. The question of repatriation was also prepared before the handover. The French municipality always tried to provide a safety net in case its personnel were laid off. This guarantee and repatriation fund were constituted long before the handover. But since 1942, because of the financial crisis, the fund was used to cover munic-ipal expenditures. Then, the consulate decided to sell plots of lands in order to refloat it. But according to article 9 of the municipality rules, this deci-sion had to be discussed with the provisional municipal commission. Since

worked for Chinese, and 6 months plus one-third of salary month by years worked for French employees.

[16] Police rules of the French Concession, 1934.

[17] ADN vol. 261, Peking Embassy, Cosmes' telegrams; French police service, Shanghai July 27, 1943.

1941 the commission members "normally" appointed by the consul-general included two belligerents and two Chinese imposed by the Nanjing government. In this condition, the consul-general Roland de Margerie with the approbation of Cosme made decisions without the commission's vote. Only the French members were informed.[18]

Finally, on July 8, 1943, Chu Minyi, the Chinese foreign minister, agreed to re-employ three-fourths of the French personnel and agreed with point 2. Then, Vichy appointed a delegation which included de Boissézon, first secretary of the French Embassy in Peking, Roland de Margerie, Salade, consul in Nanjing, and Georges Cattand, the consul appointed in Tianjin in 1943. The composition of the delegation reflected the local level of the negotiations. It was not officially the ambassador who led the negotiations but local representatives of the French Concessions.

The general principles were as follows. The new Chinese municipal authorities would:

- respect the contracts negotiated by the French municipality
- take over the liabilities
- re-engage the Chinese municipal personnel
- rehire three-fourths of the French municipality employees; the others would receive a six-month salary redundancy payment[19]
- maintain the Chinese subsidies to the cultural, humanitarian, and scholastic French or Sino-French institutions
- manage the TSF radio but allow free use for the French
- accept the Chinese as members in the Cercle Sportif

On July 30, the consul-general Roland de Margerie officially and symbolically gave the keys of the concession to the mayor of Shanghai, Chen Gongbo. Two days later, the governments of Chongqing and Vichy broke diplomatic relations. The principal question was, what is the value of an agreement with a puppet government? The answer was known at the end of the war when the surrender of Japan in August 1945 raised the question of the validity of the agreement of 1943 and opened a second round of negotiations in February 1946 with the new French and Chinese governments.

In July, the first reaction of the French community was anxiety because they had not been informed of the negotiations and feared for their future. If the agreement was made in haste, it was because most of the municipality employees did not know what it really meant to work under the Chinese administration

---

[18] ADN vol. 261, Peking Embassy, de Margerie to Cosme, May 21, 1943. Strict confidential note.
[19] MAE/ADP, War 1939–1945, Vichy-Asia, vol. 141. Cosme's telegram to MAE, July 9, 1943.

and did not evaluate the diplomatic stakes. A few days before the handover, Ambassador Cosme had organized a meeting with all the employees, municipality, and police, and had declared with a paternalist pitch:

> In waiting for the time we all long for to go back home, don't be afraid: I shall provide work to everybody. I have obtained from the Chinese administration to re-hire the three quarters of you under the same wage conditions. I have planned jobs for the other and I shall help the personnel for its dispatching or I will give it a nest egg to do it. But do not misunderstand me. There will be no unemployment allowances. Those who do not accept the job offered will not receive anything.[20]

Cosme's speech bordered on demagogy, but the French residents needed to be reassured because the end of the French Concession in the war context signaled many work-related difficulties for the employees.

After July 30, 1943, two clans appeared: the Shanghai clan and the Nanjing clan, and the political option came into sight. For some of the French, Cosme quickly lost his credibility and appeared as a supporter of the Vichy policy since 1940. The Gaullist dissidents in Shanghai had emerged in autumn 1940 when Cosme reinforced his Vichy policy and applied the shameful laws against the Jews and the Freemasons. In October, all the consular servants had to take an oath of loyalty to Pétain. In January 1941 the judge of the consular court, Kaufman, was forced to retire on suspicion of being Jewish. A few pro-de Gaulle diplomats and servants refused to support the Vichy regime. Roland Jobez, the chief of police, resigned and joined the France Libre movement in London in July 1941 with sixteen other police employees. Egal, a member of *France Quand Même*, the Gaullist movement in Shanghai, was accused of encouraging desertion. In June 1941, the embassy took various measures to prohibit the Gaullist propaganda.[21] But the question of whether or not to support the Vichy regime was not so clear from Shanghai. According to the archives and interviews, the individual conditions overtook the political debate.

For the French residents in Shanghai, the Vichy foreign ministry seemed to have prepared the retrocession with the spirit of "saving something from the wreck" and of preserving French business. In fact, the Asian department prepared the handover in trying to keep the properties and territorial rights of the French government in China. It wanted to keep commercial affairs, real estate, and extraterritoriality rights as long as possible. These last two points would be

---

[20] MAE, Nantes (ADN), vol. 180. French employees' individual files.
[21] Documents and surveys, *La France en Chine (1843–1943)*, Ouest Editions, 1997, pp. 238–239.

renegotiated in 1946. Finally, the French government lost all its properties in 1949.[22]

Concerning the employees, at first, the French municipality in Shanghai decided to pay a maximum gratification of six months' salary for good and faithful service. This gratification was not an indemnity but corresponded to the idea of the administrative transfer from French to Chinese authorities. The initial idea was that everybody retained employment but changed employer. Furthermore, the gratification was also allowed to compensate for the loss of purchasing power since 1936.[23] The intention of the French government was to keep as long as possible the French employees in the Chinese administration in order to pursue its business and reinforce its influence. The French municipality had to use its regular budget to pay the indemnities but because of its lack of funds, the municipality decided to sell tracts of land to gather money for a guarantee and repatriation fund. In the face of mounting economic difficulties, the fund was partly used to help the French employees.[24] Other problems appeared relating to the different status and role of the French employees. Actually, the employees of the Concession were divided into professional categories. Among them, differences existed between the directors of the Concession, of course, but also the employees of the colleges, the radio, the police, or hospitals. Each category had obtained a particular status or advantage. For example, the employees of the police received a housing allowance and advantages such as electricity, water, gas, and heat. In fact, the retrocession revealed these conditions, so it was difficult for the French Concession authorities to provide similar treatment for all employees. By consequence, the French consulate was accused of favoritism in integrating four employees in its services: Louis Des Courtils, Olivier de Sayve, Jean Meyrier, and Henri Brionval, who became second-class

---

[22] *Le Figaro*, Pierre Fano, 17/1/1949-27/1/1949 and private interview in 22/11/1997. Pierre Fano arrived in Shanghai in 1946 to defend his father's real estate business, the Savings Society, which financed the famous housing buildings, Dauphiné, Gascogne, etc. In his mind, leaving China in 1949 appeared to be a desertion; he always believed in the possibility of building a new China. But in 1950, it was clear that the communists did not want the "help" of the Westerners. P. Fano left Shanghai in 1955 and lost his challenge and illusions.

[23] ADN vol. 180, Repatriation and Gratification 1943. The base of cost of living in 1936 was 100, and 4,167 in 1943.

[24] Ibid.; The French Concession was never a landowner. It had a perpetual lease of land stipulated in the treaty.

consul officers.[25] The large majority of employees, however, were placed at the disposal of the Chinese municipal authorities. They had to continue their work in the same spirit despite a very uncertain future. In fact, the Chinese administration failed to use the French employees. Most of them were dispatched without a precise mission. They normally received a salary from the Chinese, but in reality the Chinese administration used only a few French and could not pay salaries to the others who had to wait for their repatriation or a French consulate solution.[26] Actually, neither the French consulate nor the embassy could enforce the agreement. Between August 1943 and January 1944, most of the French employees waited for their integration in the Chinese administration, but it was clear that the Chinese did not want foreigners in their local affairs. Even the French employed in the Chinese police under the responsibility of Sarly were disappointed and did not understand their role: Advise Chinese when they wanted to manage them as usual.

In this unequal situation, the director of the French Concession Louis Des Courtils, helped by the financial director, Olivier de Sayve, had to use the guarantee and repatriation fund to provide minimum support to the French employees. Paul Baillie, the representative of the municipal employees' association, and Roland Sarly, head and representative of the police association, wrote numerous appeals to the consul.[27] In a meeting with Cosme in Shanghai, they expressed their concern about the precarious situation of the ex-municipal staff. Cosme answered that the French government would help the employees only in case of necessity. This "wait and see" policy was partly due to the status of the Concession based on private law. The French state, therefore, did not recognize the municipal employees as civil servants and did not assume any direct responsibility regarding their employment.

P. Baillie and R. Sarly complained about the privileged treatment enjoyed by the army officers and soldiers stationed in Shanghai. Cosme recognized this fact but explained that this force was necessary and would be supported at all costs.[28] Although this policy was justified for security reasons, it generated jealousy. After the Boxers uprising, the foreign powers had obtained the right

---

[25] ADN vol. 180, French employees' individual files, February 2, 1948. The recruitment of these men was controversial. Some French citizens accused the consul of favoring those who had accepted the Vichy government. For these French, these four men were all pétainists.

[26] ADN vol. 180, 1947: Indemnities ex-employees.

[27] P. Baillie spent around thirty years in Shanghai, 1920–1948. Between 1920 and 1931, he was administrator of the Chinese post, technical director of the Concession. Then, he became its director in 1938 and adviser during the handover. ADN vol. 180, individual files, February 2, 1948.

[28] MAE/ADN: 11 March 1945, Baillie and Sarly's letters to Cosme.

to station troops in China to protect their interests. The 1,400-man French expeditionary corps (COC) in China served both as a military and a police force during the 1930s' difficulties in Shanghai. Its mission was to prevent any attack against the Concession and to contribute to public order in its territory. The COC also collaborated with the BST (Bataillon Suppletif Tonkinois) to protect the Concession. In March 1945, the Japanese would disarm the COC, which had to wait for its evacuation to Indochina.[29]

In 1945, a new phase was announced in the disappearance of the French Concession and the despondency of the French community. On March 19, 1945, all the foreign staff of the Chinese municipality were laid off. A total of 386 French employees and policemen lost their jobs in the Chinese administrative services.[30] The immediate solution proposed by the Shanghai consulate was to use them in similar services in Indochina. Their working and living conditions had been damaged since 1944. At this time the French community included five categories: the consulate group comprised consular servants, commercial adviser, court president, Jesuits, tramways, and Indochina bank directors. The "France Libre Movement" group included different businessmen and education employees. The police and municipality disbanded employees. This third category was really despondent. They lost their jobs, they lived in the Canidrome "kennels" because their apartments were requisitioned by the Japanese and then the Chinese. Then, the soldiers, who had been idle for five years, were demoralized and disarmed on March, 15, 1945. The final category included the very busy doctors and employees of Pasteur Institute, Sainte-Marie Hospital, General Hospital, and Aurore University waiting for their leave because the Chinese claimed these institutions.

In order to even out the different status levels, the French consulate decided in March 1945 to place all French personnel under a common regime similar to the army regime. Each family received a food indemnity according to its needs, payment of housing expenses (water, electricity, and gas), and support for medical and medicine expenses.[31]

Between 1943 and 1945, most of the claims and criticisms reflected a sense of having been cheated. The employees thought that they were the victims of measures which jeopardized their lives and those of their dependents. They condoned the privileges of a few and the losses of the majority. Actually, a minority of employees seemed to enjoy privileged treatment. Moreover, besides unstable

---

[29] Documents and surveys, *La révolte des Boxers et le corps d'occupation de Chine, 1901–1945*, pp. 145–159.
[30] ADP Asie, 1944–1955, vol. 14, French representation in China.
[31] ADN, Chongqing embassy, vol. 4, série B/1945.

material conditions and an uncertain professional future, several employees were charged as traitors and collaborators by the Chinese government.[32] In 1945, the municipal employees had the feeling they were regarded as suspects by the Chinese and even French authorities.[33] In the face of these complaints, Cosme decided to ask for a monthly allowance of 800,000FF from the foreign ministry to make up for the failure of the Chinese authorities to abide by the agreement. In September 1945, the new consul Baron G. Fain faced a crisis. He reported that the consulate had been paying the wages of the French officers of the Vietnamese Battalion since the beginning of 1945, following a lack of credit from the Ministry of Colonies. Moreover, the consulate also had to find a solution for the employees of the French radio station, a service closed by the Japanese. The consular authorities were overwhelmed by these unexpected problems. After eighteen months, the initial guarantee and repatriation fund dried up. It proved insufficient to pay for the repatriation of the former employees.[34] The consul asked for a monthly credit of 1,600,000FF in order to provide for the basic needs of those who had not found a job after the retrocession, those who were dismissed and could not come back to France because of the closure of maritime lines.

The capitulation of Japan and the collapse of the Nanjing and Vichy governments in the autumn of 1945 nourished new hopes within the French community and local authorities. They looked forward to a return to a peaceful life in Shanghai. This attitude reflected a complete misperception of the situation in China, namely the powerful tide of Chinese nationalism and its wish to take revenge on foreign imperialism.

ELIMINATE FRENCH INFLUENCE AND FRENCH RESIDENTS

After 1945, the Chinese authorities pursued their actions to reconquer their sovereignty. In this anticolonial context and anti-French spirit because of the collaborationist anterior period, the climate for the French businessmen who tried to preserve their activities throughout the war experienced serious tensions with the Chinese, who tried to eliminate the major French businesses. The Fonciere and Immobiliere, the Compagnie des Messagries Maritimes, or the Compagnie Française des Tramways, de l'Eau, et de l'Électricité (CFTEE) de Shanghai were all under threat and had to justify their attitudes during the occupation.

---

[32] Bergère, MC, "L'épuration à Shanghai (1945–1946)."
[33] MAE/ADN: March 11, 1945, Baillie's letter to Shanghai consul-general.
[34] MAE/ADN vol. 180: consul G. Fain to MAE, September 19, 1945.

In February 1946, the director of the CFTEE was convocated by the Shanghai court to justify his supposed collaborationist policy. The Chinese accused him of delivering motors, buses, fuel, and rails to the Japanese. The director answered that he was forced to give five motors between 1942 and 1944.[35] Because of France's political and military weakness in East Asia, the French possessions in Shanghai were particularly vulnerable. At best the French were considered the weakest of the big powers. The French themselves had to take revenge on the Vichy traitors, but it was too late; the French Concession signed its disappearance in 1943 and prepared its liquidation in 1946. There was much at stake for the CFTEE from a financial, economic, and political perspective: financially, because of the profits made during the last ten years; economically, because of its monopoly over urban transport, water supply, and electricity in the Concession; and politically, as a symbol of French power in Shanghai. The July agreement pointed out that the companies would come under Chinese law. According to these regulations, the Chinese state was to be a 50 percent shareholder of any public utility company. Behind this demand by the Chinese authorities, the Japanese were actually pressing for the eviction of all foreign interests from China. The French government proposed to sell the CFTEE to the new Chinese municipality but the Company head resisted until 1949.

What we have to consider is that the attitude of the French government in China and the Chinese aim to exclude the French from China were also directed by the French and Chinese policies in Indochina and, of course, the evolution of the war. Since May 1944 the provisional government of the French Republic (GPRF) was established under the leadership of General de Gaulle. This new political context gave the French government the opportunity to challenge the decision made by Vichy in 1943 and announced the cancellation or the revision of the retrocession agreement. In September 1944, General Z. Pechkoff was appointed head of intelligence services by General de Gaulle. He proposed to open negotiations between the GPRF and Jiang Jieshi to challenge the China policy of the Vichy government.

Strengthened by the Japanese defeat, the Chinese government accused the French local authorities of collaboration with the puppet government and strove to stamp out French influence from Shanghai. Government-level negotiations had been underway in Chongqing since September 1944. On February 28, 1946, the French government signed two treaties with the Chinese National government. The first one officially recognized the end of the French Concession

---

[35] ADP vol. 318, closing of the consular offices, January 1946–January 1949.

and the privilege of extraterritoriality. The other one arranged for the retreat of the Chinese troops from North Indochina.[36]

The government of China formally took over the duties of the Concession on June 30. The authorities established a commission of liquidation composed of four French advisers. They were selected among the residents of the Concession, not from the consulate or the municipality. The commission was set up to discuss the process of liquidation and transfer of the Concession with the Chinese.[37] Even if the first retrocession had announced the end of the French influence in Shanghai, the liquidation of French interests was not achieved and in 1945, the French local authorities and population seemed to believe in the pursuit of their commercial and cultural actions.

If the French government prepared the political handover, it failed to grasp its social and cultural impact on the French community in Shanghai. The decisions illustrated the lack of a global policy by the consulate for the personnel of the former municipality, which explains the claims and disappointments of the French community. The obligations of the ex-Concession vis-à-vis the French employees were: subsistence until their repatriation, repair of the prejudice caused by the loss of jobs, repatriation.

One of the main unsolved problems before the beginning of 1946 was repatriation. In 1943, repatriation had been put in abeyance because of the general wait-and-see attitude and because the French community, including consular authorities, did not really believe in the end of the Concession. Moreover, the evolution of the war in the Pacific did not allow transocean shipping. After the war, Italian, American, and English ships were used for the repatriation of the French population. By the end of 1945, Paris, Saigon, and Shanghai exchanged numerous telegrams about ships to be sent to Shanghai to evacuate around 1,000 persons to France and 2,200 to Indochina.[38] At this time, the *Emile Bertin* was sent to Saigon with 9 officers, 163 noncommissioned officers (NCO) and privates, 79 Vietnamese, 37 ex-policemen employed by the general governor of Indochina, and 7 undesirable persons in Shanghai – among them Carcopino, arrested for collaboration with Germany.[39] The question of

---

[36] François Joyaux, *La nouvelle question d'Extrême-Orient: l'ère de la guerre froide, 1945–1959*, pp. 119–120; Jacques Guillermaz, *Une vie pour la Chine: Mémoires, 1937–1989*, Paris, Robert Laffont, 1989, pp. 146–147.

[37] MAE/ADP, War-Vichy/Asia, vol. 252, December 1945–March 1947: Meyrier to Filliol, June 19, 1946. The four advisers were: De Courseules, Grosbois, R. P. Moulis, and at first Van Laethem replaced by de la Chevalerie.

[38] MAE/ADP, Asia-Océanie, China, vol. 38, October 1945–April 1946. French repatriation.

[39] MAE/ADP vol. 38, MAE to Haussaire, Saigon, Paris December 1, 1945. Lavabre was employed in the Chinese public works up to 1945 and received a dismissal letter and a six-month salary refund for loss of job. See also Bergère, MC, "L'épuration à Shanghai (1945–1946)."

repatriation also concerned 30,000 persons living in Indochina who asked for their repatriation.[40] Negotiations opened with the United States in May 1946 to repatriate these people.[41]

The deadline for repatriation was fixed by the French government on December 31, 1948 in Shanghai. Before that, a few individuals tried their luck in Indochina or in other colonies, some were hospitalized and could not fulfill the formalities, and employees who had married Chinese or Russians were not allowed to leave Shanghai. From 1949 to 1951, the foreign ministry dealt with these people on a case-by-case basis, but the majority left Shanghai before the end of 1948.[42] It is difficult to determine how many of those who left Shanghai went to Indochina. During the autumn of 1946, nineteen French police employees were recruited in the French police of Saigon. The Indochinese radio station also gave a six-month contract to the nine employees of the French radio station in Shanghai.[43] In practice, the re-employment policy was not well defined and most of the former employees had to wait patiently for opportunities.[44]

CONCLUSION

Employment, repatriation, and collaboration were muddled by the political context. The failure to enforce the agreement on the re-employment of 75 percent of the French former employees was due to this confused political situation. There are good reasons to argue that the Chinese (puppet or Nationalists) had no reason to please the French, that the French authorities were out of touch with reality, and that the French residents had failed to understand that times had changed. The major blunder of the French authorities, it seems, was their inability to prepare the French population for the logical end of the Concession. It seems that both the residents and the consular authorities (and perhaps the ministry itself) joined hands in wishful thinking about going back to the "good old times" after the Japanese defeat. It is clear that there was more than a technical problem of employment or repatriation. The consulate's objective remained unchanged: Maintain French influence – but it did not know how to keep it. The future of the French employees was a local affair under the sole responsibility of the French consular authorities in Shanghai. When war erupted between China and Japan, the French Concession was a privileged city within an occupied metropolis. If the French Concession was not occupied, the defeat

---

[40] MAE/ADP vol. 38: telegram of MAE to Shanghai, April 20, 1946.
[41] MAE/ADN vol. 180: this volume contained the list of names.
[42] MAE/ADN vol. 180: telegram from Hong Kong to Paris, June 10, 1949.
[43] MAE/ADN vol. 180, Haussaire to de Sayve, March 8, 1946.
[44] It is difficult to reconstruct the precise shipping passengers' transfers to France or Indochina.

of France in 1940 and the change of policy to a pro-Japanese attitude certainly were decisive factors in the evolution of the French Concession.

At this time, the fate of the concessions was compromised but the employees of the Concession still had confidence in their consulate. From Shanghai, international events seemed far away and the entire French community saw them as sheer blindness and an inability to accept change. The consular authorities themselves were not worried about the events and did not imagine the end of the Concession. They thought that the neutrality of the Concession protected them from Japanese control. This analysis postponed the awareness by French local authorities that the French presence in the Concession was over for good. Furthermore, the French government worried more about its economic and diplomatic interests in Indochina and considered the Concession a second priority. Wartime Shanghai revealed the fragility of French power in Asia, China, and Indochina. The French who left Shanghai at the end of 1948 lost view of Chinese horizons, but they failed to find their "Shangri-La," like the hero in Frank Capra's famous movie (*Lost Horizons*). They had had a good life in Shanghai, in a Concession that evaded state control. The war made them realize the artificial status of the Concession and the limited protection they could expect from the French authorities.

Part III

Chapter 11

Back to Business as Usual

The Resurgence of Commercial Radio Broadcasting in Gudao *Shanghai*

CARLTON BENSON

When the Japanese army invaded Shanghai on August 13, 1937, the career of Yan Xueting, a popular storyteller and radio personality, was briefly interrupted. Like many of his peers, Yan fled the city with his wife, children, and a few personal belongings. For a short period he found refuge in the nearby town of Zhujiajiao, but soon Japanese bombers appeared there, too, and Yan rejoined a sea of refugees flooding inland from the coast. In rapid succession he fled to Suzhou, Nanxun, and Huzhou. There he and his family rested for several days before escaping northward by boat across Lake Tai. During his flight from one temporary haven to the next, Yan performed in the region's bustling teahouses and frequently encountered other storytellers from Shanghai.

By Chinese New Year in early 1938, however, Yan began to feel homesick. He first returned to Suzhou, but the atmosphere in his native city was desolate. "To make a living," he therefore returned to Shanghai and the lucrative world of radio. "Now," he sang with relief in a signature song for his listeners:

I'm safely out of danger in Shanghai,
And reunited with everyone on the air waves
I recount my bitter tale.

But then Yan proceeded to mock his listeners for continuing to focus on idle gossip in the midst of war.

After suffering so deeply,
It's ridiculous how . . .

I wish to thank Pacific Lutheran University for a Regency Advancement Award, which funded my research.

Completely unsubstantiated rumors
Can still rivet Shanghai.[1]

Here Yan alluded to rumors that he and an accomplice had stolen a storytelling script from a fellow performer.[2] In other words, his listeners were seemingly unchanged by a bloody invasion that left thousands of people dead.[3] They still focused on petty scandals, despite the fact that Japanese invaders now occupied all of Shanghai, with the exception of the French Concession and the International Settlement.

Shanghai's broadcasting industry had indeed reverted to prewar patterns by early 1938 when Yan Xueting returned to the city. Foreign stations continued to broadcast political propaganda for the public, and underground radio operators maintained point-to-point communication with other stations. But Chinese broadcasting once again existed for two primary reasons: the dissemination of advertising and the entertainment of listeners.[4] From August to November 1937, however, local broadcasting had witnessed a patriotic interlude. For a brief period it was devoted to the dissemination of political propaganda and the orientation of a modern communications industry had been decisively shifted by war.

Why, then, did advertising and entertainment quickly replace political propaganda on the airwaves in 1938? Some contemporaries believed that greed was responsible. "Shanghai people love money more than country," observed one reporter.[5] But others blamed Western imperialism. In one cartoon from an early

---

[1] Yan's account of his life as a refugee was recorded in Chen Fanwo, "Yan Xueting tao nan" [Yan Xueting flees from calamity], *Boyin chao* 4 (undated): 20–21. Because this magazine was published by the Guohua Radio Station in Shanghai and advertised a 1938 model car radio, which had just arrived in the Guohua Electrical Appliances Store, it was probably published in 1938.

[2] The script, entitled *Yang Naiwu*, adapted for storytelling fans the story of a scandalous love affair and murder trial in nineteenth-century China. Yan's alleged accomplice was Chen Fanwo, who also composed the lyrics of "Yan Xueting flees from calamity." Many thanks to Peng Benle for identifying this allusion.

[3] Damage sustained in the Battle for Shanghai is described in Frederic Wakeman, Jr., *The Shanghai Badlands: Wartime Terrorism and Urban Crime, 1937–1941*, 6–7.

[4] On foreign stations in Shanghai, see, for example, Carroll Alcott, *My War with Japan*. On underground radio stations operated by GMD and CCP agents, see Carlton Benson, "Act Like a Ham: The Amateur Radio Operator in Republican China," paper presented at the annual meeting of the Association for Asian Studies, San Diego, March 2000. On prewar radio, see Carlton Benson, "Consumers Are Also Soldiers: Subversive Songs from Nanjing Road during the New Life Movement," 91–132; and Carlton Benson, "The Manipulation of *Tanci* in Radio Shanghai during the 1930s," 117–146.

[5] Dong Kuo, "Boyin tai shang de kumen zhe" [Depressing things about radio stations], *Shen bao*, 5 June 1940, p. 14; reprinted in *Jiu Zhongguo de Shanghai guangbo shiye* [The Shanghai

---

10. Source: from *Shanghai funü* (Shanghai Women) 1.3 (May 20, 1938), p. 16.

1938 issue of *Shanghai Women* (*Shanghai funü*), a Western gentleman representing the Shanghai Municipal Council (SMC) is depicted in an easy chair.
As he listens to a Chinese woman broadcast the correct time, news, music,
advertising, and speeches, "propaganda if any" is deposited in a wastebasket at
the gentleman's feet (see Photo 10).[6]

broadcasting industry in old China] (Beijing: Dang'an chubanshe, 1985), 478. This collection
of documents will hereafter be referred to as *SHGBSY*. The behavior of some individuals did
reflect a lack of patriotism. Pan Jinsheng, for example, established XHTM in 1938 "to broadcast
advertisements and entertainment," but in 1939 he was inspired by "Chairman Wang" to broadcast
pro-Japanese propaganda. Nevertheless, the Japanese military closed Pan's station on 8 December
1941. See "Shanghai shi tebie shi zhengfu xun ling."

6 See *Shanghai funü* 1.3 (20 May 1938), 16. Many thanks to Susan Glosser for sharing this cartoon.
On the SMC during this period, see Robert Bickers, *Britain in China: Community, Culture and
Colonialism 1900–1949*.

A strong desire to capitalize on booming demand from refugees, which is described earlier in Parks Coble's chapter in this volume, undoubtedly contributed to the resurgence of commercial radio. But the suppression of patriotic broadcasting by imperialists was also unequivocal. First, Japanese authorities placed increasing pressure on local stations to accept their supervision and stifle propaganda. And second, when Chinese broadcasters resisted Japanese demands in early 1938, the SMC cooperated with Japanese efforts to quash their resistance. Faced with censorship from Western as well as Japanese authorities, Chinese broadcasters had little choice but to substitute entertainment for propaganda – and the politicization of their industry was consequently a short-lived phenomenon. The entertainment they aired, however, was sometimes far from innocuous. In addition to comforting wartime listeners, it rallied them as a beleaguered community in protest against their enemies.

THE PATRIOTIC INTERLUDE

Before the outbreak of war in 1937, Chinese nationalists viewed the local broadcasting industry with contempt. All but two of the city's forty Chinese-operated radio stations were controlled by entrepreneurs. These individuals provided air time to advertisers for a fee, and advertisers in turn sponsored a wide variety of popular entertainment.[7] The industry was consequently attacked for pursuing vulgar fun and games when the nation's very survival was threatened by Japanese aggression. In late 1935, for example, a contributor to *Shanghai Radio* lamented the gross misuse of a vital new technology by Chinese merchants. "In this capitalist society," he fumed,

> clever businessmen quickly latched on to radio, which was successfully invented in scientific nations by people relying on scientific methods. It was then savagely violated and used for the sole purpose of promoting merchandise.[8]

Chinese broadcasters were increasingly sensitive to such criticism in the 1930s and sometimes broadcast patriotic messages, but their industry was still devoted to advertising and entertainment in early 1937.

After the Marco Polo Bridge Incident of July 7, however, most local broadcasters were prompted by a sudden burst of patriotism, by public pressure, and

---

[7] The numbers are cited in Wen Shiguang, *Zhongguo guangbo dianshi fazhan shi* [A history of the development of radio and television in China], 63. Five additional stations were operated by Westerners.

[8] Ming Cong, "Wo muguang zhong de boyin" [Broadcasting in my view], 34.

by the temporary evaporation of commercial demand for air time, to accept the leadership of nationalistic forces. The All-Shanghai Federation for the Support of Armed Resistance, which was established in Shanghai to lead the civilian war effort, orchestrated the ensuing transformation of radio.[9] The Federation consisted of several committees, including a Propaganda Committee, which announced its plan to mobilize the city's radio stations in August.

According to the Propaganda Committee's plan, which was approved by the Shanghai Guild of Private Radio Broadcasters,[10] all Shanghai stations would broadcast only eight types of programming: news about current events, programs to promote the sale of government bonds, programs to solicit donations for the Chinese army, educational programs, foreign-language propaganda, patriotic songs, stirring speeches, and entertainment produced to raise funds and spread propaganda.[11] The Committee's plan did not ban entertainment altogether, but performers would now promote nationalism instead of merchandise.

The Propaganda Committee also hoped to tightly control the content of each type of programming. News, for example, could only be gathered from pre-approved newspapers.[12] The Committee would provide scripts for speakers promoting the sale of government bonds.[13] It would determine a list of items for each station to solicit on behalf of the military.[14] And it would assign the appropriate individuals to broadcast the last five types of acceptable programming.[15]

The Committee's strong desire to oversee the effective use of foreign-language propaganda was reflected in its lengthy "Outline for Broadcasting Propaganda in Foreign Languages."[16] This outline provided general tips about skillful presentation for announcers, who were urged to adopt a polite but

---

[9] The All-Shanghai Federation for the Support of Armed Resistance is discussed in Poshek Fu, *Passivity, Resistance, and Collaboration: Intellectual Choices in Occupied Shanghai, 1937–1945,* 6–20.

[10] The Shanghai shi minying wuxiandian boyin ye tongye gonghui was established in November 1934 and represented all stations operated by Chinese broadcasters and approved by the Ministry of Communications. See Zhao Yuming, *Zhongguo xiandai guangbo jianshi, 1923–1949* [A short history of modern broadcasting in China, 1923–1949], 24–25.

[11] This plan, consisting of eight articles, is reprinted from the archives of the All-Shanghai Federation for the Support of Armed Resistance in *SHGBSY*, 265–266.

[12] These newspapers included *Shen bao, Xin bao, Shishi xinwen, Da gong bao, Shishi wukan, Xinwen ye bao, Da gong wan bao,* and *Shen wan bao.* Ibid., 265–266.

[13] Ibid., 266.

[14] The Propaganda Committee would determine this list in consultation with the Comfort Committee. Ibid., 266.

[15] Ibid., 266.

[16] This document, also produced in August 1937, is reprinted in *SHGBSY*, 271–275.

righteous tone and avoid sarcasm. The "Outline" also defined the content of foreign-language propaganda aimed at particular audiences. For Japanese listeners, it would highlight the long history of positive interaction between China and Japan, the Chinese desire for peace, equality, and national sovereignty, the belligerent role played by Japan's autocratic government, and the negative impact of war on Chinese and Japanese citizens.[17] Propaganda in English, Russian, and French would furthermore underline Japanese atrocities and Japan's desire for worldwide conquest.[18]

The All-Shanghai Federation for the Support of Armed Resistance clearly intended to mobilize radio, but were its plans and outlines merely reflections of wishful thinking, or were they actually implemented? The evidence suggests that in the heady atmosphere of late 1937 the Federation's guidelines were eagerly embraced by most local stations, which, for the reasons cited above, in fact dedicated themselves to resistance activities during the first few months of the war with Japan.

Not surprisingly, local broadcasters provide supporting testimony. Zhou Bangjun, a Shanghai merchant who established radio station XHHH in 1932 to publicize his Sino-Western Pharmacy, appeared at a meeting of the Propaganda Committee on September 7, 1937.[19] There he reported on the Committee's effort to establish contact with Shanghai stations and announced that control had indeed been established by late August.[20] Moreover, when XHHH reregistered with the Shanghai Guild of Private Radio Broadcasters after the war, its management proudly recalled the station's heroic war record:

When hostilities erupted, we immediately halted all entertainment programming in favor of news reports and rousing songs... We also disseminated propaganda for both the Comfort Committee and the National Salvation Government Bond Committee of the All-Shanghai Federation for the Support of Armed Resistance.[21]

Such postwar testimony, which should not be accepted at face value, is corroborated by contemporary print media. Newspapers reported on the activities of local radio stations and in fact praised them for broadcasting propaganda on the Federation's behalf. On August 13 and 14, *Da gong bao* printed the names of eighty individuals recruited by the Federation to broadcast speeches. These

[17] Ideally, such propaganda would persuade Japanese listeners to overthrow their government. Ibid., 271–273.
[18] Ibid., 273–275.
[19] The minutes of this meeting are reprinted in *SHGBSY*, 275–277.
[20] Ibid., 276.
[21] "Tongye dengji biao," n.p., 8 December 1945. Shanghai shi dang'an guan, S316.1.5.

individuals, including powerful gangsters like Du Yuesheng, popular writers like Yan Duhe, and prominent officials like Pan Gongzhan, each reported to local stations between August 10 and 29 and delivered a twenty- or thirty-minute speech. The speeches conformed to Federation guidelines and solicited funds for the anti-Japanese resistance.[22] *Shen bao*, likewise, hailed the Federation for actively broadcasting speeches in Japanese, English, French, Russian, German, and Korean. The propaganda was broadcast simultaneously from all Chinese-operated stations in Shanghai each night between 9:05 P.M. and 10:00 P.M. from early September until November 2, when the speeches were shifted to earlier time slots.[23]

Chinese nationalists were equally thrilled with the transformation of radio. Mao Dun reported the same phenomenon with obvious joy in *Jiuwang ribao* on August 28:

> Since the battle for Shanghai began, broadcasters have truly entered a state of war. Recordings of Peking opera, drum singing, and Hebei opera are gone from the airwaves – replaced by songs of national salvation. Sentimental storytelling songs (*kaipian*) about love affairs are also gone – replaced by new materials related to the War of Resistance. Advertisements for 'the king of longans' and cosmetics are likewise erased – replaced by news of current events and progress reports for charitable donation drives. Lectures about the *Complete Survey of Classical Prose* (*Guwen guanzhi*) have ended – replaced with speeches to promote common knowledge about defense measures during air and gas attacks.

Mao even reported listening to storytellers skillfully adapt published news items about the bravery of Chinese soldiers for radio broadcast. This method rallied the public much more effectively than reciting newspaper articles verbatim, he claimed. Therefore, stations should regularly enlist storytellers to "perform" war reports provided by the Central News Agency.[24]

One month later a second reporter echoed Mao's observation. "Privately run stations exist to disseminate advertising for shops and stores," he declared. "But such operations have all but stopped at every station and now their task is to broadcast nationalistic propaganda." He moreover added that programming was largely restricted in early October to war news, newspaper editorials, and fund-raising campaigns. XHHV, for example, had recently solicited more than

---

[22] *Da gong bao*, 13 and 14 August 1937. Reprinted in *SHGBSY*, 266–270.

[23] *Shen bao*, 3 November 1937. Reprinted in *SHGBSY*, 277–278.

[24] Mao Dun, "Duiyu shishi boyin de yidian yijian" [One suggestion concerning the broadcast of current events], *Jiuwang ribao*, 28 August 1937. Reprinted in *SHGBSY*, 460–461.

1,000 cotton-padded jackets for Chinese soldiers at the front, and its listeners had sewn into each garment an emotional message thanking the troops for their sacrifice.[25]

Radio propaganda was so effective in late 1937 in part because the number of listeners was expanding rapidly. Just as the Japanese bombing of Shanghai in 1932 had given the broadcasting industry an initial jump start, events in 1937 caused an anxious wave of city dwellers to purchase radios. Early in that year there were an estimated 100,000 receiving sets in Shanghai.[26] By January 1938, however, the *New York Times* was reporting that "war in and over Shanghai, leaving a city ruined and in chaos, lifted radio sales to a new record." Its report was based on a statement made by the Philco Sales Corporation in China, which claimed that:

> Our retail business set a new high in September [1937] and wholesale was never better. Our showrooms have been repaired... and we expect an even livelier retail trade, since the evacuees and refugees are gradually returning...[27]

By mid-1938, according to one local magazine, three or four out of ten families owned a receiving set and several hundred thousand radios were in operation.[28]

Such figures are difficult to substantiate, but the evidence suggests that a broad spectrum of the city's residents indeed composed the listening audience. If new radios were too expensive,[29] listeners purchased used radios or built their own sets with new and used components.[30] Others listened in public places. Radios were installed in government buildings, party offices, and

---

[25] Mo, "Kangzhan zhong de guangbo diantai" [Broadcasting stations during the War of Resistance], *Jiuwang ribao*, 3 October 1937. Reprinted in *SHGBSY*, 461–463.

[26] Leo Lee and Andrew Nathan, "The Beginnings of Mass Culture: Journalism and Fiction in the Late Ch'ing and Beyond," 374–375.

[27] Philco also reported that its "repair business reached an all-time record figure" during the Japanese invasion. See "Radio Sales in Shanghai Climbed as Bombs Dropped," *New York Times*, 9 January 1938.

[28] Feng Bin, "Renshen yu wuxiandian zhi bijiao" [A comparison of the human body with radio], 1.

[29] In 1938 a new radio cost from twelve *yuan* to eighty-five *yuan*. See *Wen hui bao*, 19 November 1938, di san zhang, di jiu ban. By January 1941, radios cost from $131 to $154. See the Yamei catalog in *Zhongguo wuxiandian* 9:1 (5 January 1941). By December 1941 they cost from $330 to $550. See the Yamei catalog in *Zhongguo wuxiandian* 9:12 (5 December 1941).

[30] For example, *Zhongguo wuxiandian*, a magazine published from 1933 until 1942, included a *Jiaohuan lan*, or Exchange Column. Here readers advertised used radios, new or used radio components, and radios they assembled themselves with new and used components. Instructions for the assembly of receiving sets were readily available in books, magazines, and newspapers by the early 1930s. Construction of crystal receiving sets was of course much less expensive than construction of sets with vacuum tubes.

public schools.[31] According to Carroll Alcott, an American reporter, there were also "radios in all the cafes, shops, pubs, hotels, casinos, and other gathering places. Crowds on the streets and in public rooms listened to the latest news bulletins and commentaries."[32] Local reporters were equally struck by the ubiquity of collective listening in Shanghai. In early 1939 one man lamented the pitiful condition of the city's "laboring masses," who sought "to relieve their dull gray lives" by turning to radio. "Even on minor thoroughfares," he observed, "crowds of people surround the doors of every shop with a radio and listen in."[33]

By 1939, of course, "their dull gray lives" were relieved by broadcast entertainment, but for a brief period in late 1937, when the All-Shanghai Federation for the Support of Armed Resistance supervised the airwaves, such listeners were bombarded with nationalistic propaganda. Even amidst the groundswell of patriotism, however, some broadcasters were still guided by naked self-interest. Huang Juyin, the manager of XLHN, was executed by the Shanghai Police for embezzling listener donations.[34] For other broadcasters the pursuit of profit was probably suspended by economic circumstances as much as it was by threats of violence, public condemnation, or patriotism. At a time when the local economy was disrupted and the sale of air time to commercial sponsors was almost impossible, accepting Federation guidelines involved little sacrifice. When the economy recovered and the Federation was shut down by foreign authorities on November 11,[35] local radio quickly reverted to prewar patterns.

THE REEMERGENCE OF PREWAR PATTERNS

As a result, when radio personalities like Yan Xueting returned to Shanghai in 1938, they found themselves in a familiar world of advertising and

---

[31] Arno Huth, *Radio Today: The Present State of Broadcasting*, 125.

[32] Alcott claimed that "most disturbing to the Japanese was the fact that whenever a Chungking gunman killed a puppet official or some other traitor to China, cheers went up from the crowds of Chinese gathered around a thousand public loudspeakers. But whenever Nipponese gangs killed a pro-Chiang man, the crowds hissed." Carroll Alcott, *My War with Japan*, 248.

[33] "Wuxiandian boyin yu shehui de gaige" [Radio broadcasting and the reform of society], *Shanghai wuxiandian* 40 (8 January 1939). Reprinted in *SHGBSY*, 485–486. Another man argued that radio was an effective tool for promoting adult education among the working classes, because servants listened in their masters' households and everyone listened in stores. See Pu Shuxia, "Xiang boyin tai zhuchi zhe jianyi" [A suggestion for radio station managers], *Shanghai wuxiandian* 19 (14 August 1938). Reprinted in *SHGBSY*, 467–469.

[34] Zhu Wenju, another employee at XLHN, and Xu Jinxian, an employee at XHHP, both managed to escape punishment for embezzling listener donations. Wen Shiguang, 63.

[35] Poshek Fu, 19.

entertainment. For Yan, a talented performer and active spokesman for commercial sponsors, this was a welcome relief. Yet even he was dismayed by the lingering appetite of his listeners for petty gossip about entertainers like himself. Devoted nationalists, meanwhile, were outraged when patriotic broadcasting was supplanted by entertainment soon after the withdrawal of Chinese troops in late 1937. "While the nation is poised on the brink of annihilation," the editors of *One Day in Shanghai* railed, radio's renewed focus on entertainment "reveals a complete lack of patriotic fervor."[36]

The storytelling genre known as *tanci* was still the preferred vehicle for commercial sponsors.[37] When *Shen bao* reported on the broadcasting industry in November 1938, it noted that more than thirty radio stations were providing twenty-one hours of continuous programming daily. Entertainment ruled the air waves, but *tanci*, with more than one hundred programs daily, was by far the "most popular" form of radio entertainment.[38] Local fans, struggling to restore some element of normalcy to life under Japanese occupation, tuned in for comfort to well-known storytellers like Yan Xueting, who still commanded handsome salaries for the retelling of familiar tales.[39] Yan, for example, continued to delight listeners with *Romance of the Three Smiles* (*San xiao yin yuan*), a traditional love story set in the Ming dynasty (1368–1644).

But Yan Xueting also expanded his repertoire to reflect wartime experience and strengthen bonds between him and his listeners. In "Yan Xueting Flees from Calamity," the signature song which is cited in my introduction, Yan recounted his own experience as a terrified refugee in late 1937. He also invited each of his listeners to recall their own, similar experiences during the Japanese onslaught, and thereby fostered a stronger sense of community based on "shared victimhood," as described by Frederic Wakeman. This emerging community,

---

[36] The editors noted only one station that broadcast propaganda, but XOJB was staffed by "collaborators" who aided the Japanese. *Shanghai yi ri*, di san bu, di si ji. Reprinted in *SHGBSY*, 463–465.

[37] Programming guides were often divided into categories like *tanci*, comedy, spoken drama, and Peking opera. The largest category was invariably *tanci*. See, for example, contemporary issues of *Shanghai wuxiandian*, *Shengli wuxiandian jiemu yuekan*, and *Guangbo wuxiandian*.

[38] Xin Liang, "Shanghai de boyin jie" [The world of broadcasting in Shanghai], *Shen bao*, 29 November 1938, p. 13. Reprinted in *SHGBSY*, 476–478. During the week of 17 July 1938, *tanci* was broadcast almost continuously from 9:15 A.M. until 3:20 A.M. the next morning. At 5:40 P.M., a prime-time listening hour, one could choose from seven different *tanci* programs. "Boyin jiemu fenlei biao" [Categorical listing of radio programs], *Shanghai wuxiandian* 15 (17 July 1938).

[39] Famous performers earned a monthly salary of 500 *yuan* for each forty-minute stint performed daily during prime-time listening hours between 5:30 P.M. and 11:00 P.M. *Shen bao*, 29 November 1938, p. 13. Reprinted in *SHGBSY*, 477.

however, was still riven by internal divisions. Yan himself perpetuated prewar stereotypes that divided local Chinese society by performing "The Quarreling Couple from Jiangbei." This song, a wartime hit for Yan Xueting, lampooned a Chinese man and wife from "north of the Yangzi River" (Jiangbei) as wretched migrants with extremely vulgar habits and aspirations.[40] It also underlined common bonds between Chinese listeners from "south of the Yangzi River" (Jiangnan), who pictured themselves as proper city dwellers, rather than country bumpkins with traitorous tendencies.[41]

Second to *tanci* in terms of popularity was comedy (*huaji*),[42] a form of entertainment that appealed to wartime listeners and offended Pu Shuxiu, a frequent contributor to *Shanghai Radio.* "The biggest problem with comedians," he claimed in 1938, "is their vulgar language. Extremely crude expressions like fuck off, you son-of-a-bitch (*gun na niang ge dan*) have practically become the staples of all comedy. As a result, nobler families forbid their children from listening, and comedy is only popular in middle- and lower-class society." To remedy the situation, Pu urged comedians to lampoon their victims without resorting to excess vulgarity.[43]

A popular routine entitled "Weep for the Rice-Boring Worm" (*Ku mi zhuchong*) exemplified the type of wartime comedy that Pu deplored.[44] In this routine a bitter stream of invective was aimed at the powerful "rice-boring worm," a wartime profiteer with friendly ties to the Japanese, who, as described in Wakeman's chapter, hoarded rice to manipulate the grain market and inflate prices. The routine could last for several hours and include a vast repertoire of insults.[45] One surviving script, for example, consists of several stanzas, each

---

[40] The song's popularity is noted by Zuo You, "Tan tan kaipian" (A quick discussion of *kaipian*), *Tanci huabao*, 5 March 1941. For the lyrics, see Yan Xueting, "Jiangbei fuqi xiang ma," *Boyin chao* 4 (undated, most likely 1938): 22. Also see "Jiangbei fuqi xiang ma," in *Shanghai tanci daguan* (Shanghai: Tongyi chubanshe, 1941), 46–47. For a discussion of the song, see Carlton Benson, "From Teahouse to Radio: Storytelling and the Commercialization of Culture in 1930s Shanghai," 228–236.

[41] For a complete study of ethnic identity in Shanghai, see Emily Honig, *Creating Chinese Ethnicity: Subei People in Shanghai, 1850–1980.* Honig also notes that northern workers were often "accused of being unpatriotic" because they "preferred to work in the Japanese mills." See Emily Honig, *Sisters and Strangers: Women in the Shanghai Cotton Mills, 1919–1949,* 5–6.

[42] See, for example, the "Categorical listing of radio programs" in *Shanghai wuxiandian* 15 (17 July 1938).

[43] Pu Shuxiu, "Huaji jiemu ying su mengxing" [Comedy programs should soon wake up]. Reprinted in *SHGBSY,* 473–474.

[44] Peng Benle, interview by author, 27 June 1997.

[45] For a description of one performance and a listener's response, see Amituofo, "Yun jian xiaoxi" [News from the clouds], 1–2.

ending when the comedian gleefully learns that a "rice-boring worm" has been crushed by an automobile. Each of the stanzas meanwhile hurls a barrage of insults at the speculator, whose overconsumption of luxury items is highlighted in the routine's finale:

> You build Western-style mansions, buy cars,
> And take several wives.
> In the morning you eat restoratives (*bu pin*);
> And at night before bed you eat restoratives.
> Your mouth is stuffed and it's still not enough,
> So you jam your asshole (*pi yan*) with ginseng.
> You're restored to the point where your asshole is plugged,
> And unable to shit, you panic.

Finally the speculator dies from becoming overbloated and descends into Hell.[46]

If the vulgarity of wartime comedy offended critics, listeners resented the activities of wartime profiteers like the "rice-boring worm." These profiteers indeed became a popular scapegoat for radio listeners, who defined themselves in opposition to urban fat cats as well as country bumpkins who dreamed of practicing fat cat lifestyles. Thus wartime entertainment not only helped to relieve the stress of life under Japanese occupation. It also served as a weapon for radio listeners who dared to attack their domestic enemies, if not the invader directly.

Radio listeners also cursed the flood of commercials glutting wartime airwaves. The amount of air time devoted to advertising depended on both the time of day and the season, but sometimes exceeded the amount of air time devoted to entertainment itself.[47] One listener claimed that radio stations broadcast fifteen minutes of commercials after each record,[48] while another reported that each three-minute record was followed by five to ten minutes of commercials.[49] To maximize their income, stations lined up numerous sponsors for each program, and then, "like machine-gun fire," announcers delivered a long list of endorsements during the commercial break.[50] Again, the number of sponsors varied

---

[46] "Ku mi zhuchong" [Weep for the Rice-Boring Worm], 5–7.

[47] Summer evenings were the most desirable time for advertisers. See Pu Shuxiu, "Gugeng zhi yan" [Honest words], *Shanghai wuxiandian* 25 (25 September 1938). Reprinted in *SHGBSY*, 471–472.

[48] Liu Xu, *Shen bao*, p. 15; *SHGBSY*, 480.

[49] Rui, "Zheng gao boyin diantai" [Ernest admonishment to broadcasting stations], p. 14. Reprinted in *SHGBSY*, 496.

[50] Dong Kuo, *Shen bao*, 12 December 1938, p. 14. Reprinted in *SHGBSY*, 478–479.

from five or six[51] to more than ten.[52] Not surprisingly, the audience lost patience with advertising and vented its anger publicly.[53]

Rampant commercialism was also reflected in false advertising. Pu Shuxiu reported two examples in *Shanghai Radio*. First he cited seasonal items, which were manufactured in a slipshod fashion and marketed with sensational claims. Numerous listeners were cheated and the credibility of all advertising was undermined as a result. His second example was medicine. Advertisers exaggerated the healing power of their drugs, he claimed, and consequently posed a serious health threat to the radio listening audience.[54]

Local stations were willing to produce false advertising because there were too many stations competing for the city's limited advertising revenues. In early 1938, Pu Shuxiu noted that radio stations were "sprouting like bamboo shoots after the rain."[55] By year's end, between thirty and forty stations were vying for commercial sponsors, who shrewdly played one station off against another to receive air time at reduced prices. Whereas commercial sponsors had previously paid a monthly fee of sixteen to twenty *yuan* to broadcast an advertisement one time daily, by August 1938 they paid only ten *yuan* to broadcast the same advertisement three or more times daily.[56] To cover expenses, radio stations flooded the airwaves with advertising, and listeners were subjected to a glut of commercials, just as they had been in prewar Shanghai.

---

[51] Qian Yun, "Man hua diantai guanggao" [Casual talk about radio station advertisements], *Shanghai wuxiandian* 38 (25 December 1938). Reprinted in *SHGBSY*, 484–485.

[52] Pu Shuxiu, "Gugeng zhi yan," p. 472 in *SHGBSY*.

[53] In addition to publishing their complaints in periodicals, listeners telephoned radio stations to complain. See Tang Bihua, "Boyin shenghuo" [My broadcasting life], *Shen bao*, 3 February 1939, p. 20. Reprinted in *SHGBSY*, 486–489.

[54] Pu Shuxiu, "Boyin tai yu boyin zhe zhi zijue" [The consciousness of broadcasting stations and broadcasters], *Shanghai wuxiandian* 18 (7 August 1938). Reprinted in *SHGBSY*, 465–467. Pu believed that medical advertisements placed in newspapers were regulated by the SMC's Department of Health and urged broadcasters to observe the regulations. Feng Jiao urged broadcasters to observe the *Zhongyang qudi baozhi yaopin guanggao guize* and stop advertising treatments for venereal disease. See Feng Jiao, "Boyin yuan ying zhi zhi dian" [Something announcers ought to know]. Reprinted in *SHGBSY*, 469–470.

[55] Pu Shuxiu, "Boyin tai yu boyin zhe zhi zijue," *SHGBSY*, 465. Some of these stations had been closed by the Guomindang in late 1936 or early 1937 and now reopened. See Dong Kuo, *Shen bao*, p. 14; *SHGBSY*, 478. Other stations reopened after voluntarily closing when the Japanese invaded Shanghai. See Zhi, "Shanghai boyin tai de lishi" [History of Shanghai broadcasting stations], p. 12. Reprinted in *SHGBSY*, 481–484.

[56] Pu Shuxiu, "Boyin tai yu boyin zhe zhi zijue," *SHGBSY*, 465. Pu also claimed that radio stations had previously received 120 to 150 *yuan* to broadcast one spoken drama, and frequently three enterprises had joined forces to sponsor one such program. Therefore, each paid forty or fifty *yuan*. In August 1938, each paid only fifteen or sixteen *yuan*.

THE SUPPRESSION OF CHINESE BROADCASTING

The resurgence of advertising and entertainment was determined only in part by economic opportunities and audience demand, however. It was also dictated by foreign powers. First Japanese military authorities assumed control of the air waves on November 27, 1937,[57] and four months later they adopted concrete measures to regulate local broadcasting. In March 1938 they established the Broadcast Radio Supervisory Office (*Guangbo wuxiandian jiandu chu*) in the Hardoon Building on Nanjing Road,[58] with Asano Kazuwo in charge of industry oversight.[59] On March 20, Asano announced that his office would begin supervising local radio stations and censoring radio programs on April 1.[60] Then, on March 31, he ordered all of the city's station managers to register in the Supervisory Office by April 15.[61]

Many Chinese broadcasters planned to resist Asano's order. On April 11, twenty stations located in the French Concession and the International Settlement submitted a joint letter to the SMC requesting support and guidance.[62] The SMC, however, accepted the Japanese demand[63] and urged Chinese stations located in the International Settlement to register with the Japanese.[64] The Municipal Office of the French Concession originally ordered Chinese stations located in the French Concession to disregard Asano's order,[65] but French authorities hoped to present a united front with the SMC and soon agreed to accept Japanese demands as well.[66]

Despite lack of support from the Western establishment in Shanghai, Chinese resistance continued. Only nine stations registered with Asano's office before the April 15 deadline.[67] The other stations ignored his order altogether, and a few elected to shut down voluntarily on April 20 rather than submit.[68] In response,

---

[57] *North China Daily News*, 27 November 1937. Chinese translation reprinted in *SHGBSY*, 281–282.

[58] *Xinwen bao*, 28 March 1938. Reprinted in *SHGBSY*, 282.

[59] Gongbuju jianduchu baogao," n.p., 31 March 1938. Reprinted in Chinese translation in *SHGBSY*, 291–292.

[60] The announcement, dated 20 March 1938, is reprinted in *SHGBSY*, 344.

[61] The order, dated 31 March 1938, is reprinted in *SHGBSY*, 344.

[62] The letter, dated 11 April 1938, is reprinted in *SHGBSY*, 295–296.

[63] Reported in *Shanghai meiri ribao*. Clipping filed by Gongbuju zongbanchu xuanchuanke, 14 April 1938. Reprinted in *SHGBSY*, 283.

[64] *North China Daily News*, 15 April 1938. Chinese translation reprinted in *SHGBSY*, 297–298.

[65] Ibid.

[66] *Xinwen bao*, 16 April 1938. Reprinted in *SHGBSY*, 298.

[67] The stations are listed in the Japanese consul's memorandum to the SMC, which is dated 29 June 1938 and reprinted in *SHGBSY*, 348–350.

[68] Reported in *Dao bao*. Clipping filed by Gongbuju zongbanchu xuanchuanke, 28 April 1938. Reprinted in *SHGBSY*, 284. XLHM, for example, secretly dismantled its equipment in the

Asano extended his deadline to April 27,[69] but he was already losing patience. In a letter to the SMC, he threatened military action against radio stations in the International Settlement if they disregarded his orders.[70] Nevertheless, only fifteen Chinese stations had registered with the Japanese by April 28;[71] eleven stations still refused to cooperate.[72]

In the meantime, the Shanghai Guild of Private Radio Broadcasters, which had dissolved in late 1937, was now revived to lead the stations' resistance.[73] On April 25 the Guild submitted a second request for help to the SMC,[74] and two days later, because its member stations refused to register at the Supervisory Office, the Guild suggested a compromise. It proposed that Chinese stations submit both their registration forms and signed guarantees eschewing political propaganda directly to the SMC, and the SMC would subsequently submit all of the required documents to Asano.[75] Faced with a Japanese threat of military intervention on the one hand, and Chinese intransigence on the other, the SMC was now forced to mediate between them. On April 27, the extended deadline for registration, two representatives from the SMC visited the Supervisory Office and volunteered to register radio stations that were located in the International Settlement on behalf of the Japanese.[76] The SMC also dispatched police patrols to guard the stations and prevent Japanese military action.[77]

Chinese broadcasters responded to the SMC's mediation efforts with enthusiasm. At least ten stations forwarded registration papers to the SMC by April 28, and each station guaranteed that its sole purpose for operating was the dissemination of advertising for commercial sponsors.[78] Before midnight on the same day, moreover, twenty-one Chinese stations voluntarily shut down to

---

middle of the night. See "Jiaotongbu gonghan," n.p., December 1946. Shanghai shi dang'anguan, 166.5.18.

[69] The order, dated 20 April 1938, is reprinted in *SHGBSY*, 345.

[70] The letter, dated 27 April 1938, is reprinted in *SHGBSY*, 345.

[71] Reported in *Shanghai meiri xinwen*. Clipping filed by Gongbuju zongbanchu xuanchuanke, 9 May 1938. Reprinted in *SHGBSY*, 289–290.

[72] Ibid., 289.

[73] Reported in *Huamei wanbao*. Clipping filed by Gongbuju zongbanchu xuanchuanke, 29 April 1938. Reprinted in *SHGBSY*, 285.

[74] The letter, dated 25 April 1938, is reprinted in *SHGBSY*, 299.

[75] A memorandum describing the Guild's suggestion, dated 27 April 1938, is reprinted in *SHGBSY*, 346.

[76] "Gongbuju jingwuchu baogao," n.p., 17 December 1938. Chinese translation reprinted in *SHGBSY*, 334.

[77] Reported in *Wenhui bao*. Clipping filed by Gongbuju zongbanchu xuanchuanke, 30 April 1938. Reprinted in *SHGBSY*, 286.

[78] The registration papers are reprinted in *SHGBSY*, 300–306. By 30 April, twenty-one stations had registered with the SMC. Reported in *Xinwen bao*, 30 April 1938. Reprinted in *SHGBSY*, 310.

register their protest against Japanese demands and avert the threat of Japanese military action.[79] Only three Chinese stations remained on the air, including XHHH at the Sino-Western Pharmacy. Its owner, Zhou Bangjun, initially refused to close the station for financial reasons, but after a caller went on the air to purchase medicine and suddenly shouted, "Down with Japanese imperialism!" Zhou decided to close his station as well.[80]

The Japanese response to the SMC's offer of mediation was positive at first. On April 27, when the two SMC representatives visited the Supervisory Office, Mr. Asano's assistant appeared to accept the compromise and even presented the two men with a list of unregistered stations. One day later, moreover, Asano himself expressed enthusiasm about the proposed arrangement, and his representatives subsequently entered negotiations with the SMC. This development helped to restore the confidence of Chinese broadcasters, and eight radio stations in the International Settlement consequently returned to the air waves by May 2.[81]

Unfortunately the Japanese authorities would soon reverse their decision to cooperate with the SMC mediators. Negotiations continued until the evening of April 30, but then broke down when the Tokyo government refused to grant the SMC oversight of local radio stations.[82] On May 4 Asano ordered twelve stations in the International Settlement, which had recently resumed broadcasting, to shut down immediately.[83] He also issued another order for all stations to register at the Supervisory Office by May 5. Stations that ignored the deadline would be banned permanently from broadcasting.[84]

At this point the SMC made a final effort to resolve the crisis. On May 5 its Board of Directors held a special meeting late in the afternoon. There Cornell S. Franklin, Chairman of the SMC, reported that he had successfully

---

[79] Reported in *Wenhui bao*, 29 April 1938. Reprinted in *SHGBSY*, 309. The SMC assured station managers that if they shut down, station property would become individual private property and Japanese authorities could not interfere with an individual's right to own private property in the International Settlement. Reported in *Xinwen bao*, 3 May 1938. Reprinted in *SHGBSY*, 311.

[80] See Wen Shiguang, 64. A second Chinese station refused to close because it was located outside of the protective umbrella provided by the foreign concessions. Reported in *Xinwen bao*, 30 April 1938. Reprinted in *SHGBSY*, 310.

[81] "Gongbuju jingwuchu baogao," n.p., 17 December 1938. Chinese translation reprinted in *SHGBSY*, 335.

[82] Reported in *Xinwen bao*, 1 May 1938. Reprinted in *SHGBSY*, 310–311. Also reported in *Da mei bao*. Clipping filed by Gongbuju zongbanchu xuanchuanke, 2 May 1938. Reprinted in *SHGBSY*, 286.

[83] Reported in *Shanghai meiri xinwen*. Clipping filed by Gongbuju zongbanchu xuanchuanke, 5 May 1938. Reprinted in *SHGBSY*, 287.

[84] Reported in *Wenhui bao*. Clipping filed by Gongbuju zongbanchu xuanchuanke, 5 May 1938. Reprinted in *SHGBSY*, 287.

concluded negotiations with the Japanese authorities earlier that day. According to Franklin, the Japanese wanted the SMC to assume responsibility for eliminating all political propaganda from the airwaves. The Japanese, in turn, would not adopt coercive measures against Chinese stations that failed to register. Neither Asano's office nor the SMC would register stations for the time being. In light of Franklin's report, the Board empowered its Police Affairs Division to supervise the programming of Chinese stations in the International Settlement.[85] One day later the SMC also notified the Shanghai Guild of Private Radio Broadcasters that member stations would be closed by the police if they broadcast political propaganda.[86]

News of the SMC breakthrough was immediately leaked to the local media. On May 6–7, Shanghai newspapers reported that the SMC and the Japanese authorities had successfully reached a compromise. According to the terms of their agreement, the SMC would monitor programming to prevent the broadcast of all political propaganda, and the Japanese would rescind their order for Chinese stations to register at the Supervisory Office.[87] Chinese broadcasters were of course delighted with the news, and radio stations that had not already resumed broadcasting returned to the airwaves soon after May 5.[88]

They were suddenly disappointed, however, when Japanese authorities contradicted published reports in the media. According to them, the SMC had misinformed the press about Japanese willingness to relinquish oversight of local radio to the SMC. On the contrary, the Japanese had actually broken off negotiations with the SMC and planned to adopt independent measures that would force Chinese radio stations to comply with their orders. They also forwarded a memorandum to the SMC advising it to support disciplinary actions taken by the Japanese against defiant radio stations.[89]

This advice was reluctantly accepted by the SMC, which now began to collaborate openly with the Japanese in their effort to subdue the resistance of Chinese broadcasters. To begin with, on May 13 the SMC placed a freeze on the opening of new radio stations in the International Settlement. The freeze

---

[85] Minutes of the Board's meeting are reprinted in *SHGBSY*, 313–315.

[86] The letter is reprinted in *SHGBSY*, 315–316.

[87] See *Wenhui bao*. Clipping filed by Gongbuju zongbanchu xuanchuanke, 7 May 1938. Reprinted in *SHGBSY*, 288. Also see *Da mei bao*. Clipping filed by Gongbuju zongbanchu xuanchuanke, 6 May 1938. Reprinted in *SHGBSY*, 288.

[88] Reported in *Xinwen bao*, 6 May 1938. Reprinted in *SHGBSY*, 318–319.

[89] Reported in *Shanghai ribao*. Clipping filed by the Gongbuju zongbanchu xuanchuanke, 9 May 1938. Reprinted in *SHGBSY*, 289. Also see *Da mei bao*. Clipping filed by the Gongbuju zongbanchu xuanchuanke, 9 May 1938. Reprinted in *SHGBSY*, 290.

was initiated so that prospective Chinese broadcasters would have no alternative but to approach the Supervisory Office instead of the SMC, and the Japanese authorities were predictably grateful.[90] Moreover, when the SMC refused to accept the applications of XMHJ and XHHJ, both new stations were consequently forced to register with the Japanese, and Asano expressed his gratitude in a personal letter to the Police Affairs Division.[91]

The SMC also forced Chinese stations in the International Settlement to shut down when the Japanese authorities were offended by their actions. On May 12–13, for example, the SMC police force, responding to a Japanese request, closed down XHHC and Da Guangming, two stations that refused to register at the Supervisory Office and continued to broadcast anti-Japanese propaganda.[92] Again, Asano was "very grateful," but still not satisfied. He identified six additional radio stations with "anti-Japanese tendencies" and asked the SMC "to preclude future problems" by shutting them down.[93] In response, the Chief of the Police Affairs Division volunteered to carefully monitor their programming and shut them down immediately if they broadcast political propaganda.[94]

With the SMC now serving Japanese interests, Chinese radio stations had lost their protective umbrella and now faced strict Japanese supervision. On July 15, the Japanese authorities issued their "Regulations for the Management of Private Broadcasting Stations." According to these regulations, the Supervisory Office maintained complete control over local broadcasting, and radio stations were strictly limited to four types of programming: lectures, news reports, entertainment, and advertising. If any station broadcast political propaganda, its license would be revoked, its equipment would be confiscated, and the license holder would be held responsible.[95]

Most stations yielded under the increasing pressure from Japanese authorities. By November 1938, only five Chinese stations in the International Settlement continued to defy the Japanese registration order, and Japanese officials were determined to make them submit. On November 5, each station received a notice ordering persons in charge to appear at the Supervisory Office on November 7 to discuss the registration problem. All five stations ignored

---

[90] "Gongbuju jingwuchu baogao," n.p., 17 December 1938. Reprinted in *SHGBSY*, 336.

[91] Asano's letter, dated 20 May 1938, is reprinted in *SHGBSY*, 347–348.

[92] Reprinted in *Shanghai meiri xinwen*. Clipping filed by Gongbuju zongbanchu xuanchuanke, 14 May 1938. Reprinted in *SHGBSY*, 291. Also see "Gongbuju jingwuchu baogao," n.p., 17 December 1938. Reprinted in *SHGBSY*, 337.

[93] Asano's letter, dated 20 May 1938, is reprinted in *SHGBSY*, 347–348.

[94] The Chief's memorandum, dated 30 May 1938, is reprinted in *SHGBSY*, 337.

[95] The Regulations are reprinted in *SHGBSY*, 350–352.

the order and therefore lost their broadcasting privileges in addition to their wavelengths.[96]

One of these stations was XHHG, which had broadcast continuously from the Oriental Hotel on Tibet Road since 1932. XHHG had already lost one desirable wavelength in June 1938, when the Supervisory Office reassigned its wavelength to a less recalcitrant station. XHHG had therefore occupied an undesirable wavelength at the far end of the radio band for several months, and had consequently watched its advertising revenues steadily decline. Now, in December 1938, even this wavelength was reassigned to another station and XHHG, as a last resort, was finally sold to an Englishman.[97] Thus Chinese stations were ultimately sold or shut down for refusing to register with the Japanese. In collaboration with Western authorities in Shanghai, Asano had completely suppressed Chinese resistance and thereby erased political propaganda from the airwaves by the end of 1938.

World War II had a clear impact on broadcasting in cities across the globe, but the nature of this impact was determined by local circumstances, including the character of prewar broadcasting and the degree of control established by occupation forces. In Russian cities, which successfully resisted foreign occupation, the German invasion actually triggered a "loosening of intellectual and creative controls."[98] Radio Moscow, which previously had been hamstrung by central control, now took advantage of slackening censorship to replace Soviet-style propaganda of the 1930s with more accurate news, masterly readings of Russian literary classics like *War and Peace*, and – instead of "gung-ho marches and political jingles" – patriotic music, "which meant Russian folk or classical music."[99] Propaganda was still ascendant on the airwaves, but now its tone was less stale, it was increasingly nationalistic, and it was more responsive to the needs of listeners.

In cities that were fully occupied by invading forces, on the other hand, broadcasting was subject to strict censorship and used for the dissemination of enemy propaganda. In prewar Paris, for example, broadcasting "had scarcely been used

[96] See Asano's letter to the Police Affairs Division, dated 30 November 1938, reprinted in *SHGBSY*, 352–353.

[97] "Gongbuju jingwuchu baogao," n.p., 17 December 1938. Reprinted in *SHGBSY*, 340. Also see "Tongye dengji biao," n.p., December 1945. Shanghai shi dang'anguan, S316.1.5. Here the station's postwar management claims that Japanese forces not only interfered with the station's wavelength, but also "destroyed its machinery."

[98] Richard Stites, "Introduction: Russia's Holy War," in Richard Stites, ed., *Culture and Entertainment in Wartime Russia* (Bloomington: Indiana University Press, 1995), 5.

[99] James von Geldern, "Radio Moscow: The Voice from the Center," 52.

to propagate political ideas."[100] When the German army captured Radio-Paris, however, it introduced to the city's airwaves a heavy dose of Nazi propaganda. With help from their French collaborators, German authorities continued to broadcast popular entertainment, perhaps in an attempt to pacify a population that might be prone to resistance. But the shift in Parisian broadcasting, which now disseminated propaganda as well as entertainment, was unequivocal.[101]

In Shanghai, the invasion of Japanese troops in August 1937 also had a dramatic impact on radio. Suddenly the All-Shanghai Federation for the Support of Armed Resistance employed the medium to disseminate political propaganda rather than advertising and entertainment. And suddenly political activists relied on broadcasting to inject a strong element of political consciousness into the city's popular culture and mobilize resistance. But 1937 was not a major watershed in the history of local radio because the politicization of broadcasting was a fleeting development. Unlike Paris, Shanghai was only partly occupied during the *gudao* period from 1937 to 1941. Consequently the city's radio stations, most of which were located in the foreign concessions, were not commandeered by the enemy. The Japanese were able to prohibit Chinese radio stations from broadcasting propaganda, but tolerated the dissemination of advertising and entertainment. As a result, commercial radio was again flourishing in the city by 1938, and – like the contemporaneous boom in cinema – its seemingly frivolous nature provoked the indignation of patriotic observers.[102]

Yet if local radio did not promote overt resistance to the Japanese, this was not because Chinese broadcasters were completely devoid of nationalistic sentiment. Many individuals exhibited courage by resisting Japanese demands for registration in 1938. But the Japanese occupying force, in alliance with the imperial powers that had played a leading role in Shanghai for almost a century, set the parameters within which the popular culture of radio could develop. These parameters, which restricted the freedom of Chinese broadcasters, guaranteed

---

[100] Pierre Sorlin, "The Struggle for Control of French Minds, 1940–1944," 248.

[101] Radio Luxembourg also witnessed a shift in emphasis from commercial entertainment to first Nazi and then Allied propaganda. See Erik Barnouw, "Propaganda at Radio Luxembourg: 1944–1945," 192–197. Japanese forces in Manila likewise commandeered local radio stations to broadcast propaganda as well as entertainment. See Motoe Terami-Wada, "The Japanese Propaganda Corps in the Philippines," 279–300. On Japanese activities in other fully occupied Southeast Asian and Chinese cities, see Namikawa Ryo, "Japanese Overseas Broadcasting: A Personal View," in K.R.M. Short, ed., *Film and Radio Propaganda in World War Two* (Knoxville: University of Tennessee Press, 1983), 319–333.

[102] On wartime cinema, see Poshek Fu, "Projecting Ambivalence: Chinese Cinema in Semi-Occupied Shanghai, 1937–1941," in Wen-hsin Yeh, ed., *Wartime Shanghai* (London: Routledge, 1998), 86–109.

that popular culture during the *gudao* period would not become highly politicized, but instead would retain its predominantly commercial character.

That is not to say, however, that commercial entertainment on the airwaves lacked political content altogether. Just like contemporary filmmakers, who managed to bring themes of patriotism to the screen in *gudao* Shanghai,[103] the broadcasting industry eagerly satisfied the demands of its listeners for entertainment with a sharp edge. Radio listeners certainly derived comfort from the familiar voices of professional storytellers who brought a traditional repertoire back to the airwaves in 1938. But they also relished the comic routines of entertainers who mercilessly derided notorious figures like "The Quarreling Couple from Jiangbei" and "The Rice-boring Worm," who were linked in the popular imagination with collaborationist tendencies.

BIBLIOGRAPHY

Alcott, Carroll. *My War with Japan.* New York: H. Holt and Company, 1943.
Amituofo. "Yun jian xiaoxi" (News from the clouds). *Guangbo wuxiandian* 9 (20 May 1941): 1–2.
Barnouw, Erik. "Propaganda at Radio Luxembourg: 1944–1945." In *Film and Radio Propaganda in World War II*, ed. K.R.M. Short, 192–197. Knoxville: University of Tennessee Press, 1983.
Benson, Carlton. "The Manipulation of *Tanci* in Radio Shanghai during the 1930s." *Republican China* 20, no. 2 (April 1995): 117–146.
———. "From Teahouse to Radio: Storytelling and the Commercialization of Culture in 1930s Shanghai." Ph.D. diss., University of California, Berkeley, 1996.
———. "Consumers Are Also Soldiers: Subversive Songs from Nanjing Road during the New Life Movement." In *Inventing Nanjing Road: Commercial Culture in Shanghai, 1900–1945*, ed. Sherman Cochran, 91–132. Ithaca: Cornell University East Asia Program, 1999.
Bickers, Robert. *Britain in China: Community, Culture and Colonialism 1900–1949*. Manchester: Manchester University Press, 1999.
"Boyin jiemu fenlei biao" (Categorical listing of radio programs). *Shanghai wuxiandian* 15 (17 July 1938).
Chen Fanwo. "Yan Xueting tao nan" (Yan Xueting flees from calamity). *Boyin chao* 4 (undated): 20–21.
Dong Kuo. "Boyin tai shang de kumen zhe" (Depressing things at radio stations). *Shen bao*, 12 December 1938, p. 14.
Feng Bin. "Renshen yu wuxiandian zhi bijiao" (A comparison of the human body with radio). *Shengli wuxiandian jiemu yuekan* 5 (25 June 1938): 1.
Feng Jiao. "Boyin yuan ying zhi zhi dian" (Something announcers ought to know). *Shanghai wuxiandian* 24 (18 September 1938).

---

[103] Poshek Fu cites *Hua Mulan Joins the Army* as an example. Ibid., 94–98. Contemporary stage plays like *Sorrow for the Fall of the Ming* also addressed themes of loyalty. See Edward M. Gunn, *Unwelcome Muse: Chinese Literature in Shanghai and Peking, 1937–1945*, 121–125.

Fu, Poshek. *Passivity, Resistance, and Collaboration: Intellectual Choices in Occupied Shanghai, 1937–1945.* Stanford: Stanford University Press, 1983.

"Projecting Ambivalence: Chinese Cinema in Semi-Occupied Shanghai, 1937–1941." In *Wartime Shanghai,* ed. Wen-hsin Yeh, 86–109. London: Routledge, 1998.

Gunn, Edward M. *Unwelcome Muse: Chinese Literature in Shanghai and Peking, 1937–1945.* New York: Columbia University Press, 1980.

Honig, Emily. *Sisters and Strangers: Women in the Shanghai Cotton Mills, 1919–1949.* Stanford: Stanford University Press, 1986.

Creating Chinese Ethnicity: Subei People in Shanghai, 1850–1980. New Haven: Yale University Press, 1992.

Huth, Arno. *Radio Today: The Present State of Broadcasting.* Geneva Studies, vol. 12, no. 6. Geneva: Geneva Research Centre, 1942.

"Jiaotongbu gonghan." n.p., December 1946. Shanghai shi dang'anguan, 166.5.18.

Jiu Zhongguo de Shanghai guangbo shiye (The Shanghai broadcasting industry in old China). Beijing: Dang'an chubanshe, 1985.

"Ku mi zhuchong" (Weep for the rice-boring worm). *Zui xin shidiao xinqu.* Shanghai: a small bookstore on Shandong Road, ca. 1945.

Lee, Leo Ou-fan, and Andrew J. Nathan. "The Beginnings of Mass Culture: Journalism and Fiction in the Late Ch'ing and Beyond." In *Popular Culture in Late Imperial China,* eds. David Johnson, Andrew J. Nathan, and Evelyn S. Rawski, 360–395. Berkeley: University of California Press, 1985.

Liu Xu. "Wuxiandian tingzhong de fannao" (Troubles facing the radio listening audience). *Shen bao,* 15 December 1938, p. 15.

Ming Cong. "Wo muguang zhong de boyin" (Broadcasting in my view). *Shanghai wuxiandian* 1.1 (10 November 1935): 34.

Peng Benle. Interview by author. Shanghai, 27 June 1997.

Pu Shuxiu. "Huaji jiemu ying su mengxing" (Comedy programs should soon wake up). *Shanghai wuxiandian* 26 (2 October 1938).

"Radio Sales in Shanghai Climbed as Bombs Dropped." *New York Times,* 9 January 1938.

Rui. "Zheng gao boyin diantai" (Ernest admonishment to broadcasting stations). *Shen bao,* 5 June 1940, p. 14.

"Shanghai shi tebie shi zhengfu xun ling." n.p., 6 February 1942. Shanghai shi dang'anguan, 14-1-7.

Sorlin, Pierre. "The Struggle for Control of French Minds, 1940–1944." *In Film and Radio Propaganda in World War II,* ed. K.R.M. Short, 245–270. Knoxville: University of Tennessee Press, 1983.

Tanci huabao, 5 March 1941.

Tang Bihua. "Boyin shenghuo" (My life in broadcasting). *Shen bao,* 3 February 1939, p. 20.

Terami-Wada, Motoe. "The Japanese Propaganda Corps in the Philippines." *Philippine Studies* 38 (1990): 279–300.

"Tongye dengji biao." n.p., 8 December 1945. Shanghai shi dang'anguan, S316.1.5.

von Geldern, James. "Radio Moscow: The Voice from the Center." In *Culture and Entertainment in Wartime Russia,* ed. Richard Stites, 44–61. Bloomington: Indiana University Press, 1995.

Wakeman, Frederic, Jr. *The Shanghai Badlands: Wartime Terrorism and Urban Crime, 1937–1941*. Cambridge: Cambridge University Press, 1996.

Wen hui bao, 19 November 1938.

Wen Shiguang. *Zhongguo guangbo dianshi fazhan shi* (A history of the development of radio and television in China). Taibei: Sanmin shuju, 1983.

Xin Liang. "Shanghai de boyin jie" (The world of broadcasting in Shanghai). *Shen bao*, 29 November 1938, p. 13.

Zhao Yuming. *Zhongguo xiandai guangbo jianshi, 1923–1949* (A short history of modern broadcasting in China, 1923–1949). Beijing: Zhongguo guangbo dianshi chubanshe, 1987.

Zhi. "Shanghai boyin tai de Lishi" (History of Shanghai broadcasting stations). *Shen bao*, 23 December 1938, p. 12.

Zhongguo wuxiandian 9.1 (5 January 1941).

Zhongguo wuxiandian 9.12 (5 December 1941).

Chapter 12

"Women's Culture of Resistance"

An Ordinary Response to Extraordinary Circumstances

SUSAN GLOSSER

Much of our work on occupied Shanghai focuses on the more immediate and dramatic aspects of the occupation – bombs, military checkpoints, rice-rationing, and the like. The emphasis is understandable: though political terrorism, economic desperation, and the brutality of foreign occupation were not new to occupied Shanghai, they were certainly exacerbated during the war and naturally attract our attention. While responding to these more obvious effects of the occupation, however, Shanghai residents also tended to the mundane, but no less pressing demands of daily life, and these demands were most often met by women. Given their primary responsibility for the home and for child-care, women especially found themselves trying to pursue the well-worn paths of daily life through the disruptions of war. They were the ones most often confronted with the difficulties of sustaining ordinary lives in the extraordinary circumstances of military occupation (see Photo 11).

So what was it like to be a woman living in wartime Shanghai? Despite the growing attention to gender issues in Chinese Republican history, we hardly know how to answer that question. With the exception of prostitution and female textile labor, much of our knowledge is restricted to the realm of image and ideal. Historians have effectively tapped the discourse of women's rights and roles for insights into the political and intellectual culture of the Republican period. The New Woman, for example, has ensconced herself in our historical repertoire. She appears variously as a linguistic marker of political significance (funü vs. nüxing), a shopper, a movie star, a

I am grateful to the members of the Occupied Shanghai Workshop, especially Carlton Benson, Christian Henriot, Joshua Rosenzweig, and Wen-hsin Yeh, and the anonymous readers at Cambridge University Press for their insightful comments and hard questions. I would like to thank Lewis & Clark College and the Ford Foundation, both of which funded my research for this project.

11. Woman displaced by the Japanese bombing of Pudong does her mending in the street. Source: Courtesy of the Hoover Institute's East Asian Collection at Stanford University.

sing-song girl, a student, an incipient lesbian, or the ideal wife, mother, and homemaker.[1]

Like historians of other continents and cultures, we have found our sources willing to speak volumes about what women should do, but circumspect about what they actually did. In the 1920s and 1930s, women's magazines offered readers ideals of romantic conjugal love, marital advice, tips on Westernized home decorating, child-care advice, and guidelines for a hygienic home and nutritious, economical meals. Most of the family and women's magazines published during Shanghai's occupation continued to serve up these same recipes for a happy home and family, ignoring the political chaos and material want that tested the survival skills of most of Shanghai's population. The essays and editorials made it very clear what women wanted to escape to, but gave few

---

[1] See, for example, Tani Barlow. "Theorizing Woman: Funü, Guojia, Jiating [Chinese Women, Chinese State, Chinese Family]," 132–160; Carlton Benson, "Consumers Are Also Soldiers: Subversive Songs from Nanjing Road during the New Life Movement," 91–132; Susan Glosser, "The Business of Family: You Huaigao and the Commercialization of a May Fourth Ideal," *Republican China* 20.2 (April 1995), 80–116; Kristine Harris, "The New Woman: Image, Subject, and Dissent," 55–79; Tze-lan Deborah Sang, "Translating Homosexuality: The Discourse of Tongxing'ai in Republican China (1912–1949)," 276–304.

concrete accounts of what they were escaping from. This project takes a first step toward redressing this lacuna by examining both the patriotic rhetoric and the accounts of women's activities that appeared in the occupation era periodical, *Shanghai funü*, during 1938, its first year of publication.[2]

Shanghai funü editors claimed for themselves and the women of Shanghai an important role in the resistance. But the resistance they encouraged was not one of active fighting or sabotage. Although they occasionally reported on women's heroic exploits elsewhere in China, in Shanghai, where the Japanese presence loomed large, they promoted psychological resistance. They sought to bolster women's morale and patriotic consciousness by creating a vision of a female community in which women of all classes and occupations united in their determination to support the war effort. The editors also gave prominent place to women's activities in the home and tried to convince readers that as China battled for its very survival, even the most mundane activities took on great importance. The editors' inclination to frame all of women's activities within patriotic rhetoric allows us to use this publication both to understand what counted as patriotism and to gather clues about the nature of women's experience in wartime.

Shanghai funü's reports on women's activities and experiences can be read as both tropes of resistance and reports of women's experience. The rape of women is a case in point; it was often used to symbolize the violation of China's sovereignty and its abuse at the hands of an intruder.[3] But the fact that men and women ascribed this larger meaning to rape stories does not invalidate the accounts of rape as records of women's experience. Although it will take further research to assess just how accurately the periodical depicted women's lives, *Shanghai funü* opens our eyes to their experience, their representations of that experience, and the complex relationship between the two.

SHANGHAI FUNÜ

During Japanese occupation of Shanghai, the Communist Party went underground, putting most of its effort into building coalitions with other groups,

---

[2] This periodical concerned itself exclusively with women. It made no effort to represent male experience. Accordingly, this essay focuses on women. A comparison of male and female experience will have to await further research.

[3] Many cultures have used the sexual violation of women as a metaphor for national humiliation and subjugation; China is no exception. However, accounts of rape take on a particular resonance in China because of the long tradition of associating female chastity with state virtue, political loyalism, and resistance. See, for example, Mark Elvin, "Female Virtue and the State in China," 111–52; Susan Mann, *Precious Records: Women in China's Long Eighteenth Century*, 25; Kang-I Sun Chang, *The Late-Ming Poet Ch'en Tzu-lung: Crises of Love and Loyalism*, 16–18.

publishing progressive and anti-Japanese journals, and improving worker education. *Shanghai funü* was part of that effort. First published in April 1938, the monthly periodical was edited by CCP members Guan Lu, Xu Guangping (Lu Xun's widow), and other progressive women, including Zhu Wenying, Wang Jiyu, and Jiang Yixiao.[4] The journal attempted to bolster the morale of its readers, teach a view of social and economic conditions informed by Marxism, and speak out against the Japanese occupation as strongly as it could without endangering its editors. In publishing *Shanghai funü*, these women fulfilled Party instructions to female members to write for patriotic women's magazines, work in hospitals and refugee camps, and join neighborhood sewing groups and relief associations.[5]

The magazine was printed by the Eighth Route Army Office.[6] It was quite inexpensive, costing only one *jiao* per issue on the newsstand and two *yuan* for a year's subscription. Though well printed on good-quality newsprint, the magazine's look was, for the most part, spare. I have located only five issues with their covers intact. Issue 1.4 (June 5, 1938) featured a traditional image of a Qing beauty smoothing her hair while gazing at herself in a hand-held mirror. The remaining four advertised the periodical's serious purpose; they featured

---

[4] Xiao Yang, "Guan Lu zai 'Gudao' [Guan Lu in the 'isolated islet']," 265. I am grateful to Joshua Rosenzweig for generously sharing with me the information he has gathered on Guan Lu and her activities.

After November 1937, the CCP underground sent well-known writers and other figures out of Shanghai to the relative safety of the hinterland. Only those who could remain anonymous stayed in the city to publish, organize, and run night schools. In 1932 Guan Lu joined the League of Left-wing Writers (*zuolian*), taking over Ding Ling's committee duties after Ding's arrest in May of 1933. In the early years of the Sino-Japanese war, Guan Lu became highly visible in Shanghai's progressive literary circles (Xiao Yang, "Guan Lu zai 'gudao,'" 262–265). She joined the Shanghai Association of the Cultural Circle and Women's Circle to Resist Japan and Save the Nation [*Shanghai wenhuajie ji funüjie kangri jiuwang xiehui*]. This was later called the Save the Nation Society [*Jiuguo hui*] and Guan Lu served on its board of directors (Chen Yutang, *Zhongguo jinxiandai renwu minghao dacidian* [The great dictionary of pseudonyms of historical figures in modern and contemporary history] [Hangzhou: Zhejiang guji chubanshe, 1993], 215). In the winter of 1939, she dropped out of these circles and her name disappeared from the progressive press. It was at this point that the Party sent her to infiltrate the Japanese. She was so convincing that even Party members who had known her believed she had turned coat. This service to the Party later left her vulnerable to charges of collaboration and altogether she spent almost ten years in jail for her "crimes": 16 June 1955–27 March 1957 and 1 July 1967–25 May 1975 (Xiao Yang, "Guan Lu zai 'gudao,'" 262–265). With the exception of Xu Guangping, whose biography is well known, I have yet to uncover information on the other editors. Likewise, information on *Shenghuo funü*'s contributors is sparse. Guan Lu and Xu Guangping regularly contributed essays. The identities of the other contributors are, at this point, unknown or unconfirmed.

[5] Patricia Stranahan, *Underground: The Communist Party and the Politics of Survival, 1927–1937*, 217.

[6] Ibid., 205.

a drawing of young Uzbekistani women participating in the Soviet Union's National Games, a photo of a group of women attending a lecture by a female English Labor Party leader, a photo of a schoolroom of children assembled for the anniversary celebration of the Shanghai Women's Society, and a photo collage of women making clothes for troops.[7] Advertisements were few and simple; those that included illustrations relied on modest line drawings.

The magazine's circulation reached 3,400 copies per month. Its readership is uncertain, though there are clues to suggest that the editors intended to address a fairly well-educated and affluent female audience. The vocabulary and writing style were somewhat more complicated than that of other contemporary women's magazines. Articles took a serious tone and shunned lighter topics like home decorating, fashion, and hints for a happy marriage. Moreover, many of the measures the editors suggested for improving health and hygiene were beyond the reach of Shanghai's poor. The editors also asked subscribers to phone the editorial office if an issue failed to arrive, suggesting that they expected their readers to have access to what was, for most Shanghainese, a luxury item.[8]

The editors also seem to have envisioned their readers as women who were interested in national issues but who also devoted much, if not all, of their time to work within the home. *Shanghai funü* intended to cover both the dramatic and the mundane:

> To discuss a few of women's own problems, to offer a little knowledge on managing the home and conducting oneself, to announce affairs of today that influence women's lives of every class, to reveal the suffering of women dragged into darkness, to publish a few essays by young women on literature or academic works, . . . these are the kinds of things on which this publication will focus.[9]

With the exception of their promise "to reveal the suffering of women dragged into darkness," the journal's list of topics resembled those of most other Republican era periodicals aimed at a female audience.

On December 13, 1937, the Japanese established the Shanghai Newspaper Censorship Bureau in the International Concession with the intention of regulating all the Chinese newspapers in Shanghai. Beginning on December 15, all newspapers had to submit proofs to the censors before going to press. In

---

[7] *Shanghai Funü* (hereafter *SHFN*) 2.2 (5 November 1938), 2.9 (5 March 1939), 3.2 (25 May 1939), and 4.3 (25 January 1939).

[8] Shanghai shi funü lianhe hui, *Shanghai funü yundong shi, 1919–1949* (*History of the Shanghai women's movement, 1919–1949*) (Shanghai: Shanghai renmin chubanshe, 1990), 201. "Gao changqi dinghu [To long-term subscribers], *SHFN* 1.6 (5 July 1938): 6.

[9] "Fakan ci" [Editors' opening statement], *SHFN* 1.1 (12 April 1938): 2.

response, most major newspapers closed down or moved inland.[10] *Shanghai funü* frankly acknowledged the limitations that the Japanese presence exerted on the magazine's content:

Most likely we will not, because of these [topics], break any taboos or incite anyone's hate or anger. Of course, we want to be unusually cautious, especially careful, to not discuss politics or beliefs (doctrines); in order to allow this tender sprout of this tough bud, which we hope will grow to maturity, to grow few thorns to stick people and avoid unexpectedly having the misfortune to be broken and destroyed.[11]

The editors were not interested in martyrdom.[12]

Even as *Shanghai funü* called attention to the conditions of women who worked outside of the home, it acknowledged and valued women's reproductive labor. The magazine anticipated criticism for its decision to include information on housekeeping:

As for why we want to establish a column on housekeeping advice, it is not because we side with Hitler and approve of his slogan, "women return to the kitchen," that he shouts so loudly. In actual society today housewives really still do stand in the majority. This is an undeniable fact. If our magazine wants to take up the responsibility of educating the masses of women, then we cannot forget this great majority of women. If we want them to become ardent readers of our journal, then we must suit their tastes and have a little material that is beneficial to their everyday lives. To take a step back, the young women of today who have not yet married cannot escape from stepping into the home in the future. We do not know when our ideal of constructing society so that it lightens the responsibility of the mother and wife will become a full reality. In that case, learning a little now about rearing children, cooking, sewing, medicine and hygiene, as well as home decorating etc. and daily knowledge, is not a meaningless waste of time and energy. Of course, fundamentally, we hope that there will come a day when, from our ceaseless efforts and struggle, a happy society will be created in which women do not need to take all their valuable time

---

[10] Stranahan, *Underground*, 223.
[11] "Fakan ci," *SHFN* 1.1 (12 April 1938): 2.
[12] This was the strategy endorsed by the CCP in Shanghai for most of the occupation. The decimated Party could not afford to sacrifice members through overt, and largely meaningless, activities. Instead, members were instructed to lie low, educate themselves and others, make connections with the population through unions, YMCA and YWCA, secret societies, native-place associations, factories, student groups, and professional organizations, and expand Party membership (Stranahan, *Underground*, 227–230).

and energy and while it away in the special duties of a wife and mother, a society in which they too, like men, will be able to commit themselves body and soul to the work of society and nation![13]

The editors bowed to the realities of family organization while attempting to maintain their credibility as reporters of important events and advocates for women. Although they could not immediately change the realities of women's responsibility for reproductive labor, a utopian someday promised to relieve women of that burden.[14]

Even though they carefully hid away "that which we are not permitted to say," the editors still hoped to bolster the morale of women within and without Shanghai:

> In today's profound atmosphere, one shuts the mouth and does not say anything, but just breathes in and out, trying to temporarily catch one's breath. Still one can't avoid feeling suffocated and heavily oppressed. If you want to open your throat and say a few words about what is on your mind, you may encounter the difficulty of an impenetrable atmosphere. But a person who still possesses consciousness, as long as the spirit has not been completely annihilated, if he cannot say what is in his heart, no matter what, he will always feel it is unbearable. This is the reason why we untalented women feel compelled by our good intentions to publish this magazine.[15]

In spite of this self-censorship, the editors produced an informative, and sometimes impassioned, journal. It was not, however, a journal that significantly challenged the status quo of women's place in the family or nation; most of the articles addressed familiar aspects of women's roles as wives and mothers. Nevertheless, the editors presented themselves as participants in the extraordinary, claiming a place for themselves as members of the war of resistance simply

---

[13] "Fakan ci," *SHFN* 1.1 (12 April 1938): 2.

[14] Since the late nineteenth century, Chinese intellectuals, political activists, and reformers have debated women's proper role in state and society. Throughout the 1910s, 1920s, and 1930s, New Culture intellectuals, Nationalists, Communists, feminists, and reform-minded entrepreneurs assumed that women would remain primarily responsible for child-care and housekeeping. Most participants in Republican debates about social, political, and family reform agreed that women made their most important contribution to social and national health by educating their children and supporting their husbands' productive work. In fact, they insisted that China's political survival depended on such activities. See, for example, Elisabeth Croll, *Feminism and Socialism in China*; Susan Glosser, *Chinese Visions of Family and State, 1916–1953*; Ono Kazuko, *Chinese Women in a Century of Revolution, 1850–1950*; Judith Stacey, *Patriarchy and Socialist Revolution in China*.

[15] "Fakan ci," *SHFN* 1.1 (12 April 1938): 2.

by virtue of the fact that their ordinary activities took place within a besieged city.

Others shared *Shanghai funü's* vision of itself as a force in the resistance. *Funü shenghuo* [Women's lives], a Shanghai magazine that had moved first to Hankou and then to Chongqing after the Japanese took Shanghai, described *Shanghai funü* in heroic terms.[16] It called *Shanghai funü* a "major military force in women's culture of resistance." As one of "the women's culture armies" that went to press in the wake of the Japanese attack on Shanghai on August 13, 1937 (*bayisan*), *Shanghai funü* reported on women's lives within Shanghai and kept the Shanghainese abreast of activities in the hinterland.[17] *Funü shenghuo* editors lauded *Shanghai funü's* efforts to report on women's lives in the complicated environment of Shanghai.

> As everyone knows, Shanghai is not only an isolated island, but also an international city of foreign bazaars ten miles long (*shili yangchang*). . . . There millions of women suffer all kinds of exploitation and oppression. Their lives are complicated and chaotic. To manage to completely reflect [this situation] would be an extremely difficult task. However, the efforts of *Shanghai funü* elicit a great deal of respect. It simultaneously addresses women in white and blue collar work, housewives, intellectuals, servants, dancing girls, masseuses, and women who have been dragged into enemy comfort stations (*weiansuo*), speaking out for those who live inhuman lives, it shows them the road to live and helps them solve their difficulties. This work is a very heavy responsibility and *Shanghai funü* bravely took it up.[18]

Whether high-flown or modest, the rhetoric surrounding the publication of *Shanghai funü* insisted on the magazine's role in the Chinese resistance and its position as the locus of a community in which all Chinese women participated.

---

[16] *Funü shenghuo* began publication 1 July 1935 and was first edited by Shen Zijiu, previously editor of *Shenbao's* "Women's Garden." Shen joined the CCP in 1938. After 13 August 1937, *Funü shenghuo* joined *Shijie zhishi* [World knowledge], *Guomin zhoukan* [Citizen's weekly], and *Zhonghua gonglun* [China public opinion], to publish four issues of *Zhanshi lianhe xunkan* [Wartime united triweekly]. It later moved its headquarters first to Hankou and then to Chongqing. One Cao Mengjun assumed editorship with issue 9.3. The journal ceased publication in December 1940 with volume 9, number 6. Other members of the editorial board included female luminaries from the Chinese Communist Party, Hu Ziying, and the Nationalist Party, Shi Liang and Liu Qingyang (Wang Guilin and Zhu Hanguo, eds., *Zhongguo baokan cidian: 1815–1949* [Chinese periodical dictionary: 1815–1949] [Shandong: Shuhai chubanshe, 1992], 267; Xu Youchun, *Minguo renwu dacidian* [The great dictionary of Republican figures] [Shijiazhuang: Hebei renmin chubanshe, 1991], 159–160, 434, 564, 1440).

[17] Lin Feng, "Jieshao '*Shanghai funü,'*" *Funü shenghuo* 9.3 (16 September 1940): 38.

[18] Ibid.

It bore witness to the tragedies of war; it connected women on the isolated island with their compatriots in the hinterland and sympathizers abroad; it linked the details of women's lives to the war effort. *Funü shenghuo* declared that in reporting on women's everyday lives, *Shanghai funü* bore witness to "the great historical reality of the hand-to-hand combat between all Shanghai women and the enemy and their collaborators."[19] Both periodicals elevated women's most mundane activities to the level of heroic resistance.

TAKING REFUGE

Many Shanghai residents first experienced the war in the countryside where they were threatened with torture, slaughter, and starvation. Women in the environs of Nanjing posted a continuous watch for the Japanese, as, presumably, did those living outside of Shanghai. Whenever the lookout spotted the "devils," all the women in the village hid. Women with bobbed hair faced the greatest danger because the Japanese preferred "modern" girls.[20] Despite such precautions, the Japanese sometimes took the villagers by surprise. One wedding ended tragically when Japanese soldiers burst in on a family immersed in celebrations. The bride and three other young women fled and the Japanese gave chase. Trapped between the edge of a pond and the pursuing soldiers, the women tried to drown themselves. The Japanese reportedly stood by laughing, clapping, and calling on the rest of the troops to come watch the women floundering in the water. When they were on the verge of dying, the Japanese hauled them out and raped them anyway. "The bride died lying in a pool of blood."[21]

Japanese incursions into the hinterland around Shanghai drove many refugees into the city in search of the measure of safety afforded by the European and American presence. For some, the flight to the city became a gauntlet of harrowing abuse. In the pages of *Shanghai funü*, a man related the hardships that his servant's sister had endured. The servant insisted on returning home to care for her sister who was suffering from a botched abortion. When her boss expressed his disapproval of abortion, she insisted that it had been necessary; her sister had been a widow for seven years and could not bear the shame of bearing a child out of wedlock. She was hoping to abort easily and then go to work in a cigarette factory.

---

[19] Ibid.

[20] Gui Fang, "Jinling laike yixie tan (Stories from a visitor from Jinling [Nanjing])," *SHFN* 1.11 (20 September 1938): 12.

[21] Ibid.

The master inquired further and discovered that the sister became pregnant during multiple rapes suffered at the hands of Japanese[22] soldiers as she fled to Shanghai. The six other women who took the boat with her sister were also raped many times. Each night when the boat docked, Japanese troops boarded it and raped all the women. "Not a one escaped it! . . . The old, the young, the ugly, the good-looking, all were defiled." Those who resisted were thrown off the boat into the water. No one was allowed to rescue them. One forty-eight-year-old woman was raped by four men in succession. "Twenty days after arriving in Shanghai she still cannot walk. Her private parts are bruised and swollen. A yellow fluid so noxious it makes people want to vomit flows down her leg. . . ." Another woman developed a gynecological problem two days after boarding the boat. She put some toilet paper over her vagina, thinking that the soldiers would be afraid of menstruation and leave her alone. But when they discovered she was faking menstruation they beat her with firewood and left her with a serious head wound and "she still had to dry her tears and sleep with them."[23]

SURVIVING IN THE CITY

Once refugee women arrived in the city they faced the problem of finding food, shelter, and employment. (In this respect they shared the experience of previous generations of migrants and refugees.) Those with family in the city might find room in a relative's household. Others had no choice but to enter the refugee shelters. There they joined displaced Shanghai residents. Shelters housed men and older boys separately from women, girls, and young children, exacerbating a sense of dislocation for families that had already lost everything. Some shelters did not house men at all. All were noisy, overcrowded, and provided scanty rations. Although some shelters intended to teach their residents vocational skills, it is unclear whether they were successful in helping refugees find jobs in an already oversupplied labor market.[24]

Sex Work and Wage Work

Although some women found work in factories, many were forced into sex work. In this regard, refugee women had much in common with previous generations

---

[22] The editors substituted xxx for any identifying names, but here the context makes it clear that the soldiers were Japanese.

[23] Ji Zi, "Nüren de shounan" (Women's suffering), *SHFN* 1.2 (5 May 1938): 12.

[24] "Shilian funü jiaoyang jihua," *Shenbao*, 13 October 1938, 9 [reprint 359.89].

of Shanghai's female population. Both refugees and long-time residents some-times supported themselves with sex work when necessary.[25]

Young women of hard-pressed families that had fled from the countryside to Shanghai, as well as city residents, might find themselves forced to support their families by becoming taxi dancers. In one case reported by *Shanghai funü*, a daughter's income was so important to the family that the woman's mother sued a man for taking her daughter to Hong Kong for two months. The court judged the man on moral grounds, finding him guilty of seducing a girl less than twenty years old. The young woman's mother, however, focused her testimony on her daughter's economic value, arguing that the family needed her wages to survive.[26]

Occasionally, a woman might find that her profession offered its own escape. One young woman was sent by her mother to work as a taxi dancer for the Peach River Dancing Society (*Taohuajian banwushe*). There she and a client fell in love. She left taxi dancing and went to live with him. Her mother, angered at "losing her money tree," took the man to court, most likely for seducing a girl away from her family. The court, however, found the defendant not guilty.[27] Of course, most taxi dancers did not get to live out this storybook ending. In an interview with *Shanghai funü*, a group of taxi dancers complained about the stigma that clung to their occupation. They also acknowledged that many dancers were easily seduced by customers who played the ardent suitor. These men would buy a large quantity of tickets and then spend them on one woman. Having purchased a large portion of her work-shift, he would then invite her to see a movie, have dinner, or go shopping for jewelry or fabric. Most women felt compelled to leave the dance hall with these men. In explaining why they found it difficult to refuse these customers, one woman said, "Who can tell whether he is a good person or bad? If by some small chance he were good, [and I didn't go with him] wouldn't [I] lose a chance to earn a good bit of money?"[28]

More privileged women found themselves in less desperate circumstances, but they too struggled with difficult decisions. Educated women refugees who refused to take up sex or factory work faced the possibility of finding no job at all.

---

[25] For an account of the dangers of sexual predation in women workers' lives see Emily Honig, *Sisters and Strangers: Women in the Shanghai Cotton Mills, 1919–1949*. For the history of prostitution in Shanghai see Christian Henriot, *Belles de Shanghai: Prostitution et sexualité en Chine aux xixe–xxe siècles*, and Gail Hershatter, *Dangerous Pleasures*.

[26] Han Zizhang, "Heyou yu lueyou [Seduction and abduction]," *SHFN* 1.5 (20 June 1938): 26.

[27] This woman was probably over twenty-one. Yi Xiao, "Xianzai heian zhong de jiemei [Sisters who have fallen into darkness]," *SHFN* 1.10 (5 September 1938): 2–3.

[28] "Shenghuo zixu: wunü Wei Xueshu and Yang Minshi [Telling my story: dancers Wei Xueshu and Yang Minshi]," recorded by Yi Xiao, *SHFN* 1.2 (5 May 1938), 14.

One such woman, Miss Zhang, had searched for several months for "appropriate work" before she wrote to the editors of *Shanghai funü* for advice. Her letter described three strategies for keeping herself alive: She could enter a refugee shelter, continue to look for work until she completely ran out of money, or return to the countryside to marry. The advice she received did not quite address her difficulties but reflected much about the hybridization of modern and traditional views of family and marriage that had occurred over the last twenty years. Ms. Yi, the woman who responded to the letter, reminded Miss Zhang that work and marriage did not conflict and that she was wrong to look at marriage as a way to feed and clothe herself; she should find a companion who would help her achieve her goals, not impede them. In her reply, Yi implicitly acknowledged the strong economic component of marriage, but hoped that marriage would represent a merging of more than economic interests.[29]

In addition to recounting the dangers and humiliations of sex workers,[30] *Shanghai funü* also reported on women's experience in other occupations. For example, it published women's accounts of working in factories and ran essays by and about teachers.[31] But the shortage of teaching positions and teachers' low salaries seem to have driven a certain number of women into other kinds of wage work. *Shanghai funü* occasionally featured articles that described women's experiences in breaking into male-dominated occupations. In one such article, the author described at great length her first day as a sales representative for a drug company. As "the first" female sales representative in the city, she encountered many men who treated her as the object of curiosity, contempt, and harassment. Elevator operators looked her up and down, merchants dismissed her, and hooligans surrounded and harried her as she tried to make a sale.[32] Of course, these issues and topics had appeared to varying degrees in women's journals of the previous two decades. But *Shanghai funü* distinguished itself from its Republican predecessors by the sympathy with which it reported on women of all socioeconomic classes, its strong advocacy of women's productive work, and its placement of women's work experience within the context of China's resistance to the Japanese invasion.

---

[29] Yi Xiao, "Renshi dawen: wo yingdang zuo natiao lu? [Questions and answers on human affairs: what road should I follow?]," *SHFN* 1.5 (20 June 1938): 29–30.

[30] See, for example, Lu Ti, "Tiaochu huokeng yihou: yige jinü de zishu [After jumping out of the frying pan: a prostitute tells her story]," *SHFN* 1.12: 14–15.

[31] Xue Song, "Shenghuo zishu: Jin shachan de diyi tian [Telling my story: the first day in the sand factory]," *SHFN* 1.10 (5 September 1938): 11, and Wen Ying, "Shenghuo zishu: shijinian lai de jiaoyuan shengya [Telling my story: over ten years of a teacher's life]," *SHFN* 1.7 (20 July 1938): 17–19.

[32] Yan Ding, "Nü tuixiaoyuan de kutong [The misery of a female sales-person]," *SHFN* 1.10 (5 September 1938): 10.

Reproductive Work

Feeding their families and keeping them healthy in wartime challenged most homemakers. Epidemics of cholera, dysentery, typhoid fever, para-typhoid fever, and malaria threatened the city, particularly in summer. The Shanghai Municipal Health Department offered a combination vaccine against cholera and typhoid. Vaccines were also available for dysentery and typhoid fever. Women could try over-the-counter medicines to fight dysentery and prevent malaria. They could also keep mosquitoes out of the house and ensure sanitary food preparation.[33] Of course, these practices were only tenable for those who could afford screens, mosquito coils, and clean kitchens. Under the economic pressures caused by inflation and in the crowded quarters that typified many urbanites' homes, vaccinations, medicine, mosquito-free rooms, and even clean food preparation remained out of reach for most Shanghainese.

Given the uncertainties of war, it is not surprising that women wanted information about birth control methods. In response to queries about birth control, a medical advice column in *Shanghai funü* acknowledged that in troubled times many people needed birth control. After a nod to medical authority, whose opinion was that only women with illnesses or special conditions needed birth control, the author responded with a succinct but informative evaluation of medicines, injections, IUDs, diaphragms, and condoms.[34]

Su Qing brought home the terrors of pregnancy, childbirth, and motherhood during wartime through the experiences of her protagonist in *Jiehun shinian* (Married ten years).[35] On August 9, 1937, her husband rushed home to tell

---

[33] Wu Manqing, "Jiating fangyi yundong [Home epidemic prevention movement]," *SHFN* 1.2 (5 May 1938): 33–34.

[34] Su E, Yi Xiao, and Man Qing, "Yong shenme fangfa biyun? [How does one prevent pregnancy?]," *SHFN* 1.5 (20 June 1938): 30.

Women's private interests may have contradicted the political interests of the Nationalist and Communist parties. During the war years the GMD recommended that the population continue to grow at its "natural" rate. A later *Shanghai funü* article ignored the personal aspects of birth control and denounced Malthusian fears of overpopulation as a "corrupt" concept. The author maintained that the problem of overpopulation only occurred when most land was controlled by only a few people and production was destroyed. As that was not the case for China, she encouraged population growth as part of the construction of the country: "on the one hand fight the war of resistance and on the other construct the country" (Zi Jin, "Shengyu jiezhi wenti de xin jiantao [A new review and discussion of the birth control question]," *SHFN* 1.10 [5 September 1938]: 6–7).

[35] In the issues available to me, *Shanghai funü* never covered pregnancy and childbirth. To fill this lacuna I have turned, for the time being, to a contemporary, albeit fictional, account written by the popular novelist, Su Qing. Su Qing wrote for an audience that had experienced the terrors of the Japanese invasion. I think it likely, then, that her accounts do not fall too far from the mark. Of course, in order to heighten the dramatic effect of her story, Su Qing may have embellished

her that many Shanghai residents were preparing to flee the city. Because she was only a week away from giving birth, she and her husband decided to wait until after the child's arrival to leave the city and contemplated moving to the International Concession in the meantime. Over the next three days their fears increased. Sentries lined the streets. Most of their neighbors fled. On August 11 they removed their household to the International Concession.[36]

They acted just in time. That night the protagonist went into labor and gave birth to a girl in a Concession hospital. In the early morning hours she awoke hungry and still experiencing contractions, but the nurses were too distracted to give her any attention. They seemed nervous and kept talking among themselves and looking out the window. She finally fell asleep, but before long Japanese shelling jolted her into consciousness. The woman in the bed next to her wailed that the soldiers were on their way. Others yelled for someone to hang a foreign flag on the top of the building to reduce the chance of being bombed. At the mention of more bombs, another new mother dove under her bed. Our heroine sat amid the chaos and wept because she thought she would never see her husband again.[37]

Later that day her husband did make it to the hospital. By the third day, when she was able to move about, the two decided not to risk another separation. At first her physician adamantly refused to release her. Only by making a fuss did she force the doctors to understand the gravity of her situation: "My entire family is going to flee Shanghai. If you keep me here in the hospital are you going to feed me for the rest of my life?"[38] About two weeks later, she followed her husband to Ningbo. The trip was especially hard on her infant daughter. The protagonist bottle-fed her baby and because there was no clean water to prepare formula, the little girl became seriously dehydrated.[39]

Not surprisingly, mothers wanted to help children cope with hunger, disrupted sleep, and the unexpected. One mother thought it best to start letting her children go hungry and work late into the night.[40] *Shanghai funü* editors encouraged parents to teach their children to work and be self-motivated (*zidong*); their being accustomed to "opening their mouths when tea arrives and stretching out

---

this episode with some unlikely details. It is doubtful that a hospital overflowing with wounded and sick soldiers and civilians would insist on detaining a woman who was healthy enough to leave.

[36] Su Qing, *Jiehun shinian*, 152–153.

[37] Ibid., 154–156.

[38] Ibid., 158.

[39] Ibid., 166.

[40] Wen Ying, "Zhanshizhong de ertong jiaoyu [Children's education in wartime]," *SHFN* 1.10 (5 September 1938): 2.

their hands when food appears" would not prepare them for the difficulties that might lie ahead. They offered their readers the following "concrete" guidelines:

In everyday life [you] must determinedly [teach them] to endure hardship, have them cook for themselves. Avoid soft love!
Their activities should be regulated.
Enforce frugality – start by reducing the money they spend on candy.
Teach them not to fight with their peers over small things – as an initial step in reforming "bravery in fighting for oneself but cowardice in fighting for the common good."
Encourage them to participate in work to save the country.
Teaching materials should be appropriate to the needs of wartime.
Emphasize practical education.[41]

Although we have no way of knowing just how many parents put these guidelines into practice, it is no stretch of the imagination to suppose that these concerns worried many of them.

The growing scarcity of food and groceries and skyrocketing inflation kept most of Shanghai's housewives preoccupied with feeding, clothing, and housing their families. In the spring of 1938, the Guomindang made a virtue of necessity and launched the Frugality Campaign [*jieyue yundong*]. The campaign targeted women, especially housewives. By pitching the campaign at women, the Nationalists both exploited a long-standing stereotype of Shanghai women as extravagant and incorrigible shoppers and acknowledged that women were, by and large, in charge of the families' day-to-day spending.[42]

The campaign attacked two problems. It tried to shame wealthy Shanghai residents into contributing more to the war effort – in its promotion of the campaign, the *Shanghai funü* editors frequently chastised wealthy women for continuing their frivolous spending habits and their refusal to support the war effort or to help refugees.[43] At the same time, the campaign consoled poorer urbanites by assuring them that the decreased consumption forced on them by wartime conditions was not simple deprivation but, rather, a valuable and patriotic contribution to the war effort.

An early issue of *Shanghai funü* set out the rationale and goals of the Frugality Campaign.

---

[41] Ibid., 2.

[42] Benson, "Consumers Are Also Soldiers," *passim*.

[43] See, for example, Jiang Ping, "Gaijin Shanghai nüzi jiaoyu de jidian yijian [A few ideas on improving women's education in Shanghai]," *SHFN* 1.9 (20 August 1937): 2; "Zaiyu gudao jiemei tan "jieyue," *SHFN* 1.8 (5 August 1938): 13.

What is the Frugality Campaign? For one, it means to be as frugal as possible about necessary and unnecessary expenses oneself and, moreover, urging others to be as frugal as possible about necessary and unnecessary expenses. For another, it means to purchase Chinese-made goods and not to purchase smuggled, substandard, or foreign goods.

What does it mean to carry out the Frugality Campaign?

1. Take the money that you save and buy bonds, or donate it to our refugee compatriots or the unemployed in order to strengthen the nation.

2. Get rid of unnecessary or harmful expenditures like gambling, opium, prostitution, dancing, etc. so as to avoid degradation and jadedness. Take this useful energy and give it to your nation and your people.

3. Economize where you can on necessary expenditures. Do not buy the smuggled goods that are flooding the market or substandard goods like that stuff sold by the x [Japanese]. There is no need to give them money to buy bombs with which they will kill our own compatriots. Buying any kind of foreign product increases the x's tax revenue because they have already taken over the customs houses.[44]

The author listed seven ways for readers to participate in the campaign. The wealthy should reduce expenses, buy bonds, or contribute "a large sum" to help refugees or the unemployed. The middle class, which included those in middle and lower level professions and vocations, store clerks, students, and "even" laborers, should economize as they could. Everyday they should put the money they saved into a "frugality bag" or "frugality box," which they had made themselves, and periodically donate it to the war effort. Housewives should reduce by a certain percentage the amount they usually spent on candy for the children, daily necessities, and food and give what they saved to the nation. No one should buy smuggled or foreign goods; every consumer must carefully research the origins of the products they planned to buy. If a Chinese version of a product could not be found, consumers should prefer to do without it. Readers might form Frugality Campaign Societies to encourage one another, help one another research product origins, and keep everyone informed as to product quality and provenance.[45] Finally, the author recommended that people form cooperative societies to provide everyone with Chinese-made daily necessities.[46] Of course, it is impossible to know how many Shanghai residents

---

[44] Ren Yi, "Tuijin jieyue yundong [Promoting the frugality campaign]," *SHFN* 1.3 (20 May 1938): 11.

[45] As of 19 November 1938, nineteen Shanghai branches had been established (*Shenbao*, 19 November 1938: 9).

[46] Ren Yi, "Tuijin jieyue yundong" [Promoting the frugality campaign], *SHFN* 1.1.

took this campaign seriously. On the one hand it is easy to imagine hard-pressed housewives purchasing whatever they could find. On the other, patriotic feelings ran deep.[47]

Necessity also became a virtue in that familiar ingredient of women's magazines – recipes. Even before the war, most Shanghainese could afford little meat. Once the war began, many Shanghainese found meat too expensive to buy at all. Nevertheless, in the pages of *Shanghai funü* even vegetarian recipes became emblematic of patriotic commitment rather than a sign of poverty or hardship. On the anniversary of the Japanese attack on Shanghai, Gui Fang was awakened before six in the morning by her younger sister and brother. They urged her to hurry up and write out the day's menu. They had come up with two cheap, vegetarian dishes – bean-curd strips stewed in pickles and vegetarian chicken – but still lacked a soup. Everyone gave the problem a good deal of thought. Finally her brother proudly announced his idea for a patriotic recipe. "Green vegetables represent the Nationalists, red peppers represent the Communists, bean noodles represent the United Front. If we cook them together, won't that be a great soup?" Everyone agreed and Gui Fang headed to the market, recipes in hand.[48]

On the streets national flags flew everywhere. Many stores remained closed in remembrance of August 13, 1937, the day the Japanese launched what would be their successful assault on the city. The movie theaters and dance halls stood silent. The streets were quiet. "The faces of passers-by revealed expressions different from usual: deeply pained, angry, hopeful, only the newspaper sellers were especially busy." Gui Fang finally arrived at the vegetable stands and found them particularly crowded. Business was brisk. One young man who sold bean-curd strips changed his usual song to, "eight one three, eat bean-curd strips, victorious in war, return our land" (*ba yi san, chi douban, dazhang wu dantai, difang shouhuilai*). His song moved people and everybody bought from him "as if eating his bean-curd strips would really return our land to us."[49]

When she learned about the plans for a vegetarian meal, Gui Fang's mother argued that the family should eat a whole chicken and an entire duck to wish

---

[47] Pressure to contribute something may have been high. *Shenbao* periodically published a list of the "Frugality Funds" it had collected. On 3 December 1938, for example, it listed contributions ranging from 59 *yuan* from the 24 Lehua Elementary School to dozens of one *jiao* contributions from individuals. The importance of these contributions must have been largely symbolic. After all, most contributors gave less than two *jiao* and it may have cost the paper more than that simply to set the type for each contributor's name. "Benguan daishou jieyue juankuan mingdan [Name list for frugality funds collected by our organization]," *Shenbao* (3 December 1938): 10.

[48] Gui Fang, "Wojia de sucan [My family's vegetarian meal]," *SHFN* 1.9 (20 August 1938): 18.

[49] Ibid.

the war of resistance well. But elder brother presented a more "reasonable" point of view; that meal should wait until after victory. For now they should eat vegetarian and contribute the money they saved with the frugal meal to war refugees. After dinner the younger children calculated they had saved almost six *jiao*. They planned to give it to a refugee shelter.[50]

PATRIOTIC SUPPORT OF THE WAR EFFORT

The war also presented women with the opportunity to participate in the resistance and political activism, at least vicariously. *Shanghai funü* showcased the heroism of women all over China. These women sometimes participated in combat or sabotage, but more often they supported Chinese troops by nursing the wounded and making clothes. Women who remained in Shanghai most frequently participated in the war effort through fund-raising.

Stage performances were a favorite vehicle for fund-raising. If a report in *Shanghai funü* is to be believed, in April 1938 a performance sponsored by the city's taxi dancers drew a crowd of close to nine hundred. Tickets ranged in price from one to three *yuan*, meaning that this performance collected over nine hundred *yuan*.[51] Another set of three performances sponsored by the "Shanghai women's circle" (*Shanghai funü jie*) grossed five thousand dollars. The society intended to use the net of two thousand dollars to open a factory staffed by refugees.[52]

Shanghai funü did not question the motives of those attending these events, nor did it assess the significance of the amount of money these projects raised. (It is quite likely that many, if not most, of the people attending simply hoped for a little entertainment.) Rather, it was most interested in promoting these activities

---

[50] Ibid.

[51] Qing Zhu, "Ji wunü jiunan youyi hui [Recording the taxi-dancers' variety show]," *SHFN* 1.2 (5 May 1938): 22.

Shanghai funü praised the taxi dancers' patriotic efforts, but it did criticize the plays for being too "apathetic" and failing to offer solutions to the problems they portrayed in their plays. These seem to have been different from the "agitprop plays" briefly described by Po-shek Fu. He asserts that these plays were usually put on "for a limited circle of friends and colleagues and were thus restricted mainly to the reaffirmation of patriotic fellowship" (Poshek Fu, *Passivity, Resistance, and Collaboration: Intellectual Choices in Occupied Shanghai, 1937–1945*, 95). Christian Henriot has informed me that courtesans staged performances to support famine relief in the nineteenth century and the May Fourth Movement in the twentieth. It might make more sense to view the taxi dancers' efforts as part of that tradition.

[52] Zhen Ju, "Shanghai funüjie jiunan youyi hui [Shanghai women's circle variety performance]," *SHFN* 1.5 (20 June 1938): 28. The question of where to place the efforts of the Shanghai women's circle also raises interesting issues about the intersection of class, gender, and politics and the origins of this practice.

as venues for patriotic efforts and as sources of moral support for a people living under occupation. The editors found the significance of these events in what they could be made to represent rather than in their tangible contribution to the war effort. They wanted to portray a populace that was adamant in its refusal to bow to Japanese occupation and willing to unite across class lines in order to overcome a common enemy.[53] Moreover, *Shanghai funü* implied that these activities began to erode the line separating Shanghai's educated middle- and upper-class women from female workers; it reported that upper class women began hosting dance parties in their own homes and donating the cover charge to refugees and the unemployed.[54]

Shanghai funü editors also expected women to use their informal networks to garner support for the resistance. Women who did not have income at their disposal were urged to persuade their husbands to contribute.[55] One woman wrote to the editors of *Shanghai funü* for advice on how to overcome her friends' disinterest in the war effort. The editors cautioned her against being overly zealous. They feared that an official organization and discussion meetings might repel housewives who were accustomed to informal gatherings. They advised her to relate stories that hit close to home instead. She might tell them about the husband who killed himself on the journey back to the countryside after losing everything in the war in Shanghai. Her friends would easily infer that such misfortune might lie in wait for them. Once they understood that they too might become victims of the war, she could urge them to contribute a little to the war effort. The editors also suggested that she host a dance party and charge a small admission. Afterward, she could tell her guests that the proceeds would go to the government. This might inspire them to do the same. They also suggested that she ask them to set aside part of their everyday spending money and donate it to refugees. Also, she could encourage them to participate in the Frugality Campaign, especially emphasizing frugality in food and clothing. Finally, the editors advised this would-be activist to remind her friends to spend as little as possible just in case the war continued for some time.[56]

---

[53] I suspect that the editors of *Shanghai funü* hoped to create a community of readers much like the one Zou Taofen built around *Shenghuo* (Wen-hsin Yeh, "Progressive Journalism and Shanghai's Petty Urbanites: Zou Taofen and the *Shenghuo Weekly*, 1926–1945," 186–238). The editors invited readers to write accounts of their own lives, "whether sad or happy. Nakedly written and published here, they will serve as a mirror of women's lives." They also asked that those in contact with friends or relatives in the interior submit accounts of their experiences. "Bianhou yu," [A word after editing], *SHFN* 1.10 (5 September 1938), 7.

[54] "Zenme yang quandao jiating funü [How to encourage housewives]," *SHFN* 1.7 (20 July 1938), 27–28.

[55] Ying, "Guanyu funü juankuan [Regarding women's contributions]," *SHFN* 1.2 (5 May 1938): 17.

[56] "Zenme yang," 28.

Shanghai funü editors also held women responsible for making their own moral decisions. They castigated landlords for taking advantage of the housing crisis – the unscrupulous had taken to evicting refugees and charging a premium to wealthier renters.[57] They also cautioned women not to use the old adage "marry a chicken follow a chicken, marry a dog follow a dog" as an excuse for becoming a collaborator.[58] The editors made it clear that women's preoccupation with the ordinary did not exempt them from moral responsibility; in their eyes there was no innocence by lack of association.

Political Activism

The war presented women with the opportunity to participate in political activism, but these contributions tended to be low key. In the pages of *Shanghai funü*, political activism most often manifested itself in sympathetic coverage of workers and prisoners. An occasional essay would report on a meeting of Shanghai's "female leaders" but the location and the participants were never identified. These announcements seem to have been intended to assure readers that a community of activists and resisters did exist in Shanghai.[59] For example, one article reported at length on a meeting that promoted projects that would regenerate China's economy and safeguard it from the Japanese. A "leader of the Shanghai women's world, Ms. X" called a meeting to discuss how to promote the cooperative industrial movement (*gongye hezuo yundong*). Nym Wales also spoke on the topic to the thirty to forty people present. Wales and other proponents hoped to establish three thousand branch cooperatives that would place mid-level capitalists in cooperation with workers to set up small, local factories. The factories would supply the needs of their immediate locale and so avoid the difficulties of wartime transportation. At the same time, the factories would be small enough that they could be moved in the event of Japanese invasion.[60]

---

[57] Yi Xiao, "Wei nanmin qingming" [Begging clemency for refugess], *SHFN* 1.2 (5 May 1938): 16.

[58] Qing Shaozhang, "Suiji suigou zhi bei" [The follow-the-dog-follow-the-chicken generation], *SHFN* 1.8 (5 August 1938): 20.

[59] See, for example, Lu Wei, "Teyiqu nü kanshousuo canguan ji" [A record of a visit to the women's prison in the First Special District], *SHFN* 1.4 (5 June 1938): 5–6. Lu believed that women in prison were driven to prostitution and other crimes by the economic system, lack of education, and less than ideal laws.
    The editors may well have been ascribing more importance to the meeting than it really merited. Again, *Shanghai funü* seems to have treated the promotion of the image and idea of resistance as an important end in itself.

[60] Yi Xiao, "Shanghai funü jie shangtao gongye shengchan hezuo yundong chahua hui" [Shanghai women's circle's tea reception to discuss the cooperative industrial movement], *SHFN* 1.8 (5 August 1938): 4.

The editors probably ascribed more importance to the meeting than it merited. Reports like this suggest that *Shanghai funü* editors viewed the promotion of the image and idea of resistance as an important end in itself.

CONCLUSION

The most prominent "activist" that emerged from the pages of *Shanghai funü* was the frugal housekeeper who kept her family healthy and contributed her small bit to the war effort. The values that established her credentials as a patriotic Chinese were the same ones that characterized the modern wife and mother throughout the Republican period – she was frugal, practical, and devoted to making a healthy home for her family.[61] At the beginning of the war, even those on the left of the political spectrum confirmed the importance of women's reproductive work as part of the war effort. Rather than encourage women to engage in direct political activism, *Shanghai funü* urged women to do their traditional jobs but to do them better. In fact, the pages of *Shanghai funü* suggested that in extraordinary circumstances, the pursuit of ordinary, daily sustenance of mind and body was itself heroic.

How are we to understand this ordinary response to the extraordinary? The portrayal of "life as usual" may have been, in part, an attempt to soothe anxieties about lives that had been fundamentally disrupted by war. Be that as it may, we must consider the political import that *Shanghai funü* editors attributed to ordinary reproductive labor. Were women's activities as they were described in *Shanghai funü* part of the struggle to resist the Japanese? Or did the war provide an effective justification for continuing "traditional" lifestyles and gender roles? The answer is probably yes on both counts. At some level, the affirmation of life in the pursuit of the everyday is heroic. At the same time, the first two years of war in Shanghai seem to have consolidated and strengthened a conservative strain in social life and family rhetoric that reconfirmed the importance of women's reproductive roles over and above political or productive roles.

How we understand the significance of women's behavior and roles during occupation brings us back around to the old debate over Shanghai's position in the war and the question of its loyalty. What does it mean when ordinary duties are elevated to the status of resistance? One cannot help but wonder whether such a position was merely a rationalization for less direct resistance or even passive collaboration. Contemporaries have asked similar questions of Shanghai itself. Those who left the city accused those who remained behind of collaboration.

---

[61] On the importance of frugality and the rational use of time see Wen-hsin Yeh, "Progressive Journalism," 198–214.

Those who stayed felt aggrieved at their compatriots' failure to sympathize with the hardships of living under occupation. Continued examination of the details of daily life and its representation will help us understand the complexities of life under occupation as we continue to wrestle with this question even today.

BIBLIOGRAPHY

Barlow, Tani. "Theorizing Woman: Funu, Guojia, Jiating [Chinese Women, Chinese State, Chinese Family]." *Genders*, no. 10 (March 1991): 132–160.

Benson, Carlton. "Consumers Are Also Soldiers: Subversive Songs from Nanjing Road during the New Life Movement." In *Inventing Nanjing Road: Commercial Culture in Shanghai, 1900–1945*, edited by Sherman Cochran. Ithaca: Cornell University East Asia Program, 1999, 91–132.

Chang, Kang-I Sun. *The Late-Ming Poet Ch'en Tzu-lung: Crises of Love and Loyalism.* New Haven: Yale University Press, 1991.

Croll, Elisabeth. *Feminism and Socialism in China.* Boston: Routledge & Kegan Paul, 1978.

Elvin, Mark. "Female Virtue and the State in China." *Past and Present* 104: 111–152.

Fu, Poshek. *Passivity, Resistance, and Collaboration: Intellectual Choices in Occupied Shanghai, 1937–1945.* Stanford: Stanford University Press, 1993.

Glosser, Susan. *Chinese Visions of Family and State, 1916–1953.* Berkeley: University of California Press, 2003.

Harris, Kristine. "The New Woman: Image, Subject, and Dissent." *Republican China* 20, no. 2 (April 1995): 55–79.

Henriot, Christian. *Belles de Shanghai: Prostitution et sexualité en Chine aux xixe–xxe siècles.* Paris: CNRS editions, 1997.

Hershatter, Gail. *Dangerous Pleasures: Prostitution and Modernity in Twentieth-Century Shanghai.* Berkeley: University of California Press, 1997.

Honig, Emily. *Sisters and Strangers: Women in the Shanghai Cotton Mills, 1919–1949.* Stanford: Stanford University Press, 1986.

Johnson, Kay Ann. *Women, the Family, and Peasant Revolution in China.* Chicago: University of Chicago Press, 1983.

Mann, Susan. *Precious Records: Women in China's Long Eighteenth Century.* Stanford: Stanford University Press, 1997.

Ono, Kazuko. *Chinese Women in a Century of Revolution, 1850–1950*, trans. Joshua Fogel. Stanford: Stanford University Press, 1989.

Sang, Tze-lan Deborah. "Translating Homosexuality: The Discourse of Tongxing'ai in Republican China (1912–1949)." In *Tokens of Exchange: The Problem of Translation in Global Circulations*, edited by Lydia Liu. Durham, NC: Duke University Press, 1999, 276–304.

Stacey, Judith. *Patriarchy and Socialist Revolution in China.* Berkeley: University of California Press, 1983.

Su Qing. *Jiehun shinian* [Married ten years]. Shanghai: Shanghai wenyi chubanshe, 1989 (Reprint 1944).

Stranahan, Patricia. *Underground: The Communist Party and the Politics of Survival, 1927–1937.* New York: Rowman & Littlefield, 1998.

Xiao Yang. "Guan Lu zai 'Gudao'" [Guan Lu in the 'isolated islet'], in *Shanghai "gudao" wenxue huiyi lu* [Literary reminiscences from the "isolated islet" of Shanghai]. Beijing: Zhongguo shehui kexue chubanshe, vol. 2 (1985): 262–274.

Yeh, Wen-hsin. "Progressive Journalism and Shanghai's Petty Urbanites: Zou Taofen and the Shenghuo Enterprise, 1926–1945." In *Shanghai Sojourners*, edited by Wen-hsin Yeh and Frederic Wakeman, Jr. Berkeley: Institute of East Asian Studies, University of California, 1992, 186–238.

Chapter 13

Fashioning Public Intellectuals

Women's Print Culture in Occupied Shanghai (1941–1945)

NICOLE HUANG

"Whenever she had time, my friend's mother would put on her glasses, stand in front of the window, and look out onto the streets," begins Eileen Chang (1920–1995), the most prominent woman writer from the occupation era, in a 1945 essay entitled "Qi duan qing chang" (Short on Dignity, Long on Emotion). The author continues:

> There used to be a column called "Window to Life" in the English language *Shanghai Evening Post and Mercury*,[1] full of trivial details from everyday life, very interesting, and quite indicative of the urban milieu of the time. My friend's mother could write one paragraph per day for such a column. There was one day she saw a man, dressed respectably, like someone from the long-gown class, beating a woman out there on the street. Many bystanders felt sorry for the woman and instructed her: "Send him to the police station!" The woman cried: "I don't want him to go to the police station, I want him home!" She then pleaded to the man: "Please come home with me – you can beat me there!"[2]

---

[1] An English language newspaper that was in circulation from 1929 through 1949. Starting from 1933, a Chinese edition was published concurrently with the English edition. Chinese readers were more familiar with its Chinese title, *Da Mei wanbao* (The Great American Nightly News). The publication was briefly interrupted between 1941 and 1943 under pressure from the Guomindang secret service agencies, better known as "Number 76" in Shanghai, but it resumed publication in both Chongqing and New York between 1943 and 1946. The headquarters were moved back to Shanghai in 1946 and continued publication until 1949. For a brief history of the fate of this newspaper during the war years, see Shen Lixing, *Shanghai tegong zhan* (Shanghai Secret Service Headquarters).

[2] First published in *Xiao tiandi* (Small World Monthly) 4 (January 1945); reprinted in *Zhang Ailing sanwen quanbian* (A Complete Collection of Eileen Chang's Essays) (Hangzhou: Zhejiang wenyi chubanshe, 1992), 229.

325

Here in this short episode, the form of news media functions as a metaphor for the texture and rhythm of everyday life in urban Shanghai. On the surface, Chang's essay seems to be telling some irrelevant and unconnected episodes in life; but the essay speaks more about the framing of the episodes than about the actual events themselves. It can be read as a comment on how the experience of the urban is shaped by the saturation of modern print media. Life becomes comprehensible only when placed within the framework of a printed space, and literary writing becomes a further fragmentation of an everyday life that is already flattened, fragmented, that is to say, already textualized by the mechanisms of modern print production.

Chang's essay was written on the eve of the end of the Pacific War. This was also the height of what I call a women's print culture that was made possible with the advent of war and the reality of occupation. The questions follow: What makes the cultural production of this period unique as compared to that from the previous decades? How did the experience of war and occupation affect the reading practices of a Shanghai populace? And what was the relationship between war, women, and the production of urban print culture?

The relation between war and the growing production of urban print culture can be best illustrated by a moment in Eileen Chang's 1943 short story "Fengsuo" (Blockade). The story depicts a brief encounter between a man and a woman on a streetcar during an air raid when all motion within the city is forced to a halt. There is an episode that can also be read as an extended comment on the larger cultural context of the time:

> He starts reading a newspaper. It seems like everyone else on the streetcar is following his example. Those who have a paper handy start reading; others take out their cash receipts, brochures, or name cards; and those who have no printed texts with them look out of the window at billboards and signs on the streets. They have to read something to fill up this dreadfully empty space, otherwise the mind might start spinning. To think is painful.[3]

If 'blockade' is to be interpreted as a metaphor for confined time and space particular to the besieged city during the years from 1941 to 1945, then in Chang's depiction, the practices of reading (newspapers, magazines, bestseller fiction, billboards, signs, and window displays) helped shape the everyday experience of an average reader residing in occupied Shanghai. The short story is to be read as a trope of the state of cultural production during this brief moment

---

[3] "Blockade," first published in *Tiandi yuekan* (Heaven and Earth Monthly) 2 (November 1943); collected in Chang, *Chuanqi* (Romances, extended edition) (Shanghai: Shanhe tushu gongsi, 1946), 377–387.

in modern history: Print culture of the period served to attribute meanings, a sense of stability, and structure to a life that was constantly undermined by outside forces. More questions then follow: What kind of meanings or substance were being offered through the print media to an average reader in Shanghai who had to confront the presence of war in the forms of air raids and blockades on a daily basis and, as the damage of the war deepened, had to confront the increasingly pressing issue of daily survival? And, more important, to what extent was this wartime print culture gendered? How exactly did "women" fit into the picture?

These are the main issues that I analyze in this essay. Although other scholarly discourses have highlighted the continuity of a Shanghai cosmopolitan culture throughout the Republican era,[4] I place my emphasis on a significant rupture that resulted from the war and the occupation. Cultural production from occupied Shanghai was unique compared to that from the previous decades. Most notably, women in occupied Shanghai took over the existing print space and mechanisms, created a newly defined focus on an array of issues particular to women's interests, and, most important, acquired the skills of manipulating the frame, the tone, the pace, and the structure of media representations. By naming this shifted landscape as a women's print culture, I depict the formation of a new cultural arena initiated by a group of women who not only wrote, edited, and published, but also took part in defining and transforming the structure of modern knowledge, discussing it in various public forums surrounding the print media, and, consequently, promoting themselves as authoritative cultural commentators, that is, public intellectuals of the era. I investigate why this culture had to emerge during the years from 1941 to 1945, and why it is imperative to talk about cultural construction by women writers, editors, and publishers despite an extraordinary historical moment that is conventionally characterized by themes of chaos, instability, scarcity, destruction, and transience.

THE STAGE

The beginning of the Pacific War in December 1941 divided the eight years of Japanese military presence in Shanghai into two short and yet distinctive phases, the *Gudao* (Orphan Island) era and what I will call the "post" *Gudao* era. By naming the period after the December 1941 divide as the "post" *Gudao*

---

[4] A more representative work is Leo Ou-fan Lee, *Shanghai Modern: The Flowering of a New Urban Culture in China, 1930–1945*. Lee defines the significance of Eileen Chang as "draw[ing] a kind of allegorical closure by bringing to an end an entire era of urban culture that had nurtured her creativity – an era that began in the late 1920s, reached its height of urban glory in the early 1930s, and thereafter declined until its demise in the early 1950s . . . " (269).

era, I am suggesting a radical shift in both the political and social structure as well as the realm of cultural production. The word "post" marks the two eras apart in all aspects: political, social, economic, and most important for the purpose of my study, cultural. In literary history, the 1941 divide signals the suppression of *Gudao* literary forces, which were put together by a group of leftist writers and some of the Shanghai modernists, and generally regarded as the standard model of "resistance" literature of wartime China. For many *Gudao* writers in the resistance camp, the political and intellectual atmosphere in post-1941 Shanghai resembled that of a "prison." Many *Gudao* writers either went underground or moved to the hinterland.[5] Cultural production of the period demonstrated a shift from voices of cultural resistance by a group of mostly male writers and intellectuals to a women-centered urban culture that served as the background for the emergence of a group of young women authors and artists. A convenient explanation of this shift would be that the cultural resistance camp was suppressed by the outside political forces during the occupation, while the female/"apolitical" voices found their channel of expressions free of any ideological control. What remains to be examined, I argue, are the internal connections between this emergent culture and preexisting textual traditions, particularly the marginalized Mandarin Ducks and Butterflies school (*yuanyang hudie pai*) of urban popular literature as well as discourses on domesticity formed since the earliest women's magazines from the turn-of-the-century. By highlighting a theme of cultural continuity and reconstruction, I am placing emphasis on the experience of an individual, and particularly, a woman, in the midst of a fallen metropolis, struggling to survive, to succeed, to emerge out of the ruins of history, and therefore to transcend her time.

The emergence of a women's print culture went hand in hand with the revival of the Mandarin Ducks and Butterflies literary school toward the end of the *Gudao* era; in fact, it was Mandarin Ducks and Butterflies writers, editors, and publishers who first started the societywide promotion of a new generation of urban writers, mainly, young women authors. This close connection with a preexisting print mechanism and space of urban popular culture marks the cultural presence of these women apart from other cultural productions of the wartime period and helps explain why this particular kind of print culture had to emerge during the occupation years.

---

[5] In one of his memoirs, Ke Ling, a leading leftist writer/editor of the *Gudao* era and a survivor of the occupation regime, provides us his account of the history of occupied Shanghai, which is generally considered one of the standard descriptions of the era by scholars on both sides of the Pacific Ocean. See Ke Ling, *Zhuzi shengya* (My Writing Career). For a study of resistance literature and intellectual activities during the *Gudao* era, see Poshek Fu, *Passivity, Resistance, and Collaboration: Intellectual Choices in Occupied Shanghai, 1937–1945.*

To refer to the period between 1941 and 1945 as a period of "revival" for the Mandarin Ducks and Butterflies school does not mean that writers in the group were silent during the preceding periods. The Mandarin Ducks and Butterflies school of popular fiction and the journals that it was associated with never faded from the cultural imagination of an average reader residing in Shanghai throughout the first half of the century. The most glorious days of the school were, however, back in the 1910s and 1920s when many of the Butterflies writers were themselves entrepreneurs of a modern publishing industry. These writers were the first group of professional writers who were pushed to the center stage of urban life by the ever-flourishing commercial culture shaped since the turn of the century.[6]

Cultural production by this group of writers, editors, and publishers began to lose ground during the 1930s as new generations of urban writers emerged on the horizon. Key figures in the group were categorized as "old-style literati" (*jiupai wenren*) as a contrast to those of the "new-style," that is, a younger group of *haipai* (Shanghai school) writers and publishers who were more informed by Western literary and cultural trends.[7] The prevalent linked-chapter style of fictional writing (*zhanghui xiaoshuo*) in Butterflies journals also began to lose more of its readership in its competition with the 1930s Shanghai modernist literature represented by the experiments of a group of writers surrounding the journal *Xiandai* (*Les Contemporains*).[8] By the 1940s, the readership, along with most writers from this all-male school, was rapidly aging. To incorporate a younger generation of urban writers – particularly young women authors freshly out of college – into the camp then became the central strategy adopted by key figures such as Zhou Shoujuan and Chen Dieyi in their efforts to appeal to a younger generation of Shanghai readers and to therefore reclaim the important position this school and its cultural products had always occupied in the leisure life of urban Shanghai. What I mean by "revival" then has to do with the fundamental role Butterflies journals of the period played in discovering and promoting young women writers, reclaiming and redefining the importance of popular literature, sustaining and incorporating previous literary

---

[6] For a detailed study of the formation and activities of the school, see Perry Link, *Mandarin Ducks and Butterflies: Popular Fiction in Early Twentieth-Century Chinese Cities*. For activities of representative figures in the school, see biographies collected in Wei Shaochang, ed., *Yuanyang hudie pai yanjiu ziliao* (Research Material on the Mandarin Ducks and Butterflies School).

[7] For a comprehensive study of trends in urban commercial publishing and transformation of urban literature, see Wu Fuhui, *Dushi xuanliu zhong de Haipai xiaoshuo* (The Shanghai School Fiction in the Midst of Urban Cultures).

[8] For a discussion of the fictional art and the cultural context of this group of modernist writers, see Leo Ou-fan Lee, *Shanghai Modern*, 153–266.

traditions, maintaining and expanding a wide reading public, and consequently, constructing a wartime culture that was primarily centered around practices of reading, writing, and publishing, that is, the space of modern print, during a period of time when other forms of modern life were being smashed to bits and pieces.

The most important Butterflies journal published during the occupation era was the acclaimed *Wanxiang yuekan* or *The Phenomena Monthly*. Scholarly work on cultural production of this period tends to divide the publication of this journal into two distinctive phases marked by the switching of editorship from Chen Dieyi to Ke Ling in 1943. During the first two years (1941–1943), Chen Dieyi served as the editor-in-chief and published mostly Butterflies fiction and works by other urban popular fiction writers such as Yu Qie and Tan Weihan.[9] But when Ke Ling, a leftist writer and editor who had established his literary reputation during the preceding *Gudao* era, took over the editing duties in 1943, *The Phenomena Monthly* was transformed into a stage that brought back "old" writers from the "new literature" camp such as Wang Tongzhao and Lu Yan, and promoted young writers such as Zheng Dingwen and Shen Ji who were considered as followers of the tradition of the "new literature." Scholarly work tends to highlight Ke Ling's resistance efforts during the occupation, praising his efforts in "transforming" or "correcting" a Butterflies publication and incorporating it into the mainstream literary tradition that highlights social and political consciousness in literary representation.[10]

Here I argue that *The Phenomena Monthly* remained a Mandarin Ducks and Butterflies publication even under the editorship of Ke Ling. Many Butterflies writers (e.g., Cheng Xiaoqing) and other popular fiction writers (e.g., Yu Qie) continued to publish their works in the journal. The popularity of the journal heavily relied on the fact that it was and had always been a popular journal, and had persistently catered to "the popular taste for amusement."[11] And this is also the reason why it not only survived, but also launched a major marketing success during the war and the occupation. I would further argue that Ke Ling's attempt

---

[9] Chen Dieyi joined the camp of the Butterflies school later than most of its veteran members. He was one of the editors for a 1930s fan newspaper *Mingxing ribao* (Star Daily), one of the major Butterflies publications of the period. For an account of Chen Dieyi's cultural activities during the 1930s and 1940s in Shanghai, see an interview with Chen in Shui Jing, *Liuxing gequ cangsang ji* (The Rise and Fall of Popular Songs).

[10] See Ying Guojing, "Wuni zhi zhong de jielian – *Wanxiang*" (*The Phenomena Monthly*: A Pure Lotus in the Midst of Dirty Mud) in *Xiandai wenxue qikan manhua* (Essays on Literary Periodicals in Modern China) (Guangzhou: Huacheng chubanshe, 1986), 401–405.

[11] Poshek Fu, *Passivity, Resistance, and Collaboration*, 62. Fu argues that Ke Ling transformed the monthly "from an apolitical Mandarin Ducks and Butterfly publication catering to the popular taste for amusement into a forum for symbolic resistance."

to bring in writers of "serious" literature (as opposed to "popular" literature) did not run contrary to the editorial agenda Chen Dieyi laid down when the journal was under his editorship previously. To maintain the rigid divide between the two phases in the publication of the journal is to naïvely hold on to the age-old belief in the "truth" value of the arbitrary divide between the so-called "serious" literature (literature that carries on the May Fourth tradition of social intervention and political engagement) and "popular" literature (literature that aims to entertain and to please the popular taste). In the case of 1940s Shanghai, this fictive divide was constantly undermined and eventually blurred in journals such as *The Phenomena Monthly*. The intervention by Ke Ling did not change the function of the journal in the context of popular media; rather, the changing faces of *The Phenomena Monthly* as well as other Butterflies journals from the period represent a new direction Butterflies writers and editors were gearing toward in their efforts to challenge the literary mainstream, to test the boundaries between the "serious" and the "popular," and foremost among all, to use the print medium as a way to reinvent life in wartime.

My story began in 1942 when Chen Dieyi organized two special forums, published in the fourth and fifth issues of *The Phenomena Monthly*, initiating a so-called movement of popular literature (*tongsu wenxue yundong*). In Chen's own words, what he proposes is a new kind of urban popular literature that "communicates across the barriers between the new literature and the old literature," and that "introduces new thought and correct consciousness to the ordinary readers through the medium of popular literature." Chen further argues that while popular literature can benefit from a critical edge and social/political consciousness, serious literature also needs to take into consideration the reader's tastes. Chen's concern for readership is in fact a strategy to make the so-called serious literature more "urban," and therefore more accessible to an ordinary reader. According to Chen, the importance of the new kind of popular literature he proposes lies exactly in the fact that it can serve as a bridge between two rigidly divided camps of the "new literature" and the "old literature," and therefore create something that is truly urban and modern. Here Chen's effort is to resist the equation between urban popular literature and old literature, to fight the marginal position that has been assigned to urban popular literature, to highlight the importance of this literature in representing forms of modern life, and to formally claim a mainstream status for it. Urban popular literature has been redefined as something that is both "serious" and "new" despite its many connections to old literature. Why, asks Chen, do we still want to uphold the arbitrary divide between the serious and the popular?[12]

---

[12] See Chen Dieyi, "Tongsu wenxue yundong" (The Movement of Popular Literature), 130–141.

Other successful journals associated with the Butterflies school include *Xi-aoshuo yuebao* (The Fiction Monthly), *Chunqiu yuekan* (Spring and Autumn Monthly), *Wansui banyuekan* (Ten Thousand Years Bi-weekly), and *Ziluolan yuekan* (The Violet Monthly). What these journals had in common was an important marketing strategy they used to encourage readers' involvement in the shaping of a public arena surrounding the print media. The column "Letters from Readers" (*Duzhe xinxiang*) is found in most journals, often accompanied by editors' responses. Other ways to enlarge a readership include creating columns such as "Bianhou ji" (Editorial Postscript) or "Bianji zuotan" (Editors' Roundtable Discussions), and to encourage entries by younger authors. The latter strategy was meant to attract younger readers – college and high school students – around the journals and to foster a new generation of urban writers who would in turn channel their creative energy into the making of these journals. For instance, *Ten Thousand Years Bi-weekly* set up a column called "Duzhe wenyi xizuo jiangjin" (Readers' Entry Contest); *The Fiction Monthly* created a column called "Xuesheng wenyi" (Campus Literature); and *The Phenomena Monthly* set up a column called "Xuesheng wenyi xuan" (Selected Campus Literature).

Here Zhou Shoujuan's *The Violet Monthly* should be singled out for its marked effort in promoting young women authors from the college student population. Zhou was the one who first discovered the talents of Eileen Chang – Chang's first short story "Chen xiang xie: di yi lu xiang" (Aloewood Ashes: The First Incense Brazier) was published in the second and third issues of *The Violet Monthly* in 1943.[13] But the most important contribution of the journal was its promotion of a distinctive style of writing represented by a group of less well known young women authors, many of whom were the daughters or disciples of the older generation of Butterflies writers. The list includes Shi Jimei, Cheng Yuzhen (Cheng Xiaoqing's daughter), Lian Yuanxiu, Wang Liling, Zhou Lianxia, Yang Xiuzhen, Zeng Wenqiang, Yu Shaoming, Zhou Ling (Zhou Shoujuan's daughter), and Shi Jiying (Shi Jimei's sister). This style of writing bears a distinctively "feminine" label and many ties to the so-called boudoir style (*guixiu ti*) of prose writing from the 1920s and 1930s, previously represented by women writers such as Bing Xin, Ling Shuhua, and Lin Huiyin. The difference is that the 1940s version appears to be largely "popularized" and was marketed on a much larger scale in Shanghai. In fact, this revived and reinvented style of writing created by these women writers and their editors was largely responsible for the success of many of these popular journals. Shi Jimei was the

---

[13] *The Violet Monthly*, in circulation from April 1943 to December 1944, with a total of 18 issues. The editorial preface in the second issue records the first meeting of Zhou Shoujuan and Eileen Chang.

most successful one among the group. Her reputation reached its height at one point when a good number of Shanghai readers began to call themselves 'fans of Shi' (*Shi mi*). Shi Jimei, Cheng Yuzhen, and several other young women authors of the time were graduates of the aristocratic Dongwu University, a Catholic all-women liberal arts college. Their literary careers started when they were still in school and started reading, subscribing, and contributing to popular journals at the time, most of which were Butterflies journals. After they graduated from college around the year 1943, that is, right in the middle of the wartime occupation, they attained instant success in a print market filled with journals and magazines devoted to a readership craving a new type of urban popular fiction.

Even though there were no women's voices during the 1942 discussion of "popular literature" initiated by Chen Dieyi, editors and publishers of popular journals soon discovered that promoting young women writers was imperative to the survival and the sustained success of their journals. The importance of Butterflies journals in my discussions of women's print culture taking shape in occupied Shanghai was that these journals provided an existing framework, or infrastructure, of urban media mechanisms for the staging of women writers. With the emergence of women writers came a revival of issues concerning women, particularly family, marriage, and the art of homemaking. Discussions of these women-centered issues during this period started from the Butterflies journals and gradually moved to home journals and other popular magazines. Here echoes of earlier rhetoric concerning themes such as women's education, economic independence, and social positions in general can be heard, but what marks this period apart from all the previous decades is that young women writers of 1940s Shanghai went ahead and played a central role in forging a new version of urban literature and promoting themselves as a new generation of public intellectuals.

THE ISSUES

The emergence of a new generation of urban female writers and a new kind of public intellectual also went hand in hand with the transformation of an important cultural genre – the home journal. In other words, the significance of this women's print culture is also defined by an effort to reconceptualize the notion of domesticity.

Here I am talking about home journals as a cultural genre that had evolved from the earliest women's newspapers and magazines around the turn of the century, including *Nüzi shijie* (Women's World), *Zhongguo nübao* (Chinese Women's Newspaper), *Zhongguo xin nüjie zazhi* (A Journal of a New Chinese

Women's World), *Funü ribao* (Women's Daily), and *Funü zazhi* (Women's Magazine), to a series of popular journals directed at the domestic market published by the Mandarin Ducks and Butterflies School writers during the 1920s and 1930s, including *Banyue* (Half Moon Bi-weekly), *Zilan huapian* (Violet Petals), and *Xin jiating* (The New Home), and, finally, to the stabilization of home journals as a distinctive cultural genre in the mid-1930s and 1940s marked by a sequence of publications bearing "home" (*jiating*) as their essential trademark, including several major newspaper supplements created by Xu Baiyi between 1936 and 1941.[14] And the culminating point of this generic transformation was the brief period between 1943 and 1945 that saw the simultaneous marketing success of several major publications, including *Jiating yuekan* (Happy Home Monthly), *Jiankang jiating yuekan* (Healthy Home Monthly), *Jiating niankan* (Family Annual), and, most distinctively, *Nüsheng yuekan* (Women's Voices Monthly).[15]

Women's Voices Monthly stands out among other publications in occupied Shanghai for its marked success in reaching a wide urban readership, its persistence in defining, in numerous details, the connotations of domesticity and the meanings of everyday life, as well as its conspicuous promotion of the image of a new public intellectual, that is, a "new" modern urban woman. *Women's*

[14] Among the early newspaper supplements edited by Xu Baiyi were *Dawanbao funü yu jiating fukan* (The Women and Home Supplement to *The Grand Evening News*), *Dagongbao xiandai jiating fukan* (The Modern Home Supplement to *Dagongbao*), *Shenbao yuekan jiating fukan* (The Home Supplement to *Shanghai Monthly*), and *Shishi xinbao shidai jiating fukan* (The Modern Home Supplement to *The New Daily Times*). These major newspaper supplements represent early attempts at publishing home journals in China. The editor Xu Baiyi was truly a pioneer. A large percentage of the sources published in these journals were transplanted from home journals of the West, such as *Good Housekeeping* and *Ladies' Home Journal*. Xu not only served as the editor, he also worked as a translator and writer for all of these supplements. Bian Qini was also among the earliest journalists and writers who was interested in creating a new form of modern journal targeted at the domestic market.

[15] *Happy Home Monthly*, edited by Xu Baiyi, published from January 1936 to October 1945, total 6 volumes, 72 issues. This is the most influential, popular, and long-lasting home journal published in 1940s Shanghai. The journal was originally a bi-monthly publication entitled *Kuaile jiating* (Happy Home). The English title remained unchanged even after the Chinese title was changed to *Jiating yuekan*.

Healthy Home Monthly, edited by Lu Boyu, Ding Fubao, Pan Yangyao, and Mei Fu, and later taken over by Xu Baiyi and Hongye guanggao tushu gongsi, the publisher of *Jiating yuekan*, in publication from April 1939 to June 1944, total 5 volumes, 50 issues.

Family Annual, edited by Xu Baiyi, from 1943 to 1948, total 5 issues. These mega-journals served as source books for housewives of Shanghai, the same reading community as that of *Jiating yuekan*. The first three issues (1943–1945) were all reprinted many times to meet the enthusiastic demands.

Women's Voices Monthly, edited by Zuo Junzhi (Tamura Toshiko) and Guan Lu, published between May 1942 and July 1945, total 4 volumes, 38 issues.

Voices Monthly was also the only publication from the period that was edited exclusively by women, featured mostly women authors, and proclaimed to be dedicated to serving a designated reading community of women. If the entirety of the journal can be viewed as a complete narrative, lengthy discussions of homemaking then can be regarded as narrative devices – devices of fragmentation and materialization. Here the everyday seems to be dissected and dispersed into many details. But the long list of tips for homemaking also gives the reader an impression of the endlessness of everyday life; as a result, the everyday is also maximized and glorified. If we were to list all the goods or things mentioned in one of the main columns on domesticity, entitled "Home Economy" (*Jiazheng*), we would approach the construction of a world full of details. Here we are presented with the most visible aspects of a culture. When everyday life is categorized and analyzed in such great detail, the practice of homemaking really becomes an art. Gourmet cuisine and fine clothes are turned into an expressive form for women to construct an intelligible universe, which is at once sensible, meaningful, and profoundly cultural.

Like Mandarin Ducks and Butterflies journals, editors of home journals from the period also acknowledged the ever-changing face of urban readership: A typical reader of popular journals in early 1940s was identified as a young educated woman, most likely fresh out of college and just about ready to start a career *and* a family. When Xu Baiyi started his first newspaper supplements in 1936 and 1937, that is, the "Modern Home" supplements to *Dagongbao* and *Shishi xinbao*, he intended to address a broader audience that included both genders.[16] But as the home journals were developed into the 1940s, they became more and more distinctively women's journals, especially with the participation of a group of women writers and journalists such as Su Qing (1917–1982), Pan Liudai (1922–?), Guan Lu (1908–1982), and Shi Jimei (1920–1968), and with an increasingly demonstrated fascination with the materiality of everyday life.

Home journals published during the war years also demonstrated their close ties to the market of various consumer products. For instance, the publisher of the very popular *Happy Home Monthly* was Hongye guanggao tushu gongsi (Hongye Advertising and Printing Company), an advertising agency mainly devoted to the marketing of household products.[17] Hongye also bought the publication rights of *Healthy Home Monthly* that was originally owned by Xinya, a pharmaceutical company that made a huge fortune precisely because

---

[16] See Xu Baiyi, "Zhongguo de jiating wenti" (The Family Problem in China), 4–10.
[17] See Zhu Boquan, "Fakan ci" (Foreword), 1–2.

of the surging demand for medicine and medical equipment during the war years.[18]

To be sure, the publication of home journals was not put to a complete halt after 1945. In fact, the "aftermath" of this specific cultural genre can very well demonstrate the impact it had on urban commercial printing in Shanghai. The best example of this is a journal called *Xingfu* (Domestic Bliss),[19] which resembled *Women's Voices Monthly* both in its format and its marketing strategies. The title *Xingfu* means more than just "happiness" or "joy"; judging from the content of the journal, it should be more precisely rendered as "domestic bliss." The journal was marketed as a combination of home journal and popular literary journal. The targeted readership of the first twelve issues of *Domestic Bliss* was educated middle-class women of different ages, mainly "*taitai*" (married women) and "*xiaojie*" (unmarried young women). The journal was one of the few post-1945 publications that strived to carry on the earlier attempt in forging an urban culture centered on women and domesticity. Shi Jimei, the "star" from the occupation era, published most of her post-1945 fictional writing in *Domestic Bliss*. Shi's writing, labeled and much admired as the new "boudoir style" feminine writing, is juxtaposed with numerous tips for urban housewives and aspiring housewives, such as housekeeping, cooking, cosmetics and fashion choices, pregnancy, childbearing, and numerous household health concerns represented in the two columns entitled "Xiaojie zhi ye" (The Misses' Pages) and "Xingfu jiating" (Happy Family). The promotion of a boudoir style writing is often accompanied by the visualization of a modern "guixiu," a traditional aristocratic beauty who moves freely between her inner chamber and the limelight of public attention. Among the post-1945 popular journals, *Xingfu* was unusually long-lasting. The success of the journal was built upon its brilliant promotion of a female lifestyle, a lifestyle most meticulously adorned with both words and images, which is a crossover between the realistic vision of the modern urban world and the fantastic creation of a domestic bliss. In the editorial notes of the second issue (May 1946), the editors indicate that they intend to create a "pictorial style magazine" (*huabaoxing de zazhi*).[20] This attempt has been proved to guarantee the success of home journals. Though published after 1945, journals such as *Domestic Bliss* can very well be included in the category of wartime publications, for they made use of the same editorial strategies

---

[18] See, for instance, Sherman Cochran's study of the commercialization of both popular journals and medical products in the same volume.

[19] Published between May 1946 and March 1949, edited by Wang Bo (Shen Ji) and Wang Benpu.

[20] The "pictorial style magazine" as a distinctive style can be traced back to the much acclaimed publication of *Liangyou huabao* (The Good Companion Pictorial) edited by Liang Desuo. For a discussion of the pictorial magazine, see Leo Ou–fan Lee, *Shanghai Modern*, 64–67.

and addressed the same readership, the kind of readership that was shaped by Chinese home journals during the few years under Japanese occupation, and that continued to crave the consistent catering of their "spiritual food" (*jingshen shiliang*).[21]

When imagining, designing, advertising, and marketing domesticity become the dominant themes in wartime popular print, the actual effects of such representations have gone beyond the survival demands particular to the period. What distinguishes home journals of the occupation period from those of the previous periods is that domesticity has been constructed as another kind of reality. War and domesticity, the two seemingly exclusive categories of human experiences, are brought together within the same space of urban print media. War, the bombarding presence, is dissected into fragments, channeled into the everyday; and, on the other hand, the experience of the domestic and the everyday is intensified precisely due to the threatening intrusion of the war.

What is unique about home journals of the period, that is, what marks them radically apart from women's magazines of the earlier decades, is the fact that they not only marketed a massive amount of domestic knowledge, but also served as major propaganda tools in promoting women writers, artists, and intellectuals, that is, a new generation of public intellectuals.

THE PLAYERS

The dissemination of domestic knowledge and the construction of an art of homemaking cannot be separated from a societywide promotion and infatuation with women writers and artists. In other words, women writers, editors, publishers, and readers played a vital role in defining and disseminating a body of "new knowledge," taking over the existing frame of modern print, and transforming it into a stage of their own.

Following the initial appearance of young women authors in Mandarin Ducks and Butterflies literary journals and home journals, women writers went on to generate and "occupy" other urban spaces. Between 1944 and 1945, a vast amount of media coverage, including roundtable talks, interviews, profiles, photographs, cartoons, and tabloid stories, all promoted Eileen Chang and Su Qing as two of the most important cultural figures of the era. It is unprecedented in the history of print culture in modern China that so much attention was paid

---

[21] Other post-1945 journals that are similar to *Domestic Bliss* include: *Shaonü yuekan* (The Maiden Monthly), edited by Chen Dieyi and Wen Yin, published by Diyi bianji gongsi, June 1946–June 1947; *Kangli yuekan* (Happy Couple Monthly), edited by Wu Haohao, June 1946–October 1948; and *Dajia yuekan* (Everybody Monthly), edited by Gong Zhifang and Tang Yunjing (Tang Dalang), April–July 1947, total 3 issues.

to the personal lives of women writers – their clothes, their make-up, their mannerisms, their voices, their shopping habits, the restaurants and cafés they frequented, the movies they enjoyed watching, and the men whose company they yearned for. And it is also unprecedented in the media culture of Republican China that women writers, journalists, painters, and other intellectuals were showcased together with film actresses and popular singers as important cultural icons.[22]

Su Qing in the 1940s was an even more prominent figure than Eileen Chang. A brief account of Su's journey can help illustrate the actual process and detailed mechanisms involved in legend-making. The year 1944 saw the simultaneous publication of two major works by Su that established her reputation as one of the most important – and controversial – cultural figures in occupied Shanghai. One was an essay collection entitled *Huan jin ji* (Drifting Brocade), which contains most of the essays she wrote between 1935 and 1944; the other was an autobiographical novel entitled *Jiehun shinian* (Ten Years of Married Life), which recounts the female protagonist Su Huaiqing's decade-long journey from a provincial city to the great metropolis and her metamorphosis from a wife and mother confined to everyday domestic routines to a young talented author who aspires to launch a successful career in the midst of war, marital crises, child-rearing, and other historical as well as personal turmoil. *Ten Years of Married Life* became the most debated literary work of the era for its direct references to actual events in the author's own life, its focus on family and marriage whose stability is represented as being violently threatened by the disruptive powers of modern warfare, and, most important, its intrepid revelation of female inner psyche, desire, and sexuality.

The name Su Qing was known to the publishing world of Shanghai ever since she contributed her very first essay entitled "Sheng nan yu nü" (Child-bearing: Boy or Girl) in 1935.[23] She went on to build up her writing career throughout the decade and arrived at the high point of her career by the year 1943, a year celebrated by the production of her own literary journal *Tiandi yuekan* (Heaven and Earth Monthly) and the founding of her own publisher – Tiandi chubanshe (Heaven and Earth Publisher), which printed both *Drifting Brocade* and *Ten Years of Married Life* in the following year. The public's

---

[22] Other scholars on the cultures of Republican China have studied the formation of a "star system" (*mingxing zhi*) in Shanghai during the 1920s, 1930s, and 1940s, which was a media mechanism that produced and promoted film actresses and popular singers for the purpose of urban entertainment consumption. See Andrew F. Jones, *Yellow Music: Media Culture and Colonial Modernity in the Chinese Jazz Age.*

[23] Published in *Lunyu* (Discourses) 67 (1935) and later collected in *Huan jin ji* (Drifting Brocade) (Shanghai: Tiandi chubanshe, 1944).

fascination with Su's two books then had much to do with their curiosity about the destiny of a literary press single-handedly run by a young woman author, a phenomenon unprecedented in the history of modern Chinese publishing. The publication of the two books was then a much anticipated media event, especially since some earlier episodes of the novel were first serialized in the monthly literary journal *Fengyu tan yuekan* (Chats of Winds and Rains Monthly).[24] Other major newspapers and journals had also been announcing their forthcoming publication for months before the books finally appeared on the shelves of local bookstores and at the street vendors.[25] Not only was the actual publication much awaited, the kind of impact the two books might have on the Shanghai reading public was also predicted. Both books became instant bestsellers and went through a dozen printings in a matter of six months. From initial conception to final marketing success, the entire process surrounding the production of the two books appeared to be meticulously scripted and orchestrated by a publishing community put together by newspaper and journal publishers and editors, literary and cultural critics, and the author herself.

Whereas *Ten Years of Married Life* was marketed as distinctively autobiographical, the essays collected in *Drifting Brocade* were also labeled as texts with heavy biographical contingencies. In fact, it was the author herself who suggested the "correct" way to read these two texts. While insisting that the novel should be read as "autobiographical fiction" (*zizhuanti de xiaoshuo*), with more emphasis placed on its fictionalization of personal experiences, Su Qing indicates that there are in fact more direct real life references in her essay writing, which as a whole should be interpreted as an extended narrative of an inner life in formation:

> I treasure *Drifting Brocade*, for every single essay in the collection belongs only to myself. There is no embellishment or exaggeration. My eight years of hard work is all here. Gradually, piece by piece, it has come together like this. These essays are a reminiscence of my past. I feel a little sad but my sadness will not make me cry out loud. I can't force everyone else to share my feelings, but if there is anyone out there who can understand me and feel sympathetic for me, I will shed tears because it will have brought me joy.[26]

---

[24] *Fengyu tan yuekan* (Chats of Winds and Rains Monthly), edited by Liu Yusheng, in circulation from April 1943 to August 1945.

[25] See 1944 issues of *The Miscellany Monthly* and *The Past and Present Bi-weekly*.

[26] See "*Huanjin ji* yu *Jiehun shinian*" (*Drifting Brocade* and *Ten Years of Married Life*), *Heaven and Earth Monthly* 15–16 (1945); reprinted in *Su Qing sanwen jingbian* (A Complete Collection of Su Qing's Essays), 530–534.

Rhetoric as such should of course be interpreted as a self-reflexive effort on the part of the author to invoke autobiographical contingencies and literary individualism as a discourse of legitimation that inscribes both her writing and herself within the literary mainstream of the time.

The two books together achieved exactly what both the author and her readership had hoped for: They painted a well-rounded picture of the female author, placing segments of her private life in the limelight and into wide public circulation. Her public image, the operation of her publishing house, the success of her journal, the popularity of her writing, and segments of her innermost life as a whole were subjected to public scrutiny, all contributing to her transformation into a unique urban personality during the first half of the 1940s.

Zazhi yuekan or *The Miscellany Monthly*,[27] among other major magazines of the period, stood out for its conspicuous effort both to encourage the massive attention to domestic issues as well as to showcase women writers in the center stage. One can argue that the promotion of women writers served to encourage the heated debates over issues concerning the general social status of women. The other side of the coin is also true: The debates over a variety of social issues provided a forum for the emergence of women writers. The marketing success of popular journals such as *The Miscellany Monthly* in 1940s Shanghai can largely be attributed to the fervent promotion of women writers. From the very beginning, the heated discussions on family and marriage were not merely reflections of public interest in social issues concerning women; rather, such discussions were heavily tinted with Shanghai readers' frenzy with the intimate lives of women who were placed under the limelight. And from the very beginning of their writing careers, the personal lives of these Shanghai women writers became an integral part of their public presence and reception.

It is also apparent that public attention was often directed toward the outspokenness of women writers on topics related to the ever-problematized issues of female gender and sexuality. The year 1945 saw the culmination of Shanghai readers' fascination with women writers, with the publication of a dialogue between Eileen Chang and Su Qing on family and marriage in *The Miscellany Monthly* heightening the tone of the already heated discussions of women's issues.[28] The publication of this dialogue triggered a sequence of debates over

---

[27] The journal was published by Xin Zhongguo baoshe between August 1942 and August 1945, edited by Wu Chengzhi, Wu Jiangfeng, and Fan Jugao. With a total of 15 volumes and 37 issues, *The Miscellany Monthly* was one of the most long-lasting and most successful popular journals during the occupation era.

[28] See "Su Qing Zhang Ailing duitan ji" (Su Qing and Eileen Chang Talking to Each Other), *The Miscellany Monthly* 6 (1945): 78–84.

related concerns, most of which were also published in the subsequent issues of the magazine. The editorial foreword to the Su-Chang dialogue glorifies Eileen Chang and Su Qing as "the most prominent women writers in the literary circle of Shanghai," and also indicates that female writers are the most qualified discussants of women's issues. Shanghai readers' infatuation with women writers of the 1940s can then be understood as the Chinese reading public's fascination with issues concerning women surfacing since the beginning of the century. The literary writing and the personal lives of Shanghai women writers of the 1940s became the point of convergence where issues such as women's liberation and independence, female sexual behaviors, gender roles, the mechanisms of urban families, and a variety of other gender and sexuality discourses were once again placed under public scrutiny. Though many of the themes are reminiscent of the discussions of family and marriage since the turn of the century, the specific social/cultural/political environment ensured that the talk of gender and sexuality by a group of women writers in Japanese-occupied Shanghai would move toward a different direction: While the talk of female gender and sexuality during the earlier decades served to provoke and deepen the iconoclastic spirit embraced by that generation of intellectuals, women writers in 1940s Shanghai tended to situate these issues within the materiality of everyday life experienced by an average Shanghai woman. The effect is not to shock or to disrupt the social order, but to attribute concrete forms to a vision of life that is constantly falling apart.

Most important to the purpose of this study is a series of special issues published by *The Miscellany Monthly* from March to May 1945 that was triggered by the publication of the Su-Chang dialogue. The subsequent special issues in *The Miscellany Monthly* include contributions from readers of both sexes, and of a variety of social backgrounds, from an important literary critic to an ordinary housewife.[29] The redefinition of gender and domesticity in women's literary writing of the period was directly placed in front of the reading public through the print media. These special issues also served to form an ongoing dialogue between editors, authors, and readers, which in turn contributed in

---

[29] In chronological order, these special issues include:
   "Teji: Funü, jiating, hunyin zhu wenti" (Special Issue on Women, Family, Marriage), *The Miscellany Monthly* 6 (1945): 78–90.
   "Guanyu funü, jiating, hunyin zhu wenti" (On Women, Family, Marriage: Special Issue Continued), *The Miscellany Monthly* 1 (1945): 52–63.
   "Duzhe de fanxiang" (Reader's Responses to the Special Issue on Women, Family, Marriage), *The Miscellany Monthly* 1 (1945): 64–69.
   "Tamen de yijian teji: Guanyu funü, jiating, hunyin zhu wenti" (Their Opinions: Special Issue on Women, Family, Marriage), *The Miscellany Monthly* 2 (1945): 73–82.

forging a community of social commentators during that brief moment in modern Chinese history.

In addition to special issues, there were also roundtable talks organized by journals and newspapers featuring women writers and artists, most of which were also published in *The Miscellany Monthly*. The roundtable talk was a new form of showcasing women writers by placing words (voices) and images (descriptions of their presence, and photographs) all on display. Major newspapers and journals of the period all used this strategy to advertise their publications, promote their circles of new writers, and take part in the construction of an expanded community put together by publishers, editors, writers, artists, and readers.[30]

To be sure, the most important players in this societywide promotion of women writers and discussion of women-related issues were none other than women writers themselves. Su Qing's journey already tells us that each of these women writers was indeed a self-made legend. During one of the roundtable discussions hosted by *The Miscellany Monthly* and attended by a group of women writers, Eileen Chang and Su Qing started to attribute each other's writing with a canonical position in literary history. When asked who her favorite modern women writers were, Su Qing answered: "I usually do not read works by women writers, with the only exception of those by Eileen Chang." When the same question was directed at Eileen Chang, she made the following remarks:

> Su Qing is my favorite modern woman writer. Before Su Qing, there was Bing Xin, whose feminine style was too contrived. Ding Ling's earlier works were good, but later she was simply not capable of fulfilling her ambitions. Su Qing is the first [woman writer] who can steadily grasp the appeal of life. She embodies a profound simplicity.... She understands the commonalities in human nature better than anyone else.[31]

This mutual promotion continued. In September, *The Miscellany Monthly* published another transcript of a roundtable discussion on Eileen Chang's newly published short story collection *Romances*.[32] On this occasion, Su Qing provided a more detailed appraisal of Eileen Chang's writing:

[30] For instance, a gathering of women authors on March 16, 1944 was recorded, entitled "Nü zuojia jutanhui" (A Roundtable Discussion of Women Writers). Eileen Chang, Su Qing, Wang Liling, Pan Liudai, and Guan Lu all attended the gathering. See *The Miscellany Monthly* 1 (1944): 49–57.

[31] See "A Roundtable Discussion of Women Writers."

[32] This publicized roundtable discussion was a promotional event put out by *The Miscellany Monthly* for their "star" author Eileen Chang and her first short story collection published by the same monthly. See "*Chuanqi* jiping chahui ji" (A Roundtable Discussion of *Romances*), *The Miscellany Monthly* 6 (1944): 150–155.

I am always enchanted by Eileen Chang's writing. Whenever I read it, I am always drawn into it and eager to read the entire text. It is like a piece of serene and sad music. Even just a fragment of it can move people. Her analogies are very smart and intricate. Although I do not understand some of them, I can still appreciate their beauty. Chang's writing is also like a painting because she depicts vivid colors. (Actually) Chang's heightening of colors in her writing is even more skillful than that in the best paintings. Maybe there are no such colors in the real world, and Ms. Chang is truly a "celestial genius." I admire her the most, and this is not blind flattery.

In her essay "Wo kan Su Qing" (The Way I Look at Su Qing), Eileen Chang provides us her account of the making of the coupling images in literary history:

> To underestimate the value of Su Qing's writing is equal to underestimating the cultural standards of our current era. If women writers are evaluated as a group, I really do not feel proud of being grouped together with either Bing Xin or Bai Wei. Yet I will feel perfectly happy to be placed in the same context with Su Qing.[33]

Here the reader can identify in this essay Chang's attempt to undermine the literary canon by regrouping writers and texts as well as her effort to challenge the coherency of a so-called women's writing tradition in modern China. But the significance of this mutual appraisal goes far beyond the realm of literary writing. In her essays, Su Qing frequently identifies herself as merely a "man/woman of letters" or "a member of the literati class" (*wenren*), and sometimes, "a hardworking female member of the literati class" (*jianku xiezuo de nü wenren*).[34] Eileen Chang also labels herself as someone who makes a living selling her writing.[35] Such statements can be read as a highlighted theme of wartime survival that concerns the daily living of an individual author. But when the entirety of the women writers' intimate lives was scrutinized under the limelight, their literary writing often served to supply numerous details needed for the establishment of their public images. More appropriately, the self-referentiality in their writing should be read as a strategic move on the part of the women authors in their efforts to fashion their self images. Here, one

---

[33] "The Way I Look at Su Qing," first published in *Heaven and Earth Monthly* 19 (April 1945); reprinted in *A Complete Collection of Eileen Chang's Essays*, 256–273.

[34] See Su Qing, "Guanyu wo: *Xu Jiehun shinian* daixu" (About Me: Preface to *Sequel to Ten Years of Marriage*), 542.

[35] See Eileen Chang, "You jijuhua tong duzhe shuo" (Several Things to Clarify for My Readers), 1–2.

might further argue that the societywide fascination with women writers is a largely self-made myth.

In "The Way I Look at Su Qing," Chang goes on to imagine the space that might house Su Qing, the newly constructed mythical figure of our modern era:

> I want to have a Chinese-style house in the future: snow-white painted walls, gold-plated tables and chairs, scarlet cushions, pea-green tea cups, and glutinous rice cakes piled up on the table, each decorated with a carmine dot. A Chinese house usually consists of one bright room and two dark rooms, and this [what I have just described] is certainly the bright one. A room like this carries the style of Su Qing.

Here Eileen Chang is invoking a language of domesticity to define Su Qing's public identity. It is in descriptive language as such that one can identify the connection between women writers' self-promotion in public and public discussions of various domestic issues as seen in Mandarin Ducks and Butterflies publications and home journals of the time. While domesticity becomes a public trademark, discussions of domesticity then become a public discourse, something that is situated at the center of one's political life and can no longer merely symbolize a completely enclosed structure. While the boundaries between the public and the private are further blurred and domestic issues are discussed in the space of modern media, the domestic space then is extended into the public realm. Here it is in Chang's attempt to capture a spatial moment in one's imagined private life that the imagery of a "Chinese" house becomes "modern" at the same time.

These moments depict a vivid image of a new public intellectual in the making. This public intellectual typically speaks the language of domesticity; in other words, a woman writer who speaks the language of domesticity fashions herself into a public intellectual. It is exactly here, against the backdrop of wartime destruction, that one perceives the formation of a women's print culture by pinpointing a space where discursive constructions of "women" and the "woman question" were located, political speech and social interventions by women were made both audible and visible, and a public arena was shaped in which the conceptualization of domesticity was identified as the central debates of public dialogues.

BIBLIOGRAPHY

"*Chuanqi* jiping chahui ji." *Zazhi yuekan* 6 (1944): 150–155.
"Nü zuojia jutanhui." *Zazhi yuekan* 1 (1944): 49–57.
"Su Qing Zhang Ailing duitan ji." *Zazhi yuekan* 6 (1945): 78–84.
Chang, Eileen (Zhang Ailing). *Liuyan*. Shanghai: Zhongguo kexue gongsi, 1945.

Chang, Eileen (Zhang Ailing). *Chuanqi*. Shanghai: Shanhe tushu gongsi, 1946.

Chang, Eileen (Zhang Ailing). "You jijuhua tong duzhe shuo." In *Chuanqi*, 1–2. Shanghai: Shanhe tushu gongsi, 1946.

Chang, Eileen (Zhang Ailing). "Fengsuo." In *Chuanqi*, 377–387. Shanghai: Shanhe tushu gongsi, 1946.

Chang, Eileen (Zhang Ailing). "Qi duan qing chang." In *Zhang Ailing sanwen quanbian*, 229. Hangzhou: Zhejiang wenyi chubanshe, 1992.

Chang, Eileen (Zhang Ailing). "Wo kan Su Qing." In *Zhang Ailing sanwen quanbian*, 256–273. Hangzhou: Zhejiang wenyi chubanshe, 1992.

Chen Dieyi. "Tongsu wenxue yundong." *Wanxiang yuekan* 4 (1942): 130–141.

Fu, Poshek. *Passivity, Resistance, and Collaboration: Intellectual Choices in Occupied Shanghai, 1937–1945*. Stanford: Stanford University Press, 1993.

Jones, Andrew F. *Yellow Music: Media Culture and Colonial Modernity in the Chinese Jazz Age*. Durham, NC: Duke University Press, 2001.

Ke Ling. *Zhuzi shengya*. Taiyuan: Shanxi renmin chubanshe, 1986.

Lee, Leo Ou-fan. *Shanghai Modern: The Flowering of a New Urban Culture in China, 1930–1945*. Cambridge: Harvard University Press, 1999.

Link, Perry. *Mandarin Ducks and Butterflies: Popular Fiction in Early Twentieth-Century Chinese Cities*. Berkeley: University of California Press, 1981.

Shen Lixing. *Shanghai tegong zhan*. Shanghai: Shanghai shudian, 2000.

Shui Jing. *Liuxing gequ cangsang ji*. Taipei: Dadi chubanshe, 1985.

Su Qing. "Guanyu wo: *Xu Jiehun shinian* daixu." In *Su Qing sanwen jingbian*, 539–550. Hangzhou: Zhejiang renmin chubanshe, 1995.

Su Qing. "*Huan jin ji* yu *Jiehun shinian*." In *Su Qing sanwen jingbian*, 530–534. Hangzhou: Zhejiang renmin chubanshe, 1995.

Su Qing. *Huan jin ji*. Shanghai: Tiandi chubanshe, 1944.

Su Qing. *Su Qing sanwen jingbian*. Hangzhou: Zhejiang renmin chubanshe, 1995.

Wei Shaochang, ed. *Yuanyang hudie pai yanjiu ziliao*. Shanghai: Shanghai wenyi chubanshe, 1962.

Wu Fuhui. *Dushi xuanliu zhong de Haipai xiaoshuo*. Changsha: Hunan jiaoyu chubanshe, 1995.

Xu Baiyi. "Zhongguo de jiating wenti." *Jiating niankan* 1 (1943): 4–10.

Zhu Boquan. "Fakan ci." *Jiating niankan* 1 (1943): 1–2.

Chapter 14

Women and Wartime Shanghai

A Postwar Perspective

PAUL G. PICKOWICZ

In the weeks and months after August 1945, Chinese stage and screen artists spent a great deal of time trying to come to terms with the war. Ordinary people, especially those who resided in areas that had been occupied by Japanese forces, sought straightforward explanations of the ultimate meaning of the recently concluded national catastrophe. Among other things, people wanted to know if there was a connection between wartime hardships and postwar turmoil. Plays and films produced after 1945 regarded the war as a trauma suffered by citizens throughout China, but one notices that an extremely high percentage of these early postwar narratives dealt specifically with the impact of the war on Shanghai. The favored topics included life in Shanghai before the war (*Yaoyuan de ai* [Far away love], d. Chen Liting, 1947), the wartime exodus from Shanghai (*Yi jiang chun shui xiang dong liu* [A spring river flows east], d. Cai Chusheng, Zheng Junli, 1947), the experiences of Shanghainese in the interior (*Ba qian li lu yun he yue* [Eight thousand miles of clouds and moon], d. Shi Dongshan, 1947), the fate of those who remained behind in occupied Shanghai (*Liren xing* [Women side by side], d. Chen Liting, 1949), and the depressing situation in Shanghai after the war (*Tiantang chun meng* [Heavenly spring dream], d. Tang Xiaodan, 1947).

Stage and screen artists no doubt believed that the experiences of the people of Shanghai were essentially the same as the experiences of people throughout the nation. But their emphasis on Shanghai was no accident. Most of the leading stage and screen artists were Shanghai-based before the war and they returned to Shanghai after the war. Shanghai is what they knew best. Furthermore, Shanghai was the acknowledged center of China's film and modern theater worlds. Thus, the primary audience for feature films was comprised of Shanghainese. In short, artists and consumers alike were preoccupied with Shanghai life.

Despite all the attention given to Shanghai, it is only *Liren xing* (Women side by side), among the works mentioned above, that devotes itself exclusively to life in wartime Shanghai. An elaborate stage and screen production, *Liren xing* involved many of the most important cultural luminaries of twentieth-century China. The original stage play was written in 1946 by Tian Han (1898–1968), one of the most notable playwrights to appear on the Chinese scene after the May Fourth Movement.[1] Tian Han was a veteran underground communist, having joined the party in 1932, but during the war he was in Wuhan, Changsha, Kunming, and the wartime capital of Chongqing working for a number of leading Nationalist government resistance organizations, including the political department of the Military Affairs Commission (Jun shi weiyuanhui zhengzhi bu).[2] These connections to the regime of Jiang Jieshi cost Tian Han dearly during the Cultural Revolution of the 1960s.

Liren xing was completed in Shanghai by Tian Han immediately following his return from Chongqing in 1946. The play was first performed by the well-regarded Ninth Brigade Theater Troupe (Yan ju jiu dui) in Wuxi on March 9, 1947 and later in Shanghai beginning on April 24. The play was directed by Hong Shen (1894–1955), a stellar figure in the world of modern Chinese theater, and featured a number of leading players including Zhu Lin, Zhao Yuan, and Tian Ye. Hong Shen and the Ninth Brigade were personally invited by Tian Han to come to Wuxi in February 1947 to plan the stage production of *Liren xing*. Altogether the play was performed more than fifty times and closed on May 20, 1947.[3]

As soon as the play ended, arrangements were made to convert the story into a film blockbuster. Tian Han recruited a close wartime associate, the accomplished director Chen Liting (1910–), to help him turn the stage script into a screenplay. Unlike Tian Han, Chen was not a communist, but he had worked closely with Tian and other left-wing theater activists in Nationalist cultural organizations in Chongqing during the war.[4] The film was directed by Chen Liting and featured a number of the most popular and accomplished screen actors and actresses of the postwar era, including Zhao Dan (1915–1980), Huang Zongying (1925–), Shangguan Yunzhu (1920–1968), and the brilliant Lan Ma (1915–1976). Like Tian Han, Hong Shen, and Chen Liting, all of these players had been Shanghai-based before the war and had traveled to the interior to labor in Nationalist cultural groups during the war.

---

[1] For the text of the 1946 play, see Tian Han, *Liren xing* [Women side by side].

[2] *Zhongguo dabaike quanshu: dianying* [The complete encyclopedia of China: cinema], p. 385.

[3] Zhu Lin, Zhao Yuan, and Tian Ye, "Huiyi *Liren xing* de shouci gong yan" [Recalling the first public performance of *Women side by side*], pp. 127–144.

[4] Zhongguo dianyingjia xiehui, dianying shi yanjiu bu, ed., *Zhongguo dianyingjia liezhuan* [Biographies of Chinese filmmakers], pp. 237–248.

The film version of *Liren xing* was shot in the second half of 1948 and released in January 1949 in Shanghai. The movie was produced by the Kunlun film studio, a privately owned company that served as a base for leftist artists who had served the Nationalist government in Chongqing during the war, but who were now bitterly disillusioned with the regime. *Liren xing* contained a considerable amount of material that could be considered antigovernment. But since the bloody civil war was practically over when the film came out, it is fair to say that its political impact was limited. The stage play, performed in public during an earlier and more tension-packed phase of the civil war, was more subversive than the film. Still, both texts shed light on the issue of life in Shanghai, particularly life among ordinary women, during the war.

One of the most attractive things about this narrative is its narrow focus. Unlike such epic treatments of the war as *Ba qian li lu yun he yue* (Eight thousand miles of clouds and moon) and *Yi jiang chun shui xiang dong liu* (A spring river flows east), *Liren xing* takes a decidedly microcosmic look at the war. Set in the spring of 1944, an especially difficult moment in the history of wartime Shanghai, *Liren xing* examines the daily lives of three young women.[5] Although the protagonists occupy sharply contrasting social stations, the war brings them together and causes them to forge powerful cross-class bonds of trust and mutual aid. As Vivian Shen has shown in an illuminating essay, the strategy of using the story of three young women to monitor the pulse of urban social life had been employed many times before.[6] Tian Han himself wrote the screenplay for a 1933 film entitled *San ge modeng nüxing*, or *Three Modern Women*. And in late 1935 Cai Chusheng (1906–1968), a leading leftist filmmaker of the prewar period, directed a highly influential film about three young women called *Xin nüxing*, or *New Women*. Indeed, the original working title of *Liren xing* was *Xin san ge modeng nüxing*, or *Three More Modern Women*.[7]

Jinmei, the first woman to appear in *Liren xing*, is played by the highly talented Shangguan Yunzhu. A rather meek and passive textile worker, Jinmei is not at all like the strong proletarian heroines one sees in the left-wing films of the 1930s. In the opening scene she is raped by two drunken Japanese soldiers. For the remainder of the film Jinmei tries, without much success, to regain control of her life. Rejected, in turn, by her boss and her husband, the two most

---

[5] Oddly, the film opens with a written text that identifies the setting as 1941. This is incorrect. Every other source, including the original stage play, identifies the setting as 1944, well after the end of the "orphan island" phase of Shanghai's wartime history.

[6] Vivian Shen, "Gender Politics from 'New Women' to 'Fighting Women': The Changing Role and Concept of New Women from the 1930s to the 1940s."

[7] *Zhongguo dianyingjia liezhuan*, vol. 2, p. 62.

powerful men in her life, Jinmei turns to prostitution and then, toward the end of the film, decides to commit suicide.

The second woman, Ruoying, is a well-educated, stylish, middle-class, urban woman. A former teacher, she is clearly a major beneficiary of the various modernizing drives of the late nineteenth and early twentieth centuries. Ruoying, played by the versatile Sha Li, was once married to a handsome and politically progressive young man and has a bright eight-year-old daughter. The problem is that when her husband departed from Shanghai to participate in the anti-Japanese resistance, Ruoying and the child, like many others, were left alone in occupied Shanghai to fend for themselves. Eventually, however, severe wartime shortages cause Ruoying to move in with a prosperous banker and function as his wife. Initially, the cautious banker keeps his distance from the Japanese, but soon he engages in a variety of collaborative activities that link him to the foreign aggressors. Ruoying faces an intense emotional crisis when her first husband returns from the interior. She thought he had perished long ago. Pulled by conflicting forces, Ruoying decides to stay with the banker. But when the banker rejects her for a woman who has strong connections to the Japanese, Ruoying, like the textile worker, Jinmei, decides to commit suicide.

The third woman, Xinqun (which means "*new masses*"), played by the young Huang Zongying, is a youthful school teacher who, with her live-in boyfriend, is active in the anti-Japanese underground. Many years later Tian Han pointed out that the character of Xinqun was modeled on the real life story of Mao Liying, a celebrated underground communist organizer.[8] Xinqun exhibits quiet strength throughout the film. Xinqun and Ruoying are former classmates, and it is Xinqun who comes to the aid of Jinmei following the rape. In sharp contrast to Jinmei and Ruoying, Xinqun enjoys both emotional and material security. Her relationship with the man in her life, a comrade in the underground resistance, is based on equality and mutual respect. When her boyfriend is forced to flee the city to avoid arrest, Xinqun functions with independence and effectiveness. While the rest of society seems to hold Jinmei and Ruoying in contempt, Xinqun comforts them, brings a measure of dignity to their broken lives, and gradually draws them into a vibrant network of women who are struggling to survive in wartime Shanghai. Xinqun's posture is consistently compassionate and nonjudgmental.

It is true, of course, that *Liren xing* was produced after the war rather than during the war. In brief, it is not an "authentic" wartime source. It is proper, therefore, to raise questions about the extent to which this text can provide reliable information about social conditions in wartime Shanghai. Furthermore,

---

[8] Tian Han, "Ying shi zhuihuai lu" [Recollections of the film world].

given the left-wing political orientation of many of the people associated with the production, one wonders whether the account has been distorted in ideological terms. It is hard to answer these questions. But this much is certain. Tian Han's multifaceted and rather humanistic treatment of wartime society in occupied Shanghai was politically unacceptable after 1949. This is because the most interesting and complex characters in *Liren xing* occupy the fascinating grey area between the polar extremes of "heroic resistance fighter" and "degenerate national traitor." Increasingly after 1949, it became impossible for Chinese artists to talk about the survival strategies of people who avoided overt collaboration, but remained uninvolved in the organized resistance. Tian Han's work is intriguing because, while it dwells on the indecisiveness, insecurities, and human weaknesses of such people, the protagonists remain likable and attractive. Tian Han's most compelling and convincing characters are precisely the sort of people who disappeared from the Chinese stage and screen after 1949. It is hardly surprising, therefore, that when Tian Han was identified as one of the major targets of the Cultural Revolution in the 1960s, *Liren xing* was characterized by Red Guard militants as "humanist" and "the work of a renegade, a huge poisonous weed."[9]

Indeed, Tian Han's treatment of Jinmei, the textile worker, and the working class in general, is full of surprises. Rather than portray her as a one-dimensional proletarian fighter with a high level of class consciousness, a building block of future socialist revolution, she is cast as a weak, helpless, and uneducated victim of a cruel war. But Tian Han's story is not about wartime victimization in general. It is about the special ways in which the lives of women were destroyed during the war.

It is logical, therefore, that the very first scene involves the vicious rape of Jinmei by two drunken Japanese soldiers. Rape and other forms of brutal sexual assault were used extensively by Japanese forces in China as a way of terrorizing, breaking the will of, and thus pacifying the general population.[10] The widespread raping of China's women became a symbol of national weakness and humiliation. But it was women, not men, who were the immediate victims of rape. Rape was a form of wartime violence that men, one imagines, never experienced and had little hope of fully understanding. After she is raped, all Jinmei can think about is suicide. It is the two middle-class women who convince

---

[9] Shanghai hongqi dianying zhipianchan hongqi geming zaofan bingtuan, Shanghai tushuguan hongse geming zaofan pai, eds., *Dianying xiju sishinian liang tiao luxian douzheng shilu* [A record of the forty-year two-line struggle in film and theater], p. 43.

[10] See Saburo Ienaga, *The Pacific War, 1931–1945*, for a compelling discussion of the relationship between rape and terror in wartime China. Also see Iris Chang, *The Rape of Nanking: The Forgotten Holocaust of World War II*, pp. 89–99.

her to return home and seek the comfort of her husband, Yousheng. But Jinmei knows better. Terrified, she sobs that her husband is incapable of understanding. "My husband will throw me out," she pleads. "He won't forgive me."

Yousheng is also a factory worker. Although Tian Han was a Marxist, his characterization of the burly worker is remarkably negative. Just as Jinmei thought, Yousheng explodes in anger and demands to know why she did not run away and did not resist the soldiers. It is as if Jinmei is responsible for what happened, rather than the Japanese. Jinmei begs Yousheng to kill her. Jinmei is humiliated by the Japanese and then humiliated again by her husband, whose main concern seems to be his own sense of shame. The entire scene revolves around Yousheng's anger rather than Jinmei's agony.

Apart from the two middle-class women, Xinqun and Ruoying, who befriend and comfort Jinmei, no one seems very compassionate. Once the word circulates that she has been raped by the Japanese, Jinmei is fired from her factory job by a callous boss who is embarrassed to have the mill associated with such a victim of sexual violence. Once Jinmei is viewed as the embodiment of China's national disgrace, she becomes a virtual outcast. None of the men want to deal with her.

Rather than rally around her, the broad urban masses, cast in a particularly grim and uncaring way in this narrative, prey on the young woman. For instance, owing to acute food shortages, Jinmei is forced to wait in a long line with other neighborhood women to buy a bit of rice. A group of young gangsters, all of whom do dirty jobs for the Japanese and have thus sold out to the foreign aggressor, taunt the defenseless woman. No one steps forward to protect or defend her. One of the thugs asks, "If you can do it with the Japs, why can't you do it with me?" As Jinmei is being manhandled by the group, her husband shows up. The crowd makes cruel jokes about what it must be like to be the husband of a woman who has been reduced to a sexual object by the Japanese. During a fist fight with the punks, Yousheng is blinded when a bucket of toxic chemicals is thrown in his face.

The point here is that Jinmei remains in the home not so much because her husband has "forgiven" her for the rape, but because he depends on her. With her husband blind and thus unable to work in the factory and with a sickly mother, care for the wartime family falls entirely on Jinmei's shoulders. Her husband laments, "My wife has to support me. I'm ashamed." But because of the rape she cannot get another factory job. Under such circumstances she has no alternative but to seek out neighborhood loan sharks who, like the gangsters, prey on those decent compatriots who have been victimized the most by the Japanese. Tian Han's surprising portrait of the fate of women in wartime Shanghai does not reflect very favorably on Chinese men.

When Jinmei proves incapable of repaying the loan, one of the low-life hustlers says he will get her a job in a factory provided that she supplies information about labor activists in the plant. The hustler, it seems, is also in the business of selling intelligence to the Japanese. When Jinmei refuses to betray her sisters, the other hustler says there is only one other choice. Young and attractive, Jinmei will have to start working for an "escort service," and turn over 40 percent of her earnings to the loan sharks. Furthermore, Jinmei will have to have sex every night with one of the scar-faced loan sharks. With the fate of her blind husband and sickly mother at stake, this Confucian family provider responds stoically, "It is better to have my body violated than to betray my conscience."

Worker Jinmei begins toiling as a common wartime prostitute, and the downward economic slide of the family is reversed for a time. But Jinmei's husband and her mother are suspicious about the source of her income. The mother wonders why she is out so late at night, and Yousheng asks her why she wears perfume. Jinmei decides to quit, but two days later her pimp arrives looking for her and demanding immediate repayment of her loan. He also declares in front of her family that he has not been able to sleep well at night without her at his side. The blind Yousheng goes into a rage and kills the pimp. But despite the fact that Jinmei has been buying him eye medication and providing for the entire family during one of the darkest moments of the war, Yousheng literally throws Jinmei out of the house. Once again, the personal humiliation he experiences when it comes to grappling with the sexual exploitation suffered by his wife is more than he can accept.

An even more interesting case of Shanghai women struggling to survive in the wartime environment is the case of Ruoying. In many respects, Ruoying is the most complex character in the film. It is established quite clearly at the outset that she is neither a nondescript urban housewife nor an empty-headed party animal. As Vivian Shen has argued convincingly, Ruoying is consistently portrayed as a May Fourth-type, new-style Chinese woman.[11] She has received a modern education, served for a time as a school teacher, and is highly patriotic. She is an avid reader of anti-Japanese propaganda, she takes personal risks listening to Nationalist radio broadcasts that originate in Chongqing, and she freely associates with people, like her former classmate, Xinqun, who are underground resistance activists. Her first marriage, to Zhang Yuliang, was a free-love, free-choice May Fourth-style union. Even hostile pro-Japanese elements acknowledge that Ruoying is a modern, progressive "new woman."

The problem for Ruoying is that, without much consultation, her May Fourth-type husband, Yuliang, played effectively by the famous actor Zhao Dan, left

---

[11] Vivian Shen, p. 10.

her and their small child behind in Shanghai to join the anti-Japanese resistance after 1937. As the years passed without a word from Yuliang, Ruoying assumed he had died. The challenge before her was to figure out a way to survive in wartime Shanghai and care for her daughter. One presumes that large numbers of well-educated and patriotic Shanghai women faced similar problems during the occupation.

Working in a bank, Ruoying develops a relationship with one of the managers, the politically cautious Wang Zhongyuan. In both the play and the film the relationship is described in ambiguous terms. In the play the emphasis is on the fact that they were "living together" (*tong zhu*). In the film Ruoying is almost always referred to as Wang's "wife" (*taitai*). It is clear, however, that Ruoying and her daughter live with Wang for material reasons. She has a comfortable relationship with the man, but she does not love him in the May Fourth sense of the word. She makes it perfectly clear that there is a "spiritual" void in her life that Wang cannot fill.

Wang, for his part, is fully aware of Ruoying's past. Although there are significant class differences separating Ruoying from the worker, Jinmei, one thing they share in common in wartime Shanghai is that both are involved in loveless relationships in which sexual services are exchanged for material support.

Ruoying's wartime crisis is compounded when her former husband suddenly returns from the interior and wants to see their daughter. For security reasons, the former partners meet in the apartment shared by the underground activist Xinqun and her boyfriend. During the emotional reunion, Ruoying explains that she had no choice about depending on the banker. She also makes it clear that she still loves Yuliang. But Tian Han's portrait of the returning resistance fighter is surprisingly harsh. Much like worker Jinmei's insensitive husband, Yuliang turns a deaf ear to Ruoying's bitter story. Ruoying describes her wartime hardships in great detail, but Yuliang insists that her suffering is nothing compared to the experiences of refugees at the front.

During their tense meeting, Japanese counterterrorist operatives burst into the room and arrest the couple, mistaking them for Xinqun and her boyfriend. Then they are hauled off to prison where they are subjected to the sadistic tortures of the Japanese authorities and their Chinese agents. *Liren xing* is quite violent as Republican era Chinese films go. The prison scenes are unusually graphic. At one point, for instance, a pack of frenzied German shepherds is turned loose on Yuliang, who hangs suspended from the ceiling. Terrified of life in this medieval torture chamber, Ruoying once again assumes the identity of banker Wang Zhongyuan's wife on the assumption that putting distance between herself and all people who are associated with the underground resistance is the best way to gain her release from prison. Although Tian Han's portrayal reveals a weak and vulnerable Ruoying, it is still a remarkably compassionate and sympathetic view.

When Ruoying and Yuliang are finally released from prison, the long awaited reunion between father and daughter finally takes place in a small restaurant called Petite Paris. The child wants her parents to reunite, but Yuliang believes it is essential for him to leave Shanghai once again. It is clear to Ruoying that Yuliang has no further love interest in her. Moreover, she is frightened about the prospect of leaving Shanghai. Eventually the banker shows up and pressures Ruoying to go with him to a nearby hotel. Amazingly, she gives the eight-year-old child a choice of parents, and the child chooses to go with her father. Thus, like the worker, Jinmei, Ruoying is left with no family.

Unfortunately, after checking in at the hotel Ruoying discovers that her banker husband has taken another wife, this time an entirely vamplike character who is closely connected to the Japanese invaders. In fact, she seems to have had a sexual relationship with a Japanese official named Suzuki. Indeed, Wang Zhongyuan himself appears to be working more directly with the Japanese authorities, in this case as the manager of an East Asian co-prosperity sphere publishing house subsidized by Suzuki. Following an ugly confrontation with the evil vamp, Ruoying goes off to the publishing house to confront Wang. But as she arrives on the scene, a Chinese terrorist hurls a bomb into the building, injuring Wang and his new female companion. Like the worker Jinmei, Ruoying is rejected and abandoned by her husband (in fact, by both husbands). Like Jinmei, she becomes distraught and heads down to the river to commit suicide.

Ruoying fails to conform to the idealized standard of a liberated May Fourth modern woman, and Jinmei falls far short of the stereotypical image of a militant proletarian heroine. Both exhibit character flaws and weaknesses. Yet they are the most interesting characters in *Liren xing* because they are so sympathetic and convincing. They undoubtedly reminded postwar film viewers of real people and their complicated struggles to survive in wartime Shanghai.

Tian Han's portrayals of men, like his sketches of women, contain surprises. Ruoying is clearly presented by Tian Han as a sympathetic character, but her former husband, Yuliang, the patriotic resistance fighter, seems incapable of understanding her wartime plight. Her sincere attempts to restore their prewar relationship are coldly rebuffed time and again. Yuliang has no trouble comprehending the many ways in which Japanese forces have plundered and destroyed the Chinese "nation," but he has no ability to understand that it is those same forces, not Ruoying, that are responsible for pulverizing his family life. To him Ruoying is a fallen woman. He expresses no regrets about taking their daughter away with him when he departs from Shanghai for the second time. In fact, the young girl, Beibei, identifies with her father's perspective when she chooses to go with her father rather than stay with her mother. Tian Han's representation of the resistance figher is memorable because he makes Yuliang look so cold and heartless. In this respect, Yuliang shares much in common with Yousheng, the only proletarian male to appear in the film. If anything, Yousheng's treatment of Jinmei is even less compassionate than Yuliang's treatment of Ruoying. Tian Han's primary concern was to speak frankly about social relations in wartime China, but in doing so his liberal, May Fourth concern about oppressive Confucian patriarchal norms and gender inequalities seems to have overshadowed his Marxist views on the primacy of class and class struggle.

The most interesting, indeed controversial, male character in *Liren xing* was neither Yuliang or Yousheng, but the banker Wang Zhongyuan, played masterfully by Lan Ma. It is true that by the end of the film, Zhongyuan, as manager of a Japanese subsidized publishing house, is firmly in the collaborationist camp. And it is true that Zhongyuan cruelly abandons Ruoying for a woman who never hesitates to serve the Japanese aggressors. But it is important to understand that Tian Han takes great pains to put a human face on collaborator Wang Zhongyuan, thus showing that, like most of the other leading characters, Wang is best understood as someone who occupies the vast grey area between hero and traitor.[12]

At the beginning of the film, when Wang's character is being established, he points out over and over that his attitude toward politics is one of "neutrality." He is proud of his "unaffiliated" (*wu dang wu pai*) status. He tells Ruoying that there is nothing wrong with secretly listening to anti-Japanese radio broadcasts from Chongqing, but this should be balanced by attention to the broadcasts of the Wang Jingwei regime in Nanjing. Similarly, Wang has no problem with Ruoying's interest in underground anti-Japanese publications. Wang is primarily concerned about staying out of the line of fire and protecting his own business interests and welfare.

Wang's attitude toward Ruoying's friend, Xinqun, is quite revealing. Wang is fully aware of the underground anti-Japanese actvities of Xinqun and her patriotic friends. He also makes it clear to Ruoying that he does not particularly like the highly political Xinqun. Yet he does little to block their friendship. Xinqun is seen coming and going from Wang's home all the time. In fact, at the beginning of the film, following the brutal rape of Jinmei, Xinqun comes over to enlist Ruoying's help. Xinqun even borrows books by Lu Xun that are

---

[12] For a highly nuanced discussion of different wartime modes of political behavior, see Poshek Fu, *Passivity, Resistance, and Collaboration: Intellectual Choices in Occupied Shanghai, 1937–1945.*

owned by Wang. Most important of all, Wang has many opportunities to inform on Xinqun and her friends, but he never does so, even after he starts down the collaborationist path himself. Similarly, Wang is also quite aware of the return of the anti-Japanese resistance fighter, Yuliang, to Shanghai, but does nothing to inform the authorities. Indeed, Wang is the one who tells his wife the time and place of the meeting Yuliang has requested.

One of the most forceful scenes in the film involves a long and complicated conversation between Wang Zhongyuan and the underground activist Xinqun. The encounter takes place after Ruoying is mistaken for Xinqun by the Japanese military police and placed in prison. Xinqun tells Wang that a word from him to the authorities will definitely result in the release of both Ruoying and Yuliang. The Japanese will have no reason to detain them once it is established that they have been mistaken for Xinqun and her boyfriend.

Wang claims that he is as patriotic as the next person. Xinqun acknowledges that at the beginning of the war Wang had written some articles that helped the war effort. But she wants to put his patriotism to the test. In a tense exchange, she says that Wang can prove his patriotism if he speaks to the Japanese authorities about releasing Ruoying and Yuliang. In a surprising development, Wang agrees to do so, even though his marriage to Ruoying is in ruins with the return of Yuliang. But when Wang speaks to his Japanese friends, they indicate that his request to have Ruoying and Yuliang released can be acted upon more quickly if Wang accepts the honor of helping the Japanese operate the new co-prosperity sphere publishing house. What is significant here is that Wang agrees to take the position, and thus enters into an overt collaborationist relationship with the enemy for the first time, primarily to get Ruoying and Yuliang released and to prove to Xinqun that he is, after all, a patriot. In an odd turn of events, it is none other than the recently released Yuliang who hurls the terrorist bomb through the window of the publishing house on the day it opens, thus injuring Wang Zhongyuan. The point here is that even the collaborator Wang Zhongyuan has been cast in a number of complex and sympathetic ways.

As the cases of Ruoying, Jinmei, and Wang Zhongyuan show, the politics of *Liren xing* are curiously complex. At one level, Tian Han engages in old-fashioned May Fourth politics. That is, as a male May Fourth-type feminist he speaks out against what Xinqun and others in the film call the forces of "feudal" culture in contemporary Chinese society. This is a political message that resonated with a long-standing late nineteenth century and twentieth century social and cultural agenda. With one or two exceptions, Tian Han takes the side of women who are victimized in one way or another by men during the war years. Despite the fact that Tian Han was a Marxist, and thus was predisposed to thinking in terms of class tensions, his indictment of Chinese men is far from being confined to the behavior of bourgeois men. Indeed, Wang Zhongyuan, the bourgeois man who ends up as a collaborator, seems to treat Ruoying a bit more sensitively than the proletarian man treats Jinmei and the intellectual man treats Ruoying. As a May Fourth-type political text, *Liren xing* is not concerned with the history of wartime Shanghai as such. Instead, it tells the story of the impact of the war on the kinds of urban women who had been struggling since late Qing times to achieve a modern identity. More specifically, it asks about the fate of modern women in a space now dominated by a foreign invader.

Tian Han's May Fourth message is that the strains of life in an occupied zone in the late 1930s and early 1940s was a factor that contributed to the derailing of the twentieth-century women's movement during the war years. May Fourth-type marital unions based on free choice and the establishment of small nuclear family units (*xiao jiating*) were torn apart by forces set loose during the war. The war created conditions that make women like Jinmei and Ruoying highly insecure and unusually vulnerable to male predators, Japanese and Chinese alike. When their *xiao jiating* partners are no longer able to function effectively within the framework of the modern May Fourth relationship (because they have fled to the interior, as in Yuliang's case, or because they have been destroyed by hostile forces associated with the alien invasion, as in Yousheng's case), the women are suddenly alone in a strange and ugly world and forced to fend for themselves. Independence for women was a goal of the May Fourth women's movement, but the sort of independence forced on women during the war was not what feminists had in mind decades earlier. In the modern marital relationships entered into by Jinmei and Ruoying, both husband and wife had jobs, and a significant degree of interdependence and mutual support existed within the marriage relationship. But at key points in the *Liren xing* narrative the women are called upon by cruel circumstances to provide *all* means of support for household dependents, including children, the elderly, and the disabled. *Liren xing* looks with compassion on Jinmei's decision to turn to loan sharks and prostitution and Ruoying's resolve, not once, but twice, to turn to the politically suspect banker, Wang Zhongyuan. But the men in the film exhibit no such understanding of what the war had done. According to Tian Han, the forces of "feudalism" and male domination seem to have gained strength in the wartime environment. Jinmei and Ruoying can think of no response to their humiliations other than suicide.

One feels comfortable identifying Tian Han with May Fourth-type feminism, especially the feminism embraced by intellectual men. It is important to point out, however, that this type of feminism was expressed in a variety of stereotypical ways when it found its way into popular stage and screenplays fashioned by men. In such works, many of which date to the 1920s and 1930s, tales of the victimization of women invariably focus on the many degrading sexual encounters they are forced to endure. Jinmei is savagely raped by the drunken and animalistic Japanese soldiers. Ruoying is required to sleep every night with Wang Zhongyuan, a man she does not love and who is capable only of satisfying her "material" needs. Jinmei must not only work as a common prostitute, she is compelled to have sex with her pimp every day. The only difference between Ruoying and Jinmei and the utterly negative female character who sleeps with Suzuki and Wang Zhongyuan is that Ruoying and Jinmei are acutely aware of their degradation, while the vamp appears to have no such consciousness. Here Tian Han is titillating the popular film audience in ways that were well established in the prewar years. The decision to emphasize violence against women and the degradation of wartime sexual exchanges is rather voyeuristic and made at the expense of women. In stereotypic treatments of this sort, exploited and abused women are offered few alternatives other than suicide. Jinmei contemplates suicide twice, and makes a real attempt once. At the end of the film Ruoying, too, heads down to the river to end her life.

It is true, of course, that Tian Han departs from the standard male feminist representation of victimized and weak women with his characterization of Xinqun, the always resolute underground resistance worker. But Xinqun is too perfect to be a credible alternative. Unfortunately, this character is not developed well by Tian Han, and thus suffers from a pronounced flatness. The viewer never finds out why she is so perfect and why she faces none of the suffocating problems confronted by Ruoying and Jinmei in the wartime environment. In contrast to the stage play, the film version of *Liren xing* tries to say a bit more about this character. At the very end of the movie, after Ruoying abandons her suicide plan and Jinmei is actually pulled out of the water following a suicide attempt, Xinqun is shown taking the women back to her girls' school where she tells her wide-eyed students about how Ruoying and Jinmei have been saved. The women's collective, introduced in the last minute of the film version, will presumably solve all the problems of people like Jinmei and Ruoying who have been saved by Xinqun, which means "new masses." The difficulty is that this conclusion has a decidedly tacked-on happy ending feeling that is inconsistent with the rest of the film. It is the only moment in the movie in which one of the characters looks directly into the camera and preaches to the film audience. Equally unconvincing is the sudden appearance in the last scene set in the girl's school of Jinmei's working-class husband, who now, at the last moment, sees the light and "forgives" her for the rape and prostitution. No such reunion takes place in the stage play. In the stage version, it is the patriotic intellectual, Yuliang, who reunites with Ruoying after she gives up on the idea of suicide. No such reunion takes place in the film.

The politics of *Liren xing* do, of course, bear directly on wartime controversies. During the war a question on the minds of many people in the unoccupied interior regions of China was whether people in the Japanese occupied regions, including those nominally governed by Chinese administrations that cooperated with Japanese forces, were behaving as unpatriotic collaborators and traitors. It was easy for those who had fled into the interior to imagine that flight and wartime sacrifices in Nationalist-controlled regions in the interior were the only concrete proof of individual loyalty to the nation. Any other behavior was suspect.

Liren xing argues unequivocally that ordinary people in Shanghai made extraordinary sacrifices during the war and never lost their sense of patriotism. To be sure, the film depicts the polar extremes of the high-risk underground heroics of resistance fighers and the shameless treason of those who sold out to the Japanese. But the emphasis is on the vast majority of people in the grey areas in the middle, people who were in no position to leave Shanghai and who were forced to devise elaborate and sometimes painful survival strategies. *Liren xing* reaches out to these people by reminding the broad film audience that the wartime sacrifices of noncombatants who resided in the Japanese-occupied zones should be recognized. The film points especially to the sacrifices of women. One strongly suspects that Tian Han's sensitive handling of this issue was appreciated by Shanghainese who felt they were being scapegoated in the weeks and months following the end of the war.

This leads us to the most significant of all the political thrusts of *Liren xing*, its perspective on the civil war that was raging in China in the late 1940s. At this level, the film was not about May Fourth cultural agendas or about the fate of women in wartime Shanghai. Instead the film uses the story of the war to comment on postwar domestic politics. This reading, one that Tian Han himself encouraged in the 1950s, stresses the role of the play and the film in the political and cultural destabilization of the postwar Nationalist regime. Thus, the vicious fictional rape of Jinmei by Japanese soldiers was meant to remind angry viewers of the alleged rape of Shen Chong, a Beijing student, by two U.S. Marines in 1946.[13] Indeed, the entire account of the many ways in which Japanese imperialism ravaged China was supposed to alert viewers to the fact that while Japanese imperialism may have been defeated, it had been replaced by U.S. imperialism and China was still semicolonial in character. The film implies that if imperialism is still plundering China and robbing China of independence and sovereignty, the Nationalist state must be held responsible. Indeed, the film conveys the message that the Nationalists were dependent on

[13] Zhu Lin, Zhao Yuan, Tian Ye, p. 129.

the United States in the same way collaborationist regimes were dependent on the Japanese. Of course, none of this is said explicitly, but the clever political use of the powerful tropes of rape, torture, and national humiliation made it easy for disillusioned and alienated viewers to make the connections.

The same is true of the attacks on "feudal" culture contained in the play and in the film. The unmistakable political implication is that the postwar Nationalist regime, in league with imperialism, was still very much presiding over a society that exploited women and denied them dignity, independence, and a stable and fulfilling modern family life. Xinqun's strident and self-righteous speech at the end of the film calls on the collective of women and, indeed, on all decent people, to stand up against both imperialism and feudalism. This speech is not present in the stage version of the production. It was, perhaps, a bit too explicit for the tense political environment of late 1946 and early 1947. But it does point to the contemporary political relevance of the rest of the text. This segment could be added to the film version for screening in early 1949 without much risk because the civil war was practically over and there was little doubt about which side would emerge victorious.

What is interesting, though, especially when one recalls Tian Han's communist affiliation, is the multiclass, united front character of his anti-Nationalist political appeal. Both the play and the film tell the popular audience that just as it was necessary to forge a broad, multiclass coalition of Chinese to defeat Japanese imperialism and various domestic collaborators, so too would it be necessary to maintain a diverse national coalition to expel U.S. imperialism and overthrow the corrupt and inept Nationalist regime. The industrial proletariat is not assigned a privileged or vanguard role in either the play or the film. All classes are welcome, so long as they oppose imperialism and "feudalism." If anything, the proletariat is shown to be in a weakened, almost helpless, state.[14] The class background of Xinqun, the unblemished heroine, is bourgeois and intellectual. She is the one who rescues the victims of imperialism and feudalism and leads the multiclass united front of "new" women.

These political elements of *Liren xing* no doubt contributed to the success and popularity of both the play and film. The humanistic and united front political dimensions of the work also got it into serious ideological trouble in later years. The play and film were ignored in the 1950s, even though Tian Han emerged as a major cultural leader of postrevolutionary society. During the

[14] Even Cheng Jihua, a senior film historian in China and an analyst who normally wrote glowing things about Tian Han in the pre-Cultural Revolution era raised questions about his characterization of the working-class woman, Jinmei. Cheng Jihua, Li Shaobai, and Xing Zuwen, eds., *Zhongguo dianying fazhan shi* [A history of the development of Chinese cinema], p. 233.

Cultural Revolution of the 1960s, Tian Han was attacked and perished. *Liren xing* was placed on a black list of reactionary films and banned for twelve years. It was not until 1979, the thirtieth anniversary of the release of the film, that the work was rehabilitated. But the post-Mao audience had no interest in anything that looked so old-fashioned and obscure. Few understood or cared about the dilemmas faced by such characters as Jinmei and Ruoying in wartime Shanghai.

BIBLIOGRAPHY

Chang, Iris. 1997. *The Rape of Nanking: The Forgotten Holocaust of World War II*. New York: Penguin Books.
Cheng Jihua, Li Shaobai, and Xing Zuwen, eds. 1981. *Zhongguo dianying fazhan shi* (A history of the development of Chinese cinema), vol. 2. Beijing: Zhongguo dianying chuban she.
Fu, Poshek. 1993. *Passivity, Resistance, and Collaboration: Intellectual Choices in Occupied Shanghai, 1937–1945*. Stanford: Stanford University Press.
Ienaga, Saburo. 1978. *The Pacific War, 1931–1945*. New York: Pantheon.
Shanghai hongqi dianying zhipianchan hongqi geming zaofan bingtuan, Shanghai tushuguan hongse geming zaofan pai, eds. 1967. *Dianying xiju sishinian liang tiao luxian douzheng shilu* (A record of the forty-year two-line struggle in film and theater). Shanghai: n.p.
Shen, Vivian. August 21–23, 1997. "Gender Politics from 'New Women' to 'Fighting Women': The Changing Role and Concept of New Women from the 1930s to the 1940s." Peterborough, Ontario, Canada: Trent University Asian Cinema Studies Conference.
Tian, Han. 1959. "Ying shi zhui huai lu" (Recollections of the film world). *Dianying yishu*, no. 1, January.
———. 1980. *Liren xing* (Women side by side). Beijing: Zhongguo xiju chuban she.
Zhongguo dabaike quanshu: dianying (The complete encyclopedia of China: cinema). 1991. Beijing, Shanghai: Zhongguo dabaike quanshu chuban she.
Zhongguo dianyingjia xiehui, dianying shi yanjiu bu, ed. 1982. *Zhongguo dianyingjia liezhuan* (Biographies of Chinese filmmakers), vol. 2. Beijing: Zhongguo dianying chuban she.
Zhu Lin, Zhao Yuan, and Tian Ye. 1980. "Huiyi *Liren xing* de shouci gong yan" (Recalling the first public performance of *Women side by side*), in Tian Han, *Liren xing*, pp. 127–144.

Index

abortion, 310

Academia Sinica (Zhongyang yanjiu yuan), 76–77

advertising: false, 291; medical, 83–84, 291, 291n54; radio, 11, 280, 282, 290–91; in *Shanghai funü*, 306

Alcott, Carroll, 287, 287n32

Alliance française, 265

Alliance of the New Medicine Trade and the Pharmaceutical Industry (Xinyaoye zhiyaoye lianhehui), 72n11

Allies, strategy of, 200

All-Shanghai Federation for the Support of Armed Resistance, 283–84, 287, 298

alum, 129

Archives of the Self-Defense Research Institute (Tokyo), 157n1

Arnhold, Harry, 231, 252

Asano Kazuwo, 292–93, 294, 296

Asia Development Board, 30, 34n79, 246

assassination: attempts on British officials, 244; of collaborators, 197, 235; of communist targets, 97; of Lu Bohong, 52; of Mao Liying, 99–100; reported on radio, 287n32; of Shao Shubai, 211; threats of, to Great Way Government personnel, 178–79; wars, 98, 116, 142

Associated American Industries, Ltd., 53

Association for the Chinese Labor Movement (Zhongguo gongren yundong xiehui), 219

Association for Worker Welfare (Fuyihui), 215–16, 219, 221

Association of Shanghai Industrialists (Shanghai gongye tongzhihui), 27n37

Association of Shanghai Pharmaceutical Manufacturers (Shanghaishi zhiyao changye tongye gonghui), 72

Aurore University, 271

Badlands, 224n37, 234. *See also* extrasettlement road area

Bai Wei, 343

Baillie, Paul, 270, 270n27

Bangkok, 70

Bankers' Guild, 163

banking, 47, 68, 74, 194, 203

Banking Study Society (Yinhang xuehui), 40n111

Bank of China, 54, 74, 203

Bank of Communications, 203

Banyue (Half Moon bi-weekly), 334

Baoding Military Academy, 161

Baodong, 131

baojia system: instituted by Great Way Government, 179; in model peace zones, 141–42; mentioned, 250; and rice supplies, 121n24, 127; in the Western District, 173n30

Baoshan: counterinsurgency activities in, 142n129; and Great Way Government jurisdiction, 170; pacification teams in, 160, 160n2, 174; self-government committees, 174

363

> *c J C* 321

Fuyihui (Association for Worker
Welfare), 215–16, 219, 221
Fuzhou, 121

Gander, Owen, 246, 247
gangsters: and divisions of jurisdiction in
Shanghai, 3; portrayed in film *Liren
xing*, 350; relied on in smuggling
goods to Communist bases, 93–94,
109
Gao Guanwu, 142
Gao Xinbao, 190
Gao Zongwu, 195–96
Gaoqiao, 174
Garde Indigène of Indochina, 265
Garden Bridge, *19*
Gascogne, 269n22
gasoline, 36, 121, 132, 140
de Gaulle, General Charles, 273
Gaullists, 268
Ge Sen, 138
gender inequality, theme in *Liren xing*,
355
General Hospital (French Concession),
271
General Labor Union of Shanghai West,
209
General Labor Union of the Shanghai
Special Municipality, 217–18
Geng Jiaji, 190
Geng Jizhi, 145, 145n147
glass factories, 22, 23–24
Glosser, Susan, 86
gold, 120, 125
Golden Twin Horses brand, 54
Gong Zhifang, 337n21
gongshu (offices), 183n63
government bonds, 283
grain-boring worms, 144–45, 148,
289–90. *See also* profiteering
Grain Bureau (Liangshi ju), 144, 145
Grain Control Commission (Japanese),
116n2
Grain Guild (Miye gonghui), 144
Gray, Adeline, 140n117
Great Britain, economic relations with
Japan, 36, 42

Greater East Asia Co-Prosperity Sphere,
61
Great Way (*dadao*), 165, 166–67
Great Way Government (Dadao zhengfu):
article on regime's achievements,
168–69; collapse of, 183–85; dating
system used by, 169–70; documentary
materials on, 157n1, 164; emphasis on
nation-building, 165; establishment of,
7, 157, 162; financing of, 30, 164,
180–83; first appointments of, 160;
ideology of, 163, 164–70, 185;
Japanese and Chinese role in
establishing, 163–64, 165–66, 168–69;
and the Japanese army, 157, 158,
176–77, 183; jurisdiction of, 164,
170–77; and labor, 216, 218; manifesto
of, 165–66; name of, 165, 166–67,
169, 185; obscurity of, 157–58, 164;
personnel of, 185; petitioners to,
175–76; police of, 160, 164, 177–79;
propaganda booklet published in
Tokyo, 168; recruitment by, 179,
179n50; relations with Wang Jingwei,
220; requested to reopen waterways,
183; set up Society for the Economic
Reconstruction of Shanghai, 33; and
Shanghai Citizens Action, 52; slogans
of, 185; Social Affairs Bureau, 181;
Special Service unit attached to, 167;
weakness of, 185. *See also* Su Xiwen
Great Way Self-Government Committee
(Pudong), 160n5, 171, 173
Great Way spirit (*dadao jingshen*), 161,
168
Great World Theater, bombing of, *2, 3*
Green Gang: and the Guomindang, 187,
212; and labor, 210, 226; members,
202; Nationalist guerrillas recruited
from, 138; representative at
Guangcheng pharmacy school, 77n25;
and the Shanghai United Committee,
207; threat to pro-Japanese personnel,
179; Xu Guanqun's contacts in, 71
Gu Jiatang, 202
Gu Jinrong, 225, 225n39, 225n41
Gu Jiwu, 224